IRELAND'S COURT HOUSES

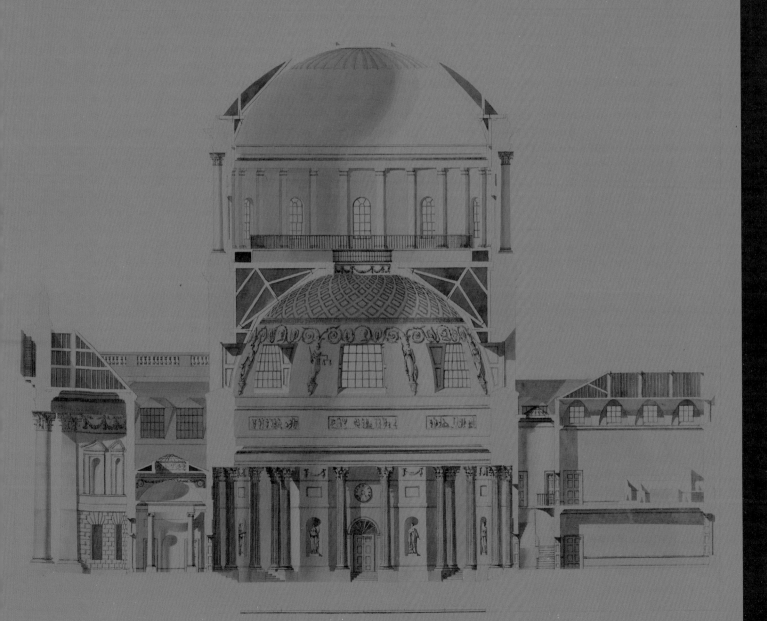

IRELAND'S
COURT HOUSES

PAUL BURNS
CIARAN O'CONNOR
COLUM O'RIORDAN

EDITORS

First published in 2019 by
The Irish Architectural Archive,
45 Merrion Square, Dublin 2

The Irish Architectural Archive gratefully acknowledges
the support provided for this publication by the
Courts Service and the Office of Public Works

An tSeirbhís Chúirteanna
Courts Service

ISBN 978-0-9956258-1-5
© The Irish Architectural Archive 2019

Designed by Daniel Morehead

Cover illustrations:
Four Courts, Dublin. Section by James Gandon, c. 1800
(King's Inns Collection, IAA)

Justice, c. 1795. Design for one of a series of eight colossal stucco figures
which once adorned the inner dome of the Four Courts, Dublin, but which
were destroyed in 1922. The drawing has the following inscription: 'Justice
when equal scales she holds is blind. Nor cruelty nor mercy change her mind'
(King's Inns Collection, IAA, 2007/10 L1)

Inside front cover illustration:
Interior of Claremorris Court House,
Illustrated London News, 26 November 1881 (IAA)

Inside back cover illustration:
Mid 19th-century engraving of courtroom interior,
Kilmainham Court House, Dublin

CONTENTS

FOREWORD

Mr Justice Frank Clarke, the Chief Justice

I am delighted to see the publication of this book which gives a comprehensive description of the historic court houses of Ireland but also the context in which they developed. We are at a time of much change in the Irish Courts system, not least in its building stock. This record of how the administration of justice has developed to where we are today, as evidenced in our court buildings, is a most valuable piece of work in that context.

I have recently participated in the official opening of some of our newest court houses and the importance of the court house buildings in their localities was very obvious at these events. So also was the pride which people take locally in their court houses. A good court house building is a positive symbol of justice within the community.

The Courts Service has worked over the last twenty years to improve the facilities in court houses around the country and a significant programme of work has been completed. We have aimed to preserve the best of the past and to enhance those buildings to provide a modern and dignified experience to those who come before the courts.

This book acknowledges the work of many talented architects, administrators and craftspeople who worked over the centuries to create the court house estate. We also pay tribute to the continuing tradition carried on by their present day successors.

I want to record my appreciation to all those involved in this excellent project.

Frank Clarke, Chief Justice, and Brendan Ryan, CEO, Courts Service

INTRODUCTION

Brendan Ryan, Chief Executive Officer, Courts Service

All through my career in the courts I have been fortunate to have been involved with the refurbishment of numerous court buildings, from those at the centre in Dublin to the smaller venues spread widely around the country. The challenges of dealing with an old estate, subject to significant underinvestment over the years, was more than balanced by the joy of working on wonderful historic building projects, each unique and many of them gems of design and workmanship. The pride of local staff in their buildings, often the finest public building in the area, has always been clear to me.

Over the years, my colleagues and I have worked to protect and enhance this heritage. The marvellous people I worked with during those times, from Courts Service staff to OPW Architects and conscientious contractors, deserve all our thanks for ensuring the projects were undertaken with due care and attention.

The purpose of this publication is to explore the architecture of the Irish court house. The essays examine the evolution of the building type from a legal, historical, and architectural perspective, while the gazetteer is a comprehensive listing of court houses across the island of Ireland from the early seventeenth to the early twenty-first centuries.

This book will be an important reference for architectural, legal and local historians and all who are interested in the administration of justice in Ireland. All the contributors to this important project are to be applauded.

THE IRISH COURTS SYSTEM AND THE COURT HOUSES

Niamh Howlin

The Courts System

At the start of the nineteenth century justice was administered at multiple levels, with various avenues of redress for civil disputes and criminal offences. Commenting on the proliferation of minor courts in the seventeenth and eighteenth centuries, McDowell remarks that '[t]hey were numerous and varied considerably in respect to jurisdiction, procedure and terminology – and by 1800 – in respect to their activity and usefulness'.[1] Civil Bill courts had operated since the early eighteenth century for the recovery of small debts.[2] A range of other courts also had jurisdiction over low-value civil cases, with variations throughout the country. These included the Courts of Conscience, established in several large towns and cities from the twelfth century.[3] Courts of Record, for the recovery of debts, were generally established by charter or patent.[4] Some larger towns, such as Carrickfergus, Galway, Waterford and Drogheda had Tholsel Courts to deal with civil disputes.[5] Others had Borough Courts,[6] often presided over by provosts and burgesses.[7] In other places there were Corporation Courts,[8] and Dublin had a Lord Mayors' Court, which dealt with minor offences and settled disputes relating to such matters as wages and apprentices.[9] Courts of piepowder (or piepoudre) determined cases which arose during fairs and markets.[10]

Manor Courts

Manor courts generally operated under patents granted in the seventeenth century.[11] Presided over by seneschals,[12] these courts, which operated both in cities and in rural areas, had jurisdiction over a range of civil, criminal and administrative matters.[13] From 1785 this included jurisdiction over the recovery of small debts by civil bills.[14] Manor courts operated both as courts leet and as courts baron. As courts leet, they generally sat twice a year for criminal offences and some administrative functions.[15] As courts baron, they sat every three or four weeks to deal with minor civil actions. McMahon points out that 'the difference between the courts leet and baron was often blurred'.[16] Their operation varied around the country, and they enjoyed considerable autonomy.[17] They tended to deal with cases worth less than ten pounds, and were primarily used for the recovery of small debts.[18] In the 1830s there were approximately two hundred manor courts still in operation.[19]

Over time, however, manor courts developed a reputation among the authorities for being 'disorderly and dangerously informal'.[20] Members of the legal profession were also critical of the way that manor courts operated.[21] In addition, as McMahon notes, they were also in competition with the assistant barristers at quarter sessions (see below), and there may also have been some local rivalry with the petty sessions (see below). Petty and quarter sessions became, from an official viewpoint, the preferred venue for 'small claims' litigation.[22] This coincided with a general move toward rationalisation of the machinery of justice under Robert Peel, manifest in reforms to policing,[23] punishment [24] and the jury system.[25] By the 1840s manor courts had fallen into disuse and they were abolished in 1859.[26]

Petty Sessions

Petty sessions (Image 1) were originally presided over by Justices of the Peace (JPs), who were essentially lay judges or 'private gentlemen'[27] without formal legal training. Some were appointed by legislation, while others 'act[ed] as justices by virtue of some office which they held'.[28] Originally Justices of the Peace acted alone, usually in private residences. Because of the poor reputation of some amateur JPs, in 1814 salaried stipendiary or 'Resident' Magistrates, better known as 'RM's, were introduced,[29] and these were extended to every county by the Constabulary (Ireland) Act 1836.[30]

The Petty Sessions Act (Ireland) 1827 [31] divided counties into petty sessions districts. A parliamentary committee noted in 1828 that the purpose of the petty sessions system was 'to give regularity and publicity to the discharge of magisterial duties'.[32] They dealt with cases of petty crime, such as poaching and illegal distilling, and took informations for cases to be dealt with in the higher courts.[33] On the civil side, they had jurisdiction over claims of trespass worth up to five pounds, and employment cases worth up to six pounds. They also dealt with such matters as licensing. Their workload grew in the 1820s and they sat more regularly.[34]

By the 1850s, as the manor courts declined, the jurisdiction of the petty sessions courts had expanded considerably. According to McCabe, up to 80% of persons in county gaols in the late nineteenth century had been summarily convicted at petty sessions.[35] Such was the frequency of the sittings

1 R.B. McDowell, 'The Irish Courts of Law 1801-1914', *Irish Historical Studies*, vol. 10, no.40 (1957), p. 375.

2 An act for the recovery of small debts 1703 (2 Ann., c. 18 (Ir.)) and the Civil Bill Courts (Ireland) Act 1851 (14 & 15 Vic., c. 57), s. 45.

3 For example, in Dublin, Drogheda and Wexford. For a more detailed discussion, see J.L.J. Hughes, 'The Dublin Court of Conscience', *Dublin Historical Record*, vol. 15, no. 2 (1959), pp. 42-9. The Court of Conscience was abolished by the Courts of Justice Act 1924, s. 78, and its jurisdiction was transferred to the District Court.

4 Examples include Bandon Bridge, Skibbereen, Clonakilty and Youghal in Co. Cork. See *Abstract return of number of courts of law in England, Wales and Ireland under name of courts of request, 1826-27*, House of Commons papers [hereafter HC], 1830 (15) xiii, 217, pp. 32-5.

5 The Tholsel Court of Fethard, Co. Tipperary, was presided over by the sovereign, and the fees were said to be excessive. See Thomas Laffan, 'Fethard, County Tipperary: its charters and corporation records, with some notice of the Fethard Everards', *The Journal of the Royal Society of Antiquaries of Ireland*, vol. 4, no.16 (1906), pp. 143–53. Some of these courts may have sat with juries: see *Tryal of David Cohen Henriks, Jun. a Jew, who was try'd at the Tholsel Court, on Monday the 18th of February, 1723* (Dublin, 1724).

6 An example is the Borough Court of Sligo town; see *Abstract Return*, pp. 32–5.

7 McDowell, p. 376, notes that about twenty-three boroughs had 'courts of limited jurisdiction presided over by the head of the corporation'.

8 For example, Enniskillen, Co. Fermanagh, and Dingle, Co. Kerry, both had Corporation Courts. See *Abstract Return*, pp. 32–5.

9 McDowell, p. 375.

10 See Charles Gross, 'The Court of Piepowder', *Quarterly Journal of Economics*, vol. 20, no.2 (1996), pp. 231-49. See also Karina Holton, 'From Charters to Carters: aspects of fairs and markets in medieval Leinster' in Denis A. Cronin, Jim Gilligan and Karina Holton (eds), *Irish fairs and markets: studies in local history* (Dublin, 2001). Patrick Logan, *Fair Day: the story of Irish fairs and markets* (Belfast, 1986), pp. 46-7 notes that Cavan town was granted a Court of Piepowder in its seventeenth-century charter.

11 Richard McMahon, 'Manor Courts in the West of Ireland Before the Famine' in D.S. Greer and N.M. Dawson (eds), *Mysteries and solutions in Irish legal history* (Dublin, 2001), p. 115. See also Raymond Gillespie, 'A Manor Court in Seventeenth Century Ireland', *Irish Economic and Social History*, vol. 25 (1998), p. 82. See J. Napier, *Digest of the Civil Bill and Manor Court Statutes* (Dublin, 1936) for a discussion of the various statutes relating to manor courts.

12 These were agents appointed by landlords.

13 See McMahon, pp. 116–8 for a discussion of the jurisdiction of these courts.

14 'An act for the more speedy and easy recovery of small debts, in the manor court within this kingdom, and for regulating the costs of proceedings for that purpose therein, 1785' (25 Geo. III c. 44 (Ir.))

15 McMahon, pp. 115–6.

16 Ibid., p. 116.

17 Ibid., p. 121.

18 *See Report from the select committee on manor courts, Ireland; together with the minutes of evidence, appendix and index*, HC 1837 (494) xv, 1.

19 T.C. Barnard, 'Local courts in later seventeenth- and eighteenth-century Ireland' in M. Brown and S. Donlan (eds), *The laws and other legalities of Ireland* (Farnham, 2011), p. 33.

20 McMahon, p. 119, citing R.B. McDowell, *The Irish administration, 1801-1914* (London, 1964), p. 118.

21 See for example W.N. Osborough, 'The Irish Legal System 1796–1877' in Caroline Costello (ed.), *The Four Courts: 200 Years* (Dublin, 1996), p. 58.

22 McMahon, p. 119.

23 For example, the Constabulary (Ireland) Act 1836 (6 & 7 Will. IV, c. 13); the Dublin Police Act 1836 (6 & 7 Will. IV, c. 29) and the Dublin Metropolitan Police Act 1837 (7 Will. IV & 1 Vic., c. 25). See further Brian Griffin, 'Prevention of crime in nineteenth-century Ireland' in N.M. Dawson (ed.), *Reflections on law and history* (Dublin, 2006) and Stanley Palmer, 'The Irish police experiment: the beginnings of modern police in the British Isles, 1785–95', *Social Science Quarterly*, vol. 56, no.3 (1975), pp. 410–24, and Ian Bridgeman, 'The constabulary and the criminal justice system in nineteenth-century Ireland' in Ian O'Donnell and Finbarr McAuley (eds), *Criminal justice history: themes and controversies from pre-Independence Ireland* (Dublin, 2003).

24 For example, the Prisons (Ireland) Act 1836 (6 & 7 Will. IV, c. 51); the Transportation (Amendment) Act 1837 (7 Will. IV & 1 Vic., c. 36); the Capital Punishment (Abolition) Act 1835 (5 & 6 Will. IV, c. 8); the Capital Punishment Abolition (Amendment) Act 1836 (6 & 7 Will. IV, c. 4); the Executions for Murder Act 1836 (6 & 7 Will. IV, c. 30); the Capital Punishment (Forgery) Abolition Act 1837 (7 Will. IV & 1 Vic., c. 84) and the Capital Punishment Abolition Act 1837 (7 Will. IV & 1 Vic., c. 91). See Tim Carey, *Mountjoy: the story of a prison* (Cork, 2000) and Henry Heaney, 'Ireland's penitentiary 1820–1831: an experiment that failed', *Studia Hibernica*, vol. 14 (1974), pp. 28-39.

25 Juries Ireland Act 1833 (3 & 4 Will. IV, c. 91). See Niamh Howlin, *Juries in Ireland: laypersons and law in the long nineteenth century* (Dublin, 2017).

26 Manor Courts Abolition (Ireland) Act 1859 (22 & 23 Vic., c. 14).

27 Hamilton Smythe, *The office of Justice of the Peace in Ireland* (Dublin, 1841), p. iii.

28 Constantine Molloy, *Justice of the Peace for Ireland: a treatise on the powers and duties of magistrates in Ireland in cases of summary jurisdiction in the prosecution of indictable offences and in other matters* (Dublin, 1890), p. 3.

29 Appointment of Superintending Magistrates Act 1814 (52 Geo. III, c. 131).

30 6 Will. IV, c. 13.

31 7 & 8 Geo. IV, c. 67. The system of petty sessions was revised by the Petty Sessions (Ireland) Act 1851 (14 & 15 Vic., c. 93).

32 *Seventeenth report of the commissioners appointed to inquire into the duties, salaries and emoluments of the officers, clerks, and ministers of justice, in all temporal and ecclesiastical courts in Ireland. Courts of quarter sessions and of assistant barristers*, HC 1828 (469) clxi, 12, pp. 1-3 & 7.

33 Richard McMahon, 'The court of petty sessions and society in pre-Famine Galway' in Raymond Gillespie (ed.), *The remaking of modern Ireland 1750–1950: Beckett Prize essays in Irish history* (Dublin, 2004), p. 101. The jurisdiction the petty sessions was set out in the Petty Sessions Act (Ireland) 1827 (7 & 8 Geo. IV, c. 67), the Petty Sessions (Ireland) Act 1851 and the Summary Jurisdiction Act 1857 (20 & 21 Vic., c. 43).

34 For a detailed list of legislation relating to petty sessions, see Desmond McCabe, 'Open court: law and the expansion of magisterial jurisdiction at petty sessions in nineteenth-century Ireland' in N.M. Dawson (ed.), *Reflections on law and history* (Dublin, 2006), p. 131.

35 Desmond McCabe, 'Law, conflict and social order: County Mayo, 1820-45' (PhD, NUI, 1991), ch. 6. See McCabe (2006) for an examination of magistrates' summary jurisdiction.

and the improved efficiency of the petty sessions during the century that '[f]or most purposes the common law was represented to the small litigant and offender by the authority of the local magisterial bench'.[36]

Police Courts

Some metropolitan areas, including Dublin, had Police Courts [37], presided over by magistrates or Justices of the Peace. These performed the functions of petty sessions, dealing summarily with minor criminal matters such as theft and public drunkenness, as well as market cases involving contaminated or adulterated food and drink.[38] Some towns also had Recorders' Courts.[39] In Dublin, the Recorder was the chief magistrate and his court sat monthly in the Green Street sessions house and had jurisdiction over a range of civil and criminal matters, such as debt cases.

Quarter Sessions

Quarter sessions (Image 2) were generally held four times per year,[40] and were presided over by Justices of the Peace, sitting in threes.[41] From 1787, legislation provided that an 'Assistant Barrister' should be appointed'[42] to act as a constant assistant to the justices constituting the court'.[43] In most instances the assistant barrister acted as chairman, and by the mid-nineteenth century they were often simply referred to as Chairmen of the Quarter Sessions.[44] Under the Civil Bill Courts (Ireland) Act 1836, an assistant barrister could act alone when dealing with criminal matters. There might be several quarter sessions districts in a county,[45] each with their own court sittings. The sittings might last for up to two weeks, but were generally around a week.[46] By the mid-nineteenth century the quarter sessions were busy; the Marquess of Clanricarde remarked in 1861 that '[a] greater amount of business was now transacted, and transacted in a satisfactory manner, in the Quarter Sessions Courts of Ireland than the public was aware of'.[47]

The quarter sessions were distinguishable from petty sessions by the presence of juries.[48] The criminal jurisdiction at quarter sessions was theoretically quite broad, but the most serious offences were generally sent forward for trial at the assizes (see below). While there was no strict division in terms of felonies and misdemeanours, the quarter sessions were mainly concerned with the latter.[49] Quarter sessions tended to be attended by attorneys (i.e. solicitors), but not by barristers. To try serious felonies at quarter sessions would therefore be 'inconvenient to prosecutors, unfair to the accused, and highly unsatisfactory to the character of the administration of the public justice of the country.'[50] The quarter sessions could also hear appeals from summary convictions by the

magistrates at petty sessions. Aside from criminal jurisdiction, the quarter sessions could deal with such issues as publicans' licences, arms licences, blacksmiths' licences, charitable loan societies and poor law rating appeals. The quarter sessions evolved into County Courts in the second half of the nineteenth century,[51] by which stage they had both criminal and civil jurisdiction. Quarter sessions continued to operate until their abolition by the Courts of Justice Act 1924.

County Assizes

The most serious criminal cases were dealt with at the assizes. (Image 3) These were held in the principal towns (or assize towns) in each county. In the nineteenth century the country was divided into six circuits, each comprising several counties. Twice a year, in early spring and summer, the twelve judges of the superior courts (discussed below) divided the circuits among themselves. They then travelled to their respective circuits in pairs, visiting each assize town in turn. The dates and locations of the assizes, as well as the judges who would be sitting, were well publicised in both the national and regional press. One judge would deal with criminal (crown) cases, while the other heard civil (nisi prius) actions. Legislation in the 1870s provided for the joining of several counties as one 'Winter Assize county', so that prisoners awaiting trial in the winter months could more speedily be dealt with.[52] However, it also meant that jurors, litigants and witnesses might have to travel significant distances, as the assize town might be located in a different county. The assizes were well publicised and were significant events, attracting crowds to the towns where they were held. McCabe notes that the militarisation of the assizes could be a source of local tension, but '[b]y the 1830s, assize ceremonial had become more restrained and less martial than in earlier decades, though the high sheriff, local dignitaries, and mounted policemen continued to parade with the judges to court on the opening day'.[53] In Dublin, instead of assizes there was a Commission Court, established in 1729.[54]

Superior Courts

In the early nineteenth century there were four superior courts in Ireland: Chancery and the three common law courts of King's Bench (or Queen's Bench, depending on the monarch), Common Pleas and Exchequer. (Image 4) There was also the Court of Admiralty, which had both civil and criminal jurisdiction [55] and the Prerogative Court, an ecclesiastical court with jurisdiction over testamentary matters.[56] Parties could appeal from the common law courts and chancery to the Court of Exchequer Chamber, which was given clearly-defined powers as an intermediate court of appeal in 1800.[57] In the 1850s, the equity side of this court was abolished, and the Court of Appeal in Chancery was established as a second intermediate court

36 McCabe (2006), p. 127.

37 The Dublin police court sat in the Chancery Street court house.

38 They were replaced by district courts by the Courts of Justice Act 1924. Two of the existing Metropolitan Police magistrates became district judges.

39 Cork, Belfast, Londonderry and Galway.

40 The times for holding quarter sessions were set out in 38 Geo. III, c. 25 and 1 & 2 Geo. IV, c. 62. See also Quarter Sessions (Ireland) Act 1945 (8 & 9 Vic., c.80). Occasionally they were held less frequently; for example, in Co. Donegal in the 1840s, the sessions at Lifford and Buncrana were held once a year, while those at Letterkenny and Glenties were held twice a year.

41 See Seventeenth report, pp. 1-3.

42 'An act for the better execution of the law, and preservation of the peace within counties at large 1787' (27 Geo. III, c. 40), ss 15, 16, and 'An act for the better and more convenient administration of justice, and for the recovery of small debts in a summary way, at the sessions of the peace of the several counties at large within this kingdom, except the county of Dublin, and for continuing and amending an act, entitled, an act for the better execution of the law and preservation of the peace within counties at large 1796' (36 Geo. III, c. 25), s. 2.

43 Seventeenth report, pp. 2-3. They were paid professionals, who were to be barristers of six years' standing. Assistant barristers could also act alone, with jurisdiction over the summary recovery of small debts. 'An act for the better and more convenient administration of justice 1796' (36 Geo. III, c. 25).

44 Civil Bill Courts (Ireland) Act 1851 (14 & 15 Vic., c. 57). Later they were referred to as County Court judges: The County Courts and Officers (Ireland) Act 1877 (40 & 41 Vic., c. 56), s. 3. In some towns and cities the Chairman was known as the Recorder.

45 For example, in 1847 there were four quarter sessions in Co. Cavan – at Cavan, Cootehill, Bailieborough and Ballyconnell. In Co. Galway, they were held at Loughrea, Tuam, Galway, Gort, Ballinasloe, Portumna, Oughterard and Clifden. Return of towns in each county in Ireland in which quarter sessions and presentment sessions are held, HC 1847 (697) lvi 329, p. 3.

46 Quarter sessions of the peace, Ireland. A return from the clerks of the peace of Ireland, of the places and periods where the quarter sessions were held, 1832 and 1833, HC 1834 (397) xlviii 641. In the Seventeenth report (1828) it was noted, p. 4, that the sessions usually lasted between six and eight or ten days.

47 Hansard 3, vol. 164, col. 1874-5, House of Lords (5 August 1861).

48 For the number of quarter sessions (and juries) dealing with criminal cases in a year, see Quarter Sessions (Ireland), Criminal Issues. Return showing the number of quarter sessions held in Ireland during the year 1895 for the trial of criminal issues; &c., HC 1896 (295) lxix 555.

49 The Seventeenth report, p. 4, noted that the misdemeanours dealt with at the quarter sessions tended to concern the public peace. These included assaults, riots, violent trespass and distraint of cattle or other goods.

50 See Smythe, p. 31.

51 Legislation included Civil Bill Courts (Ireland) Act, 1851 (14 & 15 Vic., c. 57); County Officers and Courts Act (Ireland) 1877 (40 & 41 Vic., c. 56) and the County Court Amendment (Ireland) Act 1882 (45 & 46 Vic., c. 29). See also Constantine Molloy, 'The Irish County Courts', Journal of the Social and Statistical Inquiry Society of Ireland, vol. 5, no. 38 (1869), pp. 215–17, and H. Macauley Fitzgibbon, The practice and procedure of the Irish County Courts, Quarter Sessions Courts, Local Bankruptcy Courts, and Courts of Assize, 1890–1910 (Dublin, 1910).

52 The Winter Assize Act 1876 (39 & 40 Vic., c. 57) and the Winter Assize Act 1877 (40 & 41 Vic., c. 46).

53 Desmond McCabe, '"That Part That Laws or Kings Can Cause or Cure": Crown prosecution and jury trial at Longford assizes' in Raymond Gillespie and Gerard Moran (eds), Longford: essays in county history (Dublin, 1991), p. 160.

54 'An act to provide for the more speedy trial of criminals in the County of the City of Dublin, and in the County of Dublin' (3 Geo. II, c. 15). On the Dublin criminal courts, see Constantine Molloy, 'A Central Criminal Court for the County and City of Dublin', Journal of the Social and Statistical Inquiry Society of Ireland, vol. 34 (1867), pp. 445–47.

55 In Dublin the Court of Admiralty sat in Christ Church cathedral precincts in the eighteenth century and it moved to the Four Courts building when this was completed. Having been evicted from its chamber in favour of the Court of Exchequer Chamber, it then rented rooms belonging to the Court of Common Pleas, until it moved to an office off the entrance hall to the Four Courts. Costello notes that this room 'was similar to the private chambers of the chief justices, with a bathroom attached, and probably was never intended to function as a public court room'. Kevin Costello, The Court of Admiralty in Ireland 1575–1893 (Dublin, 2011), p. 186.

56 McDowell.

57 40 Geo. III, c. 39. This court was composed of the twelve judges of the common law courts, and could hear writs of error from the four superior courts.

of appeal. Criminal appeals (on points of law) were heard by the twelve common law judges, a practice which was placed on a statutory footing in 1848.[58] The Court for the Relief of Insolvent Debtors was established in 1821.[59] Commissioners in Bankruptcy were appointed in the 1830s,[60] and both of these functions were combined in 1857 in the Court of Bankruptcy and Insolvency,[61] which had an appeal to the Court of Appeal in Chancery. The Court of Probate was also established along similar lines in 1857,[62] taking over the testamentary jurisdiction of the ecclesiastical courts.[63] The Incumbered Estates Court was established in 1848 [64] and replaced in 1858 by the Landed Estates Court.[65] From 1801, the House of Lords sitting in London was the final appellate court for most Irish cases. The Irish Privy Council [66] had appellate jurisdiction over such matters as tithe composition [67] and incumbered estates,[68] but its role diminished during the nineteenth century.[69]

Evolution and Change

After decades of upheaval in the first half of the nineteenth century, the next major reform to the courts system was the Supreme Court of Judicature (Ireland) Act 1877.[70] This radically changed the structure of the superior courts in Ireland. Within the unified Supreme Court was a High Court and a Court of Appeal.[71] The High Court consisted of five divisions: Chancery, Queen's Bench, Common Pleas, Exchequer and Probate and Matrimonial. The Common Pleas Division was subsumed by the Queen's Bench Division in 1887.[72] In 1897, the Probate and Matrimonial Divisions were also integrated into the Queen's Bench Division, along with the courts of Admiralty and Bankruptcy.[73] By the time the Irish Free State came into existence, the High Court had two divisions, Chancery and King's Bench.[74]

The Government of Ireland Act 1920 provided that the Supreme Court of Judicature in Ireland ceased to exist. On partition, the courts structure of the two jurisdictions diverged. The courts system of the Irish Free State was set out in the Courts of Justice Act 1924, in compliance with Articles 64 to 67 of the 1922 Constitution. The 1924 Act provided that there was to be a Supreme Court, a High Court, Circuit Courts and District Courts. The High Court was to be both a court of original jurisdiction, meaning that cases could be tried there at first instance, and an appellate court, hearing appeals from the Circuit Court. It could also exercise any jurisdiction (including appellate) which had previously been exercised by the previous High Court in Ireland.[75] The Supreme Court was to be a court of appellate jurisdiction.[76] A Court of Criminal Appeal could be constituted by two High Court and one Supreme Court judge. [77]

The petty and quarter sessions have been described as the precursors to the District Court and Circuit Courts,

respectively.[78] Section 47(1) of the Court Officers Act 1926 obliged the Minister for Home Affairs to divide every county into District Court Areas.[79] These were in turn grouped into Districts. There were originally thirty-one such Districts. These were reduced to twenty-four by the District Court (Districts) Order 1961.[80] Changes to population distribution and transportation meant that the work of the District Court had diminished considerably over the preceding thirty-year period. The District Court [81] had jurisdiction over lesser civil cases, and minor criminal offences which could be tried summarily without a jury. It also inherited the licensing jurisdiction which had previously been exercised by justices of the peace at petty sessions.

The Circuit Court was established by section 37 the Courts of Justice Act 1924. This act divided the Free State into eight circuits. The number and delineation of the circuits was amended several times during the twentieth century.[82] The Circuit Court had jurisdiction in all but the most serious criminal cases – that is, all indictable offences aside from treason, murder and related offences, and piracy.[83] Its civil jurisdiction was detailed in legislation.[84]

The Courts (Establishment and Constitution) Act 1961 provided for the formal establishment of the courts under the 1937 Constitution.[85] The basic structure which had been established in the 1920s was maintained. The Court of Appeal was established in 2014 [86] to hear appeals from the Circuit and High Court on civil and criminal matters.

The Government of Ireland Act 1920 also established a new courts system for Northern Ireland.[87] Dickson notes that this was closely modelled on what had previously existed.[88] There was a Supreme Court of Judicature with two divisions: the High Court of Justice and the Court of Appeal in Northern Ireland.[89] The High Court retained the same jurisdiction as had previously been exercised by the High Court of Ireland. The petty and quarter sessions continued as before.[90] Magistrates' Courts dealt with minor disputes in petty sessions districts,[91] while County Courts decided civil cases.[92]

The 1970s saw major revisions to the Northern Ireland courts system: the assizes were replaced by the Crown Court, which heard more serious offences.[93] The Crown Court sat in Belfast and in several other towns in Northern Ireland. A third division of the High Court, the Family Division, was created in 1978, and the Court of Criminal Appeal was merged with the Court of Appeal.[94] In 2009, the Supreme Court of Judicature of Northern Ireland was renamed the Court of Judicature of Northern Ireland.[95]

58 Crown Cases Act 1848 (11 & 12 Vic., c. 78). This was known as the Court for Crown Cases Reserved. See Des Greer, 'A security against illegality? The reservation of Crown cases in nineteenth-century Ireland' in N.M. Dawson (ed.), *Reflections on law and history* (Dublin, 2006).

59 Insolvent Debtors (Ireland) Act 1821 (1 & 2 Geo. IV, c. 59).

60 Bankruptcy (Ireland) Act 1836 (6 & 7 Will., c. 14).

61 Bankruptcy and Insolvency Act 1857 (20 & 21 Vic., c. 60). The Court sat at Chancery Place in Dublin. It was renamed the Court of Bankruptcy: the Bankruptcy (Ireland) Amendment Act 1872 (35 & 36 Vic., c. 58). See W.H. Kisbey, *The law and practice of the Bankruptcy Court, Ireland* (Dublin, 1884).

62 Court of Probate Act 1857 (20 & 21 Vic., c. 79). This was also accommodated on Chancery Place.

63 The ecclesiastical courts were abolished by the Irish Church Act 1869 (32 & 33 Vic., c. 42).

64 Incumbered Estates Ireland Act 1848 (11 & 12 Vic., c. 48).

65 Landed Estates Court (Ireland) Act 1858 (20 & 21 Vic., c. 72). This was accommodated in an extension to the Bankruptcy Court building on Chancery Place. See Dodgson Hamilton Madden, *The Landed Estate Court Act. Rules, forms and directions* (Dublin, 1870).

66 See Jon Crawford, *Anglicizing the government of Ireland: the Irish Privy Council and the expansion of Tudor rule, 1556–1578* (Dublin, 1993).

67 Tithes Composition (Ireland) Act 1823(4 Geo. IV, c. 99) and the Tithes Composition (Ireland) Act 1832 (2 & 3 Will. IV, c. 119).

68 Incumbered Estates (Ireland) Act 1848 (12 & 13 Vic., c. 7).

69 See further, R. B. McDowell, *The Irish administration 1801–1914* (London, 1964), pp. 106-7. On the appeal to the Judicial Committee of the Privy Council in the twentieth century, see Thomas Mohr, *Guardian of the Treaty: the Privy Council Appeal and Irish sovereignty* (Dublin, 2016).

70 40 & 41 Vic., c. 57.

71 The Court of Exchequer Chamber, the Court of Appeal in Chancery and the Court for Lands Cases Reserved were abolished.

72 Supreme Court of Judicature (Ireland) Act 1887 (50 & 51 Vic., c. 6).

73 Supreme Court of Judicature (Ireland) (No. 2 Act) 1897 (60 & 61 Vic., c. 66).

74 A detailed list of pre-1922 courts legislation can be found in the Law Reform Commission, *Consolidation and reform of the Court Acts* (LRC 97-2010), pp. 8–11.

75 The Courts of Justice Act 1924, s. 17.

76 The Courts of Justice Act 1924, s. 18.

77 The Courts of Justice Act 1924, s. 8.

78 Law Reform Commission (LRC 97-2010), p. 8.

79 See the District Court (Areas) Order 1926 (S.I. No. 52/1926). This also specified the frequency and schedule for sittings of the District Court in each area.

80 S.I. No. 6/1961.

81 The Provision of District Courts Order 1924 (S.I. No. 11,171/1924) listed the locations of District Court houses.

82 For example, The Circuit Court (New Circuits) Order 1937 (S.I. No. 309/1937) (pursuant to the Courts of Justice Act 1936, s. 13); The Circuit Court (New Circuits) Order 1960 (S.I. no. 70/1960) (pursuant to the Courts of Justice Act 1953); the Circuit Court (Alteration of Circuits) Order 1964 (S.I. No. 206/1964) and the Circuit Court (Alteration of Circuits) Order 1969 (S.I. No. 201/1969) (pursuant to the Courts Act 1964).

83 The Courts Act 1924, s. 49 and the Courts (Supplemental Provisions) Act 1961, s. 25.

84 The Courts Act 1924, s. 48.

85 See also the Courts (Supplemental Provisions) Act 1961, which set out the jurisdiction of each court. The Supreme Court that operated between 1924 and 1961 inherited the jurisdiction of the Court of Appeal of the Supreme Court of Judicature.

86 Court of Appeal Act 2014.

87 Section 40.

88 Brice Dickson, *Law in Northern Ireland* (3rd ed., Oxford, 2018), [4.6].

89 Supreme Court of Judicature (Northern Ireland) Order 1921.

90 See generally the County Officers and Courts Act (Northern Ireland) 1925.

91 See the Magistrates' Courts Act (Northern Ireland) 1964. See also the *Report of the Committee on County Courts and Magistrates' Courts in Northern Ireland*, Cmnd. 5824, 1974.

92 The Justice Act (NI) 2015, s. 1 extended the powers of each County Court and Magistrates' Court to cover the whole of Northern Ireland.

93 Judicature (Northern Ireland) Act 1978. The same Act also set up the Northern Ireland Courts Service.

94 Judicature (Northern Ireland) Act 1978.

95 This was to make way for the United Kingdom Supreme Court.

Court Procedures and the Court House

Over the two centuries considered here, the courts system, the substantive civil and criminal law, and rules of evidence and procedure were perpetually evolving. This makes a definitive statement as to the use or business of a particular court house challenging. It is possible, however, to provide an overview of the sorts of activities which took place within court buildings.

There were various actors to be accommodated in or around the courts. In the courtroom itself, depending on the level and jurisdiction, there could be one or more judges or magistrates, legal representatives, parties to a civil action, the defendant in a criminal trial, witnesses, constabulary, sheriffs, interpreters, jurors, newspaper reporters and, of course, spectators. (Image 5) Beyond the courtroom, the ideal court house also contained a deliberation room for the petty jury, a secure space or cell for prisoners awaiting trial, record rooms, and sufficient circulation space for everyone to go about their business. Court houses also had to accommodate various officers[96] such as the Clerks of the Crown, who were responsible for 'the routine functioning of the assize court'[97] and the keeping of court records. Clerks of the Peace[98] and petty sessions clerks had similar record-keeping functions which were specified in legislation.[99] Petty sessions clerks' minute books and order books were to be stored at the court house, and so storage space was required. A court house also needed space for lawyers and judges. Changing patterns of circulation and interaction from the nineteenth century on meant that there was often a separate entrance for the judge.[100] These basic requirements had changed little by the mid-twentieth century, when the Committee on Court Practice and Procedure listed as necessary: 'accommodation for consultations, a bar room for the use of the practitioners, retiring accommodation for the judge, the necessary toilet facilities for all persons including the public and a properly equipped retiring room for the jury', as well as some accommodation for the public.[101] Public waiting areas had been incorporated into some nineteenth-century designs, with the Dun Laoghaire Police Court, for example, including a separate 'waiting room for ladies'.[102]

Some buildings housed several courts.[103] Minor local courts generally did not sit in purpose-built spaces; in Dublin, for example, the Court of Conscience sat in the Tholsel for many years before moving to the City Assembly House on South William Street in the early nineteenth century. In rural Ireland, manor courts usually sat in convenient locations such as rooms in public houses or taverns.[104] Occasionally they sat in private houses.[105] In Dublin, the city sessions were held at Green Street court house, while the county quarter sessions were held at Kilmainham court house. In Drogheda, the quarter sessions were held in the Tholsel, and in Waterford they were held at the eighteenth-century Guildhall.[106]

Legislation provided for the renting of suitable premises in which petty sessions could be held.[107] If there was no court house available in which to hold petty sessions, a room and a lock-up could be rented in which to hold proceedings and store records.[108] The room had to be publicly accessible,[109] and could not be located in a licensed premises, a barracks, or 'in any building maintained in the whole or in part at the public expence'.[110] McCabe notes the simplicity of these hired rooms in the mid-nineteenth century: 'an expanse of bare floorboards, scant furniture, unevenly whitewashed walls and (in winter) a fuming turf fire'.[111] He also observes elsewhere that in pre-Famine Mayo, rooms used for petty sessions tended to lack 'the refinements expected of courts'.[112] This would appear to be typical of the smaller petty sessions court houses throughout the country.

Assizes took place in county court houses. Given the volume of business [113] and the status of the judges, ideally these were substantial buildings with prominent positions in county towns. Hill's article explains how the role of grand juries [114] in funding and overseeing court house building often led to their accommodation being prioritised. For example, an 1805 Francis Johnston design for the Armagh county court house gives almost half of the ground floor space over to the grand jury, including a room[115] in which to assemble, a dining room, a library and a secretary's room. County court houses built in the nineteenth century often included a segregated public viewing gallery. (Image 6)

Space for lawyers [116] had expanded and evolved by the nineteenth century. In county court houses they began to be provided with a variety of spaces for dining, robing, consulting and reading. Bar rooms were an important place for barristers to convene. By the twentieth century, some grand jury rooms were being repurposed as bar rooms. The bar room in Limerick court house, previously the grand jury room, was described as 'a long and graceful room with a huge old fireplace and several large windows',[117] on whose walls an old baronial map of the county continued to hang in the 1940s.[118] In both the nineteenth and twentieth centuries the standard of accommodation in bar rooms varied considerably. The bar room at the Belfast court house on Crumlin Road in the late nineteenth century was described in the following terms: 'the size of it was very small, the Light bad, and the Ventilation and Sanitary arrangements worse'.[119]

However, following refurbishment in 1907, it was 'a splendid, well-lit, and well-ventilated Bar Room'.[120] Furthermore, it was heated by a hot water system, whereas the Kilrush bar room was said to be heated by a turf fire as late as the 1980s.[121]

Various other facilities might be provided for barristers – for example, Hill Smith refers to the provision of bar wine cellars in most court houses on the North East Circuit in the late nineteenth century.[122] In other cases, barristers made use of what was available, with passages and corridors being pressed into service as meeting and consultation spaces.[123] Even in the late twentieth century, lawyers and their clients were obliged, in some parts of the country, to use local public houses or hotels for consultations, given the lack of adequate spaces in court houses.[124]

For the secure and convenient transfer of prisoners awaiting trial, many court houses, such as in Carrick-on-Shannon, Co. Leitrim, were situated adjacent to the gaol. Waterford court house, designed by Gandon, was built as part of a complex which included the county gaol. Others incorporated a bridewell [125] or had holding cells in the basement.[126] Others still were linked to gaols via tunnels. In Belfast court house on Crumlin Road, the dock in the Crown Court was 'connected with the Jail on the opposite side of the Crumlin road by a covered way which passes under the street, and so facilitates business and saves much inconvenience.'[127] Dungannon court house, County Tyrone, included cells for both male and female prisoners, as well as cells for debtors.[128] George Richard Pain's 1824 design for a court house and bridewell in County Cork clearly illustrates how accommodation for prisoners might be integrated into a court building.

In 1796 Gandon's Four Courts building on Inns Quay became the home of the superior courts. Previously, the courts had sat in the environs of Christ Church Cathedral in the seventeenth and eighteenth centuries.[129] The new accommodation appears to have been a significant improvement – 'permanent, sanitary, safe and hugely aspirational' [130] – with space and facilities for all of those who had reason to spend time in or near the superior courts. After its destruction in 1922,[131] the superior courts sat in Dublin Castle for eight years. The reconstruction of the Four Courts in the 1920s incorporated alterations which reflected changes to law and practice over the previous century.[132] For example, elaborate provision for the sequestering of jurors was evident in the redesign. The post-1922 redesign also had to take into account the Sex Disqualification (Removal) Act 1919, and included separate facilities for potential women jurors.[133] However, the use to which these spaces were put

96 See the floor plan for Carrick-on-Shannon court house, which had ample space for both the Clerk of the Crown and the Clerk of the Peace.

97 Ian Bridgeman, 'The constabulary and the criminal justice system in nineteenth-century Ireland' in Ian O'Donnell and Finbar McAuley (eds), *Criminal justice history* (Dublin, 2003), p. 117.

98 Clerks of the Crown and Clerks of the Peace were fused in 1877 by the County Officers and Courts (Ireland) Act 1877 (40 & 41 Vic., c. 56).

99 See the Petty Sessions (Ireland) Act 1851 (14 & 15 Vic., c. 93), s. 5.

100 Grand juries also sometimes had their own entrance, as at the Kilmainham court house.

101 Committee on Court Practice and Procedure, *Twelfth interim report. Courts organisation* (Dublin, 1972), p. 29.

102 See gazetteer entry for Dun Laoghaire.

103 For example, the Green Street complex housed the Dublin Commission Court, the quarter sessions, the Sheriff's Court, the Mayor's Court and the Recorder's Court.

104 McMahon (2001), p. 139.

105 For example, the manor court at Corofin, Co. Clare. It moved to a public house in 1832 following a cholera epidemic. McMahon (2001), p. 139.

106 Ibid.

107 The Petty Sessions Act (Ireland) 1827 (7 & 8 Geo. IV, c. 67).

108 Petty Sessions (Ireland) Act 1851 (14 & 15 Vic., c. 93).

109 Section 9.

110 Section 8(1).

111 See McCabe.

112 Des McCabe, 'Magistrates, Peasants and the Petty Sessions Courts 1823-50', *Cathair na Mart: Journal of the Westport Historical Society*, vol. 5, nos. 45-48 (1985), p. 48.

113 Assizes, for example, attracted significant crowds. The *Irish Jurist* noted in 1854 that it was 'a well known fact that assizes time is the harvest of the inn-keepers and owners of lodgings in the town'. Anon., editorial, *Irish Jurist*, vol. 6 (1854) (o.s.) p. 221.

114 The grand jury consisted of 'gentlemen of the best figure of the county', selected and appointed by the high sheriff at the assizes or quarter sessions. W. Blackstone, *Commentaries on the Laws of England*, 4 vols (London, 1791), vol. iv, p. 299. See also Leonard MacNally, *The Justice of the Peace for Ireland: containing the authorities and duties of that officer, and also of the various conservators of the peace*, 2 vols (Dublin, 1808), vol. ii, p. 48; and the Grand Jury (Ireland) Act 1836 (6 & 7 Will. IV, c. 116). Court house building was funded by local taxation of landowners via the grand jury cess.

115 See Armagh court house scheme 'A', 1805 (Irish Architectural Archive [hereafter IAA], RIAI Murray Collection, 92/46.4-10).

116 See for example the Mayo county court house in Castlebar, built in the 1820s and refurbished in 1860. See also the floor plan for Carrick-on-Shannon court house, which included a bar room.

117 Gerard A. Lee, *A memoir of the south-western circuit* (Dublin, 1990), p. 5.

118 Ibid.

119 George Hill Smith, *The north east bar. A sketch, historical and reminiscent* (Belfast, 1910), p. 41.

120 Ibid. Hill Smith also mentions, p. 41, that temporary measures had been introduced in 1905: 'the atmosphere of the Bar Rooms and the Courts was considerably purified and new Sewers properly laid'.

121 Lee, p. 53.

122 Hill Smith, p. 33.

123 For example, in Ennis court house, Lee observed that a wide corridor running behind each court facilitated consultations. Lee, p. 47. Kilrush court house, built in 1831, had 'an outer hall paved with flagstones', where consultations were held and settlements negotiated.' Ibid., p. 51.

124 Liam T. Cosgrave, Seanad Éireann, 10 December 1997.

125 e.g. Longford court house.

126 e.g. Swinford, Co. Mayo.

127 Hill Smith, p. 41.

128 Costello notes that in the early nineteenth century, one-third of Ireland's prison population was made up of persons imprisoned for debt, usually of small amounts. Kevin Costello, 'Imprisonment for Debt in early Nineteenth Century Ireland, 1810-1848', UCD Working Papers in Law, Criminology & Socio-Legal Studies (Research Paper No.09/2013), p. 1.

129 See Edward McParland, 'The old Four Courts, at Christ Church' and Colum Kenny, 'On holy ground: the benchers and the site of the present Four Courts before 1796' in Caroline Costello (ed.), *The Four Courts: 200 Years* (Dublin, 1996).

130 Tomás Clancy, 'The Four Courts buildings and the development of an independent bar of Ireland' in Costello, p. 82.

131 See Ronan Keane, 'A mass of crumbling ruins: the destruction of the Four Courts in June 1922' in Costello.

132 See, for example, Clancy.

133 See the floor plan for the refurbished Four Courts. IAA, King's Inns Collection 2007/10.5/2(iv).

in the ensuing half-century is difficult to state, given how few women jurors served before the Juries Act 1976.[134]

There are certain basic legal principles and procedural issues which affected court house design, although conceptions of due process have changed over time.[135] Throughout the nineteenth and twentieth centuries, the delineation of various roles within the legal process meant that space within court houses was segregated, with specific spaces assigned to specific functions. It has been observed that '[w]here different participants sit in the criminal courtroom has changed considerably over the last two hundred years'.[136]

For example, while manor court juries in the eighteenth and early nineteenth centuries sat around a table with the seneschal,[137] quarter sessions and assize courts in the nineteenth century saw an increasing physical distance between the judge and jury. It was imperative that members of the jury should all sit together, and should be able to see and hear the evidence and witness testimony. This meant that, in the courtroom, they were seated in a jury box, which was often elevated.[138] When lengthy deliberations became the norm, they required a room to which to retire. To prevent them from mixing with other court actors, this room would be accessible directly from their box, so that they did not have to walk through the passageways of the court building.

A witness had to be both visible and audible. For example, the competition specification for Tullamore court house in the 1830s stated that persons sitting in the jury galleries and the dock should be able to 'distinctly hear the Judge, Bar and witnesses'.[139] Early in the nineteenth century this was often achieved by having them testify from a chair atop a table at the front of the court.[140] (Image 7) In some places, this practice endured well into the twentieth century. For example, as late as the 1940s Galway court house had 'a witness sitting on a chair, perched on a table in front of the judge'.[141] In later court house designs, witness boxes were introduced – often elevated, and positioned so that the jury could clearly see the witness's facial expression. The placing of court furniture also affected the audibility; for example, at Tralee court house '[t]he seats were curved in a semi-circle towards the bench and the witness stand which enabled every voice to be heard clearly'.[142] Adequate lighting was an important consideration, and many nineteenth-century court houses were designed with this in mind. Tralee was described as having 'a huge window high above the bench which provided sufficient light for the proceedings'.[143] Tullamore court house was one of several to incorporate light-well courtyards to ensure adequate light, and the Police Court in Dun Laoghaire was praised when it was built in 1890 for being well-lit and ventilated.[144]

Persons who found themselves on trial in the nineteenth century generally experienced the courtroom from the dock. Docks were a relatively recent addition to the furniture of the court[145] but by the mid nineteenth century were an almost universal feature of purpose-built courtrooms. (Image 8) Usually constructed from timber,[146] sometimes they were elaborately designed, dominating the landscape of the courtroom. This left defendants isolated, often unable to see or hear witnesses or communicate effectively with their legal representatives. It also arguably had a prejudicial effect on juries. For almost as long as docks have been common courtroom features, they have been challenged by defendants.[147] Limerick city court house in the 1940s still had an old-fashioned 'dock which was topped with iron spikes'.[148] In the 1960s the Committee on Court Practice and Procedure asserted that docks were 'out of date' and incompatible with the presumption of innocence. The Committee pointed out that docks were not 'an essential part of courtroom equipment for a criminal trial',[149] and recommended that an accused person be seated so as to have 'easy and unobtrusive access to his legal advisors' while remaining visible to the judge and jury.[150] The modern trend in Irish court house design has been to move away from security docks,[151] in favour of seating accused persons near their legal representatives or in witness-style boxes. (Image 9)

Up to the late twentieth century, victims of criminal offences were not viewed as having any particular status, and no express provision was made for their involvement in the trial beyond testifying, either on a chair or otherwise. Now they are recognised as having a special status,[152] and can make victim impact statements.[153] Many court houses now have specific accommodation for victims and other vulnerable witnesses, ranging from simple rooms to suites.[154]

Other significant changes to court procedure in the twentieth century include the decreasing reliance on juries, which are only empanelled in indictable criminal trials at the Circuit and High Court, and in limited forms of civil action. Advances in technology have also impacted upon court design. Since the 1990s, it has been possible, for example, for witnesses in certain situations to testify by live video link.[155] The early 2000s saw the introduction of Digital Audio Recording (DAR), now recognised as an essential element in the design of modern court houses.

Alternative Court House Use

Mulcahy notes that '[f]or many centuries trials across legal jurisdictions within England shared space with political debates, balls and assemblies, church services, markets and theatres'.[156] The same can be said for Irish courts. Purpose-built court houses and courtrooms are a relatively new phenomenon. It can be seen from the entries in the gazetteer that, even in the nineteenth century, many court houses were in fact multi-functional spaces. Butler argues that 'in times of economic plenty and lax oversight from central government, grand juries were sometimes motivated to skim the cream of prosperity to beautify their county towns and provide ample private social spaces'.[157] Examples of such private social spaces include the Clonmel court house, completed in 1801, which incorporated a ballroom, while others incorporated assembly rooms. Billiard and reading rooms were added to the Crossmaglen court house in 1911. Rathfarnham court house, built in 1912, had moveable furniture to allow the space to be used for lectures and concerts.[158]

Aside from private entertainment, there are many examples of court buildings which incorporated other functions. As noted by Hill in this volume, many market houses built before the nineteenth century incorporated courtrooms.[159] Other juxtapositions included police barracks,[160] post offices,[161] schools,[162] or dispensaries.[163] Dun Laoghaire court house was designed in the 1870s as part of a complex which included a town hall. Into the twentieth century, it was still quite common for a range of public services and offices to be based in court houses. For example, Belturbet District Court house in County Cavan was rebuilt in 1928 to include a courtroom, county council offices, a library and concert hall.[164] The Castleisland court house in County Kerry was built in 1929 with an adjoining public library wing. Hill partially attributes such multifunctioning spaces to the frugality of the Free State government. A similarly frugal mindset was evident in the recommendation from the Committee on Court Practice and Procedure in the 1970s that courtrooms which were only in periodic use 'should be so designed as to be capable of being used for other community activities when the Court is not actually in session'.[165] The Committee's proposal included the use of moveable furniture and floors of uniform level.

Disrepair and Rebellion

Not all court houses reached ideal standards, and from time to time there were complaints about the dismal accommodation. For example, the court house at Glenarm, Co. Antrim, was said in 1827 to be in a poor state of repair,[166] and Ballyragget, Co. Kilkenny, was described in 1882 as having a 'damp fireless court house'.[167] The Dublin Jurors' Association was established

134 This piece of legislation followed the Supreme Court's ruling in de Búrca and Anderson v Attorney General [1976] IR 38 that the Juries Act 1927 was unconstitutional as it effectively excluded women from jury service because they tended not to be ratepayers.

135 Linda Mulcahy, *Legal architecture: justice, due process and the place of law* (London, 2011), p. 9.

136 Meredith Rossner, David Tait, Blake McKimmie and Rick Sarre, 'The dock on trial: courtroom design and the presumption of innocence', *Journal of Law and Society*, vol. 44, no. 3 (2017), pp. 317-44.

137 McMahon (2001), p. 139.

138 The jury in Galway county court house in the 1940s was described as being: 'in a box so high up in the air that they could not be seen or see'. Patrick MacKenzie, *Lawful occasions: the old Eastern Circuit* (Dublin, 1991), p. 92.

139 Letter dated 15 November 1832. IAA, RIAI Murray Collection, 92/46.1115. See gazetteer entry for Tullamore.

140 The floor plan for the sessions house at Dunshaughlin, Co. Meath, includes a large table. This would have served both as a platform for witnesses, and as a place for lawyers to strew their papers.

141 MacKenzie, p. 92.

142 Lee, p. 22.

143 Ibid.

144 See gazetteer entry for Dun Laoghaire.

145 For a history of the dock see Rossner *et al.*

146 e.g. the dock in the court house at Buncrana, Co. Donegal.

147 Rossner *et al*, and Linda Mulcahy, 'Putting the defendant in their place: why do we still use the dock in criminal proceedings?', *The British Journal of Criminology*, vol. 53, no. 6 (2013), pp. 1139–56.

148 Lee, p. 5. The original dock was removed from Skibbereen court house in 1956.

149 Committee on Court Practice and Procedure, *Sixth interim report: the criminal jurisdiction of the High Court* (Dublin, 1966), p. 10.

150 These views were reiterated by the Committee in 1972: see the *Twelfth interim report*, p. 30. It was stated that the presence of a dock had 'a most inhibiting effect on the general design of the courtroom accommodation as it means that the rest of the accommodation has to be designed around that central position'.

151 For a contrast with other jurisdictions, see Mulcahy (2013), and Rossner *et al.*

152 See the Criminal Justice (Victims of Crime) Act 2017 and the EU Victims Directive, Directive 2012/29/EU. See also Sheena Norton, 'The Place of Victims in the Criminal Justice System', *Irish Probation Journal*, vol. 4, no. 1 (2007), pp. 63–76, and Shane Kilcommins, Susan Leahy, Kathleen Moore Walsh and Eimear Spain, *The Victim in the Irish Criminal Process* (Manchester, 2018).

153 Criminal Justice Act 1993, s. 5.

154 For example, Tullamore court house, Co. Offaly.

155 Criminal Evidence Act 1992, s. 13.

156 Mulcahy (2011), p. 7.

157 Richard J. Butler, '"The radicals in these Reform times": politics, grand juries, and Ireland's unbuilt assize courthouses, 1800-50', *Architectural History*, vol. 58 (2015), p. 114.

158 See gazetteer entry for Rathfarnham, Co. Dublin.

159 For example, in Ballinrobe, Co. Mayo, the petty sessions were held on the first floor above an open market arcade. See also Lisnaskea, Co. Fermanagh.

160 e.g. Crumlin, Co. Antrim, built in 1832.

161 e.g. Whitehouse, Co. Antrim, and Glassan, Co. Westmeath.

162 e.g. Blessington, Co. Wicklow and Portglenone, Co. Antrim.

163 Glassan, Co. Westmeath.

164 Tullamore court house also included County Council offices.

165 Committee on Court Practice and Procedure, *Twelfth Interim Report. Courts Organisation* (Dublin, 1972), p. 29.

166 *Report from the select committee on Manor Courts, Ireland* 1837, HC (491) xv., p.123. While it was undergoing repairs, the court was held in a schoolhouse.

167 *Freeman's Journal*, 14 March 1882.

in 1875[168], partially in response to the poor state of the Dublin city and county courts. Such criticisms were not limited to the nineteenth century. Complaints about individual court houses continued throughout the twentieth century. In 1972 the Committee on Court Practice and Procedure observed that the standard of accommodation in Irish court houses was 'far from satisfactory',[169] and that it was 'almost impossible to uphold respect for the law in some of the dilapidated court houses at present in use'.[170] It suggested the design of a prototype courtroom, stressing 'the necessity for a simple design, reasonably comfortable accommodation, good acoustics and adequate heating and ventilation'.[171] It highlighted the 'comparatively modern' court house at Kells, Co. Meath, as 'a good and satisfactory example of this design'. The Courthouses (Provision and Maintenance) Act 1935 obliged county councils to provide and maintain court houses.[172] The legislation also empowered the Minister for Justice to compel a local authority to perform its duty as regards the upkeep of court houses.[173] In 1993 the Minister for Justice noted that there were twenty-six court houses in need of major repairs.[174] During debate over the Courts Service Bill, Liam T. Cosgrave recalled a judge in Kilmainham having to compete with rats, while a district judge elsewhere had to keep his overcoat on because the windows were cracked.[175] Another senator pointed out that it was common for district court judges to adjourn courts before business commenced because of 'arctic conditions in the courtrooms'.[176]

The impact of conflict on court houses, particularly in the early twentieth century, is worth mentioning. Although the 1922 burning of the Four Courts is the most well-known example, it was not the only court building to suffer during the revolutionary period. In the early days of the Free State, expenditure on court building and repairs was unavoidable. For example, the court house in Bray, Co. Wicklow, was damaged by fire in 1921 during the War of Independence, and was repaired in 1926. The court house at Tullamore was burnt during the Civil War and, according to the former Chief Justice T.F. O'Higgins, was 'rebuilt with taste and foresight'.[177]

In Northern Ireland, court houses were sometimes targeted as symbols of the State during the Troubles. For example, court houses in Antrim town, Newtownbutler and Lisnaskea in Co. Fermanagh, Keady in Co. Armagh, Downpatrick and Newry in Co. Down, Cookstown, Fivemiletown, Moy and Dungannon in Co. Tyrone and Kilrea, Co. Derry were bombed, sometimes repeatedly. As noted by Hill in this volume, court houses built or refurbished in Northern Ireland after this period tended to incorporate often extensive security features.

Conclusions

Clancy describes the opening of Gandon's Four Courts as 'a paradigm shift both in architecture and self awareness'. It heralded the beginning of a new era in court design and building. Changes to the structure of the superior and inferior courts, legal and judicial practice, rules of evidence and procedure were accompanied by changes in how the physical space of courtrooms and court houses was conceived. Much of the twentieth century, by contrast, was a period of decline. Aside from some notable (and essential) exceptions in the 1920s, development of court houses was minimal. In 1984 Senator Mary Robinson observed that, 'from an architectural and aesthetic point of view', court houses were 'important and central buildings in towns around Ireland'. However, she added, 'at the human level, they lack basic facilities. Some of them are not even waterproof and many of them have not got proper heating and wiring and there is a complete absence of privacy with regard to consulting and waiting rooms'. This can no longer be said to reflect the reality of Irish court houses. The establishment of the Courts Service in 1999 signalled another revolution in the refurbishment and remodelling of existing court houses, and the commissioning of new courts complexes, to reflect changes to trial practice and procedure.

168 *Freeman's Journal*, 30 January 1875. See further Niamh Howlin, *Juries in Ireland: laypersons and law in the long nineteenth century* (Dublin, 2017), ch. 1.

169 A minority report by two members of the Committee preferred to express this in stronger language: 'The condition of many courthouses is scandalous and not merely impairs the proper administration of justice but also makes it difficult for the ordinary layman to have any respect for the legal process.' *Twelfth interim report*, p. 37.

170 Committee on Court Practice and Procedure, *Twelfth interim report*, p. 29.

171 Ibid., p. 30.

172 Section 3. This excluded the Four Courts complex and a number of other Dublin courts which fell under the responsibility of the Office of Public Works.

173 Section 10.

174 Dáil Éireann, 13 Oct. 1993.

175 Seanad Éireann 10 Dec. 1997.

176 Denis O'Donovan, Seanad Éireann, 10 Dec. 1997.

177 T.F. O'Higgins, *A double life* (Dublin, 1996), p. 78. See also Michael Byrne, *Legal Offaly: the county courthouse Tullamore and the legal profession in County Offaly from the 1820s to the present day* (Tullamore, 2008).

--
Image

1 Petty Sessions, Ballyragget, Co. Kilkenny.
 Attributed to William Sadler, 1867 (NLI)
2 Quarter Sessions, Ballinrobe, Co. Mayo.
 Attributed to Charles William Cole, 1880 (NLI)
3 Assizes, Tullamore, Co. Offaly (Trial of Charles
 Stewart Parnell). *Illustrated London News*, 8
 January 1881 (Offaly History)
4 'Interior of the Queen's Bench Court [Four
 Courts], Dublin', *Illustrated London News*,
 18 November 1843 (NLI)
5 Interior of Claremorris Court House, *Illustrated
 London News*, 26 November 1881 (IAA)
6 Courtroom interior, Clonmel, *Illustrated London
 News*, 7 October 1848 (NLI)
7 Witness on Table. Attributed to Henry Brocas
 Junior, c. 1782-1837 (NLI)
8 Prisoner in Dock, Green Street, Dublin.
 Le Monde Illustré, 1871 (NLI)
9 Mid-20th-century courtroom interior,
 Mitchelstown, Boyd Barrett Murphy O'Connor,
 1948 (Boyd Barrett Murphy O'Connor
 Collection, IAA)

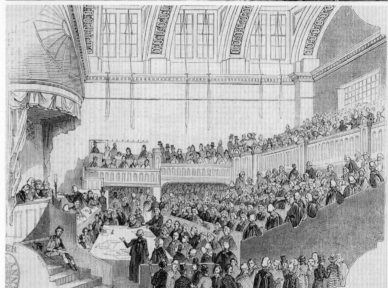

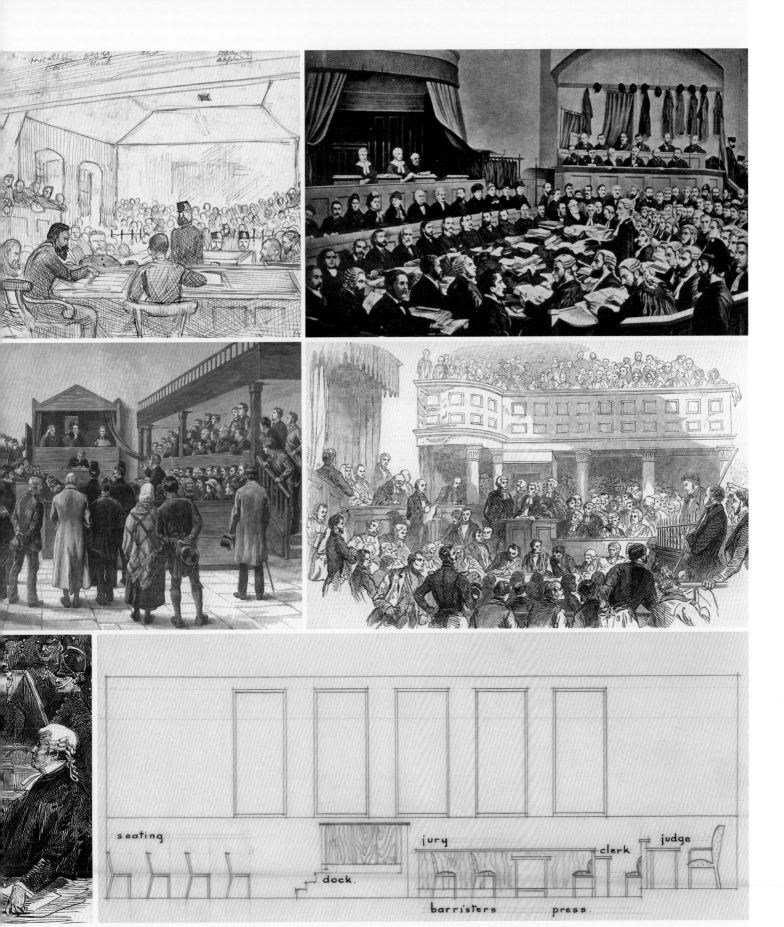

seating

dock.

jury

clerk

judge

barristers   press.

17

IRISH COURT HOUSES
A Brief Architectural History to 1998

Judith Hill

Introduction

Image and utility, the dual purpose of most buildings with any architectural pretension, are brought into particularly sharp focus when considering the design of court houses, for they must embody aspirations concerning the dispensing of justice, while allowing judicial procedure to operate in a precisely prescribed manner. These two aspects of court house architecture are the criteria that have been repeatedly used in assessing individual buildings. In 1806 the Rev. Daniel Beaufort considered the newly-built court house in Clonmel 'to be one of the most convenient & beautiful buildings of its kind & size in his Majesty's dominions'.[1] Nearly half a century later the judges who were to dispense justice in Ennis court house, completed in July 1850, were 'much surprised and delighted at the very judicious manner in which every department was arranged', while the *Clare Journal* remarked on the building's 'air of solidity and strength'.[2]

Provincial Irish court house designs display a strong family resemblance.[3] Court house briefs from the mid eighteenth to the early twentieth century almost invariably generated symmetrical plans and classical architecture. In the pre-Famine period of the early nineteenth century, when the vast majority of Irish court houses were constructed, a distinctive neoclassicism marked court houses of all sizes. This was as true of the great porticoed county court houses, such as the Greek revival court house in Dundalk, as of modest sessions houses, such as those in various Cork towns which displayed the spare concision of James and George Richard Pain's standard court house design.[4] Owing their presence to the place within the judicial hierarchy of the town or city in which they were located – their scale calibrated to the town's importance within that structure – court houses are quintessentially urban structures. In many cases the patronage of local proprietors determined their location within the town, and their design reflected their civic as well as judicial function.

Architectural historians have long recognised the impressiveness and distinctiveness of Irish court houses. In 1958 Maurice Craig identified early nineteenth-century Irish court houses as an interesting building type: homogenous, but not uniform, and presenting a 'variety of plans'.[5] In 1982 he described them as 'majestic', the 'last, and perhaps finest contribution [of the old oligarchical system] in the sphere of public buildings'. Thirty years later Livia Hurley introduced her survey of court houses by stating that they were '[a]mong the most powerful contributions made to Irish provincial architecture'.[6]

This appreciation has not been matched by research, and court houses have, until very recently, been largely overlooked by scholars. Exceptions include Charles Brett's 1973 study of Ulster structures and Christine Casey's 1982 investigation of market houses and court houses in Leinster, while Richard Butler's recent and more broadly based research has substantially opened up the subject.[7] One of the most revealing themes successively developed by these scholars has been an assessment of the extent and limitations of local elite patronage in the context of national political developments within the Union.

The comprehensive gazetteer in this volume, produced for the Courts Service in 2018/19, has provided an opportunity to review the historical development of court houses across Ireland. Using insights gained through analysis of the gazetteer data, existing scholarly studies, and some supplementary archival research, this short essay will investigate the development of the court house by considering changes in patronage, financial structure, political support and the requirements of the judiciary, and the effect of these on the planning and layout, architectural style and civic presence of the resulting buildings.[8]

The seventeenth and eighteenth centuries

The earliest surviving court houses date from the late seventeenth century. They were hybrid structures: market houses on the ground floor accessed through open arcades (usually three to five arches) with one or more rooms above, within which court sessions could be accommodated. These upper floors were not necessarily designed specifically for court use. A prominent surviving example of purpose-built accommodation for a court above market arches is the 'Main Guard' in Clonmel, commissioned by the Duke of Ormonde as part of his improvement programme for the administrative centre of his palatinate. It was completed in 1675.[9] A taste-maker with a keen sense of architecture's role in 'keep[ing] up the splendour of government', Ormonde very probably had a decisive influence on a building that combined tradition – a medieval European architectural form – with innovation: symmetry and classical detailing.[10]

When the Ormonde palatinate was extinguished in 1716 the building became the location of assizes, and thus an integral part of the developing court system. A series of parliamentary acts in the seventeenth and eighteenth centuries established a framework which enabled the construction of court houses. The system relied on twenty-three-member grand juries chosen from the pool of local landowners drawn up twice-yearly in each county for the assizes.[11] An act of 1634 enabled grand juries to levy a county cess (tax) for road-building, a measure which was extended to the construction of prisons and court houses in 1708.[12] The administration of the grand jury system, which relied on 'presentments' – a formal mechanism for publicly funded projects in which proposals for county expenditure were made by grand juries to the assize judges – was refined in a series of acts in the eighteenth century.[13]

While the market house with provision for a first-floor courtroom prevailed as the predominant typology in the eighteenth century, several trends are apparent. Architectural presence within the civic context could be achieved through classical design. This can be seen in the calm elegance of Antrim's 1726 market and court house with its long nine-bay façade capped by a finely carved dentil cornice and wide overhanging eaves.[14] It is apparent too in the Palladianism of Dunlavin's (Co. Wicklow) 1740 market and court house, in which a cruciform plan, topped by a dome surmounting an octagonal drum, resulted in a building of impressively controlled volumes and façades.

Parallel to the market-and-court-house typology were developments that prioritised the court function. In 1746 at Lifford, Co. Donegal, Michael Priestly designed one of the earliest surviving purpose-built court houses. It is a long, single-storey structure with heavily decorated windows and a central pedimented door surmounted by the royal coat of arms. In 1762 Roscommon grand jury rejected a traditional design which provided for a new courtroom in three of five first-floor bays above market arches. Instead, it signed an agreement with John and George Ensor for a building where the court provision was doubled (two courtrooms) and given primacy (the market space was located at the rear of the building), and in which the judiciary function stamped its imagery on the building.[15] This latter change is apparent in the neatly formal design (astylar doors flanking a Serliana window), which relied on strong geometries and austere

1 *Observations on a tour through Leinster, Munster and Connacht* (1806), quoted in Ann Martha Rowan (ed.), *The architecture of Richard Morrison and William Vitruvius Morrison* (Dublin, 1989), p. 70.

2 Quoted in Ciarán Ó Murchadha, *Sable wings over the land: Ennis, county Clare, and its wider community during the great famine* (Ennis, 1998), p. 257.

3 The Four Courts in Dublin (1776–1802), which house the superior courts, are exceptional in terms of planning, scale, architectural expression and status, exemplified by the great column-encircled drum crowned with a copper-clad dome. However, the neoclassicism of Thomas Cooley's and James Gandon's design allies the Four Courts to early nineteenth-century provincial court houses, the closest external architectural links being the hexastyle Corinthian portico and the use of niches on the front elevation.

4 The term 'county court house' will be used for those court houses where assizes, quarter sessions and petty sessions were held.

5 Maurice Craig, 'A note on courthouses', *Quarterly Bulletin of the Irish Georgian Society*, no. 1 (Jan.–Mar. 1958), p. 8.

6 Maurice Craig, *The architecture of Ireland from the earliest times to 1880* (London, 1982), p. 266. Livia Hurley, 'Courthouses', in Rolf Loeber, Hugh Campbell, Livia Hurley, John Montague, Ellen Rowley (eds), *Art and Architecture of Ireland, vol. IV, Architecture, 1600–2000* (Dublin, New Haven, London, 2014), p. 181.

7 C.E.B. Brett, *Court houses and market houses of the province of Ulster* (Belfast, 1973); Christine Casey, 'Courthouses, market-houses and townhalls of Leinster' (MA, UCD, 1982); Richard J. Butler, '"The radicals in these reform times": politics, grand juries, and Ireland's unbuilt assize courthouses, 1800–50', *Architectural History*, vol. 58 (2015A), pp. 109–39; Richard J. Butler, 'The history of Bagenalstown courthouse, Co. Carlow, *Carloviana*, No. 63 (2015B), pp. 201–04; Richard J. Butler, 'Cork's courthouses, the landed elite, and the Rockite rebellion: architectural responses to agrarian violence, 1820–27', in Kyle Hughes and Donald M. MacRaild (eds), *Crime, violence, and the Irish in the nineteenth century* (Liverpool, 2017), pp. 87–111. Forthcoming in 2020 is Butler's book, *Building the Irish court house and prison: a political history, 1750-1850*. Edward McParland has also written on Irish court houses in: Edward McParland, 'The public work of architects in Ireland during the neo-classical period', 2 vols (PhD, University of Cambridge, 1975); Edward McParland, *James Gandon Vitruvius Hibernicus* (London, 1985).

8 There is ample scope for more archival research and further analysis of the data provided by the gazetteer.

9 Margaret Quinlan, 'The Main Guard, Clonmel: the rediscovery of a seventeenth-century court house', *Bulletin of the Irish Georgian Society*, vol. 36 (1994), pp. 4–29. The lease of the site, dated 9 Oct. 1674, mentioned the proposed court house (Quinlan, p. 9). The upper chamber also served as a council chamber and administrative offices.

10 Quotation in Quinlan, p. 6. Quinlan observes (p. 27) that the Main Guard is one of the earliest classical buildings surviving in Ireland.

11 The grand jury system was disbanded under the Local Government (Ireland) Act in 1898, which established county councils. The grand jury system is discussed in P.J. Meghen, 'The administrative work of the grand jury', *Public Administration: Journal of the Royal Institute of Public Administration [of Ireland]*, vol. 6, no. 3 (Autumn 1958), pp. 247–64.

12 Discussed in Meghen, p. 252 and Virginia Crossman, *Local government in nineteenth-century Ireland* (Belfast, 1994), p. 25.

13 Meghen, pp. 254–8.

14 The building attracted the attention of the architect C. R. Cockerell in October 1823 (Brett, pp. 25–6).

15 Butler (2015A), pp. 113–14. The prioritising of the judicial function in the Ensors' design for Roscommon court house was first observed by Edward McParland (McParland (1975), vol. 1, p. 12).

detailing to make the judicial function of the building evident and a tone of authority implicit. This formula proved to be a harbinger of the future. However, those eighteenth-century county court houses that have survived were either elongated single-storey structures like Lifford – Carrickfergus (1779) – or presented a many-windowed, domestic image – Longford (1793), Downpatrick (1737), Drogheda (1770).[16] The exception was Waterford, which will be discussed below.

Although the market and court house combination became obsolete for large county court houses in the nineteenth century, it continued to be used for a significant number of smaller sessions houses. Examples include Arva, Co. Cavan (pre-1837), Ballybay, Co. Monaghan (1848), Castleblayney, Co. Monaghan (c.1856) (where, Brett argues, a new court house was built on top of an older market house), and Crossmaglen, Co. Armagh (1865).[17] Several nineteenth-century court houses, including county court houses, incorporated a reference to the market house formula on sophisticated front elevations: Richard Morrison's late-Palladian design for Clonmel, Co. Tipperary (pre-1801) presented a rusticated three-bay arcade with a blind arcade above, a pattern that was also used by John Hargrave in his design for Mullingar, Co. Westmeath (1824–9). James Rawson Carroll's late nineteenth-century Gothic revival design for Sligo court house returned the formula to its medieval roots with a pointed-arch arcade.

County Court Houses

Periods and politics
By far the greatest number of county and quarter sessions houses were built before the Famine (1845–49) in the early nineteenth century, with the greatest number being constructed from 1796 to the early 1830s.[18] Nearly all the county court houses were built or rebuilt in this period. It was a time of changing economic conditions, periodic rural insurrection and political reform in which the power and status of the Protestant Ascendancy, the social group that populated the grand juries and more often than not owned the land on which the court houses would be built, was challenged. Taking this into account, the historian, Richard Butler, has divided the period into three phases of court house building: 1796–1815; 1816–1829; 1830s.

The early period (1796–1815) was characterised by relative affluence. A series of acts laid the ground for the construction of significant numbers of court houses. An act passed in 1796 empowered grand juries to present sums for court house repair, enlargement and construction.[19] The Disused Public Buildings (Ireland) Act of 1808 enabled grand juries to sell redundant court houses.[20] And a clause in the 1796 act, which had restricted grand jury power to oversee the construction process and thus control the project, was removed in 1813.[21] Despite the Westminster government's awareness of the need to reform the local tax system in Ireland, parliament failed to enact effective legislation to curb the spending powers of grand juries.[22] The result was the construction of court houses that, by and large, reflected grand jury aspirations. For example, analysis of the several schemes designed between 1805 and 1808 by Francis Johnston for Armagh county court house reveals the way in which grand jury ambitions influenced the scale and impressiveness of the final design. The earliest proposal provided small courtrooms and cramped accommodation for the grand jury and administration behind a largely unarticulated façade.[23] (Image 1) In contrast, the scheme approved by the grand jury had two spacious courts, ample ancillary accommodation, a circular domed vestibule and a grand staircase to first-floor grand jury rooms, all set behind a modulated façade with a Doric portico.[24] (Image 2) A further factor is evident when the agreed scheme was executed; a limit to available financial resources ensured that the dimensions of the portico columns were reduced and the proposed dome unrealised.[25]

The years from 1816 to 1829 were a period of economic collapse, failed administrative reform and grand jury triumphalism, all of which conspired to favour impressive new buildings with substantial grand jury accommodation. With the Grand Jury Presentment (Ireland) Act of 1817 Westminster endeavoured to curb Irish grand jury power by introducing the post of county surveyor to prepare proposals for, oversee and manage public works projects.[26] However, when it became clear that there were insufficient candidates for the county surveyor posts, the provisions in this act were repealed in an amending act of January 1818, to the relief of the grand juries.[27] The economic depression that followed the end of the Napoleonic wars indirectly stimulated the Irish elite's appetite for court house building by providing credit from central government funds: the Public Works Loan Act of 1817 provided £250,000 for the alleviation of unemployment in Ireland which could be drawn down in loans for public works.[28] With the defeat of the Catholic Emancipation Bill in 1817, Irish grand juries felt that the Protestant constitution had been upheld and their position was vindicated.[29] Butler has argued that the elite's ebullience generated by these developments was manifest in an elaborate proposal commissioned by the county Dublin grand jury for a new court house at Kilmainham in 1817.[30]

Where Johnston's realised 1808 design for Armagh and Richard Morrison's designs for Naas (pre-1807) and Portlaoise (pre-1805) included impressive staircases that led from the main entrance to first-floor grand jury rooms, Henry, Mullins & McMahon's proposal for Kilmainham gave the grand jury a separate entrance at the side, impressively flanked by two-storey Ionic columns, leading to a private imperial stair. (Image 3) With the end bays on the main façade presenting engaged temple fronts over a rusticated base, the court house had a palatial image, more expressive of grand jury entertaining in its ample first-floor accommodation than of the application of the law in the courtrooms. This architectural exuberance did not prevail in the final design by William Farrell (Butler suggests that the loan which was secured for this project may have acted as a restraint on grand jury ambitions), but the grand jury retained a separate entrance at the top of a flight of steps.[31] Designs for court houses elsewhere (such as Farrell's design for Carrick-on-Shannon) included large suites of first-floor rooms for the grand juries, incorporating a room for meetings and entertaining, a waiting room and secretary's office.[32]

Butler's third period was marked by a series of parliamentary acts in the 1830s, which not only succeeded in limiting the powers of the grand juries, but also strengthened state influence at a local level. The Grand Jury (Ireland) Act of 1833 finally inserted county surveyors into the designing, executing and administering process of public works projects.[33] This act also gave cess-payers a voice in vetting expenditure, and thus enabled them to challenge self-aggrandising court house projects of the grand juries.[34] The grand jury reforming act of 1836 gave the Board of Works powers to purchase sites, build court houses and recover the cost from the grand juries.[35] This provision built on the Public Works (Ireland) Act of 1831, which had reorganized and strengthened the Board of Works, giving it the power to administer loans for court house projects.[36] There is evidence that the Board of Works used this capacity in the 1830s and 40s to exercise influence on new designs. One example concerns William Vitruvius Morrison's Carlow court house. In early summer 1832 the Board's architect, Jacob Owen, objected to the designs for the portico and roofs of the polygonal wings.[37] When the Board approved the revised designs submitted by Morrison it ensured, through the adoption of a legal instrument and inspections by the Board's architect, that the £5,000 loan would only be drawn down if the new specifications were adhered to.[38]

That the elite was learning to consider the attitudes of reformers who objected to excessively expensive court house schemes is evident from the correspondence of Charles Bury,

16 The generously fenestrated design for Drogheda was given a civic character with the addition of an impressive three-stage clock tower surmounted by a dome.

17 Brett, p. 93.

18 Butler has listed fifteen new county court houses built or planned in the period 1796–1815 (Butler (2015A), p. 137, note 30), with eight new county court houses and nineteen smaller court houses funded by government loans 1817–1832 (Butler (2015A), p. 120).

19 An act for the amendment of public roads, for directing the power of grand juries respecting presentments, and for repealing several laws heretofore made for those purposes', 1796 (36 Geo III, c.55).

20 48 Geo III, c.113.

21 Court House (Ireland) Act, 1813 (53 Geo III c.131). The act enabled grand juries to appoint overseers empowered to make building contracts.

22 Discussed in Butler (2015A), p. 115.

23 Irish Architectural Archive (hereafter IAA), RIAI Murray Collection, 92/46.10, Francis Johnston, ground floor plan and front elevation, Mar. 1805.

24 IAA, RIAI Murray Collection, 92/46.18, Francis Johnston, ground floor plan and front elevation, watermark, 1808. The lack of surviving grand jury minutes and presentment books makes it difficult to assess reasons why some schemes remained unbuilt (Butler (2015A), pp. 123, 125).

25 Butler (2015A), pp. 115–19.

26 Grand Jury Presentment (Ireland) Act, 1817 (57 Geo III, c.107). The act also restricted presentments, previously made at spring and summer assizes, to the latter assizes.

27 Grand Jury Presentments (Ireland) Act, 1818 (58 Geo III, c.67).

28 57 Geo III, c.34. Additionally, the Public Works Loan (Ireland) Act, 1818 (58 Geo III, c.88) and other acts listed in Butler ((2015A), p. 138, note 52) made it easier for grand juries to obtain loans with minimum scrutiny (Butler (2015A), p. 120).

29 Ibid., p. 121.

30 Ibid, pp. 121–3. Butler discusses an unbuilt design by Henry, Mullins & McMahon, drawings in IAA, Guinness Collection, 96/68.5.1.1–4.

31 Butler (2015A), pp. 123–4. Other examples of separate grand jury entrances and staircases can be found in John Bowden's 1813 designs for Derry (Brett, p. 17), Farrell's designs for Carrick-on-Shannon and Cavan (see note 32).

32 Harvard University, Houghton Library, William Farrell Album, MS 788, ff. 15–16, William Farrell, ground and first-floor plans for Carrick-on-Shannon court house, n.d. (copies in IAA). Farrell produced a similar scheme for Cavan (Brett, p. 55). Some grand jury suites included a dining room. An example can be found in the court house in Omagh, Co. Tyrone for which the Ordnance Survey memoir recorded a handsome dining and drawing room for the grand jury.

33 6 & 7 Will. IV, c.78. Discussed in Meghen, p. 261.

34 The roles of county surveyors and cess-payers were also spelled out in the Grand Jury (Ireland) Act, 1836 (6 & 7 Will. IV, c.116).

35 The Grand Jury (Ireland) Act, 1836 brought together and consolidated the provisions of the 1833 grand jury and other acts. Prior to the 1836 act, the Lord Lieutenant had the power to vet proposals that were to receive public works loans, but the Board of Works' power was limited to giving opinions. This is evident in a Board of Works minute dated 2 Aug. 1827 replying to a complaint by a grand jury member (Hon. Henry Westenra) that Joseph Welland's plan for Monaghan court house was 'neither so eligible or aeconomical [sic]' as Morrison's design for Tralee. A letter was sent to Westenra stating that the Board had no power 'to interfere in the arrangements or adoption of plans for goals, penitentiaries or court houses further than to report their opinion on such as may be referred for their consideration by the Lord Lieutenant'. It went on to promise that his letter would be submitted to government when the Monaghan proposal was under consideration (National Archives of Ireland (hereafter NAI), Office of Public Works (hereafter OPW), Secretariat Branch, Board of Works Minutes, I/1/1/5, p. 188, minutes for meeting on 2 Aug. 1827).

36 1 & 2 Will. IV, c33.

37 NAI, OPW, Secretariat Branch, Board of Works Minutes, I/1/1/7, minutes for meeting on 30 June 1832.

38 NAI, OPW, Secretariat Branch, Board of Works Minutes, I/1/1/7, minutes for meetings on 30 June 1832, 21 July 1832, 18 Aug. 1832, 15 Sept. 1832, 28 Sept. 1832, 9 Jan. 1833, 16 Jan. 1833, 29 Jan. 1833. The Board rejected Kilkenny county surveyor's proposals for a new court house for Urlingford in 1836 (Brendan O'Donoghue, *The Irish county surveyors 1834–1944: a biographical dictionary* (Dublin, 2007), p. 126).

Lord Tullamore, a King's County (Offaly) grand juror and the landowner in Tullamore where a new court house was proposed in 1832–3. In a letter of 3 September 1833 he explained to his mother why a classical proposal had been selected instead of a Gothic revival design which would have complemented the existing gaol in Tullamore: '[…] we have had many things to consider – economy, usage as to get the most accommodation at least cost – the plan we adopted accomplished that object and if an Elizabethan elevation had cost the same, the ignorant, the vicious, and the radicals in these Reform times, wd say Ld T [Lord Tullamore] – spent public money in ornamenting his town and squandered and frittered it away in pinnacles, carvings, to indulge in his taste regardless of the misery the poor endured in paying the tax for it'.[39]

There is some evidence for cess-payer influence in Ennis where John Benjamin Keane's proposal for a new court house, recommended by the county surveyor and presented at the spring assizes of 1842, was rejected, suggesting that cess-payers did not approve of the design.[40] But this did not prevent the building of an impressive and expensive court house. The design by Henry Whitestone, approved in 1845 and completed in 1850, was similar to Keane's proposal. Its extravagance was very clear to the philanthropist Rev. Sidney Osborne, who visited Ennis near the end of the Famine and commented, 'such unnecessary expense for such a building under such circumstances, is very foolish, if not very wrong.'[41]

Planning

Court house planning – the layout of court house buildings, the amount and type of accommodation, and the arrangement of courtrooms – changed significantly from 1800 to the 1830s. Maurice Craig's observation that two designs for Nottingham County Hall by James Gandon published in *Vitruvius Britannicus* in 1771 – one was realised; the other was adapted by Gandon for a new court house in Waterford in 1784–7 – had a decisive impact on early nineteenth-century court house building in Ireland, has been accepted by subsequent historians.[42] Both plans, which incorporated a 'Great Hall', two courts (a civil and a record court), accommodation for judge and juries and public galleries, were elegantly symmetrical. In the scheme adjusted for Waterford, the courts were parallel to each other at the rear, and the plan was contained within a rectangle, whereas in the scheme executed in Nottingham the courts flanked the hall and projected laterally beyond the façade.[43] The rationalism of these plans certainly made them exemplars for later designers, but both schemes had to be partially remodelled to accommodate the Irish situation in the early nineteenth century. Extra accommodation was needed for the grand jury (which, as we have seen, could imply an

impressive stair to first-floor rooms), court administrators – the clerk of the peace and the clerk of the crown – and the court caretaker or housekeeper. The scheme in which the courts flanked the hall was particularly flexible: a grand stair could be located on the far side of the hall on axis with the entrance, rooms for the judiciary and administrators could be built across the rear, the courts could face the front and contribute to the image of the building, and the keeper could be accommodated in a basement. Once the advantages of this arrangement had become apparent to Francis Johnston, he adopted it for Armagh; Richard Morrison adapted it for Naas, Portlaoise and Clonmel; William Farrell used it for Carrick-on-Shannon and Cavan.[44] In Dundalk Edward Parke, encouraged by the grand juror and amateur architect, John Foster, positioned his courtrooms behind the hall as Gandon had done in Waterford and created a design of impressive grandeur.[45] Where Gandon had placed a vestibule flanked by enclosed stairs in the space between the courtrooms, Parke inserted a grand bifurcating stair in Portland stone for the grand jury that was to be separated from the hall by a door. The hall was essentially an exterior space, linked to the portico by a Doric screen. When the building was constructed, the proposed door to the stair was replaced with another Doric screen, creating a monumental route, unique in Ireland, from the portico through the building to the top of the stair.

Justices, accused, witnesses, jury and public all met in court houses. In very early nineteenth-century court houses all participants passed through the hall, and throughout the period this space would retain its centrality. 'This is the main thoroughfare, waiting-place, and conversation-room for the public at assizes, sessions, general elections and other gatherings', the surveyor, John Brett, wrote in 1875, adding that it was noisy and full of bustle, quietened only when a proclamation was made for witnesses or jurors.[46] Where Gandon had provided open screens between the hall and courtrooms, nineteenth-century designers in Ireland gave their courtrooms doors to separate them from the general commotion of the hall.[47] Another concern was to separate the actors involved in court proceedings. In William Farrell's plan for Carrick-on-Shannon (c.1824) the judge entered the court directly from his chambers, the petty jury accessed galleries from side entrances and staircases shared only with court administrators and the public attending grand jury presentments, while the public visiting the court could access ground-floor seats at the rear of the courtrooms or galleries from spiral stairs just inside the entrance. (Image 4)[48] The courtrooms in this design showed clear provision for the constituent elements of the proceedings. The judge was elevated at the front, below him, also elevated, was the barrister's desk which faced the witness table surrounded by benches, while the dock was located below the bar, accessed by stairs from underground cells.

By the late 1820s these provisions were joined by newer requirements.[49] A letter of 15 November 1832 written by the overseers outlining the design competition brief for a new court house in Tullamore articulated this.[50] Apart from provision for the grand jury, petty jury, judges and officers, the brief also required extra rooms: two for grand jury committees, one for barristers and several for witnesses. This represented increased provision for the judiciary, and arrangements for the grand jury in its administrative rather than social capacity. John Brett noted that by the 1870s grand jury dining rooms were almost obsolete, and he emphasised the accommodation needed for grand jury public sessions, such as a well-ventilated room comfortable for large crowds.[51] For the courts themselves the Tullamore brief required spaciousness, designated places for each 'class' of person attending, and convenient entries for the judges, barristers, grand jury, petty jury and witnesses. It also stipulated that the jury in their galleries and the prisoner in the dock be able to distinctly hear the judge, barristers and witnesses. Brett underlined this too, as well as specifying that jury and prisoner should also have a clear, well-lit view. The brief mentioned water closets for the judge and jury, a provision that Brett amplified: his ideal court house made extensive provision for the comfort of the users with toilets and waiting rooms.

The models suggested by the competition overseers for the proposed Tullamore court house were Sir Robert Smirke's Gloucester magistrates court house of 1814–16, and William Vitruvius Morrison's 1828 design for Tralee court house, itself inspired by Gloucester.[52] These designs were notable for the clear arrangement of what had become a complex brief. The organising concept was three parallel blocks: entrance (double-height portico and hall); court business (two projecting courtrooms separated by a suite of judicial offices, also double-height); administration (a two-storey block at the rear containing offices and grand jury accommodation).[53] The courtrooms were semi-circular to facilitate multiple entries and maximise opportunities for seeing and hearing proceedings. They projected beyond the entrance portico, giving the court house a strongly three-dimensional presence. The selected design by John Benjamin Keane for Tullamore adhered to the brief and incorporated semi-circular courts, although he enclosed them within rectangular walls.[54] (Image 5) Keane gave the judiciary ample provision in the area between the courts, stretching the design laterally and creating a more relaxed, horizontal building than Morrison's court houses at Tralee and Carlow.[55] Keane inserted clerestory windows into the Crown court which threw light into the body of the courtroom.[56]

39 Quoted in Michael Byrne, *Legal Offaly: the county courthouse at Tullamore and the legal profession in County Offaly from the 1820s to the present day* (Tullamore, 2008), pp. 33–4.

40 *Clare Journal*, 24 Feb. 1842. This is discussed in Ó Murchadha, p. 255.

41 S. G. Osborne, *Gleanings in the West of Ireland* (London, 1850), p. 37.

42 Craig (1958), pp. 9–10. Craig's ideas were developed by McParland ((1975), chapter 8) and referred to by Casey ((1982), p. 18), and Hurley (p. 181).

43 McParland noted that this latter plan was similar to Sanderson Miller's scheme for Warwick Shire Hall of 1754–8 ((1985), p. 10).

44 See Johnston's schemes for Armagh, IAA, RIAI Murray Collection, 92/46.4–18. A conjectural reconstruction of the plan for Naas as designed by Richard Morrison can be found in Ann Martha Rowan (ed.), *The architecture of Richard Morrison and William Vitruvius Morrison* (Dublin, 1989), p. 136. Harvard University, Houghton Library, William Farrell Album, MS 788, ff. 15–16, William Farrell, ground- and first-floor plans for Carrick-on-Shannon Court House, n.d. (copies in IAA). Gandon's other scheme was applied in Derry by John Bowden in 1813, where offices flanked the hall and the keeper's accommodation was positioned at the rear (Brett, p. 17). Analysis of planning is hampered by the lack of extant plans with annotations giving room use.

45 Christine Casey argued that John Foster and his nephew John Leslie Foster had an input into the design and realisation of Dundalk court house (Christine Casey, 'The Greek revival courthouse, Dundalk, County Louth', *Irish Arts Review*, vol. 3, no. 2 (Summer 1986), pp. 16–20).

46 John Brett, 'County courthouses and county gaols in Ireland', *Irish Builder*, vol. XVII, no. 362–3 (15 Jan. and 1 Feb. 1875). John Brett was the county surveyor for King's County (now Offaly) 1834–65, Kildare 1865–1885 and Antrim 1885–1914. The article in the *Irish Builder*, based on a paper he gave to the Architectural Association of Ireland, appears to have been a summary of changes that had already taken place in Ireland with some personal recommendations by Brett.

47 Craig suggested that courtrooms open to the hall emulated the open-ended King's courts at Westminster and probably derived from the idea that the legal establishment was dispensing justice in public (Craig (1982), p. 267).

48 Harvard University, Houghton Library, William Farrell Album, MS 788, ff. 15–16, William Farrell, ground and first floor plans for Carrick-on-Shannon Court House, n.d. (copies in IAA). The date of 1824 is suggested by the fact that an almost identical design was used for Cavan court house, which is recorded as being built in 1824 (Brett, p. 56).

49 The basic requirements of the mid-1820s are evident in the complaint made by the assize judge of the state of Carlow court house and reported in the press: 'Upon looking round him, he could see no accommodation for the public, for the Bar, for Juries or for the Judge'. Also, 'There was no evidence of cleanliness in its condition, nor taste in its structure' (*Finn's Leinster Newsletter*, 11 Apr. 1827).

50 IAA, RIAI Murray Collection, 92/46.1174, letter from the overseers of the Tullamore court house competition to William Murray, 15 Nov. 1832.

51 John Brett, p. 25.

52 IAA, RIAI Murray Collection, 92/46.1174, letter from the overseers of the Tullamore court house competition to William Murray, 15 Nov. 1832, p. 2. Note 35 above suggests that W.V. Morrison's design for Tralee may date to 1827.

53 Keane's winning design can be compared with Murray's competition design, which was less well organised and did not adhere to the Gloucester model (IAA, RIAI Murray Collection, 92/46.1187–1192, William Murray, competition designs for Tullamore court house).

54 IAA, Lismore Castle Collection, 97/107.3.1–4, John Benjamin Keane, basement, ground and first floor plans and section, Tullamore court house, 1832.

55 This is evident in the drawing of the section (IAA, Lismore Castle Collection, 97/107.3.4, John Benjamin Keane, section, Tullamore Court House, 1832). Keane provided many separate entrances into the Tullamore court house: grand jury at the rear; public gallery staircases at the side adjacent to the entrance hall; office and witnesses entrances in the rear block.

56 William Vitruvius Morrison provided light to his crown courtroom in Carlow through a large lunette on the wall behind the judge's bench (illustrated in Rowan (ed.), p. 47).

Style

Apart from demonstrating how to rationalise court house planning, Gandon's Waterford court house also encouraged early nineteenth-century architects in Ireland to aspire to the monumental in court house design.[57] There was the grandeur of the screen walls linked to flanking pavilions. More influentially, the central block for Waterford court house had a portico and emphatic attic, and employed windowless walls animated by blind arches and plaques which lent definitive gravitas to the building. Richard Morrison, who was a pupil of Gandon, was demonstrably influenced by Waterford in his 1812 design for Galway court house. Galway in turn inspired William Farrell, who employed the shallow round-headed niches set in blind arches flanking the single-storey portico of Galway in Cavan and Carrick-on-Shannon.

A significant number of county court houses departed from Gandon's model by incorporating a pedimented portico. These varied in size, and all three classical orders were employed: Doric in Armagh (tetrastyle), Monaghan (engaged distyle), Dundalk and Tralee (hexastyle); Ionic in Derry (tetrastyle), Carlow (octostyle); Corinthian in Cork (octostyle). The success of these porticos relied on meticulously detailed ashlar stonework, which in turn had a decisive influence on the character of the building. The metropolitan character of Cork's white limestone can be compared to the local distinction of the buff and grey tones of the Carnmore sandstone used in Monaghan, while Dundalk's pristine granite distils the impression of extreme austerity implicit in the architectural design.

Many architects were concerned to express the courtrooms on the front façade, something that had not been a priority for Gandon. Johnston gave each of his courts in Armagh court house a single round-headed window on the front elevation. Richard Morrison, however, preferred the gravitas of emphatic absence: at Portlaoise and Naas he expressed his courtrooms as pedimented pavilions with large filled central arches harbouring blank windows situated between round-headed niches above which were vacant oculi. At Dundalk the courtrooms were largely concealed behind the hall and two flanking windowless staircase vestibules, but they did form a slight lateral projection (as Gandon's Nottingham courtrooms had done) and their hipped roofs sailed over the flat tops of the vestibules to flank the triangle of the portico.[58] William Vitruvius Morrison developed this sophisticated composition with the cruciform plans of Tralee and Carlow, which gave the windowless courtrooms a strong presence in the plane behind the portico from which they seemed to extend.

Versions of this style, described as neoclassical by architectural historians, were employed by landowners for their houses and estate buildings in this period.[59] There was a clear correlation between the elite's domestic and, through their role on the grand juries, public patronage. Architects such as Richard Morrison, Francis Johnston, John Benjamin Keane and James and George Richard Pain were employed for both private and public commissions. There is evidence that some grand jurors intervened to steer court house architects towards Greek revival designs, popularised for public buildings in early nineteenth-century England through the designs of Robert Smirke. Greek revival had the advantage of possessing specific antique models, many drawn in careful detail by James Stuart and Nicholas Revett in *Antiquities of Athens* published between 1762 and 1816. The inherent restraint of Greek revival appealed to the taste for simplicity, and was not prohibitively expensive.[60] The 1813 contract for Dundalk included the statement that the details 'shall be executed according to the patterns and true proportions of the Rules of Grecian Architecture as they are collected from the Ruins of the City of Athens', specifically naming Stuart and Revett's book.[61] Casey has argued that this recommendation, which was magnificently realised, originated from John Foster, a member of the committee of overseers for the project.

Neoclassical court houses were manifestly expressions of elite values.[62] Comments by contemporaries suggest that this monumental classicism carried significance as a conduit to promote respect for the legal process. This is evident in the encomium delivered on 1 April 1815 when Galway court house was opened, and the building was described as being an 'unequivocal and splendid' testimonial of 'the high respect [of the gentlemen of the county] for the laws, and of their anxiety for the due and orderly administration of public justice'.[63] State and justice were juxtaposed sculpturally on the court house: panels decorated with balance scales and a sword – symbols of justice – were set in the end bays and the royal coat of arms surmounted the attic.[64]

Quarter Sessions Houses

A network of smaller court houses in rural towns to host quarter and petty sessions developed from the late eighteenth century.[65] Where county court houses had cost anything from just over £12,000 (Ennis) to £22,000 (Carlow and Cork), sessions houses cost much less.[66] The architect, John Carr, commissioned by the Duke of Devonshire to design a court house for Lismore in 1799, presented plans for a stone building with 'proper accommodation' for the clerk of the peace and jury over ground-floor cells and market hall for about £1,000.[67] The same figure of £1,000 was given in the 1836 act as the maximum to be spent on a new sessions house.[68] This may be taken as a reasonable minimum for a decent court house. Most of the court houses built to James and George Richard Pain's standard design of May 1824 – utilitarian, spare, and, as we shall see, stylish – received just over £1,246 in loans.[69] The size of a court house that could be built for this type of figure was considered insufficient for Dungarvan, Co. Waterford, by the prisons inspector Benjamin Woodward, who reported that the grand jury's presentment of £1,200 was inadequate, adding, 'I trust that an enlarged plan will be decided on at the next assizes'.[70]

The busiest building period for new sessions houses is difficult to gauge. Examining grand jury presentments for County Carlow, Butler found that in the period from 1825 to 1835 £15,000 was spent (not including some government loans or private munificence), and that in the following ten years (1835–45) only a third of that sum was expended.[71] This pattern is confirmed in the take up of loans outside Dublin from 1818 to 1839, summarised in the House of Commons report of loans made for public works in Ireland.[72] It reveals that the vast majority of loans were made in the 1820s: two projects received loans in 1818–20; twenty in 1822–29 and four from 1830 to 1833. However, patterns for commissions in each county varied significantly. In Cavan the pattern described above is confirmed with two rebuildings before 1825 and three from 1825 to 1835. However, in County Limerick no sessions houses were rebuilt between 1825 to 1835; instead two were rebuilt before 1825, two from 1835 to 1845 and three after the Famine. In Tipperary the majority were rebuilt in 1835–45 (four), with one built before 1825, one in the 1825–35 period and one after the Famine.

The availability of public loans after 1817 was an encouragement to build new sessions houses. But there were other incentives. One was the subdivision of existing jurisdictions. Although an act of Parliament of 1787 had allowed for the doubling of sittings in every Irish county, only four counties seemed to have established new sessions towns: Cork, Kerry, Tipperary and Kilkenny.[73] Richard Butler's investigation into the establishment of seven new sessions towns in 1820s Cork has revealed that long-considered legislation to divide Cork into an east and west riding was finally enacted in 1823 because of the crisis resulting from Rockite violence and resulting pressure from the local elite.[74] Butler argues that the elite went beyond the requirements of the new government regulations in a response which incorporated prison reform together with provision for new courts in a county-wide approach initiated with a competition

57 McParland (1985), p. 146. Waterford court house is known only from drawings.

58 This is readily appreciated in a drawing in Craig (1982), p. 273.

59 Examples include the designs of James Wyatt, Francis Johnston and Richard Morrison.

60 David Watkin, *A history of western architecture* (3rd ed., London, 2000), p. 462.

61 Harold O'Sullivan, 'The court-house, Dundalk and the contract for its erection dated 30th April, 1813', *Journal of the Louth Archaeological Society*, vol. XV, no. 2 (1962), p. 139. The portico of Derry court house was modelled on the Athenian temple of Erechtheus, according to the Ordnance Survey memoir of 1837 (Brett, p. 88).

62 This has been variously interpreted by historians (Butler (2017), p. 88).

63 Words from the opening reception on 1 April 1815, quoted in James Hardiman, *The history of the town and county of the town of Galway* (Dublin, 1820; reprint. Galway, 1975), p. 300.

64 There was a similar juxtaposition in Derry court house, with figures symbolising Justice and Peace over the wings and the royal arms on the acroterium over the pediment.

65 The 1796 act did not distinguish between sizes of court houses ('An act for the amendment of public roads, for directing the power of grand juries respecting presentments, and for repealing several laws heretofore made for those purposes', 1796 (36 Geo III, c.55)). Very little research has been done on smaller court houses. Apart from sources relating to individual court houses in national and local archives, there is a great deal of data generated by the Westminster Parliament and local grand jury presentments. Examples of sources include: annual Public Works Commissioners' reports, abstracts of accounts of grand jury presentments, Public Works accounts and grand jury presentment books.

66 For Ennis see Ó Murchadha, p. 255; for Carlow and Cork see the gazetteer. The contract for Dundalk was for £16,190.10.0 (O'Sullivan, p. 133); Cavan cost £11,000 (Brett, p. 56); Omagh cost £17,000 including the later portico (Brett, p. 100); the intention was to build Tullamore for a maximum of £9,000 (letter of 15 Nov. 1832 in note 52 here); and over £30,000 in Derry (Brett, pp. 102–3).

67 It is not known if this proposal was executed, but Lismore court house is attributed to John Carr (information from the gazetteer).

68 Grand Jury (Ireland) Act, 1836 (6 & 7 Will. IV, c.116), clause 70.

69 IAA, 97/107.41, James and George Richard Pain, 'Design for a court house and bridewell to be built in the different sessions towns in the county of Cork', 6 May 1824. The figure for loans is taken from Public Works (Ireland): *Return of all sums of money voted or applied, either by way of grant or loan, in aid of public works in Ireland, since the union etc*, House of Commons papers [HC hereafter] 1839 (540), p. 44.

70 Inspectors General, *Third report on the general state of the prisons of Ireland*, HC 1825 (493), p. 22, and p. 227. The court house was built in 1832. The ambition for Dungarvan court house may have been due to the fact that Dungarvan was temporarily accommodating assize courts, and the grand jury may have been planning to apply for the role permanently, as they did from 1835 to 1837. The handsome ashlar-stone court house at Dungarvan was given loans totalling £1,566 over three years. (Public Works (Ireland): *Return of all sums ...*, HC 1839 (540), p. 44.) Costs for court houses could be higher if private patrons also supported the project. For example, Mitchelstown court house, erected by 3rd Earl of Kingston, cost £3,000 (information from the gazetteer).

71 Butler (2015B), p. 202.

72 Public Works (Ireland): *Return of all sums ...* HC 1839 (540), p. 44.

73 Butler (2017), p. 95.

74 Butler (2017), pp. 87–111. An act to divide the county of Cork, for the purposes of holding general sessions therein, 1823 (4 Geo IV, 93). The new act was enabled by the 1787 legislation.

for a standardised design, won by James and George Richard Pain in 1824. There were a number of reasons why the elite responded so enthusiastically. An economic depression caused by a banking crisis, famine, and the decline of weaving, made new building, funded by government loans, attractive. Further, the eighteenth-century concept of improvement was still alive in Ireland, and the elite was keen to ornament local towns with well-designed civic structures. This latter argument is supported by the readiness with which local proprietors made land in central locations of the designated towns available for new sessions houses.[75]

In the period after the Grand Jury Acts of 1833 and 1836 there were additional pressures to build new sessions houses. Clause 70 of the 1836 act stated that where there were no sessions houses the newly appointed county surveyors were empowered to prepare designs to be examined by the grand jury. The county surveyors appointed after 1836 were, in the main, professional and efficient, and could jealously guard their role. In an acrimonious letter to the architect William Deane Butler, Samson Carter, county surveyor for Kilkenny (1804–1860), wrote, 'Do you imagine I will, or would, tamely submit to Keane, Darley, Morrison, or even yourself stepping in between me and the body to whom I am legally appointed the professional officer and advisor, and permit them to usurp my prerogative?'[76] Some county surveyors gave design work to architects, sometimes sharing the superintendence fee.[77] Thus architects designed a number of sessions houses: for example, William Caldbeck (Newtownards, Co. Down), William Deane Butler (Callan and Urlingford, Co. Kilkenny; Clifden, Oughterard and Portumna, Co. Galway, Bray, Co. Wicklow), John Hargrave (Dungannon, Co. Tyrone and Moate, Co. Westmeath) and Thomas Alfred Cobden (Tullow, Co. Carlow).

If the county surveyors failed to enter into a contract for what the authorities deemed to be a necessary project, there was a provision in the 1836 act for the Lord Lieutenant to direct the Commissioners of Public Works to build or provide a sessions house to be paid for by the county cess. This measure was applied, though sparingly, as is evident from the involvement of Jacob Owen, Board of Works architect from 1832 to 1856, in the design of court houses in Roscrea, Co. Tipperary, Buncrana, Co. Donegal, Balbriggan and Swords, Co. Dublin.[78]

There is evidence that central government put pressure on grand juries to erect new sessions houses: for example, Samuel Jones, county surveyor for Tipperary, was directed to present plans, specifications and cost estimates for new sessions houses at Clogheen, Carrick-on-Suir, Tipperary and Roscrea, which he did in March 1837.[79] Donegal grand jury tried to resist central government pressure to build a sessions house in Glenties, arguing that it was 'unnecessary and inexpedient'.[80] When the Lord Lieutenant directed them to build it for £900, they refused to vote that particular sum, the county surveyor suggesting £650. They had, however, to eventually give way.

Planning

Quarter sessions houses contained a crown court and ancillary rooms. Planning trends towards increasingly specialised rooms, separate entrances and controlled routes followed those of county court houses. The courtroom in the late eighteenth-century court house at Dunshaughlin, Co. Meath, designed by Francis Johnston in 1799, was placed between rooms for the grand and petty jury and a multipurpose entrance hall, which Johnston labelled 'space for witnesses etc'.[81] (Image 6) By the 1820s quarter sessions houses tended to provide separate rooms for the clerk of the peace and the magistrate.[82] Some later designs also provided space for jurors and witnesses: in Bray, Co. Wicklow (1841), these players had benches behind the dock; in Glenties, Co. Donegal (1841), there was a separate jury room.[83] There was pressure to accommodate barristers in a separate room. This is evident in the 1841 plan drawing for Glenties where modifications in red ink to the ground-floor jury room and adjacent stair were proposed to squeeze in a barristers room.[84] A grand jury room was also provided in some court houses, both for larger towns such as Bray and smaller places such as Glenties.

Although symmetry was almost universally applied to the design of entrance façades, more economic internal arrangements could be achieved without symmetry. In Ballyconnell, Co. Cavan, designed with a rear gaol in 1833, the zones for gaol and court were not entirely separate (one of the gaol yards was located next to the courtroom), and the stair in the court house was accommodated by reducing the size of the barrister's room.[85] William Deane Butler's design for Bray made similar accommodations, but, by omitting the hall and by separating access in line with contemporary thinking – the public, the grand jury and the clerk of the peace entered at the rear; the chairman and magistrates through the front porch – his design was highly functional as well as economic.[86] (Image 7) The island site also allowed him to design separately eloquent elevations for three sides of the building. The blank front concealed the fact that the central entrance porch gave access to the court on one side and the magistrate's room on the other, while the side elevation gave expression to the courtroom with three large first-floor windows, and the rear elevation had symmetrically placed entrance doors.

Style

There were quarter sessions houses that fitted almost seamlessly into the townhouse façades of Irish provincial towns. An example is Ballinrobe, Co. Mayo, its civic function simply signified through scale, a central pediment and round-headed ground-floor openings. There were court houses that imitated classical temples and seemed to refer more explicitly to the estates of the proprietors who paid for them than the civic community which they served: Bagenalstown, Co. Carlow, with its deep Ionic portico, is an example.[87] The majority of quarter sessions court houses, however, were designed in an idiom that unequivocally asserted their civic function. The effect of this is shown in the words chosen by the prison inspector when he praised the new sessions houses in County Cork: 'the court houses [are] on a convenient plan, with a handsome cut stone elevation and form a very conspicuous object in the towns in which they are erected, calculated to excite a feeling of respect connected with the administration of justice at the quarter sessions'.[88]

James and George Richard Pain's standard design for the seven new County Cork sessions houses and bridewells, most of which were completed by late 1827, distilled tendencies towards restraint in a simple neoclassically inflected formula.[89] (Image 8a and 8b). The back wall of the courtroom was presented to the street. There was a two-storey block with rooms for magistrates and the clerk of the peace at the rear. The building was accessed by two small side entrance halls which also had doors to exterior passageways leading to the rear bridewell. The front façade consisted of a central pedimented block with a Venetian window to light the courtroom.[90] This was flanked by recessed entrances of the same height as the main block, each with a single door. For the central block, plain wide pilasters 'supported' a deep cornice, and proposed projecting pediments over the doors were realised with carved brackets of several variant designs. Blank plaques decorated the walls above the doors.[91] The brevity and control of the detailing, which left large expanses of blank ashlar executed in local stone, exuded a strength and distinction that was matched by few other quarter sessions houses.[92] Elements of the style appeared at Dungarvan, Co. Waterford, where it is likely that the Pains' design was taken into account, while in Killarney the new sessions house was almost a replica of the Cork standard.[93] With the large courtroom volume and multiple entrances imprinted on the façade and the stylistic restraint, these designs were unmistakable as court houses. Where court house designs imitated domestic architecture, blank openings could indicate the presence of a court house. For example, with its advanced central bay containing the entrance porch, William Deane Butler's design for Bray suggested a house, but, with the exception of the porch, the 'windows' were blind recesses.[94]

75 Butler (2017), p. 102.
76 O'Donoghue, p. 127.
77 Ibid., p. 126.
78 Jacob Owen is suggested as the designer of Buncrana (Dictionary of Irish Architects, https://www.dia.ie/architects/view/4252, accessed 09.01.19).
79 O'Donoghue, p. 218. Henry Clements, county surveyor for Galway, was asked by the Board of Works in 1837 for plans for court houses in Clifden and Oughterard, which were eventually designed by William Deane Butler (O'Donoghue, pp. 130–1). In 1837 Edward Forrest was asked to prepare plans for quarter sessions houses in Clones and Carrickmacross, to be constructed immediately. Forrest's request for a loan from the Board of Works was rejected (NAI, CSORP, 1837/1295, letter from Edward Forrest to Drummond Esq., 23 June 1837; letter from Henry Paine (Board of Works) to Thomas Drummond Esq., 4 July 1837).
80 Brett, p. 60.
81 IAA, RIAI Murray Collection, 92/46.841, Francis Johnston, 'Plan of a sessions house for Dunshaughlin, Co. Meath', July 1799.
82 IAA, 97/107.41, James and George Richard Pain, 'Design for a court house and bridewell to be built in the different sessions towns in the county of Cork', 6 May 1824.
83 NAI, OPW drawings collection, OPW 5 HC/4/396, William Deane Butler, 'Plans, elevations, sections of intended quarter sessions house for Bray', 1841; NAI, OPW drawings collection, OPW 5HC/4/398, 'Glenties Sessions House, Co. Donegal', 1841.
84 NAI, OPW drawings collection, OPW 5 HC/4/398, 'Glenties Sessions House, Co. Donegal', 1841.
85 NAI, OPW drawings collection, OPW 5 HC/4/397, 'Prison and court house Ballyconnell, Co. of Cavan', n.d. Ballyconnell is often attributed to William Deane Butler. This seems unlikely when the plan and elevation of Ballyconnell is compared to Butler's design for Bray, which is a similar but much more sophisticated building.
86 NAI, OPW drawings collection, OPW 5 HC/4/396, William Deane Butler, 'Plans, elevations, sections of intended quarter sessions house for Bray', 1841.
87 Butler (2015B).
88 Inspectors General, *Fifth report on general state of prisons of Ireland*, HC 1826–1827 (471), 11, 335.
89 IAA, 97/107.41, James and George Richard Pain, 'Design for a court house and bridewell to be built in the different sessions towns in the county of Cork', 6 May 1824. For completion dates see Inspectors General, *Sixth report on general state of prisons of Ireland*, HC 1828 (68), 12, 349. New sessions houses: west riding; Macroom, Bantry, Skibbereen, Clonakilty; east riding; Mallow, Midleton, Kanturk.
90 Mallow is an exception: it had a single, round-headed opening for the courtroom.
91 This detail was not shown in the proposal.
92 The proposal had no pilasters on the central block; instead, it showed niches flanked the Venetian window. The design as realised conveys a stronger image.
93 Butler (2017), p. 109. Killarney had lower entrance wings and the Venetian window had a larger arch. Elements of the style also appeared in Boyle court house.
94 NAI, OPW drawings collection, OPW 5 HC/4/396, William Deane Butler, 'Plans, elevations, sections of intended quarter sessions house for Bray', 1841.

In a design of c.1825 for Tullow, Co. Carlow, Thomas Alfred Cobden employed a slightly different, though equally spare, vocabulary for a plan which aligned the side of the courtroom with the street, and provided entrances at either end.[95] Cobden's semi-circular courtroom windows were unusual, but the lateral alignment of the courtroom became the basis of the 'standard' design that was current after 1836.[96] This was usually a five bay, two-storey block – the end bays generally slightly advanced – flanked by recessed single-storey entrance wings. Five rectangular or round-headed windows at first-floor level lit the central double-height courtroom and flanking stairs, grand jury room, and judge's chamber, while, on the ground floor, small windows in the two outer bays framed three blank bays decorated with plaques. An emphatic platband usually incorporated the sills of the first-floor windows, dividing ground and first floor, a division that was accentuated in some cases by rustication on the ground floor.[97] The design was flexible, as the variations alluded to above suggest. It also allowed for different scales: smaller five-bay court houses – Newcastle West, Co. Limerick, Youghal, Co. Cork, Tulla, Co. Clare, Westport, Co. Mayo – did not have separate wings for the flanking doors.[98] Levels of architectural decoration varied; Carrick-on-Suir had small windows without architraves, while Clones had finely decorated window surrounds and projecting pediments over the doors. The design for the 'standard' was less architecturally stylish than the neoclassically informed designs by the Pain brothers for Cork, but the strictly formal symmetry, the areas of blank wall and, above all perhaps, the fact that the plan could be read on the façade, set these buildings apart and proclaimed their function in the small communities in which they often had a central location.

A striking effect of standardisation was recognition. This was commented on by visitors such as the novelist William Thackeray, who encountered the County Cork court houses 'as usual'.[99] For those involved in the judicial process, familiarity could smooth proceedings. Standardisation also equated to savings for those commissioning buildings. Apart from the examples discussed above, there are examples of local standardisation. In Wexford, a single-storey, single-bay, T-plan court house design for Gorey (1819) and Enniscorthy (1820), probably by the same architect, was also used twelve years later in New Ross (1832). A nicely balanced court house and bridewell design with a two-storey central block flanked by single-storey wings with gable chimneys, accessed by a central arched gateway in the low street wall, was used in Glin, Co. Limerick, and not so distant Milltown and Tarbert, both Co. Kerry.

Petty Sessions Houses

Petty sessions were held in the smallest and most numerous court houses.[100] An act passed in 1827 provided for the division of counties into petty sessions districts, and enabled grand juries to present an annual sum (capped at £10) to rent a public justice room.[101] Many of the buildings in which petty sessions were held have now gone, but of those that survive a large proportion were terraced houses in the centres of small towns and villages. Evidence that houses were rented survives in the Ordnance Survey memoir for Tandragee, Co. Armagh, where an end-of-terrace house was rented for £10. School houses were used in several places by petty sessions courts (Kinnitty, Co. Offaly, and Dundrum, Co. Tipperary, are examples), while in Fethard, Co. Tipperary, the early seventeenth-century almshouses were converted into a market and court house in the nineteenth century. There are also several examples of petty sessions being held in prominent market house buildings. In Rockcorry, Co. Monaghan, the 1805 market house, built as part of the village improvement scheme by the proprietor Thomas Corry, was the location for petty sessions, as was the multi-purpose hall designed in 1854 by John Skipton Mulvany for Portlaw, Co. Waterford, as part of the village improvement financed by the Malcomson family.

Apart from the courtroom, buildings used for petty sessions could also provide jury rooms (at Ballybot, Co. Armagh, two jury rooms flanked the courtroom), and there could also be a barristers' room.[102] Petty sessions courts were often held in buildings adjacent to constabulary barracks (Clonmacate, Co. Armagh, and Hospital, Co. Limerick, are examples) and some incorporated cells. A few purpose-built petty sessions houses survive, almost all examples of nineteenth-century vernacular buildings. At the end of a single-storey terrace in Lorrha, Co. Tipperary, a four-bay building with two entrances flanking a pair of small windows indicates that this was a court house. In Castleconnell, Co. Limerick, a small rubble-stone building set back from the road with an irregular façade – a single camber-headed first-floor window roughly positioned above a door flanked by windows – is another purpose-built or adapted petty sessions court house.

The Late Nineteenth Century

Although relatively few new court houses were built after 1850, there was considerable pressure to extend court house buildings and redesign courtrooms. Lack of maintenance had resulted in deterioration in some cases – by 1835 a leaking roof had seriously damaged stuccowork in Armagh court house, for example – but there were also demands to modernise buildings.[103] The design standard set by William Vitruvius Morrison in the late 1820s at Carlow and Tralee, which had influenced Keane and his patrons at Tullamore in the early 1830s, lay behind much of the criticism in the later nineteenth century. In 1850 the county surveyor of County Down objected to the 'boarded compartments' of the courtroom at Newry.[104] His suggestion that the existing seats and dock be replaced by a circular row of level seats on a raised platform so that 'the voice can be heard more distinctly' evoked the layout of Carlow and the aspirations of the Tullamore brief. At the 1871 spring assizes in Naas, Co. Kildare, the judges explicitly cited Carlow. Having complained about the wretched accommodation in the court house, they advised the County Surveyor, John Brett, to inspect Carlow and adopt some of the features in Naas.[105]

One aspect of Naas court house, designed by Richard Morrison before 1807, had in fact already been modernised. In 1861 John McCurdy's two-storey extension to the front had been completed. It had increased accommodation for the judiciary by providing rooms for the court clerks, crown solicitor, witnesses and grand jury committee as well as providing a double-height entrance hall.[106] Extensions to house public offices, committee rooms, accommodation for witnesses and police were built to many county court houses, mainly in the 1860s and 70s. John Brett's 1875 essay not only outlined the desirability of rooms for each functionary and member of the judiciary, but he also looked for designated space to house an expanding bureaucracy that sustained deputy clerks and magistrates' clerks, and looked for the convenience of waiting rooms and safes.[107] In several cases the blocks were added to the rear – Henry Davison, the County Surveyor, in association with the architect, Thomas Turner, built a rear wing onto Armagh court house, which was completed in 1863. However, in Omagh, Co. Tyrone, a five-bay, three-storey block designed by William Barre was added to the south in 1866, extending the front elevation.[108] Court houses with eighteenth-century roots still needed basic additions in the late nineteenth century; Wicklow, first built in the 1770s had been altered and extended in 1824, 1842 and 1866, but the record court, designed by John Brett, was not added until 1876.

Courtrooms were redesigned to improve audibility and visibility, provide specified places for those involved in the proceedings, encourage separate access and improve lighting and ventilation. The changes intended for the Crown Court in Armagh in the early 1860s have been recorded: the

95 Tullow court house was completed by 1827: Inspectors General, *Fifth report on general state of prisons of Ireland*, HC 1826–1827 (471), p. 11, p. 335.

96 The 'standard' design may have been derived from the two court house designs for Co. Laois (Borris-in-Ossory and Stradbally), dated to 1828 and attributed to William Deane Butler, the architect most commonly used to produce 'standard designs' after 1836. It has long been evident that there is the strong possibility of a standard design for sessions houses (see Casey (1982), p. 37). Twenty-seven sessions houses designed between 1826 and 1844 present subtle variations on a readily appreciated formula. Most post-date the 1836 act, which suggests that, although there was no provision in the legislation for a standard design, the Board of Works may have prepared one. It is perhaps significant that when Samson Carter's plans for Urlingford and Callan were rejected by the Board of Works in 1836, the approved plans, designed by William Deane Butler, conformed to the standard formula (O'Donoghue, p. 126).

97 Channelled ashlar was used for the ground floor in Newcastle West, Co. Limerick and for the end bays of the central block in Clones, Co. Monaghan.

98 The court house for Portumna, Co. Galway, has four bays.

99 Quoted in Butler (2017), p. 106.

100 Petty sessions were also held in county and quarter sessions houses.

101 'An act for the better administration of justice at the holding of petty sessions by justices of the peace in Ireland' (7 & 8 Geo. IV c.67).

102 Information from the gazetteer.

103 The complaint about Armagh court house was made by the county surveyor, H.L. Lindsay, and recorded in the grand jury records (Brett, p. 37).

104 Quoted in Brett, p. 72. Newry court house was completed by 1841.

105 O'Donoghue, p. 116. This experience probably inspired the paper John Brett gave to the Architectural Association of Ireland, published in the *Irish Builder* in 1875 (John Brett, pp. 25–6).

106 NAI, OPW drawings collection, OPW 5HC/4/402, R.J.S[tirling], J.H.M[ellon] & E.T.O[wen], survey: ground, upper floor and basement plans and front elevation, Naas court house, stamped 8 Dec. 1870.

107 Waiting rooms for the crown solicitor, clerk of the crown, grand jury, and the committee rooms, and safes for the county treasurer and clerk of the peace featured on Keane's 1832 plans for Tullamore court house.

108 Robert McKinstry, Richard Oram, Roger Weatherup and Primrose Wilson, The buildings of Armagh (Belfast, 1992), pp. 153–4.

barristers' pews were placed in front of the dock to face the judge; accommodation was provided for jurors in waiting; the public was to enter the gallery from an outside entrance to prevent them passing through the hall; and the courtroom was to be lit by 'sunburners' at night.[109]

Environmental and sanitary improvements to court houses pioneered in the 1830s became more commonplace in the later nineteenth century. The 1870 survey drawings of Naas court house include four water closets adjacent to the two jury rooms and one next to the county treasurer's office, all retrofitted into the original rear block.[110] The new quarter sessions court house at Ballyshannon, Co. Donegal, designed in 1880–81 by Board of Works architects Enoch Trevor Owen and his son, Alfred Richard Owen, incorporated a water closet in the front court yard and a second adjacent to the jury room.[111] Another aspiration was effective heating and ventilation. Brett, outlining his preferred system for courtrooms, described the admittance of fresh air at ground and basement level to be heated by hypocaust pipes and discharged through vents in the ceiling.[112] Such a system was incorporated into the new county court house in Sligo completed in 1879. Vents were provided for the admission of fresh air, which was heated by hot water pipes and ducted under the seating in the courtroom.[113] The air was extracted through ducts around the central light fitting and taken to the tower, from which it was expelled. Several new quarter sessions houses incorporated vents in their roofs: there were two discreet ventilating dormers on the tall roof of Keady market house and a prominent stack for Lurgan, both in County Armagh.

Newly constructed court houses were rare in late nineteenth-century Ireland. The only new county court house was built in Sligo. Of the few quarter sessions houses that were built, most were constructed in the 1870s and 80s. The classical tradition was maintained, but the most innovative designs were in Gothic revival styles.[114] These styles were the preferred choice for public buildings in Britain – and to a lesser extent in Ireland – in this period. Those with steeply pitching roofs, deep arcades, tall chimneys and prominent towers evoked northern European medieval urbanism. The buildings also added colour and richness to the urban landscape with their dramatic silhouettes, polychromatic and carved decoration. Thomas Turner designed court houses for Magherafelt, Co. Derry, and Lurgan, Co. Armagh, in 1874. Both used polychromatic materials to good effect: Lurgan, built in yellow brick and ornamented with bands of red brick, was particularly effective. It is the massing of Magherafelt which is impressive. A collection of towers, arcades and gabled chimneys, it evokes a community in which each element plays a part; the gabled keeper's house, the overarching central court, the judge's door. The new court house in Dun Laoghaire was part of a larger town hall project designed in 1874 by John Loftus Robinson costing £16,000. With campanile, balconies, broad eaves and round-headed windows decorated with alternating red and black voussoirs, this building, which addresses the street, refers directly to northern Italian urban architecture. Sligo, built with a Board of Works loan of £15,000, was quasi-ecclesiastical and northern European in its resonance. It impressed through the use of contrasting stonework and sculptural detail: the moulded arches to the ground-floor arcade; the frieze of cusped lancets; the corbelled turrets; the fleur-de-lys finials. The tower was used to good effect on a site where three roads meet, giving the building emphatic presence.

The Twentieth Century

Burnings and their aftermath

Between the passing of the Government of Ireland Act in 1920, which was the British government's final piece of Home Rule legislation, and the Courts of Justice Act of 1924, which established the courts system for the Irish Free State, there was a period of insurrection in Ireland which impacted on existing court buildings.[115] At least forty-three structures, not including the Four Courts complex in Dublin, were damaged or destroyed, with the majority of the attacks occurring in Munster and Leinster.[116] Nearly all the attacks occurred during the Anglo-Irish war of 1919–1922. The county court houses were sandbagged and defended by British troops, so that only two – Tullamore and Wexford – appear to have been successfully targeted.[117] Most of the damage was sustained by small quarter and petty sessions courts. There is evidence that some Irish Volunteers targeted court houses in their localities; Nicholas Carroll, in his witness statement to the Bureau of Military History, recorded that the local battalion of Volunteers explicitly targeted Kilmaganny court house, Co. Kilkenny, to prevent it being occupied by British military and police.[118] Sometimes court houses were included as targets with adjacent RIC barracks, as happened in Sneem, Co. Kerry.[119] There is at least one recorded case – the court house in Templemore, Co. Tipperary – of an attack by the British army.[120] The civil war of 1922–1923 was initiated when Free State troops besieged the Four Courts occupied by the Republican 'irregulars'. However, relatively few provincial court houses suffered during the civil war; exceptions include the county court house in Tullamore, Co. Offaly, Maam, Co. Galway, Bantry and Clonakilty in Co. Cork, Enniscorthy, Co. Wexford, and a number in Dublin including Dundrum and Tallaght.

Many of the court houses were repaired and restored to their original appearance in the 1920s. Given the Free State government's lack of financial resources, this suggests that damage had been relatively light and mostly internal. However, the investment represents a clear indication that the new state was anxious to maintain continuity between the old legal system and the new.

Building

New court houses have been planned and some built since the 1920s.[121] Perhaps the most ambitious was that proposed by Patrick J. Sheahan for Limerick city in 1939. (Image 9) An imposing court house was proposed as part of an extensive riverside civic centre in a stripped classical style, all of which was unrealised. The few new court houses which were built were mostly constructed to extremely tight budgets, but there has been a variety of approaches and briefs. The 1930s was a period of revived classicism and the gradual adoption of modernism. Modest references to these styles are apparent in small rendered district court houses from the late 1920s to early 1940s. A very simple classical formula was used for three similar court houses in County Mayo constructed in 1938 – Achill, Kilkelly and Ballycroy – while the new district court in Carlingford, Co. Louth, gestured towards a modest stripped classicism, and the flat concrete canopy over the entrance to the new rendered court in Templemore of 1937 referenced modernism.

International modernism prevailed for new public buildings in the 1960s and 70s, though most new court buildings, such as the single-storey court house in Rathdowney, Co. Laois, which could be mistaken for a small office, were extremely modest versions of this style. Early signs of modernism are apparent in the flat roof and asymmetric massing of the otherwise traditional redbrick court house in Mitchelstown, Co. Cork designed by Boyd Barrett Murphy-O'Connor and constructed between 1951 and 1953. (Image 10) Kilcock court house, Co. Kildare, of c.1965 stands out for its three-dimensional design – the curved timber front of the double-height courtroom roof rises above the single-storey entrance – and the use of a textured grey brick.[122] In the 1980s it was felt that modernism should be rendered in a less industrial aesthetic. Vernacular forms and materials were introduced into modern briefs for offices and industrial units. An example of such architecture applied to court houses can be seen at Bray, where Cooney Jennings designed a brick-built, hipped-roof linked courtroom and office block in 1984. In order to facilitate car users – a growing consideration – the court was located on an industrial estate where the court structures blend in with the surrounding buildings, rather

109 Ibid.
110 NAI, OPW drawings collection, OPW 5HC/4/402, R.J.S[tirling], J.H.M[ellon] & E.T.O[wen], survey: ground, upper floor and basement plans and front elevation, Naas court house, stamped 8 Dec. 1870.
111 NAI, OPW drawings collection, OPW 5HC/4/395, E. Trevor Owen & Alfred R. Owen, contract drawings, Ballyshannon court house, Co. Donegal, for contract signed 16 Aug. 1881.
112 John Brett, p. 26. Brett also recommended good ventilation in grand jury rooms where public sessions were held (ibid., pp. 25–6).
113 Lynda Mulvin, 'Administering justice in Gothic revival Ireland: a study of the Sligo assizes courthouse', in Michael McCarthy and Karina O'Neill (eds), *Studies in the Gothic revival* (Dublin, 2008), pp. 191–2.
114 The majority of the Gothic revival court houses were built in the northern part of Ireland.
115 Raymond Byrne and Paul McCutcheon, *Byrne and McCutcheon on the Irish Legal System* (Bloomsbury, 6th ed., 2014), p. 36. The Government of Ireland Act 1920 was unacceptable to Irish nationalists and never recognised by them.
116 The figures are derived from the gazetteer entries and are not definitive. The counties experiencing most attacks were Cork (eight) and Limerick (six). Smaller concentrations occurred in Kildare (four), Donegal and Tipperary (three each). Elsewhere – Galway, Louth, Wexford and Wicklow – there were two attacks.
117 Witness statement of Mr Justice Cahir Davitt to the Bureau of Military History (http://www.bureauofmilitaryhistory.ie/reels/bmh/BMH.WS0993.pdf#page=1, p. 26, accessed 13.02.19).
118 http://www.bureauofmilitaryhistory.ie/reels/bmh/BMH.WS1705.pdf#page=1, p. 6, accessed 13.02.19.
119 http://www.bureauofmilitaryhistory.ie/reels/bmh/BMH.WS0958.pdf#page=1, p. 4, accessed 13.02.19.
120 Information from the gazetteer.
121 Grand jury responsibility for the erection of court houses ended with the Local Government (Ireland) Act of 1898 when the administrative powers of the grand juries were invested in the newly established local authorities. The Courts of Justice Act of 1924 established the present courts system. The Courthouses (Provision and Maintenance) Act, 1935 stated that the provision and maintenance of court houses was the responsibility of local authorities, with a role for the Minister of Justice. The Department of Justice, Equality and Law Reform has commissioned a number of court houses which were designed and built by the Office of Public Works, most notably, Smithfield, Dublin (1987) and Carrick-on-Shannon, Co. Leitrim (1997) (The Office of Public Works, *Building for government: the architecture of state buildings, OPW: Ireland 1900–2000* (Dublin, 1999), pp. 182–5).
122 Kilcock court house had deteriorated badly by 2016. A number of Carnegie libraries were converted into court houses in the early to mid twentieth century. Examples include: Millstreet, Co. Cork, Rathkeale, Co. Limerick (1970s) and Castleisland, Co. Kerry (1929).

than, as nineteenth-century courts did, stand out from them.[123] Postmodernism, which revived classical formality, represented an alternative response to modernism. With its formal symmetry, undecorated pillars and 'quotations' from interior features, the façade of the children's court house at Smithfield, Dublin, partakes of the postmodernist spirit of the period.[124] But to judge the design from this single perspective is to underestimate its seriousness as a public building. It is an early example of effective contextualisation in an urban context: the corner building is designed to fit into two existing streets while addressing the public space of Smithfield. The articulation of the interior volumes, and the primacy given to the route through the building, bring a modernist sensibility to the tradition established in the county court houses of the early nineteenth century (Image 11).[125]

Elsewhere, the intention has been to downplay the public role of court buildings. In the late 1990s at Carrick-on-Shannon, Co. Leitrim, Burke Kennedy Doyle's brief was for 'a modern courthouse' that was 'both dignified and unintimidating'. It was located in a new estate on the edge of the town and designed to project inclusiveness with a curved façade protected by an over-sailing roof, and a curved colonnaded interior space that separates entrances, offices and courtrooms. The trend to bring civic and judicial functions together in a multipurpose building began in the frugal 1920s and 30s when, for example, the rebuilt court house in Bruff, Co. Limerick, incorporated a library. It blossomed in the late 1980s and 90s with large civic centre schemes. In Burke Kennedy Doyle's design for Limerick city, the court house and council chamber are distinguished from the city council offices by the use of stone, sloping roofs and the riverside location.[126] In the late 1990s and early years of the twenty-first century several major projects for circuit (former county) court houses combined refurbishment to modern briefs with conservation: McCullough Mulvin Architects' work on Sligo court house is notable, while Murray O Laoire inserted attic windows into a new zinc roof in Limerick county court house.

Northern Ireland
A new high court, built in central Belfast from 1928 to 1933 by the British Government, was constructed under the Government of Ireland Act of 1920. A large building that fills a city block, it was designed in what might be regarded as an imperial classicist style employed by architects such as Aston Webb, Sir Edwin Lutyens and Sir Herbert Baker for public buildings in Britain and its empire.[127] With thirteen bays articulated by giant Corinthian columns and a relentless line of attic windows, its effect is intimidating rather than impressive. This feeling is reversed inside, where the marble-lined hall

with its heavily coffered ceiling is definitively grand, and the courtrooms, decorated in timber and cork, are comfortable.

Mid-twentieth-century rebuilding, undertaken by the Ministry of Home Affairs and Ministry of Finance, was more ambitious in Northern Ireland than in the Republic. In a number of cases modernist sensibility dictated that decaying nineteenth-century court houses should be demolished rather than repaired. In Newtownards, Co. Down, Caldbeck's 'standard' court house was replaced by a bland 21-bay, flat-roofed structure that Brett, not unreasonably, likened to a 'justice factory', while in Lisburn, Co. Antrim, John McHenry's elaborate 1884 building, based on Palladio's Villa Ragona, was demolished in 1971, to be replaced by an extremely spare, elegantly designed concrete modernist box.[128] In this period a new petty sessions court house was erected in Belfast almost opposite the high court. A three-storey, flat-roofed structure with a twelve by three grid of windows interrupted solely by the asymmetrically-placed entrance, it was accurately described by Brett as a 'judicial office-block'.[129]

Bomb damage during the Troubles (prominent examples include Antrim, Newry, Crossmaglen, Downpatrick and Derry) led to the widespread appearance of security lodges and fencing, and new buildings in a style that emphasised security. This is clearly evident in the court house constructed on an island site in Antrim in 1994, which consists of three brick-built pyramid-roofed blocks with small introverted windows surrounded by a high security fence. The brick extension to the rear of Newry, Co. Down, built in 1995, has rounded corners and windows seemingly embedded in the walls, its utilitarianism in marked contrast to the classical elaboration of the walls of Thomas Duff's 1843 structure and the civic-mindedness of its cupola. The prominent and accessible Laganside courts complex in Belfast was completed in 2002 in a time of peace. Although corporate rather than civic in tone, its architecture points to a more optimistic future, though its bottle-green bulletproof windows reveal that the legacy of the immediate past remains potent.

Re-use
The last few decades have seen the decommissioning of many court houses in both Northern Ireland and the Republic. One trend has been to interpret and present court houses in the context of a museum. The mid-nineteenth-century market and court house of Cushendall, Co. Antrim, has been relocated to the Ulster Folk and Transport Museum at Ballycultra, while the distinctive mid-eighteenth-century court house of Hillsborough, Co. Down, built by the Marquess of Downshire, has been converted into a heritage centre. In the Republic,

the court and bridewell in Tarbert, Co. Kerry, was opened as the Bridewell Visitor Centre in 1993, and Kilmainham court house joined the successful Kilmainham gaol museum and visitor centre in 2016 as a visitor destination. Elsewhere, the distinctiveness of the buildings and their central location have made redundant court houses prime locations for arts centres and libraries: examples include Kinsale regional museum, opened in 1958, Bagenalstown court house, opened as a library in 1992; while the court houses in Tinahely, Co. Wicklow, and Carrick-on-Shannon, Co. Leitrim, were converted into arts centres in 1996 and 2005 respectively.

Conclusion

Irish provincial towns have a potent legacy in their court houses. Quintessential civic structures, often centrally placed, designed to concentrate attention, and exemplary in their use of materials and in the sturdiness of their construction, they have survived as the focus of many towns. Early nineteenth-century court house patronage is complex. Although it can be shown that grand jury patronage does not fully explain the flowering of court house design in the early nineteenth century, it is clear that the aspiration of grand juries to embody their authority in new court house buildings was crucial for the appearance of an architectural type made distinctive through the adoption of the restraint and rhetoric of neoclassicism. This legacy was not significantly developed in the later nineteenth and twentieth centuries. A modest, pared down aesthetic prevailed in new classical and modernist designs, but it is largely the survival of the early nineteenth-century buildings, adapted and extended to accommodate developments in the judicial system, that ensured the continuation of the early nineteenth-century legacy. Meanwhile, the older market house formula survived as a current in court house design, experiencing a renaissance in the few prominent Gothic revival designs of the late nineteenth century.

This brief history of court houses to the end of the twentieth century has demonstrated something of their ability to adjust to developing briefs. Perhaps the most significant proof of the adaptability of court houses has been their transition from official structures of the Union to official structures of Independent Ireland. Apart from the shedding of royal coats of arms, and the burning of a few structures, these buildings, many of which display an architectural language which effortlessly complements the order and restraint of the eighteenth- and nineteenth-century buildings and urban spaces that form the core of most Irish towns, have made the leap from embodying the justice system of Britain to that of an independent Ireland, while projecting, through architecture and sculptural representations, the ideal of justice.

123 Mildred Dunne and Brian Phillips, *The courthouses of Ireland: a gazetteer of Irish courthouses* (Kilkenny, 1999), p. 62.

124 *Building for government*, p. 182; Ciaran O'Connor and John O'Regan (eds), *Public works: the architecture of the Office of Public Works 1831–1987* (Dublin, 1987), pp. 58–61. The architects' statement described the design: 'The square entrance façade is designed to … make this new public building intelligible by translating the linear sequence of the plan onto the vertical arrangement of the elevation. Elements of the façade such as the pair of columns and the glass canopy refer to key elements of the interior expression of the building' (O'Connor and O'Regan, p. 59).

125 Plans, isometrics and projections, which reveal the design proprieties, are shown in O'Connor and O'Regan, pp. 59–61.

126 The trend continued into the twenty-first century: in 2003 a new civic centre in Tobercurry, Co. Sligo, designed by McCullough and Mulvin, incorporated a court house, as did a mixed use development in Cavan.

127 Belfast high court was designed by J.G. West of the Board of Works. For discussion and illustrations see Brett, pp. 50–51.

128 Ibid., pp. 74, 76.

129 Ibid., p. 50.

Image

1 Armagh Court House. Proposed elevation
and plan by Francis Johnston, 1805
(RIAI Murray Collection, IAA)

2 Armagh Court House. Proposed elevation
and plans by Francis Johnston, 1808
(RIAI Murray Collection, IAA)

3 Kilmainham Court House. Proposed side
elevation by Henry, Mullins and McMahon,
1817 (Guinness Collection, IAA)

4 Carrick on Shannon Court House. Ground
plan by William Farrell, 1820
(Houghton Library, Harvard)

5 Tullamore Court House. Ground plan by
J.B. Keane, 1833 (Lismore Collection, IAA)

6 Dunshaughlin Court House. Plan by Francis
Johnston, 1799 (RIAI Murray Collection, IAA)

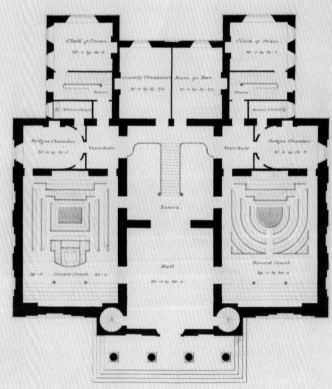

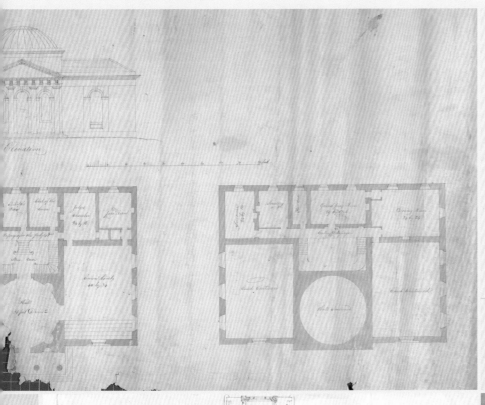

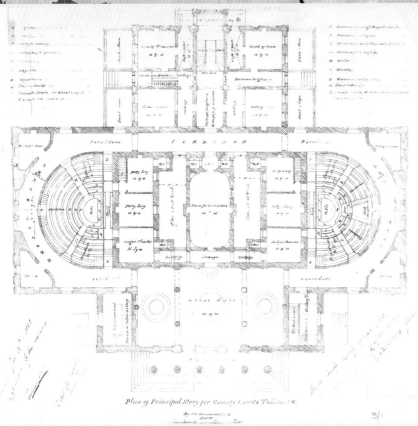

Plan of Principal Story for County Courts Tullamore.

3/1

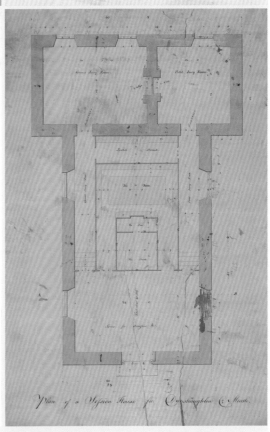

Plan of a Session House for Castlenaughten, Meath.

--

Image

7 Bray Court House. Plans, sections and
   elevations by William Deane Butler, 1841 (OPW
   Collection, NAI)

8a *Design for a court house and bridewell to be built
   in the different sessions towns in the County of
   Cork*, George Richard Pain, 6 May 1824, plan
   (Lismore Papers, NLI)

8b *Design for a court house and bridewell to be built
   in the different sessions towns in the County
   of Cork*, George Richard Pain, 6 May 1824,
   elevation (Lismore Papers, NLI)

9 Proposed Civic Centre and Court House,
   Limerick, by Patrick J. Sheahan, architect.
   Perspective view by Cyril Farey, 1939 (IAA)

10 Mitchelstown Court House. Section and plan
   by Boyd Barrett Murphy O'Connor, 1951 (Boyd
   Barrett Murphy O'Connor Collection, IAA)

11 Smithfield Court House. View of circulation
   space by John Tuomey, 1987 (O'Donnell and
   Tuomey Collection, IAA)

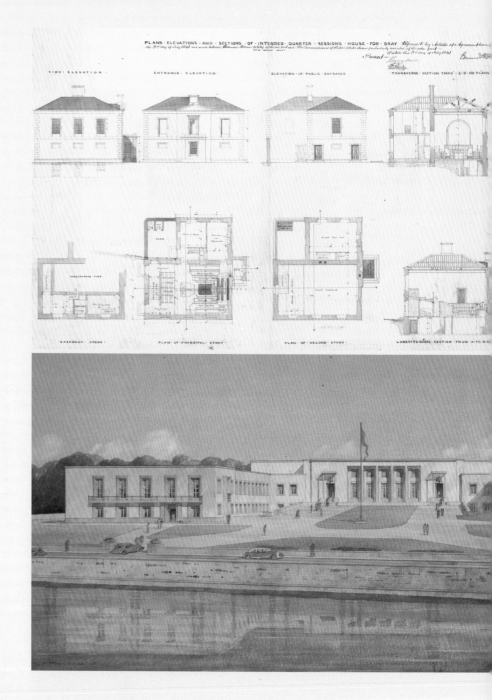

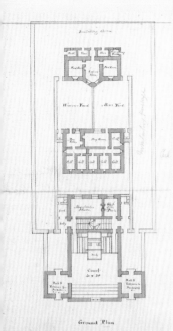

Ground Plan

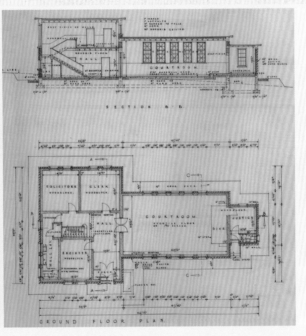

SECTION b b.

GROUND FLOOR PLAN.

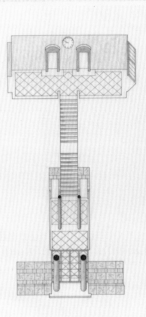

THE COURTS SERVICE BUILDING PROGRAMME SINCE 1999

Paul Burns

Background

The Courts Service was established in 1999 following the enactment of the Courts Service Act 1998. The service inherited a large network of court buildings – around 270 still active in 1999. Prior to this legislation the primary responsibility for the upkeep of court buildings fell to local authorities. This large estate of buildings was generally in poor condition as the investment by local authorities over many year had been minimal.

The poor condition of the estate was one of the factors that gave rise to the establishment of the Courts Service. The first report of the Working Group on a Courts Commission in April 1996 contains the following statement:

"The administration of justice is a solemn act of government. It should take place in dignified, suitable and fully equipped buildings. The current deplorable state of many courthouses is the most striking visible manifestation of the absence of adequate funding over the last 70 years to provide the necessary resources for the administration of justice."

Court House improvement projects

Continuing the work commenced by the Department of Justice in the early 1990s, the Courts Service in its early years commenced planning and implementing a significant programme of investment in projects with funding provided by Government. Combined with this there was a rationalisation of venues, with poor quality venues located close to suitable alternative venues being closed and amalgamated. The projects undertaken in this period included those set out in table 1.

Main Projects Completed 1998 to 2015

| **1998** |
| Ennis, Co. Clare (also in 2004) |
| Chancery Place (Four Courts), Co. Dublin |
| Tallaght, Co. Dublin |
| **1999** |
| Portlaoise, Co. Laois |
| Cork, Washington Street, Co. Cork (also in 2005) |
| **2000** |
| Trim, Co. Meath |
| Mallow, Co. Cork |
| Listowel, Co. Kerry |
| Baltinglass, Co. Wicklow |
| **2001** |
| Carrickmacross, Co. Monaghan |
| Athy, Co. Kildare |
| Carlow, Co. Carlow |
| Sligo, Co. Sligo |
| Cloverhill, Co. Dublin |
| **2002** |
| East Wing, Four Courts, Co. Dublin |
| Phoenix House, Smithfield, Co. Dublin |
| Castlerea, Co. Roscommon |
| **2003** |
| Limerick Circuit Court, Co. Limerick |
| Dundalk, Co. Louth |
| Accessibility works, Four Courts, Co. Dublin |
| **2004** |
| Castlebar, Co. Mayo |
| **2005** |
| Ballyshannon, Co. Donegal |
| **2006** |
| Nenagh, Co. Tipperary |
| Longford, Co. Longford |
| Bray, Co. Wicklow |
| **2007** |
| Dolphin House, Co. Dublin |
| Tullamore, Co. Offaly |
| Belmullet, Co. Mayo |
| Fermoy, Co. Cork |
| **2008** |
| Ardee, Co. Louth |
| Blanchardstown, Co. Dublin |
| **2009** |
| Thurles, Co. Tipperary |
| Youghal Offices, Co. Cork |
| **2010** |
| Kilkenny, Co. Kilkenny |
| Monaghan, Co. Monaghan |
| Gorey, Co. Wexford |
| Kilmallock, Co. Limerick |
| **2015** |
| Court of Appeal, Four Courts, Co. Dublin |

Delivering the court house building programme

The work undertaken in the building investment programme was regarded as an important function and has been overseen by a subcommittee of the Courts Service Board called the Building Committee. The involvement of the judiciary in this committee, which is usually chaired by a High Court judge, has been an important aspect of it, ensuring that all designs are developed in a way that is acceptable to, and supportive of, the role of the judiciary.

In the building programme the Courts Service was assisted by the Office of Public Works which provided a range of services: from architectural and engineering design to project management and site acquisition. The Courts Service also worked closely with local authorities: in acquiring space in court house buildings and in some cases in joint venture building projects, such as Tubbercurry in County Sligo, Ardee in County Louth, Gorey in County Wexford and Kilmallock in County Limerick. In developing court houses by way of Public Private Partnership, the Courts Service has been assisted by the National Development Finance Agency.

Court houses in Ireland Design Guide

An important factor in the development of new or refurbished court houses in the last 20 years has been the production of a standard design guidelines in the "Court houses in Ireland Design Guide" which was produced jointly by the Courts Service and the Office of Public Works. This sets out standards which were expected in any new court house or any major refurbishment works, such as: types of facilities to be incorporated, the space requirements, and general layouts for the different types of facilities. The areas which the design guide covers include:

- **General planning and design principles** to ensure a court house fulfils its basic function which is to provide an environment conducive to the efficient and effective administration of justice;

- **Building design and construction** which provides general guidance on legislation, regulations and standards to apply;

- **Schedule of accommodation**, listing the room types required for the various types of court buildings; and

- **Data sheets** setting out a room-by-room listing of the schedule of accommodation.

The process of developing the design guide involved discussions between architects and courts staff and involved the input of judges through the Courts Service's Building Committee.

While the requirements that the design guide sets out may not be capable of being met in all court houses, in particular in heritage buildings, the guide sets out an objective at which architects in such projects must aim.

Courtroom layouts

The courtroom layouts in the design guide were designed following discussions between architects and courts staff and judges. The layouts are intended to ensure that court hearings can operate fairly and efficiently with all participants able to see and hear the court proceedings.

While the general layout of courtrooms has not changed significantly over the years, in recent years courtrooms have become brighter, with more effort to bring natural light into the courtroom and the use of lighter coloured materials: wood, stone, carpets and furnishings.

Separate circulation

The design guide requires that there should be four separate circulation routes within a court house for the following: the public, judges, jury members, and persons in custody. These four categories of persons should only meet in the courtroom where a case is being dealt with. In a traditional court house there was some limited separation, for example with a judge having a separate entrance to the side or back of the court house. In general all other participants would come through the public entrance. The separate circulation routes are designed to ensure that there is no contact between persons in the four categories while in the court house, other than in the courtroom when the case is being heard. Contacts other than in the courtroom could in certain circumstances be seen as prejudicing a trial.

Custody access is designed to be, where possible, away from public view. This is to avoid persons in custody being seen or photographed while in handcuffs.

Accessibility

Traditionally court houses were built to impress, or even to intimidate, those coming to them. Externally this often involved the court house being located on a height with a long flight of steps to access the building. Internally courtrooms involved people being located at different heights within the courtroom and significant steps being involved to access various different locations (judge's bench, registrar's bench, witness box, jury box and custody area). All of these different levels and steps present difficulties for people with accessibility issues.

In modern court house design every effort is made to eliminate these challenges as far as possible. Sometimes where heritage buildings are involved it may only be possible to lessen the challenge, if not to fully eliminate it. Provision of ramps, lifts and movable platforms can help in making even heritage courtrooms more accessible.

Modern courtroom design will, through careful layout of facilities and the use of ramps and lifts, allow people with accessibility issues, to access any area of the courtroom, be they judges, courts staff, jurors, witnesses, legal practitioners, persons in custody or members of the public. In a modern courtroom the layout of furniture takes account of the requirements of turning-circles for people in wheelchairs and as a result modern courtrooms are less "cluttered" in appearance than many older courtrooms.

Signage is designed as far as possible to be legible even by people with sight issues and induction loop systems are provided to assist people with hearing difficulties.

Victim support and vulnerable witness facilities

In the past the position of a victim of crime in a court case was very much secondary to the prosecution and defence parties. The victim may have had a role as a witness in the case but otherwise had limited involvement. This has changed in recent years and the facilities in modern court houses have changed to reflect this. A modern court house contains a victim support suite with a range of facilities. These include a waiting area, with toilet and kitchen facilities, where a victim can wait during the course of a trial without fear of meeting the accused in the public areas. There are facilities for victim support organisations to provide their services in this area. There is an area where a child witness can wait, which is child-friendly in layout and furnishing. The suite also includes a video-link room, from which a vulnerable witness can give evidence in court without having to appear in the courtroom and have to face the accused.

More recent developments in this area include the provision of screens around the witness box in a courtroom, to allow a vulnerable witness to attend in person in the courtroom, be seen by all involved in the case but be prevented from seeing the accused.

The "dock" and custody facilities

The use of a "dock" or custody holding area in a courtroom has changed in courtroom design over the years. In a traditional court house a person in custody would usually attend court in a dock: an area directly accessed from the cell area, which was usually located below the dock. They were accompanied by police or prison officers and in some cases were in handcuffs.

In more recent times courts have moved towards a situation where the accused is no longer in a separate area and is permitted to sit in the body of the court. This is particularly so in the case of jury trials where arrangements for the accused person which could be seen as calling into question the presumption of innocence are to be avoided.

In the case of non-jury trials where a single judge (in the District Court) or a group of three judges (in the Special Criminal Court) are presiding, there may be security arrangements around persons in custody – such as a glass screen surrounding the custody area in the courtroom – as this would not be expected to influence the decision making of the judge or judges involved.

Courtroom technology

In a traditional courtroom up until recent years, the extent of courtroom technology was the use of microphones on the judge's bench and for witnesses and legal practitioners, to enhance the transmission of sound around the courtroom. Today there is a range of technologies in use in a modern courtroom. All courtrooms have digital audio recording equipment which have a number of uses: allowing the replay of evidence in the courtroom or jury room, and enabling the production of transcripts remotely without the presence of a stenographer in court. Many courtrooms have evidence display systems which enable CCTV footage to be played in court and electronic documents to be displayed. Some equipment also allows physical evidence to be shown on screen. Video conferencing equipment in some courts allows witnesses to appear from remote locations. These include persons in custody who can appear from prisons for bail and remand hearings. Witnesses who are abroad can appear by video as can expert witnesses from any location with access to video-conferencing facilities.

A more recent development has been the installation of wifi systems in court houses to allow those participating in a court case to have access to the internet and to a range of information systems.

The Criminal Courts of Justice

In 2006 the Courts Service embarked on its most ambitious project to that date, the Criminal Courts of Justice in Dublin.

This involved the use of Public Private Partnership as a means of delivery of the project and the holding of an international competition for the design, build, operation and finance of the project. The Criminal Courts of Justice commenced operation in November 2009 in a landmark building on Parkgate Street, beside the Phoenix Park. The building was delivered by the PPP Company Amber Infrastructure. Architectural design was by Henry J Lyons Architects and the main contractor was PJ Hegarty Construction. The building's design is innovative and is unlike any previous court house building in Ireland. It does however incorporate elements, such as the central Great Hall, which is reminiscent of, though larger than, the Round Hall in the Four Courts.

The economic recession commencing in 2008 saw a change in the building activities of the Courts Service. Projects underway before 2008 were completed (Kilkenny, Monaghan and Gorey) but no new projects were to commence for a number of years. In this period there was also a significant reduction in the size of the Courts Service's building estate, as small, unsuitable and infrequently used venues were closed, their workload being amalgamated into more suitable nearby venues.

The Courts PPP Bundle

During the period from 2008 the Courts Service continued planning for new venues and in 2012 a Government Investment Stimulus Package was announced, to be provided by way of Public Private Partnership. The Courts Service had seven projects ready for inclusion in a "Courts Bundle": Cork (Anglesea Street), Limerick (Mulgrave Street), Waterford, Wexford, Mullingar, Letterkenny and Drogheda. These were all locations where a site for a new court house, or space for the refurbishment and extension of an existing court house, was available.

The Courts Service had worked with the Office of Public Works to prepare outline plans for the proposed buildings and to bring the proposals through the planning process. The National Development Finance Agency undertook the procurement and project management of the project and BAM PPP were chosen as the developers. The buildings were all delivered in 2018-2019. Combined together into a single bundle, these seven buildings represent the largest single contract ever entered into for new court facilities in Ireland, with a total capital value of around €150 million.

Future development proposals

The Courts Service continues to plan for future developments. In Dublin plans are at an advanced stage for a new Family Law Court complex, including the Children Court and the Supreme Court, on a site at Church Street and Hammond Lane. This location beside the Four Courts will consolidate business within the "Legal Quarter" of central Dublin. Outside Dublin plans are being made for five new or refurbished city and county town venues: Galway, Tralee, Wicklow, Portlaoise and Roscommon.

Combined with the significant investment made in new and refurbished court buildings over the last twenty years, it is essential that a proper programme of maintenance is put in place to keep these buildings in a proper state. During the recent economic recession funding for maintenance work was extremely limited and work was undertaken on priority issues, such as those relating to health and safety. In order to get a clear picture of the state of court buildings the Courts Service is in 2019 undertaking a survey of its existing building stock. This will assist in the development of a proactive maintenance programme for the remaining venues. The Courts Service wants to ensure that the court house stock does not return to the "deplorable state" that was a feature in much of the twentieth century.

Conclusion

In the twenty years of its existence the Courts Service in partnership with the Office of Public Works and the National Development Finance Agency has delivered a significant improvement in the courtroom facilities that are available to all court users. This was done with the support of Government in funding this programme, which is greatly appreciated. The Courts Service values the ongoing support of the Department of Justice and Equality in ensuring that appropriate court accommodation is available throughout the country, and looks forward to continuing investment to improve facilities into the future.

DESIGNING COURT HOUSES: AN ARCHITECT'S ANALYSIS

Ciaran O'Connor

Context and vision, aspirations and ambitions

Courts are more than four walls and a roof. They embody the concept of justice, of right and wrong – an aspiration that is deeply human and enduring. There is a primal need for redress for an injustice done. Citizens seek to be treated equally, want respect and to be afforded dignity. We the citizens have aspirations and are the electorate who choose our elected representatives who pass laws by which we are governed. An independent judiciary is fundamental to the rule of law in a democratic society. The design question is how such a triumvirate of carefully balanced power is acknowledged in a court house design.

Architecture embodies many different realms from the social, political, economic, to design ideas and their technical execution. Together they affect the context in which architecture occurs. In the golden age of 19th-century court house building there were nearly 200 offences for which a defendant could be hanged. Stealing a sheep or a different political view could get you deported to a penal colony in Australia. Yet for a short period of historical time aspirations and ambitions rhymed for court houses.

When Ireland had its own limited parliament in the late 18th century, there were aspirations backed by finance to articulate a vision for the island. While acknowledging the aristocratic and undemocratic realities of that time, it is clear that certain enlightened steps were taken in architecture and planning terms. The Wide Streets Commission was founded in 1757 to transform Dublin into a 'modern and prestigious city'. In 1793 the Irish Parliament passed an act which decreed that all public buildings paid solely from the public purse were to be placed under the control of 'His Majesty's Board of Works'. This act appointed an Architect Inspector of Civil Buildings 'who shall superintend the execution of all public works', and brought more architectural and administrative structure to public building. This position was held in the 19th century by a number of significant architectural personalities including Francis Johnston (1760-1829), who was Architect and Inspector of Civil Buildings for the Board of Works from 1805 to 1826.

Francis Johnston designed Kells and Armagh court houses, the GPO and the Chapel Royal in Dublin Castle. He oversaw the approval of court houses by other architects in the early 19th century. Records show that his comments were less than complimentary on some of the court house designs submitted to the Board of Works. He was not shy to send back drawings 'for further development'.

The influence of the 18th-century Grand Tour of classical Rome and Greece should not be underestimated. The Grand Tour was a type of 'finishing school' for the aristocracy and landed gentry for about two hundred years, until the advent of rail travel in the mid-19th century. It involved the acquisition of knowledge, culture and 'taste' through visiting the roots of Western civilisation in the classical world of Italy, France and Greece. Individuals such as James Caulfeild, Earl of Charlemont (Casino at Marino), Frederick Hervey, Bishop of Derry, and Howe Peter Browne, 2nd Marquess of Sligo (Westport House), undertook Grand Tours and were impressed by what they saw. It gave neoclassical design an historical authenticity and moral authority when it came to state and other prestigious buildings. Architectural publications by James Gandon and Robert Smirke influenced design theory and practice in a similar direction.

Until the local government reform in the late 19th century, the county Grand Jury was the client for court houses and the Board of Works the loan granting agency. The Grand Jury was made up of the local landlords and business barons who controlled their areas as fiefdoms. Some wanted court houses that reflected their importance, other were parsimonious and mean spirited.

Consolidation of court house design

A court house design vocabulary evolved that was tested over time. Formative ideas from Gandon, Morrison, Smirke, Keane and Johnston led to organisational concepts. An understandable, almost archetypal, pattern of court house design emerged in the early 19th century, with incremental technical and environmental improvements over time.

Daylight, fresh air, heating, lighting and improved sanitation kept pace with other public buildings. The hierarchy of court house spaces, circulation, and the interface of the judge with the court, the jury, the prosecution, defence and the public became architecturally defined and reflected power, attitudes towards justice, and social norms of the period.

Jacob Owen (1778-1870) was Principal Architect of the Board of Works from 1832 to 1856. He acted in a similar manner to Francis Johnston, approving court house plans for grant aid. He also designed smaller local courts in Roscrea and Buncrana, and directly influenced other projects, notably Carlow. It is likely he was also involved in the standard plans for local courts during his tenure of office. Owen was involved in the large programme of expansion to the Four Courts where he was responsible for the north block in the 1830s. E. Trevor Owen and R.J. Stirling were designers of the Probate Court of 1861, the Bankruptcy Court of 1864 and the innovative Record Repository built to the west of the Four Courts proper in 1864-67. The siege of the Four Courts in 1922 that heralded the outbreak of the Civil War destroyed most of the two Owens' works and much of Gandon's and Thomas Cooley's Four Courts.

The late 18th and first half of the 19th century saw significant design achievements at the Four Courts, in Clonmel, Carlow town, Cavan town, Cork city, Ennis, Galway city, Kilkenny city,

Monaghan town, Mullingar, Naas, Tralee, Waterford town and many other smaller venues throughout the country. The latter part of the 19th century saw less court house building and those built were not major courts for the most part. This is not surprising since the Famine of the 1840s dramatically reduced the population of Ireland, which continued to fall until the 1960s. There were a few exceptions such as Sligo town (1874-77) court house by Rawson Carroll. This three-storey over basement building is a flamboyant example of free form Gothic carried through with verve and conviction. The hegemony of classical design was broken but it remained a potent design force into the 20th century.

Post-independence

During the War of Independence and Civil War that followed most court houses escaped serious damage, with some notable exceptions, such as the Four Courts and Wexford. The Four Courts were to be rescued from the ashes by T.J. Byrne, Principal Architect of the new state's Office of Public Works.

After independence, local authorities were given responsibility for courts except for a number of state-owned buildings such as the Four Courts. Courts now fell between the administrative cracks of government and the local authorities, the latter having neither funds nor special interest in looking after court houses. When new small court houses were constructed there was a wide disparity of quality. Bruff, Co. Limerick (1925) sports a clumsily columned portico aping a classical building. Templemore, Co. Tipperary (1935) and Ballynacarrigy, Co. Westmeath are detached single storey buildings not unlike a standard vocational school of its time. Mountrath, Co. Laois (1960) District Court had a strong visual resemblance to a public convenience. The nadir of court house accommodation was reached in the prefab provision at Tobercurry, Co. Sligo in 1973.

From stagnation to rejuvenation

The long slow decline of the physical fabric of the courts system could not continue. The Department of Justice knew it and the judiciary experienced it. The need for a Courts Service to take a direct role in this area was recognised. Some two hundred years after the first golden age for courts that gave us the Four Courts, aspiration and ambition once again rhymed for court houses.

The articulated vision of the Courts Service found a reciprocal response in the OPW. There was a rational and considered analysis of the steps and issues involved in bringing the court estate up to a recognisable standard after seventy-five years of decline. Its analysis was much more than a perfunctory property review. It sought to extract all the potential value, both hard and soft, from a property. A particular challenge of the last twenty years was to develop new court facilities and court types for a growing population, and to close or repurpose court houses no longer viable in caseload terms.

Where possible, existing court houses of architectural quality were retained, restored, refurbished and extended. This approach supported existing town and city urban renewal. If this approach was not feasible, then a brown field site was chosen whenever possible, an approach which supports sustainability, urban permeability and connectivity.

There are many subtle advantages to an extended client/architect relationship. The architect becomes intimately familiar with the client, not just their physical environment but how that environment is really used, and how the client really functions. Jim McCormack, Brendan Ryan, Paul Burns and their staff, supported by successive Chief Justices, deserve special mention. They coupled vision with strategy and matched aspirations with good implementation goals. The Court Houses in Ireland Design Guide developed in 2005 by Michael Haugh, former Assistant Principal Architect in OPW, and Shay Kirk, former Head of the Estates and Buildings Unit in the Courts Service, along with the members of the Courts Service Building Committee, is seminal. It is a 'living document', continually adjusting over time. It absorbed, adapted and reinterpreted the knowledge base of each organisation. Since then, dialogue and problem solving have led to sensitive and sometimes surprising results. Use and experience met ambition and vision, making good decisions contagious. Challenges were turned into valuable insights. There was a conscious effort to see the building brief and specific site in a complementary relationship such that the civil and civic aspects of society are represented alongside the 'dignity of the Court'.

Unity in diversity

The architectural design teams for each court house met frequently to discuss and share ideas. We sought a consistent sensibility, not a singular design hand. I called it unity in diversity. We defined the brief, researched the site, studied its historical, physical and cultural context, to determine possible solutions. We interfaced with the client.

The function, shape, form and technics of court house design also occur within a context. That context is social, judicial, economic and physical. Problems and aims need to be perceived, defined and articulated before shaping the solution. Architecture is more than satisfying the purely functional requirements of the brief or building programme. Architecture needs to promote functionality, elicit responses and communicate meaning.

Today, architectural design is neither entirely a creative or psychological experience, nor a functional and procedural operation. It is a multi-layered transformation in which reality is imaginatively changed, while remaining rational and contextual in principle. Architecture as a response and not just a statement. Design must stand up to both scrutiny and indifference. It must find the hinge or fulcrum point to tip the balance in favour of quality and real value. This is how to achieve architecture that has cultural resilience and economic sustainability.

As previously noted, classical architecture had a set of rules or a vocabulary with its own syntax and grammar. It set out the principles of composition, hierarchy of form, space and materials that should constitute a court house or other important public buildings. Most of the neoclassical court houses of the 19th century followed the classical rules of antiquity. We sought a variety of ways to investigate and interpret that history. We looked to reveal the latencies of the site and its physical history. Then we pursued a way to weave these latent and physical characteristics into the future design, a sort of empathetic reckoning with the past that was both explicit and implicit. For example, in the Limerick project we worked with the 'as found' historical fragments of the site and knitted them into the new court house fabric at the main entrance. In Waterford, a more explicit interface with history led to specific site and plan relationships.

It is not only the present that needs roots in the past; the past, if it is not to be fossilised, needs to be continued into the present. We need to keep our architectural inheritance open to the future. Cultural heritage needs contemporary creativity for a deeper reciprocal relationship.

Part of a continuum

Neoclassical court architecture had connotative meaning, associate values and symbolic content. Over time, cultural interpretation can change. For example, the Monaghan court house has a royal insignia on its main façade and there were demands that this be removed during our restoration and new work. Our aim was for a continuous architectural history that makes the past part of the present. We cannot change the past, but nor should we try to erase it. We are all part of a continuum. Culture can shape our identities and define our viewpoints. It oscillates with time, place and social values. For some the Monaghan royal insignia is a reminder of a negative colonial past. For others it is a memento of times past or of carving craftmanship. The coat of arms remains in place.

Restoration can be less about the achievement of a particular end state than about an ongoing dynamic process of remaking – an interface with the past that is not subservient. An example would be the interface between the new Cork court house set behind the best 19th-century Model School. Both buildings are enhanced rather than diminished by each other's presence.

Process of delivery

In the set of recent projects that follow are a cross section of the architectural issues and solutions discussed here. Some court houses were delivered by 'traditional' or normal government contract. Others were delivered by the Public Private Partnership (PPP) method. The PPP system is a form of lease-back over twenty-five years. In a conventional PPP there is a set of procedures with set timelines such that the preconstruction period can be longer than a normal traditional contract. To assist the Courts Service and the National Development Finance Agency in shortening that timeline, I suggested a variation, a so-called 'smart-PPP', whereby a set of design drawings, with specifications and design details, was used. This helped maintain design intent for the client without the loss of the developer inputs. Effectively you had the Design Architect leading the design team for the client and an Architect of Record leading the developer's design team while attached to his or her construction team. Seven projects were delivered under the 2015 courts bundle PPP.

A collaborative undertaking

Without the support of the Courts Service Building Committee, my fellow OPW Management Board members, professional and administrative colleagues, these illustrated projects would not have been a success. Designing and building are collaborative undertakings. The architect works with the structural and civil engineers, mechanical and electrical engineers, quantity surveyors, contractors, specialists and, most importantly, the client, to deliver a court house befitting a democratic republic.

Conclusion

Courts have come a long way, both in terms of a building type and the administration of justice. In the early Norman period, the furniture in the Great Hall of Trim Castle was rearranged to accommodate a trial at which the lord presiding was effectively judge and jury. Similarly, the Archbishop of Dublin in the medieval Palace of St Sepulchre (later site of the old Kevin Street Garda Station) had his own ecclesiastical and temporal courts, prison and gallows. Later courts found rooms above the town market hall, as happened in Kinsale and Clonmel, but the administration of justice still largely rested with the local elite.

The golden age of court house design and construction in the late 18th to mid-19th centuries saw the emergence of a recognisable building type for which the clients, the county grand juries, were drawn from the upper echelons of society, while the state was the provider of loans.

Electoral and judicial changes brought in a new modern era of reform. A courtroom today is a place to seek vindication, to face justice, to pass judgement, to work within, or to visit and witness the independent rule of law. As the following short case studies show, the contemporary court house must rise above pure utility, beyond basic construction, to combine all that is practical and necessary to function with a design that is meaningful and humane, that enriches the present and honours the past.

--
Image
1 Section by James Gandon, *c.* 1800, showing original decorative scheme for dome (King's Inns Collection, IAA)
2 Law Library interior (IAA, *c.* 1900)
3 Aerial view with Four Courts in the middle ground (J.V. Downes Collection, IAA, *c.* 1950)
4 Damage to centre block (T.J. Byrne Collection, IAA, July 1922)
5 Plasterwork figure of Mercy from dome interior (C.P. Curran Collection, IAA, *c.* 1900)
6 River front following bombardment. The rear area was even more damaged (T.J. Byrne Collection, IAA, July 1922)

Thomas Cooley began the general Inns Quay design in 1776 but he died in 1784 with one wing of his public offices complete. James Gandon took over the project to which were added the courts of justice. He retained and respected Cooley's contribution while adding his own tour-de-force of the temple portico, rusticated arcades, courtyards, and four courtrooms leading off an impressive rotunda under the dome at the heart of the building. A coffered interior dome terminated with an oculus or circular opening. The space between the inner and outer domes was used for storing court documents. A series of ropes and pulleys allowed documents to be lowered from the dome store to the rotunda below.

DUBLIN

THE FOUR COURTS
A PHOENIX FROM THE ASHES

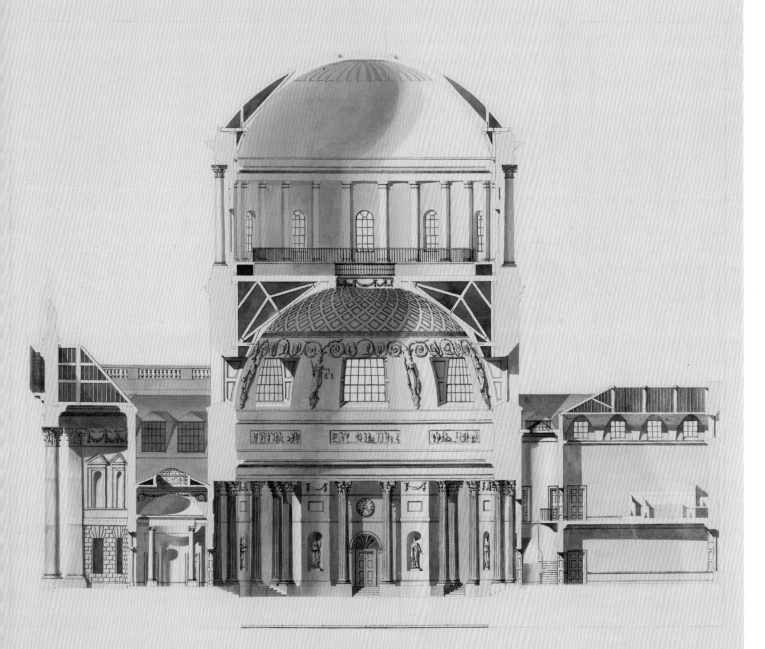

In June 1922, the Civil War began with an artillery attack on the Four Courts to compel the surrender of anti-treaty forces which had occupied the building for two months. After almost three days of fighting, the building was so heavily damaged that the OPW engineering advice was to demolish what remained. However, the new OPW Principal Architect, T.J. Byrne (1923-1939) used his quiet, persuasive powers to convince politicians (he knew W.T. Cosgrave well), the judiciary and the Department of Finance to restore, refurbish and rebuild the Four Courts.

The severely damaged building needed major interventions to repair and stabilise it. Steel framing was used to brace the external walls and carry new reinforced concrete floors. Roof lighting to the individual four courts and a new Supreme Court room, on axis with the portico, were added. Internal circulation was reorganised and room-through-room access was replaced by corridor circulation. Lighting, heating and sanitation services were modernised.

Externally the end building pavilions were set back 3.6 metres, making them almost flush with Gandon's arcade screens, and causing them to lose some of their visual impact. This was done to facilitate pavement and road widening. Granite and Portland stone was patched and matched into the external façades.

The great dome was rebuilt as a reinforced concrete shell which Byrne used to stabilise the damaged structure. Byrne designed the concrete dome structure and reinforcement himself. He inventively used a construction elevator, possibly for the first time in Ireland, to hoist and hand pour all the concrete in a 30-hour unbroken shift by 20 men. Externally, Byrne used Portland stone in the reconstruction of the rotunda to the dome. To save costs, he rotated damaged capitals to face inwards while the formerly internally facing and generally less damaged capitals were turned outwards. Irish materials such as Killaloe and Carrick-on-Suir slates were used alongside Kerry sandstone internal linings to the foyer. The mammoth task was completed in October 1931.

T.J. Byrne was assisted by OPW architects Cooke, Geoghegan and Ward. The Chief Justice Hugh Kennedy complimented the OPW, and Byrne in particular, on the restoration of 'the main architectural features of the Gandon masterpiece'. It is to a fledgling new state's credit that it supported Byrne in his vision to retrieve such an important building from potential oblivion.

In the mid-1990s refurbishment work and court/administrative reorganisation were completed in time for the bicentenary celebrations. More recently, in 2015, the part of the Public Records Office that survived the 1922 explosions and fire was converted into courtrooms and support facilities for the new Court of Appeal. The damaged capitals to the dome are currently being restored. As we approach the centenary of its near total destruction in 2022, a new masterplan is needed to chart a new future for the Four Courts and the Courts Quarter.

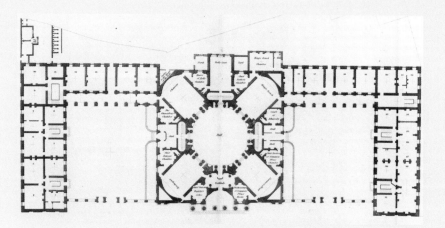

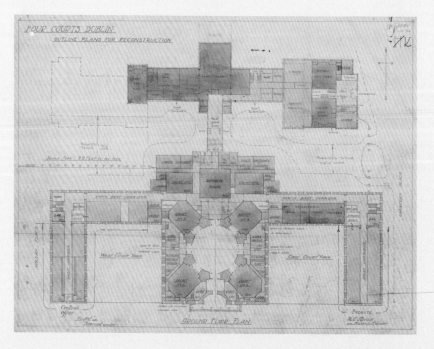

--
Image
1 The Great Hall, a central rotunda
off which the individual courtrooms
are disposed
(Joshua St John, 2010)
2 Main entrance off Parkgate Street
(Enda Kavanagh/Gareth Byrne, 2010)

It had become clear by the end of the 20th century that the Four Courts could not manage the rising volume of civil and criminal court cases. The solution was to separate these two basic forms of judicial work, with civil cases remaining in the Four Courts and criminal cases moving to a new criminal court.

The OPW provided the 0.95 hectare site at the junction of Infirmary Road and Parkgate Street near the Phoenix Park, helped to write the brief with the Courts Service, and gave architectural input through the Public Private Parnership (PPP) process. *The Court Houses in Ireland Design Guide* had recently been completed by the OPW Architectural Services and the Courts Service and this helped the development of the project brief.

Relocation from the iconic circular dome of the Four Courts to the circular new Criminal Courts of Justice (CCJ) was not without its detractors. Objections were many and varied, from the location to the proposed scale of the development and most things in-between.

DUBLIN   CRIMINAL COURTS OF JUSTICE

Na Cúirteanna Breithiúnais Coiriúla
The Criminal Courts of Justice

The largest court project since the 1796 Four Courts, the CCJ has 600 rooms, including 22 courts over 11 floors and basements, amounting to some 25,000 m² of building. Some 150 barristers are catered for, plus offices for the Director of Public Prosecutions, the Probation Service, An Garda Síochána, the Law Society and press. There are special spaces for judges' chambers, jury rooms, court administration, together with significant detention facilities.

Enabling works on the site found military/naval ordnance that had to be carefully removed. An uncharted water culvert taking surface water from the Phoenix Park also had to be diverted. The steep, sloping, small site has a 10-metre difference in height between the north and south boundaries. This required architectural and engineering skills to resolve which were not found wanting.

The large scale of the building is visually reduced by the use of glazed panels that are two-storey in height, thereby giving the impression of a smaller building. This and other lower street-level scaling devices, and choice of base materials, all help to reduce the physical impact on the adjacent streetscape.

The relatively simple circular external form belies a more complex internal plan. The public enter from the lower Parkgate Street side while judiciary, staff and defendants enter the discrete yet secure Infirmary Road entrance. Once inside the building, the central circular space acts as a huge organising device. The judiciary, jury and persons in custody all have their own separate circulation routes. There is an air of importance within this central space yet there is also dignity and calm. Good light and acoustics work with discreet and effective security segregation. Some legal wags have dubbed this tall central space 'the Pantheon' because of its great height which is some four times that of the Four Courts' central space.

The courtrooms have natural light without the loss of visual security. A perforated bronze anodized aluminium mesh is sandwiched between two layers of glass to give this security, while modulating internal light levels and avoiding glare. The jury rooms are well crafted while the judges' chambers at the top of the building enjoy views of a roof garden, the Phoenix Park and the skyline of Dublin.

In November 2009 the CCJ opened its doors. The then Chief Justice, John Murray, described the building as a 'magnificent construction'. Peter McGovern of Henry J. Lyons Architects commented that architecturally there is 'no house style' involved, rather a representation of functional requirements. However, it is far more than a functional utilitarian construction. It is a major public building executed with architectural skill and technical competence. The contractor, PJ Hegarty and Sons, deserves credit for the quality of finish and the manner in which they executed a demanding building on an unforgiving site.

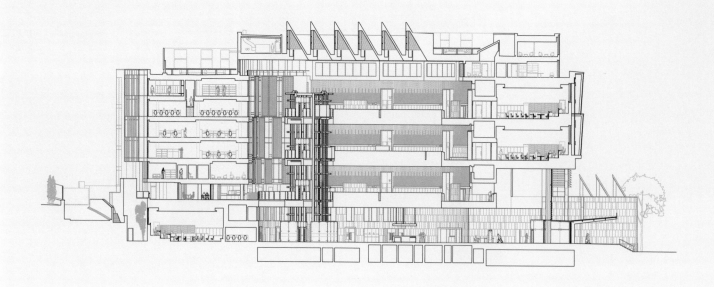

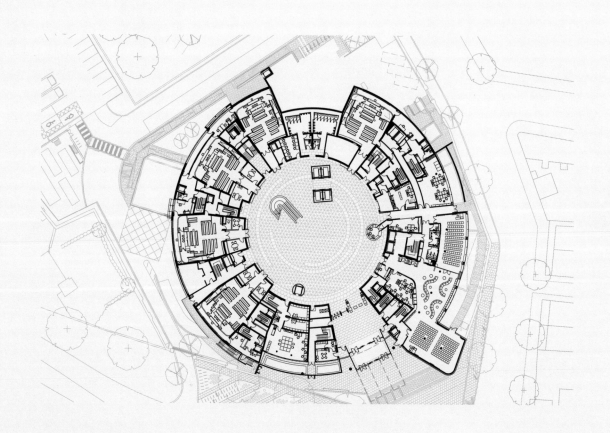

1B21

3026 Tallaght

--
Image
1 Atrium space with access to new
courtrooms, viewed from original building
(Donal Murphy, 2010)
2 New entrance from John's Bridge
(Donal Murphy, 2010)

This historic two-storey-over-basement building became a court house in 1792. It was built over the remains of the 13th-century Grace's Castle and a 16th-century gaol. The architect, William Robertson, provided a classical façade c. 1830 which gave some unity to the much altered earlier buildings. Further building works were executed over the course of the 19th century. A 1980 'refurbishment' was unsatisfactory and in the OPW design of 2008 a number of these insensitive alterations were reversed.

KILKENNY   COURT HOUSE

Teach Cúirt Chill Chainnigh
Kilkenny Courthouse

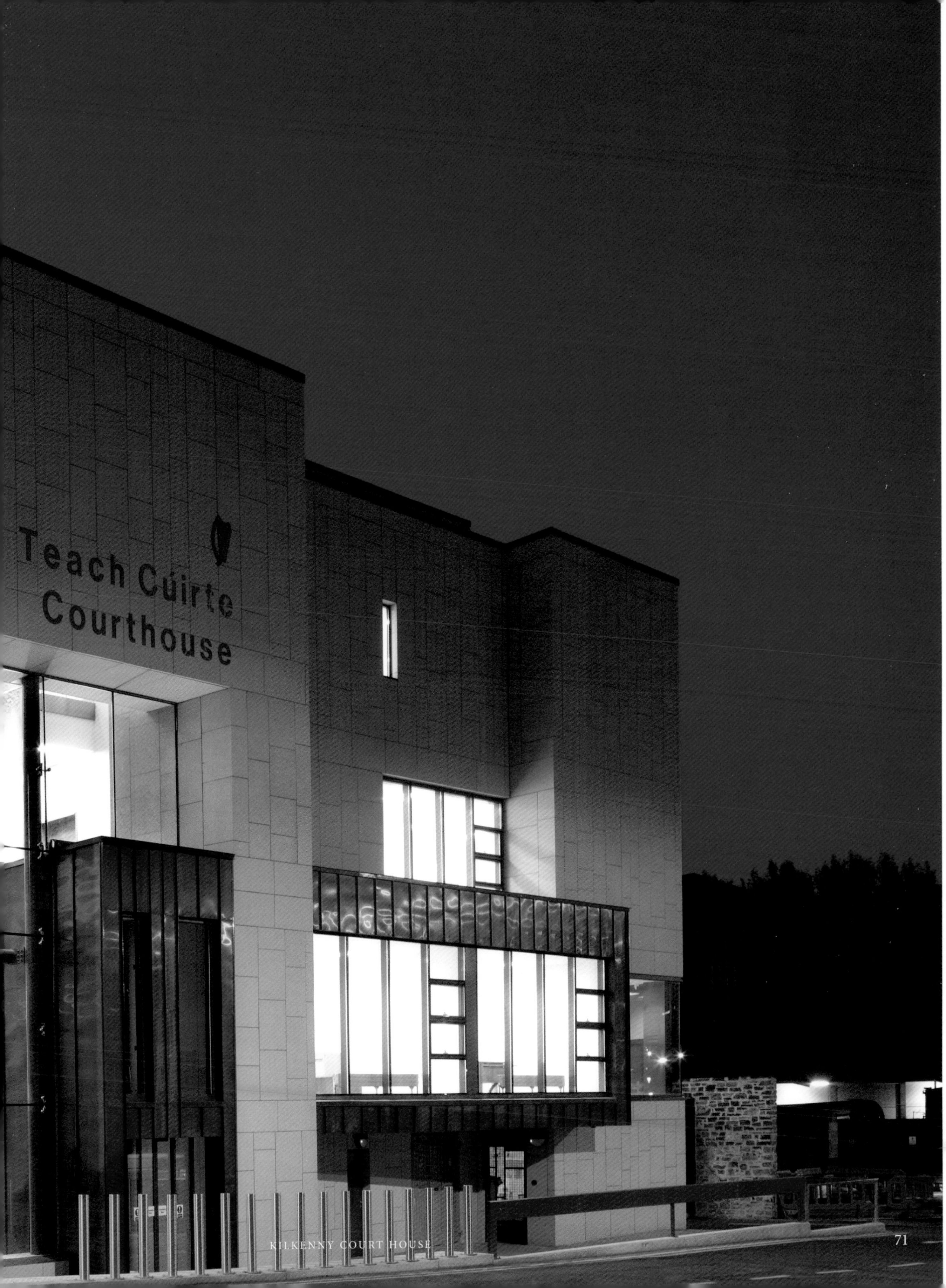
Teach Cúirte
Courthouse

--

Image

3　Atrium between old and new
　buildings (Donal Murphy, 2010)

4　New grand staircase
　(Donal Murphy, 2010)

5　Artwork in atrium
　(Donal Murphy, 2010)

6　View from new building
　across atrium to old building
　(Donal Murphy, 2010)

7　Original entrance hall, with
　new elements clearly identified
　(Donal Murphy, 2010)

8　Restored original façade, with new
　civic space to Parliament Street
　(Donal Murphy, 2010)

The new 3,000 m² extension could have overpowered the original building. Instead, the new and old relate to each other by virtue of their relative proportions, use of materials and lighting, and thoughtful interfaces. A new atrium for universal access acts as an intermediary between old and new and serves as a new public entrance. The resultant contrast works well. One can read the layers of history as one progresses through the building and the old entrance is also retained.

The 2008 archaeological excavation to the rear of the site found twenty-three burials. The damp site preserved many objects, even wooden shingles used in medieval timber buildings. Seed and pollen samples gave us a history of nearly 1,000 years of food eaten and vegetation grown on this site.

Most importantly, Kilkenny has retained and extended its historic court house in its very heart and thereby significantly strengthened its civic centre.

KILKENNY COURT HOUSE

This court house (1827-30) reflects both the turbulent history of Ireland and the architectural aspirations of its designer Joseph Welland (1798-1860). The site is a prominent location. Previously it housed the old county gaol but now the court pairs with St Patrick's Church (1831-36) to create an important civic centre within Monaghan town. During the Civil War the building was occupied by opposing forces and suffered damage. During the Troubles, the court house suffered an arson attack in May 1981 and was gutted. The local authority did some repair works in 1986. Some twenty years later the Courts Service sought OPW help in returning the damaged old court house to full order with two large jury courts and one family court, with all the attendant modern requirements.

The front façade of cream-coloured local sandstone needed restoration, cleaning, new stone grafts and stabilisation. The original Bragan Quarry had ceased operations so OPW architects sought information from the Geological Survey of Ireland to assist in sourcing a compatible stone for restoration work. The GSI assistance led to Rossmore Quarry in County Fermanagh. The cleaned and restored stone façade, combined with the removal of inappropriate extensions to the front of the building, gives us back the original 1828 Joseph Welland design fronting onto a new paved forecourt to Church Square. A memorial to the victims of a car bomb attack in May 1974 is nearby.

MONAGHAN COURT HOUSE

MONAGHAN COURT HOUSE

Internally, the remains of the original court house are lined with oak and limestone.
A new circulation scheme separates judge, jury, defendant, staff and public areas.
A new central core houses separate public and defendant circulation while judge,
jury and staff circulation is to the rear. These interventions resolve contemporary
court issues while also respecting the integrity of the original design.

Within the courtrooms, the flush detailed timber panelling is organised around a
horizontal datum of oak battens which resolved varying heights of doorways. This
gives a calm composition to what would otherwise be an uncoordinated jumble
of wall and furniture elements. This holistic interior design approach was used as a
template for the later seven smart PPP projects.

The court house was reopened in February 2011. It retains its royal coat of arms to the
tympanum as part of its long history. Previously described as displaying 'imperial solidity
and establishment', it is now a vital part of the urban renewal of Monaghan town.
It also displays the skill of those who originally designed it and those who worked
on its restoration and renewal and thereby gave it a new history, one of dialogue
rather than monologue, as befits a democratic republic.

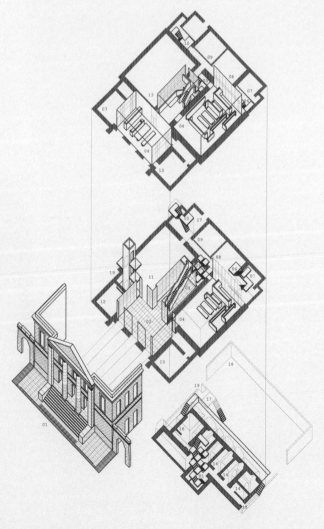

MONAGHAN COURT HOUSE

Interior design and furniture have always been a significant element of court house architecture; Green Street court house in Dublin is an early example. The 1797 building, designed by Whitmore Davis, has a double-height courtroom at its centre. The space is both side- and roof-lighted, giving a high quality of natural daylight to a powerfully moulded interior made up of built-in furniture. The steep sloped stepping of the furniture, combined with sweeping curves, creates an amphitheatre for the oratory of Senior Counsels. Presiding over the space is the judge, ensconced in a timber-panelled apse overhung with its own importance-defining canopy, akin to a medieval cathedral pulpit. Elevated side galleries complete the well composed interior configuration.

Green Street courtroom can be appreciated for its clarity and quality of design. It integrates all of the requirements of courtroom design and orchestrates all the disparate elements into a cohesive whole where each supports and accentuates the other.

COURTROOM INTERIORS

In recent court houses, particular attention has been paid to the courtroom layout. Architectural volume is crucial to good courtroom design and performance, and can be vital to the wellbeing of all who attend, particularly in the case of jury trials which sometimes attract public interest.

Sight lines, universal access, good acoustics and quality lighting are combined with integrated technology and, most importantly, a human scale. Acoustic control is incorporated into the timber wall panelling. Slatted panels are backed with acoustic absorption material. Sound reflectance and reverberation are carefully studied, adjusted and altered to suit a particular courtroom size and volume.

In consideration of how a democratic republic should represent itself through its furniture design, the interiors of Kilkenny and Monaghan court houses, incorporating both restored and new furniture, were a useful starting point. These designs formed the basis of the template for later PPP court interiors. The use of native oak rather than the more imperial mahogany gives a visually lighter touch while also acknowledging species-sustainability. Detailing is contemporary yet acknowledges traditional timber craft and custom.

--
Image
1 New court house and St Mary Magdalene
  Dominican Church viewed from St Mary's
  Bridge (Richard Hatch, 2018)
2 Chute providing daylight to courtroom
  (Richard Hatch, 2018)
3 Judges' chair and state emblem
  (Richard Hatch, 2018)
4 Detail of riverside façade (Richard Hatch, 2018)
5 View from St Mary's Bridge
  (Richard Hatch, 2018)
6 The new civic space to riverside is built over a
  sterilised main drain zone (Richard Hatch, 2018)
7 Exploded view showing stacked courtrooms.
  The public plaza incorporates the town wall
  discovered by archaeological excavation
  (OPW, 2017)
8 New court house viewed from Dominic's Bridge
  (Richard Hatch, 2018)

This two-courtroom court house is located at St Patrickswell Lane within the old walled area of Drogheda, which dates back to the late 12th century. Indeed, archaeological excavation uncovered the base of the previously demolished town wall at the periphery of the court site. The outline of this wall was incorporated into the public realm design. Other constraints included local authority main drainage pipes transversing the site and sterilising significant parts of it. In essence, the footprint available for building was very restricted. In addition, the building needed to be elevated above the flood plain of the river Boyne, and this gave rise to access issues. Ramped access was used in a creative way to maintain universal access yet provide discreet separation between the public plaza and the private, secure court entrance.

The public plaza has good views over the river Boyne and leads to the public hall from where there is access to the smaller ground-floor court. The larger jury court is on the first floor, where additional volume can be provided. The light-filled interior has views of many Drogheda landmarks including the Mary Magdalene church.

DROGHEDA   COURT HOUSE

The site constraints and the important historic riverside location have been turned to best advantage. The bend on the river location required a building of some vertical scale which the two-court brief would not normally provide. However, by stacking the courtrooms on top of each other and compacting the building footprint, a sufficient civic scale was achieved. The contemporary interpretation of the traditional court portico and its colonnade suitably addresses the public plaza and its important riverside location. The court house has an assertive civic quality through the use of limestone similar to other local civic buildings.

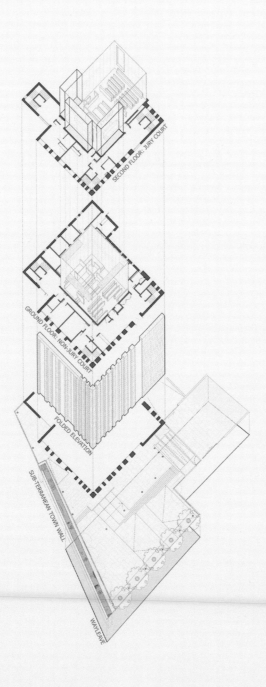

SECOND FLOOR: JURY COURT

GROUND FLOOR: NON-JURY COURT

FOLDED ELEVATION

SUB-TERRANEAN TOWN WALL

WAYLEAVE

IRELAND'S COURT HOUSES

DROGHEDA COURT HOUSE

The new six-courtroom court house is located on the site of a former British artillery barracks built in 1807 adjoining Mulgrave Street and Roxboro Road. The artillery barracks was one of four in a heavily army-occupied city. Historic maps show this district to have been an 'institutional' one. The county prison, lunatic asylum (as it was called in the 19th century) and municipal cemetery meant that this area of the city was neither prominent nor prosperous. While the prison site remains in use today, much of the artillery barracks it adjoins was destroyed by fire during the Civil War. The institutional, wall-enclosed, feel of the derelict barracks needed to be rethought and repurposed for a contemporary court house.

The new design incorporates the once derelict gatehouses and magazine store that survived the 1922 fire. The gatehouses integrate the main entrance and security facilities before a glazed link joins them to the main court building behind.

LIMERICK COURT HOUSE

--
Image
1 The building steps with the steep site
  (Paul McGuckin, 2019)
2 The foyer space outside each
  courtroom is modulated by stair
  cores and linking glazed bridges
  (Niall Warner, 2017)

The site of the court house was formerly occupied by a local authority leisure centre and swimming pool; the building had been demolished and replaced by a car park. The steeply sloping site had rear gardens and ill-defined backs of buildings on two sides. The other two sides have a two-storey millennial cultural centre and an earlier separate theatre with adjacent car park that was not landscaped in a coherent manner. The entrance off High Road was narrow and uninviting. In essence it was a back-lands site which, at first glance, presented few urban design opportunities. On the positive side, it had good elevated views towards Ramelton Road and Port Road, with the valley of the river Swilly stretching away to the south east.

Following a detailed survey and analysis, it was found that the existing site gradient created difficulties for designing for universal access. In addition, the Courts Service brief required two courtrooms and support office accommodation to be located at the main entrance level. The solution was to regrade the levels. To keep the solution economical, the OPW utilised the existing fill and spoil to re-contour the site and create a new entrance level.

LETTERKENNY COURT HOUSE

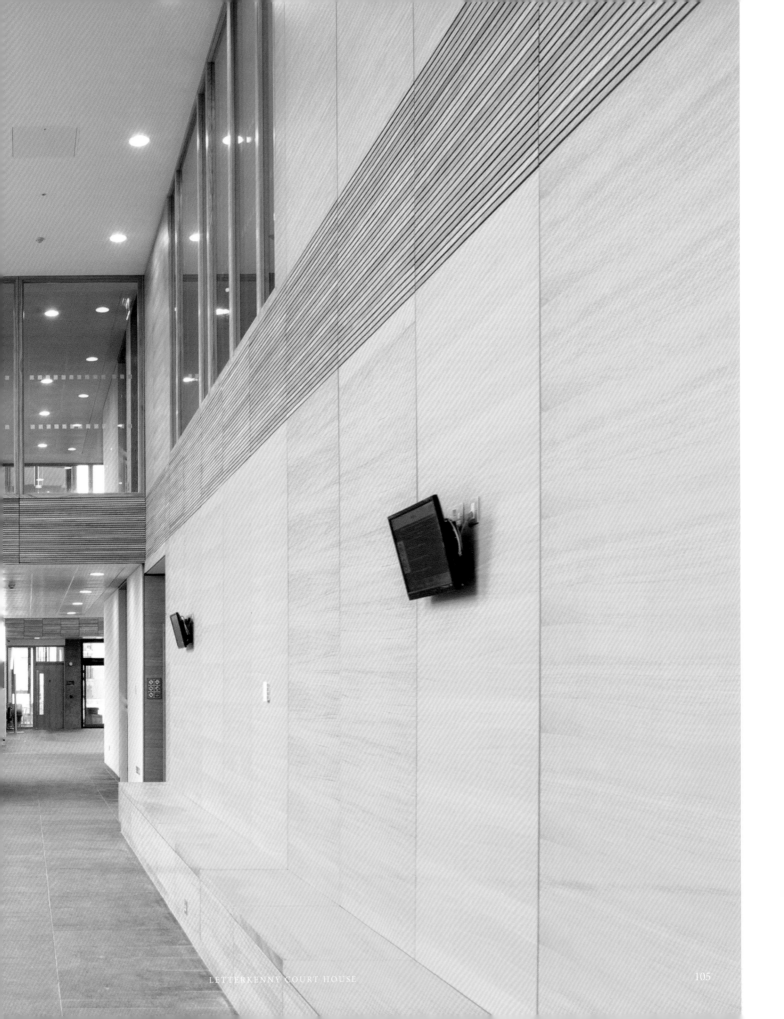

--
Image

This new entrance level is located one floor above the old ground level. This design strategy allowed the OPW to meet the brief requirements and comply with universal access. In addition, the strategy allowed for the secure car parking, judicial entrance, service access and custody entrance to be discreetly located below the main entrance level without the cost of excavating a basement. A significant urban design benefit was the opportunity to create a public pedestrian plaza as a forecourt to the main public entrance and interlink it with a pedestrian route connecting the High Road to the lower Port Road and the regional bus depot, via the two cultural buildings.

The re-contoured site has a carefully thought out hard and soft landscape plan which strengthens and enhances the overall site strategy, while also providing cohesion to the previously fractured and incoherent back-land location. The main entrance of the pedestrian plaza is defined by the hard and soft landscaping. The reception area is linked to the staff offices. Beyond is an enfilade of spaces

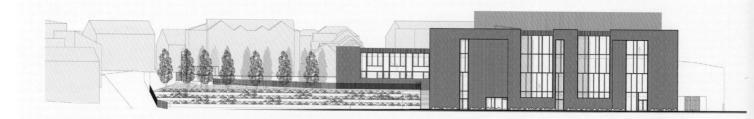

providing access to the consultation rooms and courtrooms on one side and opening out on the other side to the views of the town below and the valley of the river Swilly beyond. This is a calm restful space, helped by the proximity of the landscaped exterior which forms what the Romans would have called *rus in urbe* or the countryside in the town.

The building responds to the clear functional requirements of the brief, the different user groups and the site orientation. The four-storey, 5,500 m² building now sits carefully, respectfully and with civic ease on a site that originally seemed to offer very little. Through skill and imagination Letterkenny has gained a new court house to replace the 1831 building which will be used by Donegal County Council for administrative and tourism functions. The Mayor of Donegal, Councillor Gerry McMonagle, described the new court house as 'impressive and iconic' at its official opening in early 2018.

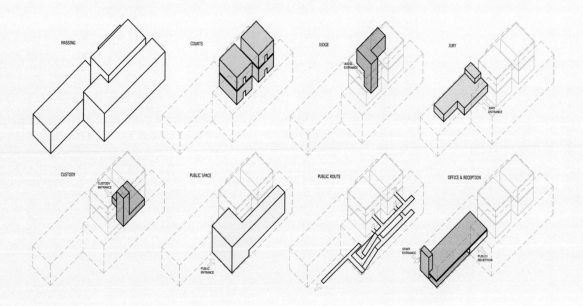

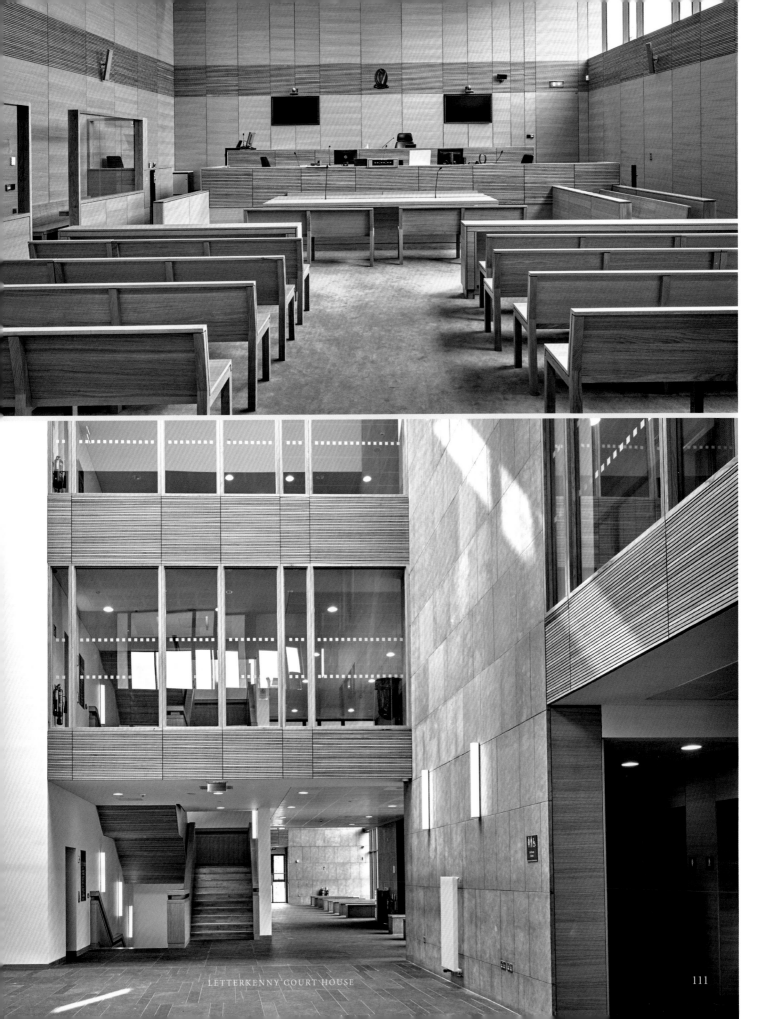

TEACH CÚIRTE LEITIR CEANAINN
LETTERKENNY COURTHOUSE

--
Image
1 New extension to side and
rear of original court house
(Neil Warner, 2018)
2 The original façade
presented many difficulties
during restoration
(Neil Warner, 2018)

The original and distinctive Italianate classicism of this court house, built *c.* 1824-29 and attributed to John Hargrave (*c.*1788-1833), is an accomplished design. The equally accomplished restoration, refurbishment and extension is a credit to all, especially architect Michael Grace of Newenham Mulligan & Associates.

Hargrave's plan put the entrance hall in the centre between the courtrooms, in a manner similar to Richard Morrison's court houses in Naas, Portlaoise and Wexford. Hargrave also designed Omagh (1814), Moate (1828) and Letterkenny (1831) court houses, and extended Mullingar gaol adjacent to the court house. Unfortunately, the forecourt to the court house was reduced at the time of the demolition of the gaol between 1910 and 1913.

MULLINGAR   COURT HOUSE

In January 1839 Mullingar court house was badly damaged in a storm known in Irish folklore as 'the night of the big wind'. The latent evidence of this damage would be revealed some 175 years later when opening-up works were done.

The restoration, refurbishment and extension of the court house is as successful as the original design. It peels back the layers of history in an erudite and scholarly manner, yet makes confident new insertions such that the extended court house is better than the sum of its individual parts. The forecourt and front elevation have been improved by hard landscaping and new glass and stone finishes to the extensions. Inside, daylight to the courts animates the timber finishes. A new family court is inserted on a new floor. The 3,300 m² court house gives Mullingar back a worthy civic building and an important part of its built heritage.

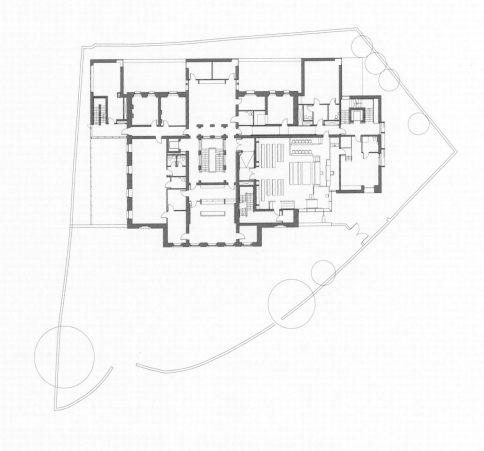

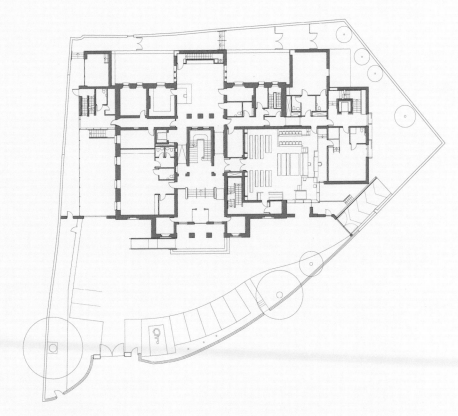

Waterford court house dates from 1849 and was designed by the architect J.B. Keane. It is located on the site of the long-vanished 12th-century Augustinian Priory of St Catherine. Set in mature parkland which falls gently to a river on three sides, its granite neo-classical front façade is its most important surviving feature.

The original structure had fallen into serious disrepair by the late 1970s, making it necessary in 1977 to demolish some two-thirds of the original Keane building. Only the front façade and the shell of the two courtrooms, with their linking concourse, remained. The present refurbishment has been careful to retain and enhance this core arrangement of spaces.

The kernel of the approach taken by the OPW architects has been to reinstate the court house as a neo-classical 'villa-in-parkland', honouring the original setting devised by Keane. This concept had been undermined by a variety of unthinking alterations over time: the forecourt to the main portico façade had been turned

WATERFORD COURT HOUSE

into a disorganised car park, while an adjoining 20th-century fire station also had a negative impact on the building's setting. Fortunately, the local authority agreed to move the fire station to a new site, thereby opening up the possibility of solving on-site parking and of re-landscaping the park/court house interface. As a result, the riverside park is enhanced and the old and new court house given an appropriate public realm setting.

The Keane design was the starting point for the new building in both conceptual and physical terms. The surviving form has been extended to the north, with four classically inspired elevations. The west and east planes of the existing building now contain contemporary façades, thereby recreating what architectural scholars might term 'the solid closed cubic block of the neo-classical ambition' of court houses of that era. The newly formed 'cubic block' now contains some 6,400 m^2 of accommodation, including six courtrooms.

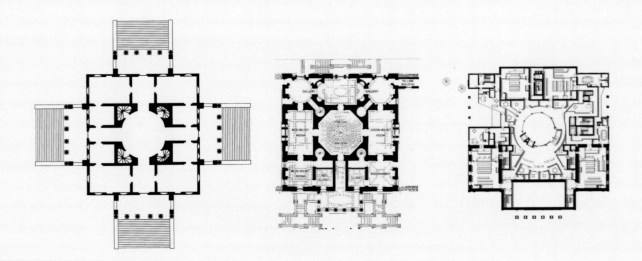

The new Wexford court house combines a listed building known as the Tate School with a new contemporary extension on Belvedere Road. The red-brick Tate School was opened in 1867, funding having been willed by William Tate, a Wexford man who ran two plantations in Jamaica. The 'Charity School' existed from 1867 to 1949, when Wexford Corporation purchased the site and building.

The new extension and the original Tate School are combined in a three-dimensional manner to deliver the building brief while respecting the architectural quality of each element. The new entrance via a stone 'goal post' canopy sets up the dynamic between old and new which is orchestrated throughout the interfaces of plan and section. The composition of the new respects the existing Tate building and uses similar stone and brick materials in a contemporary manner.

WEXFORD COURT HOUSE

--
Image
4 The elevated site provides views of the waterfront from both the restored and new facilities (Newenham Mulligan & Associates, 2018)
5/6 Ground and first floor plans (Newenham Mulligan & Associates, 2018)

Internally, the building is organised around the public circulation route, which is glazed on one side. There are two courtrooms on each floor and their central location ensures the functional ease of separate circulation for judges, jurors and those in custody. Support facilities and offices are located at ground-floor level and within the existing Tate building, which enjoys good views down to the waterside.

Wexford court house remains in the centre of the historic town. An old protected structure and a confident new building unite to form a modern county court house which also contributes to Wexford's regeneration and further evolution. Cultural resilience and economic sustainability combine with judicial need.

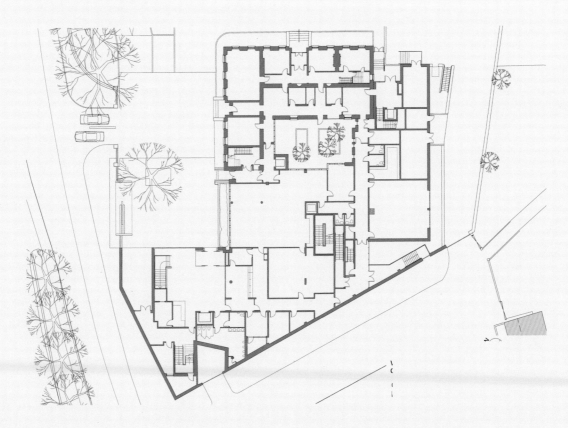

Like Dublin, Cork now has separate locations for civil and criminal cases. The 1836 Washington Street court house hears civil cases while the new criminal court house is on Anglesea Street opposite the modern extension to Cork City Council, Cork fire brigade and the major Garda station in the city. This six-court, 8,500 m² building also provides a vulnerable witness suite, a victim support room, a legal practitioners' room, a jury reception room and consultation rooms, as well as the judge, jury and custody facilities, all served by separate circulation.

Cork Model School was designed by James Higgins Owen or Enoch Trevor Owen with assistance from draughtsman Robert A. Gibbons, of the OPW in 1862 and construction began the following year. It opened in 1865 and closed in 1990. The building was converted to court use by the OPW in 1994. As detailed in surviving contemporary drawings, this was an example of what would come to be called 'total design'. From the Italianate-inspired elevation, which is both civic and civil, to the careful plan and thoughtful sections, the attention to detail is exemplary. The tower served as an observation point for shipping at Cork quays.

CORK

COURT HOUSE
ANGLESEA STREET

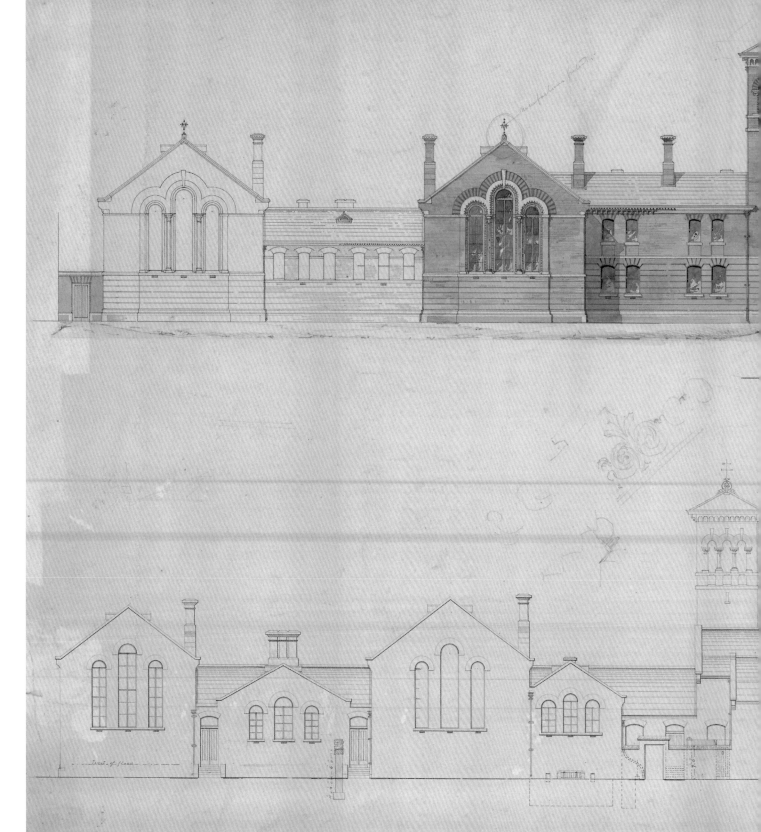

8 feet to one inch

ONT ELEVATION _____

Note. For dressings to door and window Opes.
Also for Main Cornice Chimneys Caps &c.
See detail drawings.
All ceilings for ventilating floor and Roor
timbers to be placed as directed.

ERE ELEVATION

After the school closed in 1990, the OPW and the Department of Justice saw the potential of using the building for court and administrative purposes. It was used as a District Court from 1995 until the present development started in 2016. The Cork Model School was thus saved from dereliction

The new development was made possible because the OPW donated its adjacent maintenance facility site which, combined with the old school yard, provided just sufficient space to accommodate the large new court facility. One enters the new combined building through the original campanile entrance. The restored Model School is used for support facilities where a variety of functions, compatible with

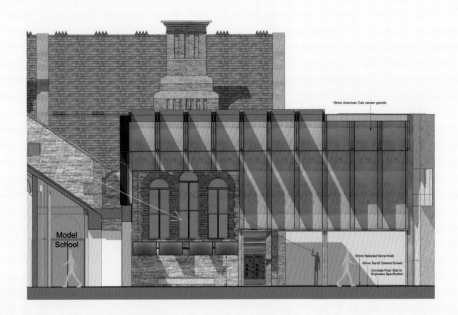

the original design, are housed. A small landscaped courtyard separates the old and new buildings, while a carefully crafted link engages both on axis with the campanile.

While the intention was to restore the Model School, the approach to the larger new building was a contemporary one. However, a common link was desired. Areas of the old school had Cork limestone and this was chosen to create the visual connection between old and new. Unfortunately, Cork limestone is no longer quarried but a matching limestone from Lecarrow, Co. Roscommon, was found. The main height of the new building takes its cue from the old campanile.

Given that the original building was an architectural tour de force, any new addition had to be of a similar standard. The sequence of spaces is important. Daylight is brought deep into the building, materials are appropriate to both use and longevity and, like the Model School, plan and section work with form and function to give Cork an exemplary new court house.

MOD NAT SCHOOL

Details of Entrance Porch.

Front Elevation

Section

Timbers to be wro't & exposed

B — B

A

Tiles

A.A. × ½ Plan at B.B.

¼ Plan of Roof

¼ Plan at C

Down Pipe

C

D

Side Elevation

Details of Tower.

Scale ½ an inch to a foot.

Details of Entrance Door to Girls and Infants
Chimney Caps &c.

½ Plan below Caps.

½ Plan showing
projection of Caps.

Outside Elevation.

¼ Plan of Roof Timbers.

¼ Plan at D.D.

Circular windows
in front & side of Tower.

From top of Plinth. 22 . 9

--
Image
1 Restored courtroom with
   'witness chair' on top of the table,
   and contemporary chandelier
   (Ros Kavanagh, 2016)
2 Elevation of restoration proposal
   (OPW, 2014)

Kilmainham court house was designed by William Farrell and completed in 1820. It had a long and varied use but was eventually closed in 2008. As part of the 1916 centenary commemorations it was restored, refurbished and, most importantly, repurposed, as part of a visitor support facility for Kilmainham Gaol.

Visitors to the gaol had to queue at the small prison entrance. However, increasing visitor numbers made this increasingly difficult and unsafe. Repurposing the court house allowed this issue to be addressed, but for the court house to properly function as a visitor centre a number of new elements and adjustments were needed. And, of course, it was essential that the new use for the old court house would be implemented in such as way as to enhance rather than diminish the historically significant Gaol.

KILMAINHAM COURT HOUSE
A COURT HOUSE REPURPOSED

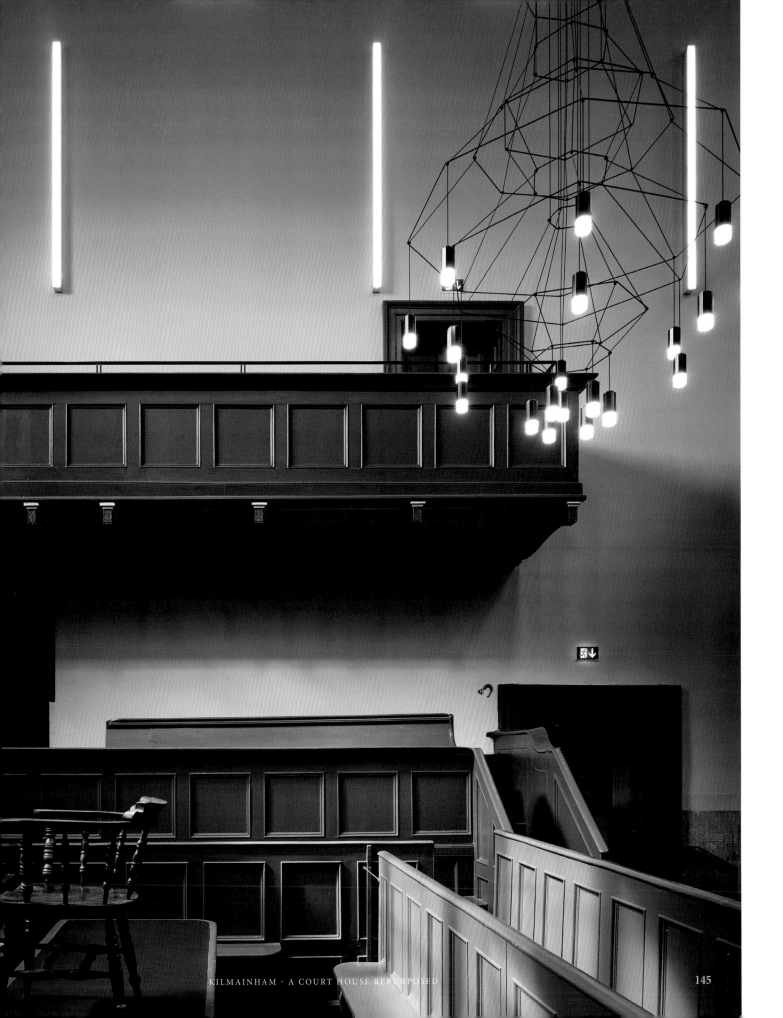

Previously separated Grand and Petty Jury first floor rooms have been connected by a 'bridge' without affecting the volume of the entrance hall negatively, and the necessary café and bookshop are placed discreetly not to affect the flow of people. All the new elements are well resolved with a reserved and restrained architectural language, in the spirit of the original court house. The former coach house was converted as ancillary buildings. A new public plaza adjacent to the court house integrates Richmond Gate with Kilmainham Gaol and completes a pedestrian link to the Royal Hospital Kilmainham and the Irish Museum of Modern Art.

The repurposing of the court house has worked on many different levels from an improved public realm and better visitor experience and management, to an exemplar of how to combine old and new uses and materials in such a way that both benefit from each other's presence.

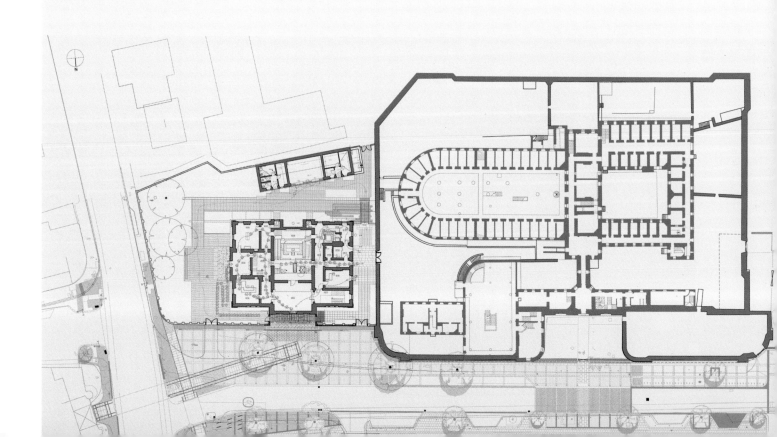

IRELAND'S COURT HOUSES

By and large, no place became a District Court location that had not previously been a petty sessions location and so there is a substantial continuity of court house use into the mid-20th century. However, many petty sessions locations ceased to exist under the new dispensation. In 1842 the twenty-six counties which would later constitute the Republic of Ireland were divided into 468 petty sessions areas (out of a total of 566 across the island). In 1924 those same twenty-six counties were divided into 353 potential District Court Areas. This was reduced to 338 when the precise geographic extent of those areas was defined in 1926 and 1927.

When a court house in a county in the Republic of Ireland is referred to in the gazetteer as a 'petty sessions court house', this means that it ceased to be used as a court house by 1924.

A further rationalisation of District Court Areas occurred in 1961 and the number of locations dropped to 227. From the mid-1990s, and in particular in the post-Celtic Tiger era, the number of District Court locations has been reduced still further to just under seventy by 2017.

In Northern Ireland, there was less immediate rationalisation after partition. Although some reorganisation took place, and some petty sessions areas were redrawn or abolished, by 1946 there were still 101 petty sessions locations in the six counties. This had reduced to ninety-seven by 1959, while modernisation in the early 1960s reduced the number still further to seventy-six by 1967. The impact of the Troubles led to further consolidation. In 1978 there were fifty-eight petty sessions areas across Northern Ireland. Major reform came in 1979 when the number was reduced to twenty-six, and

the boundaries redrawn to match those of the existing local authorities. By 1994, the number was down to twenty-one and rationalisation has continued into the 21st century.

From a high of over 600 buildings in use as court houses in the 1880s, there are now fewer than 120 across the island.

When a District Court, or petty sessions location, was abolished, and the Electoral Division which constituted the District Court Area amalgamated into another, the court house ceased to have a judicial function. Some – Newtownmountkennedy, Co. Wicklow, for example – were demolished but most were repurposed. Even when a District Court Area was maintained, its court house might be closed and court sittings moved to other available venues within the Area. Poor physical condition was often the reason for closure, as local authorities throughout the 20th century seemed to have spent minimally on court house maintenance. Lack of use could also lead to closure. In some Areas, court sittings might have taken place on as few as six days in a year. It was simply more cost effective to hire alternative venues on an *ad hoc* basis than to maintain a permanent court house. Such alternative venues included hotels, community halls, sports facilities, even public houses (though this has occurred extremely rarely) and while these buildings may be noted in the gazetteer, they have not been given separate entries.

Also excluded from the gazetteer are the buildings used in the period 1919–1921 by so-called Sinn Féin, Dáil or Republican Courts. These buildings were summarised by Cahir Davitt in his Bureau of Military History witness statement as 'halls of some kind or another, public buildings such as County Council Offices, Workhouses, hospital buildings or schools, or Sinn Féin Club premises… creameries, farmhouses, outhouses, barns, and any place with four walls and a roof that could be made ready and reasonably usable for the purpose' (Bureau of Military History WS 993). The only actual court house used for sittings of these courts would appear to have been the Four Courts, on the grounds, Davitt claims, that it was the last place the authorities would expect to find such a court sitting.

The compilation of the gazetteer has been a desk-based exercise with little field work or building visitation. In the first instance it utilises the resources of the Irish Architectural Archive, and in particular the *Dictionary of Irish Architects* (www.dia.ie), created and edited by Ann Martha Rowan. The gazetteer also relies on previous court house gazetteers including Sir Charles Brett's seminal *Court Houses and Market Houses of the Province of Ulster* (Belfast, 1973), Christine Casey's 1982 MA thesis 'Courthouses, Markethouses and Townhalls of Leinster', and *The Courthouses of Ireland* compiled by Mildred Dunne and Brian Phillips (Kilkenny, 1999). It also draws on the published volumes of the *Buildings of Ireland* series: Alistair Rowan, *North West Ulster* (London, 1979), covering Derry, Donegal, Fermanagh and Tyrone; Alistair Rowan and Christine Casey, *North Leinster*, (London, 1991), covering Longford, Louth, Meath and Westmeath; Christine Casey, *Dublin: the city within the Grand and Royal Canals* (London, 2005); and Kevin Mulligan, *South Ulster, Armagh, Cavan and Monaghan* (London, 2013). These published sources have been supplemented by a variety of resources including online copies of historic OS maps (available via Geohive.ie and the Public Record Office of Northern Ireland), Google Street View and other digital image resources, the online surveys of the National Inventory of Architectural Heritage (NIAH, www.buildingsofireland.ie), and the Northern Ireland Historic Buildings database.

Images have been included for a considerable sample of the buildings in the gazetteer. A great many of these are drawn from the collections of the Irish Architectural Archive, and some new photography has been undertaken for the project by Denis Mortell and Paul Tierney. Images marked *NIAH* are reproduced courtesy of the National Inventory of Architectural Heritage, those marked *Courts Service* are reproduced by courtesy of the Courts Service, those marked *Crown DfC Historic Environment Division* are reproduced by courtesy of the Historic Environment Record of Northern Ireland, and those marked RTÉ Archives are by courtesy of RTÉ Archives.

A particular debt of gratitude is owed to Dr Richard Butler who very generously shared his research on the county court houses of Ireland. His own publication on this topic will be a significant addition to the subject.

Special thanks too are due to Paul Burns and Eva Font of the Courts Service, and State Architect Ciaran O'Connor from the Office of Public Works (OPW).

As with everything the Irish Architectural Archive does, the production of the gazetteer was very much a team effort and our thanks go to Aisling Dunne, Anne Henderson, Simon Lincoln and Ann Martha Rowan.

For such mistakes and omissions as remain, we take full responsibility.

Main Sources and Abbreviations

Brett's *Court Houses of Ulster* - Sir Charles Brett, *Court Houses and Market Houses of the Province of Ulster* (Belfast, 1973)

The *Buildings of Ireland* - The *Buildings of Ireland* series: Alistair Rowan, *North West Ulster* (London, 1979), covering Derry, Donegal, Fermanagh and Tyrone; Alistair Rowan and Christine Casey, *North Leinster*, (London, 1991), covering Longford, Louth, Meath and Westmeath; Christine Casey, *Dublin: the city within the Grand and Royal Canals* (London, 2005); and Kevin Mulligan, *South Ulster, Armagh, Cavan and Monaghan* (London, 2013).

CSORP - Chief Secretary's Office Registered Papers

DIA - *Dictionary of Irish Architects* (www.dia.ie)

Griffith's Valuation - Richard Griffith, *Valuation of Ireland 1847-1864*

HC - House of Commons papers

IAA - Irish Architectural Archive

Lewis's *Topographical Dictionary* - Samuel Lewis, *A Topographical Dictionary of Ireland* (London, 1837)

NAI - National Archives of Ireland

NIAH - National Inventory of Architectural Heritage (accessible via www.buildingsofireland.ie)

NLI - National Library of Ireland

OPW - Office of Public Works

OS - Ordnance Survey

OS *Memoirs* - Angélique Day and Patrick McWilliams (eds), *Ordnance Survey Memoirs of Ireland* (Belfast, 1990-2002)

Parliamentary Gazetteer - *The Parliamentary Gazetteer of Ireland, adapted to the new Poor Law, Franchise, Municipal and Ecclesiastical Arrangements, and compiled with special reference to the lines of Railroad and Canal Communication, as existing in 1844-45* (Dublin, 1846)

Petty Sessions Return - *A Return from every Petty Sessions in Ireland, showing the Number of Days, and Date thereof, on which Petty Sessions were or ought to have been held in 1842* (London, 1843)

PRONI - Public Record Office of Northern Ireland

RIAI - Royal Institute of the Architects of Ireland

Ordnance Survey (OS) map dates

County	First edition 6-inch	25-inch
Antrim	1831-33	1900-06
Armagh	1835	1905-07
Carlow	1839	1905-06
Cavan	1835-36	1908-11
Clare	1840-42	1893-97; 1913-18
Cork	1841-42	1896-1904
Derry	1830-32	1904-06
Donegal	1834-36	1900-05
Down	1835	1900-03
Dublin	1843	1863-67; 1905-07
Fermanagh	1835	1907-07
Galway	1838-39	1890-1900; 1912-16
Kerry	1841-42	1892-98; 1914-15
Kildare	1837-38	1907-09
Kilkenny	1839-40	1899-1902
Laois	1838-41	1906-08
Leitrim	1835-36	1907-09
Limerick	1840-41	1897-1903; 1918-24
Longford	1836-37	1911-12
Louth	1835	1907-09
Mayo	1837-39	1893-99; 1913-17
Meath	1836	1908-11
Monaghan	1834-35	1907-09
Offaly	1838	1908-10
Roscommon	1838	1888-92; 1911-13
Sligo	1837	1909-12
Tipperary	1839-41	1901-05
Tyrone	1832-34	1904-07
Waterford	1839-41	1903-05; 1922-23
Westmeath	1837	1910-13
Wexford	1839-40	1902-05; 1921-22
Wicklow	1838	1907-09

How to use this gazetteer

A selection of some significant court houses is presented in chronological order. This is followed by the rest of the court houses, listed alphabetically by county and alphabetically within each county. For locations with more than one court house, the order is alphabetically by street address, and chronologically where building have been replaced on the same site.

When a court house in a county in the Republic of Ireland is referred to in the gazetteer text as a 'petty sessions court house', this means that the building ceased to be used as a court house by 1924.

[] indicates that the name of an architect has yet to be identified.

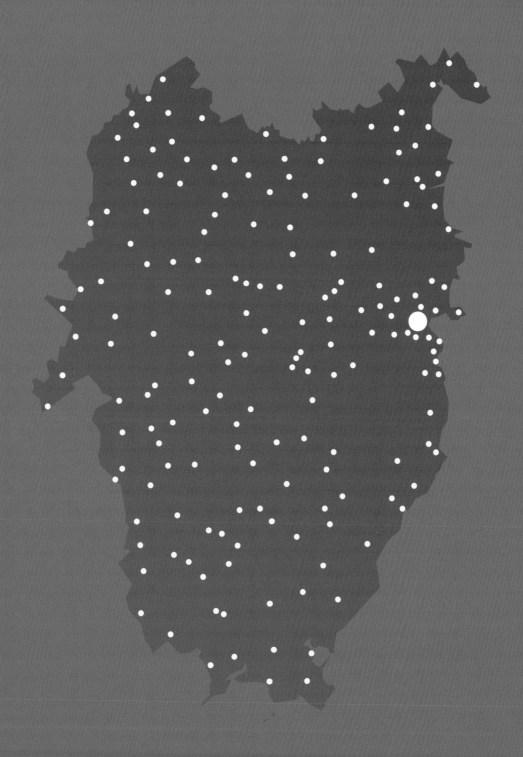

IRELAND'S COURT HOUSES
GAZETTEER

SOME SIGNIFICANT COURT HOUSES
A CHRONOLOGICAL SELECTION

SOME SIGNIFICANT COURT HOUSES

A CHRONOLOGICAL SELECTION

1608	DUBLIN, Four Courts (old)
1675	CLONMEL, Main Guard
1737	DOWNPATRICK, County Court House
1740	DUNLAVIN, Market House and Court House
1746	LIFFORD, County Court House
C. 1750	WICKLOW, County Court House
1784-87	WATERFORD, Court House and Gaol
1785-1802	DUBLIN, Four Courts
C. 1790	KILKENNY, County Court House
1793	LONGFORD, County Court House
C. 1795	ENNISKILLEN, County Court House
1801	CLONMEL, County Court House
1802	KELLS, Court House
1805	PORTLAOISE, County Court House
1805-09	ARMAGH, County Court House
1807	NAAS, County Court House
1807-09	LIMERICK, County Court House
1810	TRIM, County Court House
1812-15	GALWAY, County Court House
1813-17	DERRY/LONDONDERRY, City and County Court House
1813-20	DUNDALK, County Court House
1814-20	OMAGH, County Court House
1820-22	CASTLEBAR, County Court House
1824	CARRICK-ON-SHANNON, County Court House
1824-25	CAVAN, County Court House
1824-27	ROSCOMMON, County Court House
1824-29	MULLINGAR, County Court House
C. 1826	MACROOM, Court House
1827	MONAGHAN, County Court House
1828-33	TRALEE, County Court House
1828-34	CARLOW, County Court House
1833-37	TULLAMORE, County Court House
1835	CORK, City and County Court House
1840-44	NENAGH, County Court House
1841-43	GLENTIES, Court House
1845-50	ENNIS, County Court House
1848-49	WATERFORD, County Court House
1848-50	BELFAST, County Court House
1874-79	SLIGO, County Court House
1928-33	BELFAST, High Court/Royal Courts of Justice
1987	DUBLIN, Children's Court House
1994	CORK, Anglesea Street Model School/Court House
2007-09	DUBLIN, Criminal Courts of Justice
2015-18	WEXFORD, Tate School/County Court House

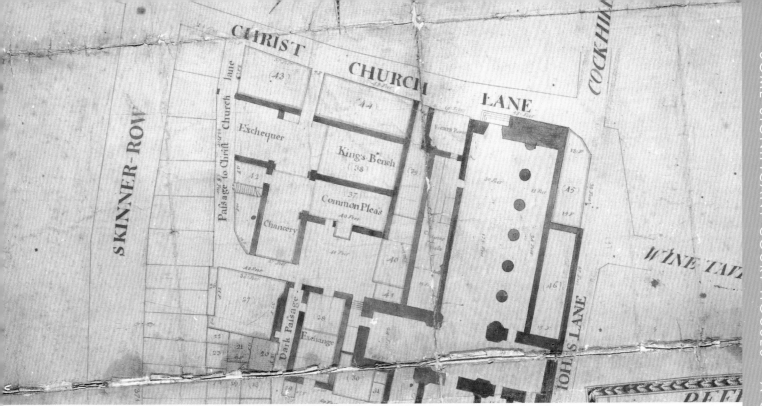

DUBLIN
St Michael's Hill
Four Courts (old)
Samuel Molyneux; Sir William Robinson;
Thomas Burgh; Pierce Archibald
1608; 1695; 1705-06; 1750s

--
Image
St Michael's Hill, Old Four Courts. Detail from
A Map of the Liberty of Christ Church Dublin.
Surveyed in October 1761 by Thos Reading (RCB)

In their *History of the City of Dublin* (London, 1818), J. Warburton, Rev. J. Whitelaw and Rev. Robert Walsh note that 'there are no records of the proceedings of the law courts of Dublin before the establishment of the first inns of court in the reign of Edward I. These were erected outside the city walls near Dame's Gate, on the south side of Great George's-street, and Exchequer-street, where also the superior courts of justice were held'. Subject to raids from beyond the Pale, the courts transferred to the safer environs of Dublin Castle, and even on occasion to Carlow, 'which town, on the frontiers of the Pale, appears to have been the strongest fortified place in Ireland possessed by the English'. In 1542, the courts moved from the Castle to the dissolved Dominican monastery which stood on the site now occupied by the Four Courts.

From the early 17th century until 1796, the most senior courts in Ireland were located in a precinct to the south of Christ Church Cathedral, now occupied by the Cathedral gardens, and the much widened street formerly known as Skinner's

Row, but now called Christ Church Place. Samuel Molyneux constructed a broadly cruciform but irregular, multi-level courts building *c.* 1608 in which, due to the gradient of the site, the courts of Chancery and Common Pleas were on one level, with the court of Exchequer set higher, and King's Bench higher again. Molyneux's court house was rebuilt on a similarly irregular plan in 1695 by Sir William Robinson with 'competent classicism and baroque flourishes' (Edward McParland, *Public Architecture in Ireland 1680-1760* (London, 2001)). Chancery, Common Pleas and King's Bench were on the same level with Exchequer set higher. The building was accessed from Christ Church Lane (Winetavern Street) via a passageway beneath the Exchequer Court, known as Hell, which was lined with small retail premises. It was famed as Dublin's toy shop district. Thomas Burgh carried out alterations from 1705 to 1706, and Pierce Archibald carried out repairs on a number of occasions in the 1750s. The building was demolished in the early 1800s following the transfer of the courts to Gandon's new Four Courts across the river in 1796.

CLONMEL, CO. TIPPERARY

Sarsfield Street

Main Guard

[Sir William Robinson/Captain John Archer];

Margaret Quinlan Architects

1675; 2000-04

Prominently positioned to close the vista down the town's Main Street (now O'Connell Street), the Main Guard in Clonmel was commissioned as a court house for the County Palatine of Tipperary by James Butler, 12th Duke of Ormonde. The Palatine rights of Tipperary, extinguished in the Cromwellian period but given back to Ormonde following the restoration of Charles II in 1660, included the authority to administer justice in the county. A building for court purposes had existed behind the site of the Main Guard in the early 17th century, but by 1673 Ormonde was in correspondence with Clonmel Corporation regarding a new court house. As testified by two carved stone panels set into the front wall, bearing the arms of the town and the Duke of Ormonde and the date, the Main Guard was completed in 1675.

Samuel Lewis's *Topographical Dictionary* (1837) says that the Main Guard was 'built after a design by Sir Christopher Wren', which is not the case. The building has also been attributed to Sir William Robinson, though Margaret Quinlan, whose research into the building began in 1990, considered Captain John Archer as circumstantially a more likely contender. When constructed, the building was arcaded at ground floor, in the manner of a market house. The main floor was above the arcade and consisted of a single large chamber for the courtroom, perhaps with a lobby or antechamber.

The Palatinate of Tipperary was extinguished by Act of Parliament in 1715, after which the Main Guard continued to be the court house for county assizes. These transferred to Morrison's court house on Nelson Street *c.* 1801 and the Main Guard subsequently became an army barracks. It was then that it acquired the name by which it is still known. In the first or second decade of the 19th century it was redeveloped for commercial use, resulting in radical alterations, including the replacement of the ground floor arcade with shops. Additional floors were inserted and the single set of windows to the front was replaced by two rows of windows.

The Main Guard was acquired by Clonmel Corporation in 1984 in poor condition, and might have been largely demolished had not Quinlan's investigation, supported by Borough Engineer Jim Keating, revealed that it still contained substantial 17th-century fabric. A major restoration programme by Margaret Quinlan Architects was completed in 2004, returning the building in large measure to its 17th-century configuration. As it stands now, the Main Guard is a two-storey, five-bay structure with an open arcade of semi-circular arches to ground floor supported on massive cylindrical columns. Above this are five large square-headed windows set in dressed sandstone walls. A limestone cornice with central pediment contains a clock. The hipped roof is topped by a tall octagonal turret with copper cupola and weathervane. The building is now a museum.

--

Image

Clonmel, Main Guard (Margaret Quinlan, 2004)

Clonmel, Main Guard. Ground plan in context by Margaret Quinlan (Margaret Quinlan, 2004)

River Suir

Site Plan

DOWNPATRICK, CO. DOWN

English Street
County Court House
Hugh Darley; John Benjamin Keane; Henry Smyth
1737; 1833-34; 1855-59

ImageDownpatrick, County Court House
(IAA, 2000)

A 1708 survey of Downpatrick by John Maguire records 'a good convenient Session House with apartments for the Grand and Petty Jury and a private room for the Judges'. Built in the 17th century to replace a court house established in the former Franciscan church, it was in turn replaced on the same site in 1737 by the first manifestation of the current building. Walter Harris, in his *Antient and present state of the County of Down* (1744), describes this as 'designed and well executed by Mr Hugh Darling of Dublin', by whom he meant Hugh Darley. He went on to record that it contained 'two handsome Court Rooms, one for carrying on the Business of the Crown, and the other for the Dispatch of civil Causes; with Rooms also for Grand Juries, Petty Juries, and Juries of Matrons [a special jury which adjudicated whether or not a party to a legal action was pregnant], well contrivd, either against Spectators, or other impertinent Folks'. The cost is reported to have been between £2,000 and £3,000.

By 1832 the building was in a poor condition. It was repaired and extended in 1833-34 by contractor John Lynn to designs by John Benjamin Keane. The OS *Memoirs* considered the result 'a fine and capacious building, its length in front being 120 feet and its greatest breadth is 80. It is conspicuously situated and is a great ornament to the town. The front is faced in imitation of stone, 2 statues and a carved representation of the royal arms are placed on the top and the building altogether is a handsome one, though very plain in its architecture'. The courtrooms were 'capacious and lofty'. Extended again in 1841, the building was badly damaged by fire in 1855 and was substantially rebuilt by Henry Smyth, County Surveyor, from 1857 to 1859. Smyth provided a new crown court, Grand Jury room and offices, a new public staircase to galleries and an enlarged hall. The front porch was added by Bernard Murray in 1870. Damaged by a bomb in 1971, the building was repaired and again refurbished in the early 1990s.

As it stands now, this is a rendered two-storey, nine-bay building set behind a high fence on a hill-top site with a multi-bay coursed rubble extension to the rear. The centre three bays of the entrance elevation are advanced, fronted by a vermiculated porch with urns, and topped by the statues and coat of arms recorded by the OS *Memoirs*. Three arched recesses to the ground floor of the end bays on each side, the centres containing entrances, the others having blind windows with architraves. Plain windows to first floor resting on a sill-level platband. Three-bay side elevation to the front block and five bays to the sides of the rear extension, with a second vermiculated porch on the west side. The windows in the main façade of the extension are set in red-brick surrounds. Still used by Magistrates' Courts, County Courts and Crown Courts.

WICKLOW

Market Street and Kilmantin Hill
County Court House
[]; []; []; Henry Brett; John Henry Brett; []
c. **1750**; 1824; 1842; 1866; 1876; 1943

Image
Wicklow, County Court House (IAA, 2019)

Wicklow acquired a dedicated court house, and adjoining gaol, sometime in the mid-18th century. By a 1774 Act of Parliament (Stat. 13 & 14, George III, cap. 18 sect. 16) the Grand Jury of Wicklow was 'impowered to present such sum or sums, as they shall think necessary, for the purchasing of a plot of ground, house or houses, adjoining the court house and gaol of said county for the purpose of enlarging and rendering the same more convenient for doing the business of said county'. Expenditure was capped at £400. The gaol section of the complex was substantially altered and enlarged by William Vitruvius Morrison from 1817 to 1820 at a cost of £3,996 to provide thirty male and six female cells behind a high wall. Additions were carried out to the court house in 1824, so extensive that Lewis's *Topographical Dictionary* actually gives this as the date of construction of the building, adding that it 'is a plain but commodious edifice, with sufficient accommodation for all requisite purposes'. Further repairs were required in 1842, after the Grand Jury described the court house as dilapidated and in need of replacement. At the same time a block of forty more cells was added to the gaol. This is now the only part of the gaol to survive. Yet more alterations and improvements were carried out to the court house by County Surveyor Henry Brett in 1866. A decade later his son, John Henry Brett, added a record court at a cost of £1,800, and the building was further extended in 1943.

The result of this ongoing building programme is an unsurprisingly uninspiring three-storey, nine-bay range divided into three blocks and forming one side of Market Square. Rusticated stone at ground or 'basement' level where the three end bays on each side have arched recesses containing round-headed windows and entrances. The middle section is slightly set back and has a raised round-headed entrance accessed by a double flight of opposed steps. Above the door are three stone panels while flanking it are lunette windows, set at the same height as the fanlight to the door. The upper storeys are rendered. A continuous bracketed stone cornice above the first floor suggests that the top storey is an addition. The three end bays on each side are quoined with round-headed windows at first floor level and square-headed at second; the middle three bays have round-headed windows to the second floor. The building contains double-height courtrooms. That on the right was altered in 1985 but that on the left, added by John Henry Brett in 1876, retains its original fittings and furnishings, including a Gothicised pilaster screen behind the judge's bench and a public gallery on cast-iron pillars.

In July 2010, Wicklow County Court House was closed on health and safety grounds, with all court sittings transferred to the newly completed court house in the Civic Centre in Bray. The reopening of the court house remains under active consideration.

DOWNPATRICK, CO. DOWN

English Street
County Court House
Hugh Darley; John Benjamin Keane; Henry Smyth
1737; 1833-34; 1855-59

ImageDownpatrick, County Court House
(IAA, 2000)

A 1708 survey of Downpatrick by John Maguire records 'a good convenient Session House with apartments for the Grand and Petty Jury and a private room for the Judges'. Built in the 17th century to replace a court house established in the former Franciscan church, it was in turn replaced on the same site in 1737 by the first manifestation of the current building. Walter Harris, in his *Antient and present state of the County of Down* (1744), describes this as 'designed and well executed by Mr Hugh Darling of Dublin', by whom he meant Hugh Darley. He went on to record that it contained 'two handsome Court Rooms, one for carrying on the Business of the Crown, and the other for the Dispatch of civil Causes; with Rooms also for Grand Juries, Petty Juries, and Juries of Matrons [a special jury which adjudicated whether or not a party to a legal action was pregnant], well contrivd, either against Spectators, or other impertinent Folks'. The cost is reported to have been between £2,000 and £3,000.

By 1832 the building was in a poor condition. It was repaired and extended in 1833-34 by contractor John Lynn to designs by John Benjamin Keane. The OS *Memoirs* considered the result 'a fine and capacious building, its length in front being 120 feet and its greatest breadth is 80. It is conspicuously situated and is a great ornament to the town. The front is faced in imitation of stone, 2 statues and a carved representation of the royal arms are placed on the top and the building altogether is a handsome one, though very plain in its architecture'. The courtrooms were 'capacious and lofty'. Extended again in 1841, the building was badly damaged by fire in 1855 and was substantially rebuilt by Henry Smyth, County Surveyor, from 1857 to 1859. Smyth provided a new crown court, Grand Jury room and offices, a new public staircase to galleries and an enlarged hall. The front porch was added by Bernard Murray in 1870. Damaged by a bomb in 1971, the building was repaired and again refurbished in the early 1990s.

As it stands now, this is a rendered two-storey, nine-bay building set behind a high fence on a hill-top site with a multi-bay coursed rubble extension to the rear. The centre three bays of the entrance elevation are advanced, fronted by a vermiculated porch with urns, and topped by the statues and coat of arms recorded by the OS *Memoirs*. Three arched recesses to the ground floor of the end bays on each side, the centres containing entrances, the others having blind windows with architraves. Plain windows to first floor resting on a sill-level platband. Three-bay side elevation to the front block and five bays to the sides of the rear extension, with a second vermiculated porch on the west side. The windows in the main façade of the extension are set in red-brick surrounds. Still used by Magistrates' Courts, County Courts and Crown Courts.

MARKET-HOUSE OF DUNLAVIN,

DUNLAVIN, CO. WICKLOW
Market Square
Market House and Court House
[Richard Castle]; Mark Cross
1740; 1835

--
Image
Dunlavin, Front (IAA, 1951)
Dunlavin (*Dublin Penny Journal*, 26 December 1835)

A sophisticated exercise in Palladianism, Dunlavin market house was erected for local landlord James Worth Tynte, who signed an agreement relating to the building with one Thomas Gilbert in 1737. The Knight of Glin attributed it to Richard Castle ('Richard Castle, architect, his biography and works', *Bulletin of the Irish Georgian Society*, vol. 7, no. 1, Jan.-Mar. 1964), though Maurice Craig considered it 'too clumsy to be the work of an academically accomplished designer' (*The Architecture of Ireland from the earliest times to 1880* (London, 1982)). The ground floor was used for markets with the first floor accommodating court sittings. A detached, rusticated granite building with a cruciform plan, open Tuscan colonnades with full entablature at each corner, and a fluted stone dome sitting on an octagonal drum pierced by oculi, two of which – one facing north and one south – contain clocks. Two-storey, seven-bay east and west side elevations, arcaded at ground floor and with the centre three bays prominently advanced to form the transept of the cruciform. The ground floor arches of the centre bays contain round-headed windows with small square-headed windows to first floor. The north and south end elevations are expressed as single-bay compositions. The tall arched recesses were formerly open and gated but are now enclosed, that to the north containing an entrance and that to the south a window. Full-width pediments sit at impost level on pairs of Tuscan corner pilasters. Above is a second, plain, pediment.

In 1835 Lady Tynte Caldwell commissioned Mark Cross to carry out repairs to the building at a cost of £500. The *Dublin Penny Journal* commented that 'Mr Cross has left a lasting example of good taste, and well-directed judgement, inasmuch as he has adhered with the greatest precision to the original design of the building'. However, it would appear that Cross moved court sittings to the ground floor, creating a double-height courtroom under a barrel-vaulted ceiling. Renovated in 1998. On the abolition of the District Court in 2007, Dunlavin became part of Baltinglass District Court Area. The market and court house, which had been shared with the local library since the early 1980s, is now exclusively used by the library.

LIFFORD, CO. DONEGAL
The Diamond
County Court House
Michael Priestley; []
1746; *c.* 1985

--
Image
Lifford, County Court House (Alistair
Rowan/Buildings of Ireland, 1971)

The very early county court house in Lifford is a detached eight-bay (seven principal and one additional at the east end), single-storey over basement building. A bridewell is located in the basement, hidden by a low screen wall. A plaque with the coat of arms of George II above the central Gibbsian door records the date, 1746, and the architect, Michael Priestley, to whom the Grand Jury made a payment of £23 4s 6d in 1754 as reimbursement for his work.

The building was repaired and extended in the 1790s and again in the 1830s and a new heating system was installed in the 1870s which, according to correspondence of 1875, 'when properly attended to does very well indeed'. Rendered with Gibbsian surrounds to round-headed

windows. Dressed-sandstone quoins and string-courses. Venetian windows on river side. Little of the original interior survives. Brett's *Court Houses of Ulster* considers this 'one of the finest buildings in the north, and one of the most neglected', while the *Buildings of Ireland* worried that it could 'soon be added to an already long list of Lifford losses'. Fortunately, the building was renovated *c.* 1985 with an internal mezzanine and extension to rear. Vacated by the court in 1997 when Lifford District Court was amalgamated with Letterkenny, it is now a popular visitor centre and also houses the local community library.

WICKLOW

Market Street and Kilmantin Hill
County Court House
[]; []; []; Henry Brett; John Henry Brett; []
c. **1750**; 1824; 1842; 1866; 1876; 1943

Image
Wicklow, County Court House (IAA, 2019)

Wicklow acquired a dedicated court house, and adjoining gaol, sometime in the mid-18th century. By a 1774 Act of Parliament (Stat. 13 & 14, George III, cap. 18 sect. 16) the Grand Jury of Wicklow was 'impowered to present such sum or sums, as they shall think necessary, for the purchasing of a plot of ground, house or houses, adjoining the court house and gaol of said county for the purpose of enlarging and rendering the same more convenient for doing the business of said county'. Expenditure was capped at £400. The gaol section of the complex was substantially altered and enlarged by William Vitruvius Morrison from 1817 to 1820 at a cost of £3,996 to provide thirty male and six female cells behind a high wall. Additions were carried out to the court house in 1824, so extensive that Lewis's *Topographical Dictionary* actually gives this as the date of construction of the building, adding that it 'is a plain but commodious edifice, with sufficient accommodation for all requisite purposes'. Further repairs were required in 1842, after the Grand Jury described the court house as dilapidated and in need of replacement. At the same time a block of forty more cells was added to the gaol. This is now the only part of the gaol to survive. Yet more alterations and improvements were carried out to the court house by County Surveyor Henry Brett in 1866. A decade later his son, John Henry Brett, added a record court at a cost of £1,800, and the building was further extended in 1943.

The result of this ongoing building programme is an unsurprisingly uninspiring three-storey, nine-bay range divided into three blocks and forming one side of Market Square. Rusticated stone at ground or 'basement' level where the three end bays on each side have arched recesses containing round-headed windows and entrances. The middle section is slightly set back and has a raised round-headed entrance accessed by a double flight of opposed steps. Above the door are three stone panels while flanking it are lunette windows, set at the same height as the fanlight to the door. The upper storeys are rendered. A continuous bracketed stone cornice above the first floor suggests that the top storey is an addition. The three end bays on each side are quoined with round-headed windows at first floor level and square-headed at second; the middle three bays have round-headed windows to the second floor. The building contains double-height courtrooms. That on the right was altered in 1985 but that on the left, added by John Henry Brett in 1876, retains its original fittings and furnishings, including a Gothicised pilaster screen behind the judge's bench and a public gallery on cast-iron pillars.

In July 2010, Wicklow County Court House was closed on health and safety grounds, with all court sittings transferred to the newly completed court house in the Civic Centre in Bray. The reopening of the court house remains under active consideration.

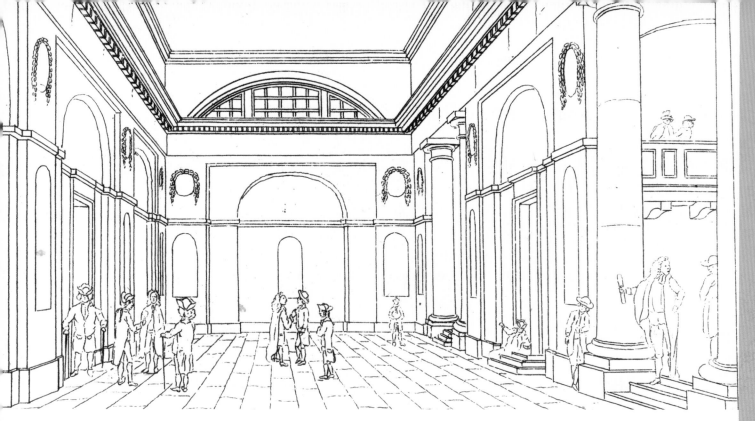

WATERFORD

Ballybricken Green

Court House and Gaol

James Gandon

1784-87

--

Image

Waterford, Court House and Gaol.

Engraved Interior after James Malton, c. 1800

(Maurice Craig Collection, IAA)

Mid-18th-century Waterford had two separate court houses, one for the county on High Street and one for the city on Broad Street. Neither of these court houses survive. In 1784 work began on a new combined court house and gaol designed by James Gandon and the building was completed in 1787. Constructed on the site of an old barracks and terminating the vista down Mayor's Walk, Gandon's court house was unprecedented in an Irish context. In the words of Edward McParland, 'No earlier court house… had so effectively rationalised its plan, and none was as monumental inside and out' (Edward McParland, *James Gandon: Vitruvius Hibernicus* (London, 1981)). The main façade consisted of a central courtroom block linked by screen walls to end pavilions. In plan, the building followed Gandon's proposal for Nottingham County Hall which he had published in *Vitruvius Britannicus* in 1771. A large entrance hall took up the full width of the building; opening off, and indeed open to, this were two parallel courtrooms separated by circulation and office space.

Gandon's court house became a model which was followed repeatedly in the first decades of the 19th century. Externally William Farrell's court houses at Carrick-on-Shannon and Cavan were based on it, as was Richard Morrison's Galway County Court House. The floor-plan was adopted by Morrison at Clonmel, Portlaoise and Naas. Following the completion of the new City and County Court House in 1849, parts of Gandon's building were pressed into service as a chapel and workroom for the adjoining gaol. By 1860 the decision had been taken to replace the gaol and the old court house was demolished to make room. This new gaol was itself demolished c. 1950 and Waterford Garda station now occupies the site.

DUBLIN
Inns Quay
Four Courts
Thomas Cooley, James Gandon; Jacob Owen;
Sir Thomas Drew; Thomas Joseph Byrne
1785-1802; 1835-39; 1894; 1925-31

Image
Four Courts (David Davison, c. 1975)

The Four Courts stands as James Gandon's second masterpiece after the Custom House, and one of Ireland's finest buildings. Construction began in 1785 on a site already partially occupied by a public office building designed by Thomas Cooley in 1776 and incomplete when Cooley died in 1784. Gandon adapted and altered the two standing wings of Cooley's building as the west end office ranges of his own courts complex, duplicated these to the east and, slightly set back between them, placed a square courtroom block. The two courtyards created by this arrangement were enclosed by arcaded screens and central triumphal gates surmounted by the arms of Ireland in Portland stone. The three-storey over basement office ranges, with their rows of square-headed windows, had ashlar granite fronts, rusticated at ground floor and arcaded along their south sides. The three-storey over basement granite courtroom building was fronted by

a hexastyle Corinthian portico in Portland stone with a plain pediment topped by statues of Moses, Justice and Mercy by Edward Smyth. Seated figures of Wisdom and Authority, also by Smyth, were placed at the corners of the balustraded parapet. Paired Portland stone Corinthian pilasters framed first floor niches on either side of the portico beneath which the walls curved towards the single fanlit entrance. The building was crowned by its most distinctive feature, a flat copper-clad dome on a tall drum encircled by twenty-four free-standing Corinthian columns, again in Portland stone, a dramatic addition to the Dublin skyline.

Four large courtrooms had to be provided – Chancery, King's Bench, Common Pleas and Exchequer – and Gandon placed them in a radial arrangement around a central circular hall set between eight massive piers supporting the dome. Above

the hall was an inner dome and oculus, while opening directly off it, and indeed open to it, were the double-height, apse-ended courtrooms, their entrances demarcated by paired columns. In the angles between the courtrooms were placed circulation spaces, staircases, judge's chambers and offices, while projecting to the rear was a Chancery chamber. This was converted to the Rolls Court in 1801.

None of Gandon's interiors survives but they are recorded in a small number of photographs and in drawings for some of the sculptural elements which decorated the drum and inner dome. Eight giant plaster figures representing *inter alia*, Justice, Wisdom, Eloquence and Mercy, lined the dome below which were decorative panels recording the history of law from William the Conqueror establishing the courts of justice to James I abolishing Brehon law. The hall accumulated a number of statues over the years including one of Lord Chief Justice James Whiteside by Thomas Woolner (1880), which survived the destruction of 1922, and Richard Lalor Sheil by Thomas Farrell (1884) which did not.

Courts began operating in the building from 1796, though works continued until 1802 as changes and additions were being suggested as building progressed. Francis Johnston proposed various alterations including the fire-proofing of the courtrooms in 1821. William Murray made drawings for sundry minor works in 1826-27. In 1832, Frederick Darley proposed adding a replacement Rolls Court and a Nisi Prius Court to the rear. These additional double-height courtrooms were in fact added from 1835 to 1839 by Jacob Owen, architect to the Board of Works; the Rolls Court on the west and the Nisi Prius on the east. The contractors were Henry, Mullins and McMahon. Between the courtrooms at ground floor was a hall above which, on the first floor, Owen provided a top-lit Law Library. In 1894, the Law Library moved to the first floor of the north range on the east of the courtroom block. This was fitted out by Sir Thomas Drew, who created a long double-height space with a coffered ceiling supported by rows of Corinthian columns between which were balustraded balconies.

The OPW annual report for 1922/23 laconically recorded that 'at the end of June 1922, the group of buildings known as the Four Courts, which has for some weeks – since 14th April 1922 – been occupied by Irregulars under Roderick O'Connor, was besieged and taken, and in the process was almost completely ruined'. The *Irish Builder* with more emotion ranked this event as 'among the worst outrages in the history of architecture'.

Proposals for the site in the immediate aftermath of the destruction ranged from the creation of a new park to the building of a Catholic Metropolitan Cathedral but Thomas Joseph Byrne, Chief Architect of the Office of Public Works and a man who had the ear of W.T. Cosgrave, President of the Executive Council for the Irish Free State, successfully made the case for the rebuilding of the Four Courts.

By March 1923 the OPW was 'carrying out works of repair whose purpose is to restore the outer shell of the central part of the building, viz., the portico, the central hall, and the drum and roof over it, to something like their original appearance'. In 1926, the OPW could report that 'it was settled that the Four Courts building would be reconstructed for the use of the Supreme Court and High Court, and the general lines of a plan of reconstruction were approved. The plan adheres as closely as possible to the central conception of Gandon's original design'. Externally the principal alteration made by Byrne was the shortening by over 3.5m of the east and west office ranges to bring them flush with the screen wall and portico. Steel and concrete were used to rebuild the ranges themselves, their roof profiles were altered, the arcades on the south sides were filled in, and the interior layout was rationalised. The dome was also replaced in steel and concrete, the capitals of its peristyle of columns turned where necessary to hide any damage. The external statuary was repaired and returned. Internally, the arrangements of the central block were replicated, with four now apse-less courtrooms fitted out where their predecessors had been, though now closed off from the central hall. Three new top-lit courtrooms were added to the rear where Jacob Owen's Rolls and Nisi Prius Courts had been, including one for the Supreme Court. The central hall was reinstated, and a pared back classicism adopted for the internal finishes.

The High and Supreme Courts returned to the building in 1931 and remain in situ, though building works have continued on a semi-regular basis ever since. James Ryan and Son repaired the external stone work and the dome in 1969. Tyndall Hogan Hurley carried out alterations to the basement in 1986-87. Costello Murray Beaumont inserted new courtrooms in the west wing in 1997-98, and refitted T.J. Byrne's east courtroom to the rear as a second Supreme Court to be known as the Hugh Kennedy Courtroom. The dome was repaired by the OPW 2018-19. With the proposal to construct a new Supreme Court building on the Hammond Lane site, the precise nature of the future judicial use of the Four Courts is yet to be decided.

KILKENNY
Parliament Street
County Court House
[]; William Robertson; []; []; OPW
c.1790; c. 1830; 1855; 1895; 2007-10

Image
Kilkenny, County Court House
(Courts Service, 2010)

Kilkenny County Court House is an imposing two-storey, seven-bay edifice, set back from Parliament Street and approached by flights of steps at either end, leading to a full width balcony at first floor level. The first building on the site, fragments of which remain in the basement, was built c. 1210 for the Grace family, hence the name still in use, 'Grace's Old Castle'. This was substantially altered in the 1560s to transform it into a gaol. Cells are still visible in the ground floor arcade beneath the balcony, and the building continued to function as a bridewell into the 20th century. Substantially altered again c. 1790, possibly for Sir Jerome Fitzpatrick, to accommodate court use, the first assizes were held in the building in 1792. It was given its current external appearance by local architect William Robertson c. 1830. He added the balcony and staircases, and transformed the front elevation at first floor level, creating the three central square-headed entrances, topped by plaques decorated with roundels and swags, and framed by an engaged Tuscan tetrastyle pedimented portico. The end bays are also framed by engaged Tuscan columns and have square-headed windows. These are topped by panels and entablatures with swags, while between the end bays and the central entrances Robertson placed segmental relieving arches surmounting square-headed tripartite windows.

In 1855 Richard Burnham, architect, won a competition for additions but declined to accept the terms by which the competition premium would be deducted from his fees. The Grand Jury consequently decided to have no architect, 'leaving the building in the hands of the contractor and clerk of works'. In 1875 a judge declared that it was 'the most disgusting and abominable court-house he was ever in'. Partially rebuilt 1895, after a fire, so that internally only the main hall with its barrelled ceiling remains from Robertson's interior.

Although the two double-height courtrooms were extensively upgraded c. 1980, in 2002 the building was designated by the Courts Service for complete refurbishment and expansion. Plans were finalised by the OPW in 2007, with Michael O'Boyle of Bluett and O'Donoghue acting as conservation architect, and works were completed in 2010 at a cost of €17 million. The main contractor was Michael McNamara and Co. During the renovation process court sittings transferred to a speculative office building on Parnell Street and to Kilkenny Castle. The renovated court house now has a 3,000m² extension to the rear, the faceted, panelled, John's Bridge façade of which makes extensive use of glass and copper and is a deliberately contemporary counterbalance to the older building. Together, old and new provide improved accommodation for all court users, including three new courtrooms to complement the refurbished original two, judges' chambers, and office accommodation for the Courts Service.

LONGFORD
Main Street
County Court House
[]; James Bell; Deaton Lysaght Architects
1793; 1859; 2004-06

--
Image
Longford, County Court House
(Lawrence Collection, NLI, late 19C)

Longford, County Court House
(Courts Service, 2006)

Presenting as the substantial Georgian townhouse it originally was, Longford court house was built in 1793. Already in court use by the time the first-edition OS map was produced, the building was enlarged in 1859 by the Longford County Surveyor, James Bell, who also added a now-lost Italianate tower. Five-bay, three-storey over raised basement structure, with rendered façade and dressed-stone string-course, quoins, and architraves. Central pedimented Doric doorcase, with freestanding columns and full entablature, approached by a flight of six steps and flanked by tall round-headed windows. Above the entrance is a Venetian window, on either side of which are two square-headed windows. The third floor is part of the mid-19th-century additions and makes the building, in the words of *The Buildings of Ireland*, 'tall and ungainly'. Here are two segmental-headed windows on either side of a double window with deep sill supported on three stone consoles. Above this is an eaves pediment with oculus window, obscured in the late 19th century by the insertion of a clock. The internal arrangements are those devised by Bell: a double-height entrance hall with twin wrought-iron staircases leading to two top-lit courtrooms at the back of the building. The half basement contained the bridewell, and this was extended to the front *c.* 1900 by the addition of two small blocks, one on either side of the entrance steps.

The court house closed in 1994 because of its poor condition and from 2004 to 2006 a conservation and extension programme was carried out by Deaton Lysaght Architects. The rear of the building was reconfigured and extended in a contemporary idiom, and the licensed premises immediately adjacent to the south was acquired to provide additional floor space. The street front was refurbished, the bridewell extensions, which had become shops in the mid-20th century, were removed, and suitable railings installed. Internally, the former Grand Jury room was converted to a family law court and a suspended glazed gallery added to the entrance hall to facilitate access to the mezzanine level courtrooms. The building now has two large courtrooms, a family law courtroom and court office accommodation. Consultation rooms, victim support room, media room and holding cells for prisoners have also been provided.

ENNISKILLEN, CO. FERMANAGH
Bridge Street, East
County Court House
[]; William Farrell; Roderick Gray
c. **1795**; 1821-22; 1861-62

--
Image
Enniskillen, County Court House
(Alistair Rowan/Buildings of Ireland, 1970)

Lewis's *Topographical Dictionary* reports of Enniskillen that the 'assizes for the county and quarter session of the peace are held in the county court-house, which is a plain building near the eastern bridge'. Located on a curve of Bridge Street, East, the court house was first constructed *c.* 1795. It was reconstructed in 1821-22 by Henry Lambert to designs by William Farrell at the then considerable expense of £3,000. Further repairs and alterations were carried out in the early 1860s by Roderick Gray, Fermanagh County Surveyor. For the *Buildings of Ireland*, the court house has 'the most distinguished façade in the city, but now no more than that', the interior having been gutted in the 1970s when the building was under threat of demolition.

Arguably the most understated of the county court houses, this is a five-bay, two-storey structure, with square-headed windows to ground floor and tall round-headed windows above. These retain a delicately intricate glazing pattern, a contrast to the robust single-storey tetrastyle Doric portico added by Farrell in the early 1820s. Rendered, with stone quoins and window surrounds. Hipped roof with broad modillioned eaves and a central ventilator. Refurbished in 1982, it is now designated as a Court Hearing Centre (a feeder court from which proceedings may be transferred to a specified Civil Trial Centre).

CLONMEL, CO. TIPPERARY
Nelson Street
County Court House
Sir Richard Morrison; Deaton Lysaght Architects
1801; 1996-98

Image
Clonmel, County Court House, courtroom
(IAA, 1986)

Clonmel, County Court House
(Maurice Craig Collection, IAA, 1982)

Described by Rev. Daniel Beaufort in his *Observations on a Tour through Leinster, Munster and Connacht* (1806) as 'allowed to be one of the most convenient & beautiful buildings of its kind & size in his Majesty's dominions', Clonmel court house was built by 1801 to replace the Main Guard as the county court house for Tipperary. Set back slightly from the street behind railings with massive stone piers, it was designed by Sir Richard Morrison who had set up his architectural practice in Clonmel in the early 1790s. For the court house Morrison chose a refined late Palladian style, most obviously expressed in the five-bay, two-storey front façade. This is rendered, with stone detailing. The centre three bays are advanced with a ground floor rusticated arcade containing the fanlit entrances. Above stand four half-engaged Ionic columns supporting the dentil-lined pediment. The columns frame a second arcade, this time containing three large square-headed windows which are set in finely detailed architraves and fronted by balustrades. A sill-level string-course extends the full width of the building. The end bays have arched recesses to ground floor, continuing the motif of the central arcade, and decorative panels are located above and below the first floor windows.

The seven-bay side elevations are plainer, with arched recesses to the ground floor of the end bays, above which are square-headed windows, some blind. The centre three bays have square-headed windows in arched recesses at first floor level, providing light to the courtrooms. The pedimented two-storey, seven-bay rear façade is more sophisticated than the backs of court houses usually are. It is rendered, with five round-headed windows to the first floor of the advanced centre bays. The two single-bay, single-storey ground-floor protrusions are later additions.

Internally the front entrances lead to a hall, above which is a ballroom, a rare, but not unique, court house feature. Beyond the hall a broad central corridor, top-lit at first floor, separates and gives access to the two courtrooms and leads to a stair hall providing access to the first floor and the courtroom galleries. To the rear are offices and the first floor former Grand Jury room which has a coved ceiling and frieze with crowned harps, lions and unicorns. The courtrooms themselves are two-storey chambers with deep coved ceilings. Both courtrooms have been altered over time. The current arrangement of galleries and seating generally dates from the late 19th century, though some original elements remain such as the Corinthian columns framing the recess for the judge's bench in the District Court.

Refurbishment works mainly to the exterior were carried out in the 1980s and from 1996 to 1998 a further comprehensive programme of restoration and extension by Deaton Lysaght Architects resulted in significant improvements to the courtrooms, staff accommodation and ancillary facilities. The court house now has three courtrooms and includes provision for High Court and Family Court sittings, in addition to the Circuit and District Courts.

KELLS, CO. MEATH

Headfort Place

Court House

Francis Johnston

1802

--
Image
Kells (Paul Tierney, 2018)

Kells petty and quarter sessions court house is an imposing gable-fronted building by Francis Johnston. The pedimented three-bay entrance front of ashlar limestone has an arcade at ground level, consisting of a recessed central fanlit entrance flanked by recessed round-headed windows. Above are three square-headed windows. Rubble six-bay side elevations whose first and last bays are blind and advanced while the centre four bays reverse the window arrangement of the front: square-headed below and round-headed at first floor level. The rear elevation is similar to that in a drawing signed by Johnston and dated February 1802 (IAA, RIAI Murray Collection, 92/46.894).

The interior was substantially altered in 1948 by Simon Aloysius Leonard of W.H. Byrne and Son to whom the unusual glazing pattern of twenty-four over twenty-four small panes has been attributed. However, the pattern is shown on the practice's survey drawings of the building which predate their alterations. The court house remained in use until the 1990s when court sittings were transferred to the former VEC building on Bective Street, a classically proportioned, detached, nine-bay, two-storey technical school designed in 1929 by Michael Grace. This was in turn closed in 2013 when the Electoral Divisions in the Kells District Court Area were transferred to the Areas of Navan and Trim. The original court house became the Kells Heritage Centre in 1999 at which time the 9th-century high cross known as the Market Cross was moved to stand in front of the building under a glass and steel canopy. The centre closed in 2009, but reopened in 2018.

PORTLAOISE, CO. LAOIS

Main Street

County Court House

[Sir Richard Morrison]; James Rawson Carroll; David Slattery

1805; 1875; 1999-2000

--
Image
Portlaoise, County Court House (IAA, 2000)

Attributed to Sir Richard Morrison, primarily because of similarities with his court houses at Naas and Wexford, this neoclassical county court house was completed in 1805. Three-bay, two-storey centre block with imposing Doric limestone doorcase with full entablature, square-headed windows, limestone platband at first floor sill-level and decorated plaques. On either side are two pedimented rendered courtroom pavilions with stone plinths and round-headed niches flanking central arched recesses, each containing a blind ashlar limestone window. Platband at impost level, while above the niches are oculi containing decorative discs. Carriage archway to east.

The entrance hall, like that at Naas, has doors to the courtrooms on either side framed by columns set in shallow recesses. Beyond this is the stair hall with curved stone staircase. Altered and extended by J. Rawson Carroll in 1875. Extensively renovated and refurbished by David Slattery, architect, for the Courts Service, 1999-2000, at a cost of IR£2 million. Works included rationalisation of internal circulation, installation of a new lift and escape staircase, repair of historic fabric, and refitting of the court rooms. The building officially reopened in 2002.

Morrison linked the court house by means of a curved wall to the adjoining County Gaol on Church Street, designed in 1789 by Richard Harman who had acted as clerk-of-works on James Gandon's Custom House, Dublin. Practically all that remains of the original gaol fabric is the seven-bay, two-storey front façade, the central three bays of which step forward and are dominated by six giant pilasters, each with bands of stylised vermiculation, supporting a deep cornice and central plaque. The pilasters frame three round-headed windows at ground level with vermiculated surrounds set in a rusticated wall. At first floor level is a central round-headed window with further vermiculation, on either side of which are square-headed windows. At the same time as the court house was renovated, the former gaol, which had served as a library, was converted into a theatre and arts centre.

ARMAGH
College Hill
County Court House
Francis Johnston; Henry Davison, with Thomas Turner and Thomas Drew; Richard Henry Dorman; Chief Architects Office, Department of Finance NI; Stephen Leighton
1805-09; 1861-64; 1909; 1965-71; 1994-99

Armagh Grand Jury began planning to replace the existing court house in the city from as early as 1804. That building, located at Market Street and Market Place and attached to a gaol, had survived a fire in 1704 and had been substantially rebuilt in 1735, but had come to be considered very inconvenient. In January 1805 Francis Johnston prepared his first scheme for the new court house and surviving drawings make it possible to trace the evolving sophistication of his design through at least five further stages. The physical culmination of this progression was completed in 1809 at a cost of £6,000.

Prominently sited at the end of the Mall, Johnston's court house presents as a single-storey, five-bay classical building of ashlar limestone. A pedimented Roman Doric portico on a stepped plinth shelters an arcade of three full-height arches with prominent keystones. The centre arch contains a tall entrance topped by a window, while those on each side have lower entrances topped by niches. The court designations are inscribed on the lintels above these secondary doors, 'Record Court' on the left and 'Crown Court' on the right. A sharply detailed cornice extends from the portico across the façade, around the slightly recessed, quoined corners and down the random-coursed stone three-bay side elevations. Tall round-headed windows in dressed-stone surrounds provide light to the double-height courtrooms which are accessed from a central entrance hall.

The architect did not supervise the construction of the court house and was not entirely happy with the results. In a letter of February 1820 he complained that 'I sent a plan for the new Session House (erected there about seven years ago) but it has not been followed; the Managers (an Attorney and others) were prevailed upon by some of the workmen to reduce the diameter of the columns (I suppose for the greater convenience of getting the stones of which they are composed) and have thereby ruined the portico'.

In 1835 the County Surveyor Henry L. Lindsay reported that the court house was falling into a state of dilapidation. Major works were carried out from 1861 to 1864 to designs by Henry Davison, with Thomas Turner and Thomas Drew, at a cost of £2,500. The interior was reordered and a three-bay by five-bay, three storey, pedimented office extension was added to the rear. Further offices were added in 1909 by Richard Henry Dorman, while a second major refurbishment was carried out under Albert Neill, architect with the Chief Architects Office, Department of Finance NI, from 1965 to 1971. This, according to Brett's *Court Houses of Ulster*, was 'on the whole a great success'. However, the court house was badly damaged by a bomb in 1993 necessitating a third major rebuilding, undertaken by Stephen Leighton, architect, from 1994 to 1999 at a cost of £8 million. It was then that the tall railings to the front were added, and a single-storey security lodge. Although closure has been considered, Magistrates' Courts and County Courts continue to sit in the building.

Image
Armagh, County Court House.
Unexecuted proposal by Francis Johnston, 1805
(RIAI Murray Collection, IAA)

SOME SIGNIFICANT COURT HOUSES – A CHRONOLOGICAL SELECTION

NAAS, CO. KILDARE

South Main Street
County Court House
Sir Richard Morrison; John McCurdy; John Henry Brett; Deaton
Lysaght Architects
1807; 1860-61; 1870s; 1997

--
Image
Naas, County Court House
(Denis Mortell, 2018)

The county court house in Naas is a substantial, detached, seven-bay, two-storey over basement classical building. Originally built in 1807 to designs by Sir Richard Morrison, and probably very similar to his court houses at Portlaoise and Wexford, though here Morrison added an impressive portico. Altered and enlarged in 1860-61 by John McCurdy who reused Morrison's giant columns in his three-bay tetrastyle pedimented entrance portico, the entablature of which now bears the inscription 'Naas Courthouse Teach Cúirte an Nás' and the official harp emblem.

The recessed elevation beneath the portico has pilasters on each side of a central doorcase with a square blank panel above. Round-headed windows in lugged surrounds to ground floor. Segmental-arched windows to first floor with prominent keystones. Double-height entrance hall beyond which is Morrison's original rectangular single-storey hall with doors flanked by columns leading to the two double-height courtrooms on either side, a plan adapted from James Gandon's 1780s Waterford court house. Between the courtrooms is an oval stair hall with double-return main stairs. The building was altered and extended by John Henry Brett in the 1870s. It was damaged by fire in the 1950s and subsequently repaired. Extensively refurbished and enlarged in 1997 by Deaton Lysaght Architects at a cost of IR£2.25 million to provide four courtrooms for District and Circuit Court. Still in court use.

SIGNIFICANT SELECTION   183

LIMERICK
Merchants Quay
County Court House
Nicholas and William Hannan; James and George Richard Pain;
Patrick Joseph Sheahan; Murray O'Laoire Architects
1807-09; 1820; 1957; 2001-03

Image
Limerick, County Court House
(Tom Cleary, c. 2005)

In the 19th century Limerick had a City and a County Court House, while records also survive for a separate Police Court, a Children's Court and a petty sessions court for the Liberties of Limerick.

The first County Court House in Limerick was built in 1732 on the site of a former Franciscan friary at the confluence of Courthouse Lane, Long Lane, Sheep Street and Gaol Lane. Shown on the 25-inch city map of 1870, it was subsequently demolished; the site is now beneath Island Road/Sráid Seámus Ó Cinneide. The old court house fell out of use following the erection of the new County Court House on Merchants Quay. The foundation stone was laid on 1 September 1807 and the court house, designed by brothers Nicholas and William Hannan, opened on 17 July 1809, though the portico was not completed until five years later. The cost was £13,000, with the portico adding an extra £700 to the final amount.

Built on an axis with St Mary's Cathedral, the County Court House is a classical freestanding structure designed to be seen from all sides but with two principal elevations – the entrance or east front and the south side. The five-bay, two-storey entrance front is dominated by a tetrastyle Doric portico, flanked at ground floor by arched recesses containing round windows. Beneath the portico are three round-headed entrances set in rusticated stone. At first-floor level five large square-headed windows are framed by plain stone architraves. Nine-bay, two-storey side elevations, the centre five bays advanced. On the south side the advanced bays are framed by giant-order stone Doric pilasters, on the north they are more simply demarcated by quoins. Six-bay, two-storey west or river front elevation, again with advanced centre bays demarcated by quoins. Square-headed windows with stone architraves to ground and first floor of side and river elevations, aside from the end bays on the river front and the first advanced bays on the north where round-headed openings are set in recessed arches on the ground floor.

Internally, a large entrance hall to the front gave access to two double-height courtrooms, the Crown Court on the north side and the Record Court on the south. Jury rooms, judges' chambers and offices were to the rear.

The Pain brothers carried out alterations to the building in 1820, and Patrick J. Sheahan carried out repairs in 1936. He proposed replacing the building in 1938 with a new civic centre for Limerick incorporating a new court house. While this scheme came to naught, Sheahan did reconstruct the court house within its external walls in 1957 at a cost of £100,000, replacing the original pitched roof with a flat concrete roof. Further major restoration works were carried out by Murray O'Laoire Architects 2001-03, at a cost in excess of €9 million, the most visible external manifestation of which is the addition of a zinc-covered roof and attic level. This scheme won a Plan-Expo Conservation Award in 2003.

TRIM, CO. MEATH
Castle Street
County Court House
Sir Richard Morrison; Newenham Mulligan and Associates
1810; 2000-01

--
Image
Trim, County Court House
(Newenham Mulligan & Associates, 2001)

In 1810 Meath Grand Jury paid Sir Richard Morrison £100 for 'making plans and estimates for the repairs and improvements of the County Sessions House in Trim'. It is unclear whether this refers to an 18th-century court building or to the hall of the Franciscan friary which stood on the site from the 14th century and was converted to court use *c.* 1618. Morrison provided a classical, seven-bay, two-storey court house with three-bay pedimented central breakfront. Rendered façade with dressed-stone quoins and square-headed windows set in distinctive architraves. Stone surround and lintel to central entrance. The pediment contains a clock. 'A dull building for this architect', says the *Buildings of Ireland*, 'though presumably the fault lies in the parsimony of the Grand Jury who commissioned it'.

Abutting the early-19th-century building to the south is a modern two-storey extension, 2000-01. According to its architects, Newenham Mulligan and Associates, 'the architectural concept for the extension to the courthouse is for an expressive contemporary design which through form and material refers to the medieval and historic context of the site as well as unashamedly expressing its place as a court building for the 21st century'. A modernist white-rendered block with horizontal glazing sits above a rough stone wall, a nod to the nearby castle, and is anchored by a zinc-clad tower structure.

The 19th-century building was refurbished as part of the extension project. Works included the restoration of the interior of the old District Court courtroom and the reinstatement of the double-height entrance hall which had been subdivided in the late 19th century. In combination, old and new structures contain four courtrooms available for sittings of the High, Circuit and District Courts, extensive ancillary and support facilities and modern office accommodation. Trim court house won the Plan Expo Opus Building of the Year Award in 2001 in the over £2.5 million category.

GALWAY
Courthouse Square
County Court House
Sir Richard Morrison; James Perry; O'Riain and Yates Architects
1812-15; 1895-97; 1995

--
Image
Galway, County Court House
(Lawrence Collection, NLI, late 19C)

Galway County Court House was designed by Sir Richard Morrison and built on the site of the Franciscan Abbey to replace the Tholsel in Shop Street where court sessions had been held until it burned down. Construction began in 1812 and the building opened on 1 April 1815 when it was adjudged as an 'unequivocal and splendid' testimonial of 'the high respect [of the gentlemen of the county] for the laws, and of their anxiety for the due and orderly administration of public justice'.

The monumental stone front façade, facing the former Town Court House, is dominated by a tetrastyle Doric portico whose entablature attic is now missing the Hanoverian coat of arms with which it was once topped, while the entablature itself retains its four lion-head roundels. The central entrance is framed by round-headed recesses containing windows. The end bays, which step forward slightly, are blind with niches set in shallow arched recesses above which are carved panels decorated with symbols of justice. On the two-storey over basement rendered side elevations the main block is demarcated by stone quoins. The first two bays now have robustly mullioned windows while the middle three bays have ground-floor windows set in tall arched recesses. The two-storey over basement six-bay rear elevation looks across the Salmon Weir Bridge (1818) to the site of the former prison (now occupied by Galway Cathedral). Each of the pedimented end bays has a fanlit entrance at ground floor and a round-headed window above. The four recessed central bays have square-headed windows at ground and first floor, surmounted by a plain pediment with clock.

James Perry carried out extensive alterations, 1895-97, and the royal coat of arms was removed in the 1920s. The court house was renovated in 1995 by O'Riain and Yates Architects who retained many of the surviving 19th-century details including the grand staircase and the barrel-vaulted ceiling to the original courtrooms. The building is still in use, though the process of finding a replacement began in 2017.

DERRY/LONDONDERRY
Bishop Street
City and County Court House
John Bowden; Arthur Charles Adair; Matthew Alexander
Robinson and Charles Littleboy Boddie
1813-17; 1896-97; 1902-03

Image
Derry, County Court House
(Maurice Craig Collection, IAA, 1947)

'A scrupulous Greek Revival block' according to the *Buildings of Ireland*, Derry court house was designed by John Bowden and built by contractors Henry, Mullins and McMahon from 1813 to 1817 at the instigation of local MP Sir George Fitzgerald Hill and with the support of the Irish Company. The cost is recorded by Lewis's *Topographical Dictionary* as '£30,479 15s including the purchase of the site and furniture'. Prior to the construction of Bowden's building, court hearings had taken place in the 1691 'Town House' or 'Exchange' in the centre of the Diamond, an ornate classical building designed by Captain Richard Neville. This was replaced in 1823, and this replacement was itself demolished following the construction of the Guildhall in 1890.

Two-storey, seven-bay court house in sandstone and Portland limestone with a tetrastyle Ionic portico on a stepped podium. The five centre bays, three of which are behind the portico, are slightly recessed. Rusticated ground floor with a single, central, square-headed entrance. Square-headed windows to first floor in simple architraves. The fluted columns of the portico, derived from the Erechtheion in Athens, are mirrored by Doric pilasters, with further paired pilasters framing the windows in the end bays. A sill-level platband extends across the front to meet the sills of the first floor windows on the first six-bays of the eight-bay side elevations. (Only the first four bays are now visible on the south side, the remainder swallowed up by the 1890s extension.) The final two bays of the sides were recessed, de-emphasising the rear office

section of the building. A royal coat of arms, on the back of which Bowden placed his name, tops the pediment. In the middle of the end bays, above the cornice and partially balustraded parapet, are statues of Justice and Peace occasionally attributed to Edward Smyth. However, as Smyth died in 1812 they are more probably by his son, John.

Internally, the plan was, and remains, conventional with an entrance hall and two parallel double-height courtrooms. These have been much altered over the years, leaving them, in the judgement of Brett's *Court Houses of Ulster*, 'on the whole rather nondescript'.

Following years of complaint about inadequate space and indifferent sanitation, the court house was altered and extended in 1896-97 by County Surveyor Arthur Charles Adair at an estimated cost of £6,289. He added the large lanterns to both courtrooms and provided an office extension on the south side, using this to link the court house to his sandstone and brick county offices building which was under construction at the same time. Further alterations, including a reroofing, were carried out by Matthew Alexander Robinson and Charles Littleboy Boddie, 1902-03, at a cost of £3,500. Damaged repeatedly by bombs during the Troubles, the court house acquired railings and a security lodge and was the subject of a major restoration in the 1990s which included the cleaning of the façade. It remains in use for sittings of Magistrates, County and Crown Courts.

DUNDALK, CO. LOUTH
Market Square
County Court House
Edward Parke, John Bowden; John Neville; Thomas Walsh; Brian O'Halloran and Associates
1813-20; 1846 & 1855; 1930; 1998-2003

--
Image
Dundalk, County Court House.
Elevation by Owen Fahy, c. 1820
(Guinness Collection, IAA)

Intended to replace a 1736-40 sessions house by William Elgee which stood on the same site, the first call for designs for a new County Court House in Dundalk was issued in 1802. Sir Richard Morrison submitted proposals in 1804, 1810 (with John Behan) and 1812. These were rejected and in 1813 designs were commissioned from Edward Parke. In April of that year the builder William Moore signed a contract to complete the building within three years for £16,190 10s. After construction began, Parke fell out with the Grand Jury. He had wanted to be able to appoint individual craftsmen to the works; the Grand Jury demurred, preferring to retain such patronage to itself. Parke was replaced as supervising architect by John Bowden and as works proceeded the design would appear to have evolved. The builder, Moore, sued for an additional £12,000 in 1819 because of 'additions to or alterations in the original plan'. In 1820, the year of completion, he received £3,500 in settlement of his claim.

The 1813 contract for the construction included a stipulation that the new court house should conform to 'the patterns and true proportions of the rules of Grecian architecture as they are to be collected from the ruins of the city of Athens'. The driving force behind this requirement was John Foster, member of the Louth Grand Jury (and last Speaker of the Irish House of Commons), who had such an influence on the development of the building that its design has on occasion been attributed primarily to him. His stipulation was certainly obeyed. Set behind a low wall and railings, Dundalk court house is a severe Greek Revival building in ashlar granite, with an impressive Portland stone hexastyle Doric portico. The portico is derived from the Hephaisteion or 'Temple of Theseus' in Athens via Stuart and Revett's *Antiquities of Athens* (1762). However, as *The Buildings of Ireland* observes, this is not just a pattern-book copy; 'the design is far more accomplished… This sophistication is seen particularly in the decision to set two massive columnar screens *within* the portico; their effect is to lend movement to the façade and to draw the onlooker deep into the hall'.

Flanked by two smaller halls, which provide access to the public galleries, the open entrance hall leads to the central top-lit stair hall containing Portland stone stairs with wrought iron railings. On either side are double-height courtrooms, with the jury rooms and judge's chambers to the rear and the Grand Jury room on the first floor.

Additions and repairs were carried out by County Surveyor John Neville in 1846 and 1855. Further additions by Thomas Walsh were completed in 1930 and a glass curtain wall was installed in the portico in 1980. The building was extensively refurbished by Brian O'Halloran and Associates for the Courts Service from 1998 to 2003, and a new three-storey building fronting onto Crowe Street was constructed to provide two additional courtrooms and modern court facilities. A two-storey glazed atrium links the old building to the new. An upgrading project to Market Square by Nicholas de Jong and Associates was completed in 2011, a scheme which extended across Clanbrassil Street to include the immediate curtilage of the court house.

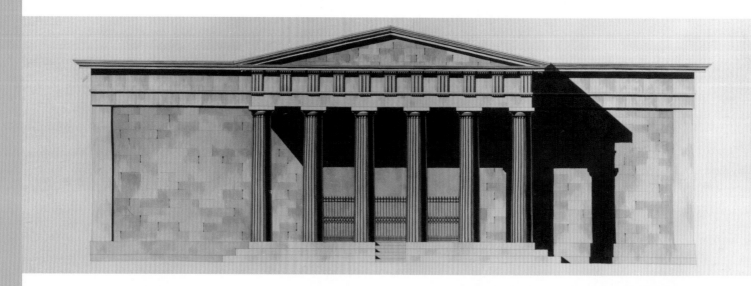

OMAGH, CO. TYRONE
High Street
County Court House
John Hargrave; William Joseph Barre; Francis John Lynam
1814-20; 1863-66; 1906

--
Image
Omagh, County Court House (IAA, c. 1950)

Sitting prominently across the top of High Street and enclosed by wrought-iron railings, Omagh County Court House was built in 1814 on the site of the former gaol. Designed in a Palladian style by John Hargrave, and built at a total cost of £17,000, it replaced an earlier court building destroyed by fire in 1742. Originally a five-bay, two-storey over basement block, it acquired its tetrastyle Tuscan portico, also by Hargrave, in 1820.

Approached by a flight of twelve steps, the tall, thin columns of the portico – 'very lanky' in the opinion of the *Buildings of Ireland* – support a pediment containing a clock and surmounted by a monumental royal coat of arms. Four Tuscan pilasters divide the façade which is rusticated at ground floor level with five round-headed openings – a wide central entrance and four windows. A platband separates the rustication from the plain ashlar of the first floor, where the square-headed windows have lugged architraves and sills which merge to form a continuous string-course. The ground floor rustication continues on the George's Street side elevation, with six tall round-headed windows to the rendered first floor, set in stone Gibbsian surrounds. A pedimented entrance, approached by a flight of steps, is squeezed in between the last two windows.

Internally, as the OS *Memoirs* reports, the court house 'contains a large vestibule opening into Crown and civil courts, retiring rooms for the judge and juries, a large room for the grand jury and a handsome dining and drawing room for their accommodation, with a kitchen and lock-up place for prisoners on the underground floor. The Crown court has 2 galleries for the accommodation of the public and one for the grand jury, whose official room opens into it. The civil court is small, without a gallery, and has little space appropriated to the people'.

From 1863 to 1866, William Joseph Barre extended the court house to the south by adding a five-bay range. Barre replicated the detailing of Hargrave's original design, including the rustication, platband, string-course and lugged architraves, giving unity to the whole though leaving it somewhat unbalanced, while the slope of the site required Barre to make his extension three-storey. Round-headed windows are in line with Hargrave's but below them, separated by decorative panels, are square-headed windows flanking a Doric entrance porch.

The *Irish Builder* reported in its 25 August 1906 edition that the court house was to be further altered 'to the plans of the County Surveyor, Mr. F.J. Lynam'. In particular, old wood and glass domes were to be replaced, 'Messrs. Helliwell & Co., Ltd, of Brighouse, Yorkshire, and 17 Nassau Street, Dublin, have been asked to supply and fix their patent glazing'. Some restoration work was carried out in the early 2000s, with other minor works in 2014 and 2018, though some Troubles-era security infrastructure remains in place. Magistrates', County and Crown Courts continue to sit in the building.

CASTLEBAR, CO. MAYO
The Mall
County Court House
[]; George Papworth; George Wilkinson; Mayo County Council
1807; **1820-22**; 1858-60; 2002-04

--
Image
Castlebar, County Court House
(IAA, 2004)

Castlebar, County Court House, Judge's canopy
(Frederick O'Dwyer, c. 1995)

From 1820 to 1822 an existing court house in Castlebar which dated from 1807 was substantially altered, or rebuilt, to designs by George Papworth. A seven-bay, U-plan, single-storey building with two courtrooms in what the *Dublin Builder* described as 'plain wings'. Between the wings, and projecting just beyond them, Papworth placed a hexastyle Doric portico made, unusually, of cast iron. In a particularly back-handed compliment, J.P. Lawson noted in his *Gazetteer of Ireland* (1842) that the façade was 'of an original order of architecture, only known to Irish professors of the art of building'. He was clearly unaware that Papworth had been born and trained in London. Lawson also described the Green onto which the court house still faces as 'a swamp… surrounded by an iron chain, judiciously placed there, I imagine, to prevent cattle and children being lost in the morass'.

The court house served briefly as a temporary hospital during the cholera epidemic of 1832. A competition for improvements to the court house was held in 1858 and won by Edward Henry Carson. Although a call for tenders to execute Carson's proposals was made in May 1858, this scheme was not proceeded with. Instead the job of altering the court house went to George Wilkinson, best known for constructing most of Ireland's workhouses. He retained Papworth's portico but raised the courtroom wings by a storey, giving them their limestone pediments and the Venetian windows to the jury rooms. The *Dublin Builder* reported in 1860 that Wilkinson's 'internal arrangements comprise a central hall with a long flight of stairs leading to the upper storey, the Record Court being at one side, and the Crown Court at the other, with judges', barristers' apartments &c'.

Refurbished *c.* 1940 and again *c.* 1975, when a single-storey extension was added to the rear. From 2002 to 2004 a substantial programme of repair and extension was carried out by Mayo County Council architects department. The project was divided into the restoration of the porticoed front block, and the construction of an entirely new extension to the rear. Linked to the older building by a top-lit atrium, this provides two new courtrooms, Courts Service offices and consultation and meeting rooms. Two existing buildings on Spencer Street, acquired in 2000/01, were also incorporated into the scheme to provide additional offices and archives stores. The original courtroom layout was retained, including the wooden balconies, but all furnishings were replaced. Still in court use.

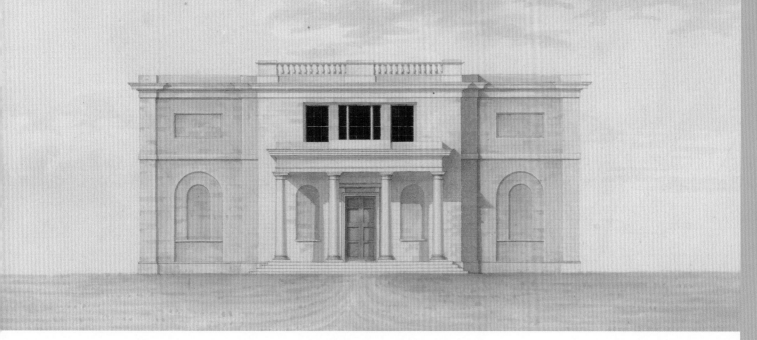

CARRICK-ON-SHANNON, CO. LEITRIM

St George's Terrace
County Court House
William Farrell; Coady Architects
1824; 2004-06

--
Image
Carrick-on-Shannon, County Court House.
Front Elevation by William Farrell, 1820
(Houghton Library, Harvard)

On a stepped plinth adjacent to the former county gaol, Carrick-on-Shannon court house is a substantial almost square classical building completed by 1824. Designed by William Farrell, whose drawings for the building survive in an album held by the Houghton Library, Harvard. Almost identical to Cavan court house, which is consequently also attributable to Farrell. Two-storey over basement with a five-bay main façade. Set-back end bays with blind arched recesses at ground floor level and rectangular panels above. Central entrance with dressed-stone surround, flanked by two round-headed windows. Above these are three windows grouped in a long rectangular recess. Four-bay rendered side elevations with tall round-headed windows above basement level square-headed windows in arched recesses. Office wing to rear. The building originally had a parapet balustrade, gone by the early 1970s, and a single-storey tetrastyle Doric portico but this was dismantled in 1982.

Internally a large entrance hall separated two courtrooms, shown on Farrell's plan as the 'Crown Court' and the 'Record Court'. Behind the courts were the judges' chambers while

beyond the entrance hall was the stair hall with a single flight of steps leading to a gallery landing providing access to jury rooms – 'Grand' and 'Petit' – and courtroom galleries.

Aside from court use, the building also accommodated the chamber and offices of Leitrim County Council for many years. Altered in the 1950s with the removal of one courtroom and the insertion of a new first floor to provide additional council accommodation. Poor maintenance over the course of the 20th century led to the vacating of the building by both courts and council in 1994 when its demolition was briefly contemplated. After standing empty for several years the court house was converted to arts use by Coady Architects, reopening in August 2005. Alterations included ramp access and a replacement for Farrell's lost portico, a modern canopy consisting of three steel sails supported on four tall posts.

CAVAN
Farnham Street
County Court House
William Farrell; Patrick Joseph Brady; []
1824-25; 1928; 1987-89

--
Image
Cavan, County Court House
(Tom Cleary, c. 1990)

Cavan County Court House is a classical, detached building, set back from the street behind railings by Richard Turner. The *Parliamentary Gazetteer* says it is 'a graceful structure, erected at a cost of £11,000, after a design by [John] Bowden'. However, the building is now generally attributed to William Farrell, not least because of its striking similarity to Farrell's court house in Carrick-on Shannon. It was built by Williams and Cockburn of Dublin.

Monumental two-storey, five-bay, sandstone façade. The middle three bays are advanced and are fronted by a single-storey tetrastyle Tuscan portico. This shelters three square-headed doorcases, the outer two of which are blind while the centre contains the principal entrance. Above the portico are three square-headed windows, grouped in a rectangular recess, surmounted by a pediment, which lost its coat of arms *c.* 1930. The end bays are blind, with tall arched recesses at ground floor and rectangular panels above. Rubble side elevations with tall round-headed windows to first floor.

Originally four bays deep but substantially extended in 1987-89 when the interior, which had previously been reworked by Patrick Joseph Brady in 1928, was also substantially reconstructed. The arrangement of twin courtrooms separated by a circulation hall was retained, but the height of the courtrooms was reduced to provide additional accommodation for county council offices. The building remains a venue for Circuit and District Court sittings.

ROSCOMMON

Abbey Street
County Court House
Richard Richards; Christopher John Mulvany
1824-27; 1883 and 1904

A new county gaol was built in Roscommon, 1814-18, designed on a radiating plan by Sir Richard Morrison with Thomas Colbourne and Richard Richards as contractors. Once the gaol was complete, efforts intensified to replace the existing court house. The new court house, designed by Richard Richards, was built beside the gaol from 1824 to 1827 at a cost of at least £5,310.

John Parker Lawson in his *Gazetteer of Ireland* (1842) considers Richards' building to be 'without architectural pretention', though Lewis's *Topographical Dictionary* is more impressed: 'The new court-house… is a handsome and spacious structure with a Doric portico in front; and contains, besides two well arranged court-rooms for criminal and civil business, a superb room for the Grand Jury, an apartment for the use of the judges, a room for the barristers, refreshment rooms, and accommodations for persons having business at the assizes or sessions, with complete ranges of requisite offices'.

Richards' court house was destroyed by a fire in June 1882. A temporary court house was provided to designs by James Perry, while consideration was given to finding a permanent replacement. A number of schemes were submitted, including one by William Kaye-Parry and Henry A. Cheers, but the task was given to the Roscommon County Surveyor, Christopher John Mulvany. In 1883, he rebuilt the court house on the same site, to a nearly identical plan, at a cost of over £11,000.

The resulting building is a detached, five-bay, two- and three-storey over basement block set on a prominent elevated site. The centre three bays of the two-storey front façade are modestly advanced and fronted by a single-storey hexastyle Doric portico with fluted columns (retained from Richards' 1820s building). Beneath the portico is a central fanlit entrance flanked by two round-headed windows set in channelled walls. At first floor level are three large, square-headed windows and above these a small rectangular pediment, now missing its royal coat of arms, and a domed bellcote. The ashlar end bays have arched recesses to ground floor and square-headed windows above, framed by full-height channelled pilasters. Nine-bay side elevations, with round-headed windows to the courtrooms. Two-storey rear elevation with two flights of stone steps bridging the basement area to access fanlit entrances. Internally the original plan is retained, a columned entrance hall leading to a stair hall off which are two large double-height, galleried, courtrooms.

Mulvany carried out alterations in 1904 and for much of the 20th century the building has accommodated both court and local authority services, the county council meeting in the former Grand Jury room on the first floor. Michael Scott carried out repairs in 1950 and further extension took place *c.* 1965 with the addition of a now demolished office wing. While a major refurbishment has been planned since 2000, this has yet to take place. Court use continues, though the county council has relocated to the adjacent Áras an Chontae by Ahrends Burton Koralek (ABK) Architects, completed in 2016.

MULLINGAR, CO. WESTMEATH
Mount Street
County Court House
John Hargrave; Newenham Mulligan and Associates
1824-29; 2015-18

Built in the late 17th century, Mullingar market house accommodated petty and quarter sessions and the county assizes. In 1815 it was described as 'an oblong, two-storeyed block, with an open space in front and rere, with eight gateways but no gates', the ground floor occupied at night by drunken men, including soldiers in uniform, and women who were 'outcasts of society' (James Woods, *Annals of Westmeath* (Dublin, 1907)). Perhaps unsurprisingly, by 1820 the Grand Jury considered the building no longer satisfactory. A new court house was built *c.* 1824-29 at a cost of £11,626. It can be attributed on stylistic and circumstantial grounds to John Hargrave, who had completed Mullingar gaol in 1821.

Set behind railings on a corner site, Hargrave's court house is 'a handsome and highly literate Italianate' building according to the NIAH. Ashlar limestone, seven-bay, two-storey classical structure, originally with flanking carriage arches. The centre five bays are prominently advanced. Rusticated at ground floor with an arcade of round-headed arches. The centre three arches are open to form a porch in front of the recessed entrance which is flanked by round-headed windows. The outer two arches of the advanced section contain round-headed windows while those in the set-back end bays are blind. At first floor is a second arcade of recessed round-headed arches, carried on Doric pilasters and with prominent keystones, each containing a window. Shallow, hipped roof behind a continuous cornice and parapet with a scrolled rectangular tablet over the centre bays. The advanced block contained the entrance hall, main stairs and offices while the recessed wings held the Crown and Record courts, lit from square-headed windows set high in the side elevations.

The court house doubled as headquarters for Westmeath Grand Jury, and Westmeath County Council from 1898, until the new council offices and library complex by Bucholz McEvoy Architects – built on the site of Hargrave's gaol to which the court house had once been linked by a tunnel – was completed in 2009. The court house was renovated in the 1970s, when one of the courtrooms acquired new built-in furniture, and again in the 1990s.

Planning for a major refurbishment of the court house began in 2005 and the building was included in the 2015 Courts Bundle Public Private Partnership (PPP) project. The construction company BAM carried out a comprehensive €14m remodelling and extension to designs by Newenham Mulligan and Associates. Bluett and O'Donoghue were conservation architects on the project. The historic building was conserved, with a glass-clad addition on the south side and a stone-clad contemporary structure on the north, linked to the old building by a glazed section. During the works District Court sittings transferred on a temporary basis to St Loman's GAA Clubhouse, Delvin Road. Circuit court sittings had previously been transferred to Tullamore court house. Court sittings resumed on a phased basis from August 2018. The building now has three courtrooms, improved custody capacity, court offices and associated facilities. It officially reopened on 23 November 2018, the final court house in the 2015 PPP bundle to be completed.

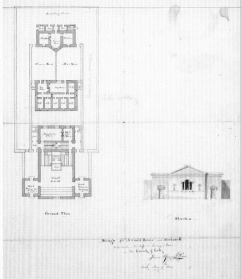

MACROOM, CO. CORK
Barrack Lane
Court House
George Richard Pain
c. 1826

--
Image
Macroom
(Denis Mortell, 2018)

*Design for a court house and bridewell to be built in
the different sessions towns in the County of Cork,*
George Richard Pain, 6 May 1824
(Lismore Papers, NLI)

In December 1823 local landlord Phillip Harding of Firville, Macroom, wrote to the Chief Secretary opposing plans to build a new bridewell and court house in Macroom, noting that the existing facilities were adequate and had been recently improved (NAI CSORP/1823/2211). Nonetheless, a new court house was built, one of seven petty and quarter sessions court houses built in Cork to George Richard Pain's *Design for a court house and bridewell to be built in the different sessions towns in the County of Cork*, dated 6 May 1824. The others are in Bantry, Clonakilty, Kanturk, Mallow, Midleton and Skibbereen. Killarney court house in Kerry is also based substantially on this design.

Macroom was described by J.P. Lawson in the *Gazetteer of Ireland* (1842) as 'new built'. It is a classical building with a three-bay stone façade, the centre bay advanced and pedimented with a Venetian window between two broad plain pilasters. Pedimented entrances, with blank panels above, in the shallow end bays. Ashlar walls to front and to part of the sides before giving way to rubble masonry with square-headed windows. Bridewell to the rear. The double-height courtroom was altered *c.* 1975. A renovation project was completed in 2011 resulting in improved accommodation for legal practitioners, judges, staff and other court users. It remains in court use.

MONAGHAN

Church Square
County Court House
Joseph Welland; John P. McArdle; []; OPW
1827 and 1837-8; 1930; 1986; 2007-10

--
Image
Monaghan, County Court House
(Maurice Craig Collection, IAA, 1957)

William Deane Butler exhibited a design for Monaghan court house in the Royal Hibernian Academy in 1826. However, it was Joseph Welland who received the commission for the building the following year, despite his scheme being unfavourably compared by the Board of Works with Morrison's Tralee court house proposal. Welland produced an essay in academic Greek classicism which the *Buildings of Ireland* notes was his 'most conspicuous debt to his master John Bowden, and one of the few classical buildings attributable to him'. Lewis's *Topographical Dictionary* considers the result 'a handsome modern building of hewn stone, containing spacious court-rooms and all requisite offices, and in every respect well adapted to its purpose'.

On the site of the former gaol, the court house is raised on a podium above Church Square and approached by a flight of nine steps. Built from Carnmore sandstone, quarried at nearby Eshnaglogh, this is a five-bay, two-storey building, the front façade elongated by robust single-storey carriage arches at either end. Engaged, three-bay, distyle portico with squared antae and fluted Doric columns rising through two storeys to support a deep plain entablature and pediment containing a finely carved royal coat of arms. Channelled ashlar ground floor with blind end bays and a central entrance flanked by a pair of square-headed windows, all now behind contemporary screens. Two string-courses separate the floors, and above these are five square-headed windows in lugged architraves.

The side elevations, and internal layout, are similar to William Farrell's court houses at Cavan and Carrick-on-Shannon; rubble walls with tall round-headed windows at first floor providing light to the two double-height courtrooms separated internally by a central corridor.

Welland carried out repairs and alterations to the court house, 1837/38. The building was again altered and also extended by John P. McArdle in 1930. Besides court use, the building came to accommodate a library, County Council offices and Monaghan Museum. Badly damaged by fire in 1981, it was essentially rebuilt within the exterior walls in 1986. Completely refurbished from 2007 to 2010 by the OPW for the Courts Service. The external fabric was repaired, the entrance hall upgraded, and a top-lit central circulation atrium created, dominated by a new public staircase. Three new courtrooms were provided, two for jury courts and one family courtroom. The building officially reopened in February 2011 and won the Public Building of the Year at the 2011 CMG Building and Design Awards.

In front of the court house stands the Monaghan Memorial by Ciaran O'Cearnaigh, a sandstone and metal pillar erected in 2004 in memory of the seven people killed in the Monaghan bombing on 17 May 1974. This has since been joined by the Hive of Knowledge, a sculptural piece made at the International 'Forge-In' held in Monaghan in 2011.

TRALEE. CO. KERRY

Ashe Street

County Court House

William Vitruvius Morrison; Donald Alfred Tyndall; O'Sullivan
Campbell Architects

1828-33; 1953; 1980-81

--
Image
Tralee, County Court House (IAA, late 19C)

A pre-1750s market house in the Square, no longer extant, functioned as Tralee's court house, gaol and market house from the mid-18th century. A new gaol was provided in 1788 and from at least 1807 onwards there were calls for a new court house. Another new gaol was built 1812-17, and the site of the 1788 gaol identified as suitable for the proposed court house. An architectural competition was held in 1828. This was won by William Vitruvius Morrison and the new court house was built from 1830 to 1833 at a cost of at least £9,350.

Closely related to Carlow, this cruciform building of local limestone consists of an extended transverse block, with apse-like ends, set on a high podium with a three-storey rectangular administration block to rear. The courtrooms are disposed at either end of the building, enclosed in curved external walls with pedimented windows. To the front is a monumental hexastyle Ionic portico with plain entablature and pediment, approached by a broad flight of steps. William Vitruvius Morrison's name is inscribed on the entablature at the south end of the portico. Flanking the steps are cannons

on decorated plinths, war memorials commemorating men of Kerry killed in wars in Russia, India and China 1834-60.

Internally, as with Carlow, there were two D-plan top-lit courtrooms, circumscribed by a circulation corridor and lit by large internal lunette windows. The judges' benches were set in broad arched recesses under the lunettes. Between the courtrooms were judges' chambers and a stairwell.

Repaired in 1953 by Donald Alfred Tyndall but vacated by the courts in the 1960s due to the poor condition of the building. Major repairs were undertaken in 1980-81 by O'Sullivan Campbell Architects. The southern courtroom was removed and replaced by a garden. The pedimented windows to the external curved walls of the courtroom ends were filled in and an inappropriate two-storey configuration was created under the portico, with reduced-height doors surmounted by domestic scale windows. It is currently proposed to develop a new court house in the town, with various alternative sites being explored.

CORK
Washington Street
City and County Court House
James and George Richard Pain; William Henry Hill; Cork City Council Architect's Department
1835; 1891; 2003-04

James and George Richard Pain shared first premium with Thomas Deane in the 1830 architectural competition for a new court house for the City and County of Cork. The Pains' design was chosen for execution. The contract was awarded in 1830 and the building was completed by December 1835. Following a devastating fire in March 1890, a second competition had to be held in 1891 for rebuilding the court house. This was won by Cork architect William Henry Hill. The contractor was Samuel Hill of Cork, and works were completed in 1895 although the building was not formally opened until 3 September 1896. The eventual cost of the rebuilding was £27,000: £5,000 more than the Pain brothers' original building.

One of Cork's architectural jewels, and one of the finest neoclassical buildings in the country, the court house occupies an entire block between Washington Street and Liberty Street. The south façade or entrance front is dominated by a magnificent pedimented octastyle Corinthian portico surmounted by a sculptural group by Thomas Kirk, comprising Hibernia, Justice and Commerce. The giant unfluted columns rise from a platform approached on three sides by a flight of eleven steps. The railings which once protected these steps were removed in the early 1960s. Behind the portico rises a copper-clad dome. A deep cornice, circumscribes the building. Corinthian pilasters articulate the recessed bays flanking the portico as well as the east and west sides where

the first two bays at each end are three storey. Between these bays is a two-storey section containing a single pedimented entrance above which is a set of five windows, separated by short pilasters. Below the windows is a cornice with triglyphs and guttae while above the central window is a pediment and swags. Two deep, and one shallow, oriel windows, supported on robust brackets, enliven the three-storey north or rear elevation.

Internally, a marble-clad, arcaded entrance foyer rises three storeys up through the building to be crowned by the dome. Each floor is demarcated by pilasters of a different order – Doric at ground level, next Corinthian, and finally Ionic. The inner hall contains the grand staircase giving access to the first floor where the two double-height main courtrooms, originally the City Court in the east wing and the County Court in the west, retain many of their 1890s fixtures including wooden mouldings and architraves, and cast-iron Ionic columns.

Vacated for nearly a decade due to its poor condition, a major €26 million restoration programme was undertaken by Cork City Council Architect's Department in 2003-04. This included glazing the internal courtyard and adding a tunnel to facilitate prisoner transfer, and the provision of three additional courtrooms, ten consultation rooms, a family law office, and a victim support suite with video link room.

NENAGH, CO. TIPPERARY
Banba Sqaure
County Court House
John Benjamin Keane; John Moynan and Walter Glynn Doolin (portico); Costello Murray Beaumont Architects
1840-44; 1890s and 1909-10; 2004-06

--
Image
Nenagh, County Court House
(Courts Service, 2006)

Nenagh, County Court House
(Courts Service, 2006)

Following the decision to divide Tipperary administratively in two in 1836, Nenagh saw off competition from Thurles to become the location for the county assizes for the North Riding. Assizes were initially held in the old court house situated beside a gaol on Pound Street (now Sarsfield Street). No longer extant, the Orchard Heights local authority housing development now occupies the site.

Architect John B. Keane exhibited his design for a replacement court house in the Royal Hibernian Academy in 1840, the year after a Board of Works loan for the construction was secured by the Grand Jury. Peter Street (later Kickham Street) was laid out c. 1839-40 and a new gaol was built from 1839 to 1842. The court house was placed in front of the gaol to terminate Peter Street and was completed in 1844 at a cost of over £7,000.

Cruciform in plan and standing two-storeys over basement in its own railed grounds, Nenagh court house has an advanced three-bay central block flanked by two courtroom wings. Approached by a flight of steps, a full-height, pedimented tetrastyle Ionic portico gives a pronounced classical emphasis to the building. Beneath the portico are three tall, round-headed entrances set in ashlar walls. The hipped-roofed courtroom wings have rusticated ground floors sitting on an ashlar plinth. Pairs of full-height Doric pilasters frame windows – round-headed above square – and support a plain cornice. The main entrances opened into a double-height hall beyond which were circulation spaces, judges' and jury rooms and a light

well, with the main stairs to the rear. The two courtrooms were polygonal double-height spaces, with columned balconies.

A tunnel was built between the new court house and gaol c. 1843, and the portico repaired by John Moynan and Walter Glynn Doolin in the 1890s. Moynan carried out further alterations and repairs in 1909-10. The *Irish Builder* reported in October 1966 that the building, which had also come to accommodate Tipperary South Riding County Council, was to be reconstructed at a cost of £31,500. The court house had to be closed for safety reasons in 1999.

From 2004 to 2006, the court house was extensively refurbished by Costello Murray Beaumont Architects for the Courts Service at a cost of €11.5 million. Most of the 20th-century accretions were removed and the office wing to the rear extended by the addition of a contemporary, zinc-roofed, square-windowed block. The courtrooms were refitted and the former Grand Jury room, which had been the council chamber of South Riding County Council, was converted to a Family Court. Circulation was improved by the addition of a lift, while the original main staircase, which served only the ground and first floor, was replaced with a new staircase in a more central position.

As part of the reconstruction, a new statue of Justice was set on the acroterion at the apex of the pediment. Replacing a statue which had been removed at the end of the 19th century, the figure was created by Newbridge, Co. Kildare-based artists Anna and Barry Linnane.

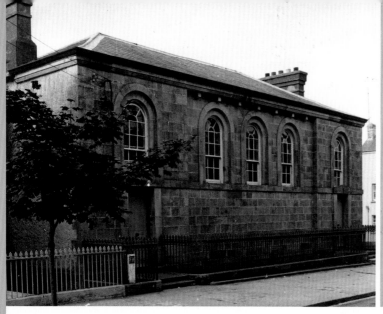

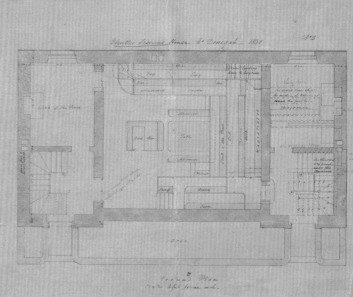

GLENTIES, CO. DONEGAL
Mill Road
Court House
1841-43

--
Image
Glenties
(Alistair Rowan/Buildings of Ireland, 1971)

Glenties. Ground floor plan, 1841
(OPW Collection, NAI)

Glenties court house is a variant of the standard late-1830s – early-1840s petty and quarter sessions court house. There are twenty-seven court houses throughout Ireland which can be regarded as modifications of a common or standard design, beginning with early prototypes at Borris-in-Ossory and Stradbally, Co. Laois, 1826-30, and ending with Carndonagh, Co. Donegal, in 1873. They were, in the main, constructed under the supervision of local county surveyors, though William Deane Butler was also involved in several. William Caldbeck, to whom many have been attributed, designed only one – Newtownards, Co. Down. As Hill notes in her essay in this volume (fn. 96, p. 29), most 'post-date the 1836 [Grand Jury] act, which suggests that, although there was no provision in the legislation for a standard design, the Board of Works may have prepared one'.

An unsigned drawing for Glenties dated 1841 is in the OPW collection in the National Archives. The subject of a dispute between the local Grand Jury and the Lord Lieutenant – the former being unwilling to spend the money the latter demanded on the court house – the building was not completed until 1843. It is a two-storey over basement (containing bridewell), five-bay detached structure set back from the street behind iron railings. Hipped roof with prominent eaves. Ashlar façade with projecting end bays containing entrances in dressed-stone surrounds, the pedimented tops of which sit proud of a platband which merges with the sills of the first floor windows. These are round-headed and set in recesses. The timber-panelled double-height courtroom retained much of its original furnishings. Court use ceased in September 2015 when District Court sittings moved to a community centre across the street, a closure precipitated by a shower of hail falling on court attendees.

ENNIS, CO. CLARE
Lifford Road
County Court House
Henry Whitestone; Dermot and Sean Merry Architects with
Deaton Lysaght Architects
1845-50; 2000-04

Image
Ennis, County Court House
(Courts Service, 2012)

Ennis, County Court House, courtroom
(Courts Service, 2008)

The architect John Benjamin Keane prepared plans and specifications in 1840 for a new court house in Ennis to replace the 17th-century building on Abbey Street. Modelled on his Tullamore court house, this scheme was rejected by the Grand Jury. Keane was also unsuccessful in the architectural competition which the Grand Jury organised in 1845. This was won by Henry Whitestone, whose scheme is not dissimilar to Keane's Tullamore building. Construction of Whitestone's court house began in 1846. The contractor was Burgess of Limerick and the cost was £12,000. The court house opened in 1850.

Set back from the adjacent Gort and Lifford Roads, this imposing detached classical court house is dominated by its impressive full-height hexastyle pedimented Ionic portico approached by a flight of nine steps. Seven-bay, two-storey-over-basement front elevation of fine ashlar limestone, rusticated at basement level. Advanced broad centre bay contains pedimented entrances. More modestly advanced end bays with pedimented windows at ground-floor level. Five-bay side elevations, again with advanced end bays. Two internal courtyards, and two double-height, galleried, U-plan courtrooms at each end of the building.

The building was re-roofed in 1998 and the courtrooms, which retained many of their original fittings, were upgraded and modified from 2002 to 2004 to improve accessibility and acoustics. This was part of an €8.57 million refurbishment for the Courts Service and the OPW by Dermot and Sean Merry Architects, with Deaton Lysaght Architects working on the roof. An additional courtroom for civil and family law was added to the lower ground floor, along with judges' chambers, practitioners' rooms, consultation rooms, jury rooms, victim support facilities, media facilities and public waiting areas. The court house can now accommodate the High, Circuit and District Courts.

In the entrance hall is a statue of Sir Michael O'Loghlen (1789-1842), Master of the Rolls in Ireland, by Joseph Robinson Kirk (1821-94), while outside is a large Russian cannon, a trophy of the Crimean War.

WATERFORD
Catherine Street
County Court House
John Benjamin Keane; []; OPW
1848-49; *c.* 1984; 2015-18

--
Image
Waterford, County Court House
(Maurice Craig Collection, IAA, 1954)

Waterford, County Court House (Courts Service, 2018)

Waterford, County Court House (IAA, c. 1895)

Following the prevention of the transfer of the county assizes to Dungarvan in 1837, discussions began on replacing the existing Waterford City and County Court House. Architect William Tinsley exhibited a design for the new court house at the Royal Hibernian Academy in 1846, the year the Grand Jury submitted a loan application to the Board of Works, but it was a design of John B. Keane which was executed. The site chosen on Catherine Street required the demolition of the last of the ruins of the Augustinian Priory of St Catherine. Construction began in 1848 and the first assizes were held in the completed building in July 1849.

Very similar to Keane's previous court houses in Tullamore and Nenagh, as well as the court house in Ennis, Waterford is a two-storey over basement, classical granite building set back from the street, its grounds demarcated by iron railings. The broad main façade is dominated by a full-height pedimented hexastyle Ionic portico approached by a flight of steps. The portico, once topped by a royal coat of arms, screens an ashlar granite wall with an arcade of five round-headed recesses, the centre three containing entrances. The end bays are recessed, with pedimented ground floor windows and terminating paired pilasters. The side elevations were originally six bays long with tall round-headed windows to first floor providing light to the two courtrooms. These were accessed from a large vestibule to the front while between them were judges' chambers, light wells and circulation spaces. To the rear was an office wing.

By 1977 court use had ceased because the building was in serious disrepair. Extensive works *c.* 1984 allowed court use to resume but saw the building substantially truncated. All that remains of Keane's court house now is essentially a U-plan block formed by the external walls of the two courtrooms and their linking hall. The portico survived, though the royal coat of arms was removed. A utilitarian extension was added to the rear.

As part of the 2015 Courts Bundle Public Private Partnership project, BAM, with Wejchert Architects, carried out a comprehensive €26m remodelling to designs by the OPW. Michael O Boyle of Bluett and O'Donoghue acted as conservation architect. The 1980s extension and a redundant fire station were removed, and the remains of Keane's building completely refitted using a simple palette of materials – granite, copper, glass and oak. A new classically proportioned, four-storey, 6,000 m² cube was added to the rear. This is accessed via a paved courtyard and a contemporary colonnade, a subtle acknowledgement of Keane's classical portico, while at its core is a full-height circular atrium around which six new courtrooms are arranged. The building is universally accessible and contains the necessary facilities of a modern court house. The fifth building in the PPP package to be delivered, Waterford court house officially reopened on 9 April 2018, five days after the first court sittings had been held there.

During the building works court sittings moved on a temporary basis to Grace Dieu Manor on the Tramore-Waterford Road, an 1840s house remodelled by Albert E. Murray from 1892 to 1894 in an Italianate style for T. William Anderson and later used as a retreat house.

Aside from the assizes, and the borough quarter and petty sessions, in the 19th and early 20th century Waterford also had a police court for which order books survive for 1851-97 and 1902-13, and St Patrick's Hall petty sessions, with order books surviving for 1851-1913.

BELFAST, CO. ANTRIM
Crumlin Road
County Court House
Sir Charles Lanyon; Young and Mackenzie
1848-50; 1905-07

Image
Belfast, Crumlin Road, County Court House
(IAA, c. 1980)

Lewis's *Topographical Dictionary* records the variety of courts which sat in Belfast in the 1830s. These included a manorial court, courts leet, petty sessions held by the seneschal and, separately, by the stipendiary police magistrate, a magistrate's court, and quarterly assizes. Buildings which accommodated these courts but are no longer extant included the tholsel, the assembly rooms above the original market house, an 1817 sessions house in Howard Street, adjacent to a gaol and described as being in poor condition and unfit for purpose in 1828 (NAI CSORP/1828/645), and an early 1840s police building in Poultry (later Victoria) Square.

In the late 1830s Belfast finally succeeded in wresting the county assizes away from Carrickfergus and consequently a new county court house had to be provided. In 1841 a site was acquired on Crumlin Road, newly laid out in 1836. A new county gaol was constructed directly opposite this site to designs by Sir Charles Lanyon from 1843 to 1845. In 1848 work began on the court house, also designed by Lanyon and built by James Carlisle at a cost of £22,000. The building which opened in 1850 was a reduced version of Lanyon's highly ambitious original proposal which took its cues from the Parliament House in Dublin but which was rejected on cost grounds. Only the hexastyle portico, with its thirty-foot high columns topped by fine Corinthian capitals, its tympanum with the royal arms, and its statue of Justice by Joseph Robinson Kirk, remain to testify to what might have been.

Beneath the portico three tall doors provided access to a galleried central hall. Beyond this were two courtrooms, Record and Crown. 'Each of these', William McComb reports his 1861 *Guide to Belfast* 'is fifty-five feet in length by forty-one in width, and about thirty in height… The courts are excellently lighted and ventilated, but are decidedly defective in acoustic properties'. For Sir Charles Brett, the courtrooms gave the impression of 'a cross between an anatomy lecture theatre and a Presbyterian church' (*Buildings of Belfast 1700-1814* (London, 1969)). To the rear were the Grand Jury room, judges' chambers, bar rooms and offices. The building was linked by an underground passage to the gaol across the road.

The court house was extended in 1905-07 at a cost of £14,850 by architects Young and Mackenzie, who retained Lanyon's portico, courtrooms and hall, though the gallery was replaced by a corridor and offices. The internal circulation was adjusted and two wings were added, elongating and flattening the façade. Single-storey blocks were inserted to the rear of the wings, flanking the courts on the east and west sides. Closed as a court house in 1998, it was gutted by fire in 2009. In 2018 planning permission was granted for the conversion of what remains into a 'luxury hotel'.

SLIGO
Teeling Street
County Court House
James Rawson Carroll; McCullough Mulvin Architects
1874-79; 1998-2000

James Rawson Carroll won the 1874 architectural competition for the new court house in Sligo with an exuberant Gothic revival scheme. The builder was P. Morris, and the clerk of works a Mr Hutchieson. The original estimated cost was £14,450 and construction was financed via a loan from the Board of Works. The first assizes were held on 5 March 1879, when the court house had only been completed for a few days.

In his *History of Sligo County and Town* (Dublin, 1892), W.G. Wood-Martin provides a detailed description of the court house. 'The style of architecture is Gothic, freely treated. In the front, towards Albert-street, the central feature on the ground floor is an open porch with circular pillars in the centre, and square piers at the angles, carrying three pointed arches; above these there is a group of seven windows with cusped heads and mullions, the whole finishing with a high pitched gable… An important feature in this front is the octagon ventilating tower, which is about 60 feet high to the roof parapet; it has four storeys, and is covered by a slated roof with two ranges of dormers alternating on each of the eight sides, the whole finishing by an iron finial about twelve feet high'.

Internally, Wood-Martin continues, the entrance porch leads 'by a short vestibule to the public hall, which forms the principal means of communication with the courts and the several public offices on the ground floor'. The hall has

'stone staircases leading to the upper floor, enclosed by stone-pointed arcades which continue round the corridor above' and a top-lit, open timber hammer-beam roof. The Crown and Record Courts 'are behind the central hall, with entrances for the public direct from it; they are divided by a wide corridor which leads to the two judges' rooms beyond… Attached to each court are two petty-jury rooms… Both the courts are lighted by windows placed high up in the walls, and they are heated by hot-water pipes'.

From 1998 to 2000 McCullough Mulvin Architects undertook an extensive refurbishment of the building for the Courts Service at a cost of €7.8 million. The fabric was carefully conserved – with special attention given to preserving the character of the existing courtrooms – and sensitively updated to provide the requisite services and facilities for contemporary court use including two new courtrooms, family law facilities, consultation rooms, judges and jury facilities and expanded offices. A new limestone-covered staircase was installed, as was a lift, to improve circulation routes. The south courtyard was revitalised as an urban space for the town, and a new Family Court suite, designed in a clearly contemporary style, was inserted into a derelict block to the rear. Since its official reopening in 2002, the court house has been the recipient of several awards including an RIAI Regional Award, 2002; an Irish Joinery Award for Conservation, 2002; a Europa Nostra diploma, 2003. It was highly commended at the RIAI Conservation and Restoration Silver Medal Awards, 2011.

BELFAST, CO. ANTRIM
Chichester Street
High Court/Royal Courts of Justice
Sir James Grey West
1928-33

--
Image
Belfast, Chichester Street, Royal Courts of Justice
(*Irish Builder*, 1932)

The *Irish Builder* (8 June 1933) reported on the recent opening of the new Royal Courts of Justice in Belfast. The building's 'full beauty is now revealed, and the edifice, which is in the traditional Italian style, with column and pilaster treatment to the main elevations, reflects credit on its architect, Mr J.G. West, O.B.E., of H.M. Office of Works, London. The forecourts towards Chichester Street and May Street, enclosed by low stone balustrades with carriageways to the entrances of the building, and the unpaved portions laid out as grass plots, enable the building to be viewed to advantage from these streets, and are a transformation for the dusty potato market, with its rows of low offices, that formerly occupied the site'.

An exercise in what Brett's *Court Houses of Ulster* calls 'the Recessional-Imperial style of British architecture', the High Court building, as it is more commonly known, was built between 1928 and 1933 to designs by Sir James Grey West, in fulfilment of the requirements of the Government of Ireland Act, 1920. As with its near contemporary, the Northern Ireland

parliament building at Stormont, its vast presence seems inversely proportionate to the size of the state for which it was built. It is a large, steel-framed, Portland stone-clad, hollow (above first floor) rectangle, three storeys to entablature with a fourth above. Thirteen-bay north (Chichester Street) and south (May Street) fronts, with ranks of three-storey engaged and freestanding (at the entrances) Corinthian columns and pilasters. Projecting corner pavilions distinguished by segmental-headed windows in arched recesses at attic level. Plainer, nineteen-bay side elevations, now partially obscured to public view by security walls, with long rows of windows whose architraves diminish in elaboration, floor by floor. The inner-facing walls of each side are of red brick. Cavernous Travertine marble-panelled entrance hall with coffered ceiling, Corinthian pilasters and carved coats of arms above monumental doors at either end. Teak-panelled courtrooms. Damaged by a bomb in 1990, it was subsequently restored and now houses the Northern Ireland Court of Appeal, the High Court of Northern Ireland and the Crown Court in Northern Ireland.

DUBLIN
Smithfield
Children's Court House
OPW
1987

--
Image
Smithfield, Children's Court, courtroom
(OPW, 1987)

Smithfield, Children's Court, side elevation
(OPW, 1987)

In 1973 the Minister for Finance, Richard Ryan TD, announced approval for an architectural competition for the design of a new courts complex to house the Dublin Metropolitan District Court and the Children's Court (which sat in Dublin Castle) on the former Irish Distillers site in Smithfield. Nothing came of this proposal but just under a decade and a half later, in 1987, the Children's Court House was completed in Smithfield to designs by John Tuomey, then of the OPW. It is a three-storey, three-bay by ten-bay building on the corner of Smithfield and New Church Street. Taking its height from a former Jameson warehouse, which adjoins it to the rear, and the Victorian buildings on Smithfield to which it is attached, this is a post-modern red brick court house with a limestone-clad ground floor. The central bay on the narrow entrance front is recessed. Plain columns flank the entrance, above which is a balcony. A second smaller balcony on a concrete strut sits in front of the second floor window above which is a steel and glass pediment-like canopy. The limestone benches which were integrated into the façade on either side of the entrance were removed in the 2000s. Square-headed windows to the side elevation where the courtroom wall is recessed above ground floor and a secondary entrance is marked by a tall triangular oriel window. Beyond the entrance is a large hall with stair access to the first floor where two parallel courtrooms are located, each wood-panelled and with vaulted glazed ceilings. The building won an Architectural Association of Ireland award in 1987.

Immediately adjacent to the court house on Smithfield are two three-storey over basement Victorian office buildings which have been in court use. Red-brick façades, with square-headed windows to basement, ground and second floor, and segmental windows with mouldings and keystones to first floor.

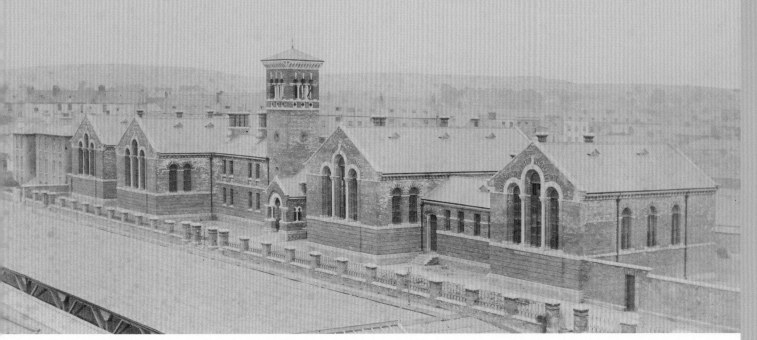

CORK

Anglesea Street

Model School/Court House

James Higgins Owen or Enoch Trevor Owen; OPW

1864-65 (School); **1994**; 2015-18

--
Image
Cork, Anglesea Street, Model School
(IAA, 1866)

The new Model National School on Anglesea Street, Cork, was designed by James Higgins Owen of the OPW, or possibly Enoch Trevor Owen (probably no relation), to whom J.H. Owen assigned his design responsibilities in 1863 and who signed two of the surviving drawings for the building held by the OPW. Red brick Italianate structure with campanile and black brick and stone dressings. Four projecting gable-fronted classroom bays. Tripartite round-headed window in each gable with dressed-stone arches and marble pillars. Construction began in January 1864 and was completed by August 1865.

The building was converted to court use in 1994 by the OPW with two double-height courtrooms inserted into the former classrooms. It closed in 2015 to undergo an extensive €34 million refurbishment and expansion carried out as part of the Courts Bundle Public Private Partnership (PPP) project with construction firm BAM. The architects for the project were the OPW, with Cork-based Wilson Architecture acting for the contractor. The school building was carefully restored to accommodate offices and support facilities, and a new six-storey limestone-clad building was inserted to the rear. The exterior of this new block, completed in April 2018, with its deep window-reveals and use of stone, conveys the impression of a building hewn from one solid mass. Six new courtrooms are provided, their walls clad in European oak balancing the oak furnishings. The court house reopened in May 2018.

DUBLIN
Parkgate Street
Criminal Courts of Justice
Henry J. Lyons
2007-09

Image
Parkgate Street, Criminal Courts of Justice, main hall
(Joshua St John, Courts Service, 2010)

Parkgate Street, Criminal Courts of Justice
(Joshua St John, Courts Service, 2010)

The business case for a new criminal courts complex was made by the Courts Service in 2003. The site adjacent to the Royal Infirmary (Department of Defence) on the corner of Infirmary Road and Parkgate Street, formerly the location of a Garda vehicle pound and the proposed location for a new headquarters for the Department of Arts, Gaeltacht and the Islands, was identified in 2004. The new building was procured via a design and build public private partnership, one of the first such arrangements to be completed in Ireland. In May 2006 a consortium led by Amber Infrastructure Ltd with P.J. Hegarty and Sons and Henry J. Lyons architects was announced as the preferred bidder. Construction began in May 2007 and courts began sitting in the completed building in November 2009, though the official opening did not take place until January 2010.

Standing ten storeys over basement, with 23,000m² of accommodation, the Criminal Courts of Justice is the most significant Irish court house to be erected since the Four Courts and draws unambiguous inspiration from its illustrious antecedent. The new building's cylindrical form reflects the great drum of the Four Courts while its great top-lit, full-height, circular central hall is an even more blatant homage to Gandon's masterpiece. Despite this, the Criminal Courts of Justice is overtly contemporary. Squared-off on its north

side by a concrete and flush-glazing office wing, the primary external expression of the cylinder is a faceted glass and metal façade. Between this and an inner glass layer is a membrane of patterned and folded bronze-anodised aluminium. This complex skin is an integral part of the building's climate control system.

The entrance, beneath a broad glass canopy, is set above the street level, and leads to the large circular atrium containing a black-clad sculptural staircase. A seven-storey window looks out over the Phoenix Park. Around this central space, twenty-two courtrooms are arranged in three balconied layers. These accommodate the Dublin Metropolitan District Court and Dublin Circuit Court, the Central Criminal Court, Special Criminal Court, and the criminal division of the Court of Appeal. The courtrooms are double-height spaces, naturally lit, with walnut panelling and furnishings. Segregated circulation is provided for judicial, professional, custodial and public users. Writing shortly after the building was completed, architect Des McMahon suggested that it 'will doubtless come to symbolise the Irish Justice System in its modernity as did the Four Courts in its time' (*Architecture Ireland*, vol. 250). The Criminal Courts of Justice won the Public Choice Award and Best Accessible Award in the RIAI Architecture Awards 2010.

WEXFORD

Belvedere Road
Tate School/County Court House
Sandham Symes; Edward O'Brien;
Newenham Mulligan and Associates
1864-66 (Tate School); 1905 (Tate School); **2015-18**

--
Image
Wexford, County Court House
(Newenham Mulligan & Associates, 2018)

Wexford, County Court House
(Newenham Mulligan & Associates, 2018)

The refurbishment of the Wexford County Court House at the former county gaol had been under consideration since 2001, but the confined nature of the site limited what was achievable. In 2007 the former Tate School on Belvedere Road was acquired by the Courts Service as a site for a new county court house for Wexford. When William Tate, a Wexford-born Jamaican sugar plantation owner, died in 1795/6, he left instructions in his will for the establishment of a charity school in Wexford for as many pupils, girls and boys, regardless of religious persuasion, as could be admitted. Because of legal disputes, it was not until 1859 that the Court of Chancery could make an order to execute the will and in 1867 the Tate School opened, though – contrary to Tate's wishes – it would only admit Protestant boys. The initial school building was constructed from 1864 to 1866 to designs by Sandham Symes, at a cost of £1,650. It was expanded by Edward O'Brien in 1905. A nine-bay by seven-bay, two-storey, L-plan, red-brick pile with stone quoins to corners, shallow-arched windows and central recessed segmental entrances, the building closed as a school in 1949 and was subsequently used as municipal offices.

The €14 million redevelopment of the school as a court house formed part of the 2015 Public Private Partnership Courts Bundle project. Designed by Newenham Mulligan and Associates for the OPW, with Wejchert Architects acting for the contractor BAM, the school building has been rehabilitated and a substantial new structure added to the rear. Two tall off-set blocks are oriented around an internal courtyard framed by the L-plan school and linked by lower, mainly glazed, elements. The selective use of red brick pays due deference to the existing structure while coloured metal, extensive stone cladding, and distinctive vertical fenestration and ventilation, in particular in the taller elements, provide an overall coherence to the composition.

Four wood-lined, well-lit, double-height courtrooms have been provided in the new building, two at first floor level and two at second. Support facilities, which are located on the ground floor and in the former school, include a public office, a vulnerable witness suite, victim support room and legal practitioners' rooms, enhanced custody facilities, a jury reception room, media room and consultation rooms. It was the third of the Courts Bundle PPP buildings to be delivered. Court sittings commenced on 23 January 2018 and the building was officially opened by Charles Flanagan TD, Minister for Justice, on 19 February 2018.

BELFAST

Chichester Street

Belfast Petty Sessions Court House

Chief Architects Office, Department of Finance NI

1966-67

Designed by the Department of Finance Chief Architects Department, Belfast petty sessions court house was a three-storey, twelve-bay, flat-roofed office block of 1966-67, whose rigorous façade was enlivened by a canopy over the offset three-bay entrance. Built on the site of the former police courts building, the petty sessions court house was in turn demolished to make way for the Laganside Courts Complex.

BELFAST

Chichester Street

Belfast High Court/Royal Courts of Justice

See Significant Court Houses – A Chronological Selection   **P207**

BELFAST

Chichester Street

Laganside Courts Complex   **#006**

Hurd Rolland Architects

2002

Opened in 2002, the sixteen-courtroom Laganside Courts Complex was designed by Scottish architects Hurd Rolland to replace facilities at Newtownabbey court house, Belfast Magistrates Court and the Crumlin Road court house. At the time, it was the largest Private Finance Initiative project in Northern Ireland. The façade facing the Royal Courts of Justice nods in the direction of the earlier building in its extensive planes of Portland stone and the column-like fins to the large central glazed section which could be an entrance but is not. The Oxford Street elevation, with a curved wall of Portland stone and long expanses of bottle-green glazing, is more corporate than civic in appearance, while the opposite side is clad with terracotta façade-system panels. The building was awarded the Liam McCormick Prize for Building of the Year and an Royal Society of Ulster Architects (RSUA) Design Award in 2002.

#004 | Ballymena (Crown DfC Historic Environment Division, 1973)

#005 | Ballymoney (Crown DfC Historic Environment Division, 1973)

#006 | Belfast, Laganside Courts Complex (IAA, 2019)

BELFAST
Victoria Street
Town Hall (former)   #007
Anthony Jackson
1869-71

Standing on the corner of Victoria Street and Chichester Street, the former town hall in Belfast is a two-storey, broadly E-plan, nineteen-bay, red brick pile, with red sandstone dressings. It was completed in 1871 to a competition-winning design by Anthony Jackson. With its mansard roof with balustraded parapet, round-headed windows, and shallow gabled porches to entrances, it is described by Paul Larmour as 'a kind of Franco-Italian job but rather dull' (*Belfast: An Illustrated Architectural Guide* (Belfast, 1987)). Too small, and too modest, once Belfast acquired city status in 1888, it has served various functions since being usurped as the seat of local government by the City Hall in 1906. The building was the headquarters of the Ulster Volunteer Force during the Home Rule Crisis (1913). It has also housed offices of the Provincial Grand Orange Lodge of Ireland and the Ulster Women's Unionist Council. From 1927 to the early 1970s it was primarily in educational use but by 1977 Belfast petty sessions were sitting here. Renovated in 1983 to house a recorders court and ancillary offices, it was severely damaged by a bomb in 1985. The building was restored c. 1999 to accommodate Belfast's Youth, Family and Domestic Proceedings Court.

BUSHMILLS
Main Street
Court House
c. 1835

Looking like a fine townhouse, Bushmills petty sessions court house stood three bays wide, three storeys tall, with its most distinctive feature being the columned and pedimented entrance porch. The court house was built c. 1835 for Sir F.W. Macnaghten. With the courtroom on the first floor, the building also accommodated police and prisoners. It became a private residence in the early 20th century, and has been dilapidated since the 1960s. Bushmills petty sessions were abolished in 1965.

CARRICKFERGUS
Antrim Street
Court House (Town Hall)   #008
Richard Drew
1779

The Franciscan friary in Carrickfergus was built c. 1230. Following disestablishment, it was used for a variety of civic purposes, including as a court house. It survived until the 1560s. The parish church of St Nicholas was also used briefly as a court house, as was the upper floor of the market house built in Market Place in 1755 and still standing, though much altered. Sir Arthur Chichester, who was governor of Carrickfergus from 1598 and became Lord Mountjoy in 1604, had Joymount House built on the friary site in 1613. This was demolished in 1768 to make way for a new court house and gaol. Terminating the view down High Street, the court house is a well-positioned, seven-bay building of 1779 by the otherwise unknown Richard Drew. The three central bays of the single-storey Antrim Street façade are advanced and this façade is enriched by quoins and a cornice with dentils. The pediment above the Doric entrance bears the building date. The large windows, with their original glazing pattern and architraves, are also pedimented, while on the parapet are ball finials and a central curlicued pediment containing a clock. The hipped roof is topped by a copper vent. The Joymount façade is two storeys with a Doric porch to the main entrance, and architraves to the windows. Following the transfer of the county assizes to Belfast in 1850, the building was acquired by the military and used as an artillery barracks. The adjacent gaol was demolished in 1897 to be replaced by an ordnance store. Expanded on a number of occasions, the building became Carrickfergus Town Hall in 1935, in which use it remains. Carrickfergus remained a petty sessions location until 1976, when the court relocated to Newtownabbey court house.

CLOGH/CLOUGH
Court House
c. 1766

Lewis's *Topographical Dictionary* says that Clogh 'is the head of the manor of Old Stone, and contains the manorial court-house, in which the court was formerly held once in three weeks; but the court leet only is now held there. The court-room is large and of good proportions; adjoining it is a jury-room, and underneath are two rooms for debtors, against whom decrees have been issued out of the manor court'. It was reportedly a reconstruction of c. 1766 of an earlier court house, but no building in the village now corresponds exactly to this description, though Brett's *Court Houses of Ulster* considered the Orange Hall or the former dispensary as most likely to incorporate the court house remains.

CRUMLIN
Main Street
Court House
1832

The OS *Memoirs* recorded that Crumlin petty sessions court house was 'situated near the centre of the town. It is a neat, little 2-storey building, erected in January 1832 at the expense of 190 pounds, defrayed by the county. The understorey is suitably fitted up as a court house for holding petty sessions. The upper storey is fitted up as [a] police barracks and contains accommodation for 4 men'. No trace remains.

CUSHENDALL
Market House and Court House
1858

In 1979, the Ulster Folk and Transport Museum took down Cushendall market and court house originally located on the south side of Mill Street, and re-erected it in Ballycultra, the Museum's re-creation of a 'typical' Ulster town. It is a plain, two-storey, five-bay sandstone building with a central, arched entrance at ground floor. According to the Museum, the combined market and court house was built about 1858 by the local landlord, Mr Turnley. The courtroom was on the first floor, and the current re-creation is based on the memories of a solicitor who recalled his father, also a solicitor, defending clients in this room.

DERVOCK
Castlecat Road
Court House

Dervock court house is shown on the third-edition OS map (1900-06) as the first building in a long terrace of two-storey houses on the west side of Castlecat Road, just north of the market house. No longer extant.

DUNMURRY
Glebe Road
Court House

In 1837 the OS *Memoirs* reported that attached to the rear of the 1779 Presbyterian meeting house in Dunmurry was 'a session house, 1-storey high and slated, It measures 19 and a half by 15 and a half feet inside and is lit by 3 oblong windows'. However, Lewis's *Topographical Dictionary* fails to mention Dunmurry petty sessions and Dunmurry was not listed in the 1842 *Petty Sessions Return*. By 1880, a petty sessions area of Legoneil was being listed and in 1897 this area's name was changed to Dunmurry. The third and subsequent editions of the six-inch OS maps show that the court sat in the manse and hall adjacent to the Presbyterian meeting house. The court house remained in this location until 1971, when sittings of Dunmurry petty sessions were transferred to Lisburn before being abolished in 1974.

GALGORM
Court House
1821

The OS *Memoirs* recorded that the only public building in Galgorm was 'the court house which was erected in 1821 by Lord Mountcashel, the proprietor, for holding manor courts and courts leet for the recovery of debts not exceeding 4 pounds 6s 8d by civil bill'. No longer extant.

GLENARM
Toberwine Street
Market House and Court House   #009
pre-1757

Incorporating walls from the medieval Glenarm Castle, the building at the corner of Toberwine Street and Castle Street was originally Glenarm market and court house. There is a reference to repairs being carried out in 1757. The ground floor market was filled in after 1833, and an early tower re-clad as an Italian campanile, noted by Thackeray in his *Irish Sketch Book* of 1843. The imposing two-storey five-bay Toberwine Street stone façade has two impressive pedimented doorcases and windows with unusual hooded architraves at ground floor and large sash windows with lugged architraves above. Glenarm petty sessions were abolished in 1971. The building is now a Baptist church.

KILLAGAN
Court House

Killagan court house stood isolated on the west side of what is now the A6, 1km west of Cloughmills and c. 300m south of Drumadoon House. No longer extant. Killagan was listed as a petty sessions location in 1882, and from at least 1883 as Killagan, Finvoy. It remained a petty sessions location until 1964.

LARNE
Victoria Road
Court House
Samuel Patrick Close
1903

Designed by Samuel Patrick Close, Larne petty and quarter sessions court house is a gable-fronted building facing Victoria Road. It has a large recessed segmental window taking up most of the façade, glazed at ground floor, blind above, and incorporating a shield bearing the date 1903. The keystone to the arch is topped by a small curved pediment, echoing in miniature that of the grand Gibbsian entrance to the right-hand side of the building. Court sittings ceased in 2013, on the transfer of business to Ballymena. Court offices continue to use the building.

LISBURN
Railway Street
Court House   #010
John MacHenry
1884

Based on Palladio's Villa Ragona at Ghizzole, Montegaldella, in the province of Vicenza, the elaborately pedimented, columned and pilastered petty and quarter sessions court house in Lisburn was designed by John MacHenry and cost £4,000 to build in 1884. It replaced a mid-18th-century court house which had itself been rebuilt c. 1830. A tetrastyle Corinthian portico on the two-storey, five-bay entrance front framed a pedimented doorcase above which the central three bays were recessed to form a loggia at first floor level. The tympanum was fully filled by a coat of arms. Corinthian pilasters to corners and a three-bay pedimented side elevation, with large round-headed windows to first floor, and a tympanum containing a simpler coat of arms. Demolished in 1971.

Belfast, former Town Hall. Engraved perspective, *The Builder*, 9 April 1870 (IAA) | **#007**
Carrickfergus (Crown DfC Historic Environment Division, 1974) | **#008**
Glenarm (Crown DfC Historic Environment Division, c. 1970) | **#009**

ANTRIM | ULSTER   219

LISBURN

Railway Street

Court House   #011

Chief Architects Office, Department of Finance NI

c. 1975

Designed by the Chief Architects Office, Department of Finance NI, Lisburn court house was built c. 1975 in a Brutalist idiom on the site of its demolished 1884 predecessor. Flat-roofed, two-storey, and square in plan, it has panelled concrete walls with centre bays of dark glazing. The offset entrance is indicated by a small concrete-roofed porch. It was designated for closure as a court house in 2016, but the decision was deferred and the court house is still in use.

NEWTOWNABBEY

Church Road

Court House

Newtownabbey petty sessions area was created in 1958 on the renaming of Whiteabbey. From 1976, court sittings took place in a facility on Church Road. This was replaced by the Laganside Courts Complex in 2002.

PORTGLENONE

Court House

c. 1795

According to the OS *Memoirs*, Lord O'Neill built a court house in Portglenone c. 1795 for manor court and petty sessions sittings, 'a plain low building 40 feet long and 22 feet wide'. It was also used from 1822 as a schoolhouse. The first-edition OS map shows a school on the east side of the Ballymena road, just to the south-east of the town, but it is not clear if this is the court house and school to which the *Memoirs* refers. The site of the school is now occupied by a Freemasons' hall. Portglenone remained a petty sessions location until 1964.

#010 | Lisburn (demolished) (IAA, c. 1970)
#011 | Lisburn (c. 1975) (Paul Tierney, 2019)'
#012 | Portrush (Lawrence Collection, NLI, late 19C)
#013 | Randalstown (IAA, 2000)

PORTRUSH
Kerr Street/Mark Street
Town Hall   #012
Lanyon, Lynn and Lanyon; A.J.H. Clarke
1872; 1930

Portrush petty sessions area was created in 1879. The sessions were
held in the Town Hall, built by contractor Thomas Stewart Dickson
in 1872 to designs by Lanyon, Lynn and Lanyon, with alterations and
additions in 1930 by A.J.H. Clarke, Portrush Town Surveyor. Red brick,
with black and yellow brick string-courses and black brick detailing,
this is a two- and three-storey Scots-Baronial building featuring an
apse-like end, a stair turret, and stepped gables topped by ball finials.
Portrush petty sessions were transferred to Coleraine in 1969 and
abolished in 1979. Still in local authority use.

RANDALSTOWN
New Street
Market House and Court House   #013
1831

Randalstown had a court house built in 1770, according to the OS
Memoirs, but this is no longer extant. The market house is dated to 1831
and was noted in Lewis's *Topographical Dictionary* as having rooms for
holding court sittings. Two-storey, five-bay detached building, with
recessed single-storey wings, topped off by a cupola with clock. Built
of dark basalt blocks, the ground floor has an arcade of five arched
recesses, the outer two containing fanlit entrance doors and the middle
three round-headed windows. Square-headed windows to upper floor.
Randalstown petty sessions were abolished in 1940. The building now
houses the local library.

RASHARKIN
Moneyleck Road
Court House and Constabulary Barracks

The combined court house and constabulary barracks in Rasharkin
stood on Moneyleck Road at the junction with Bridge Street. The petty
sessions, which had been established in 1844, were abolished in 1936.
A pair of modern houses now occupies the site.

TEMPLEPATRICK (PARKGATE)
Antrim Road
Court House

The OS *Memoirs* noted that Parkgate petty sessions court issued
878 summonses in the period 1833 to 1837, operating from a small
room in a private house 'fitted up for the purpose'. Listed in the 1842
Petty Sessions Return, Parkgate petty sessions area had been renamed
Templepatrick by 1882. By the early 20th century, as shown on the
third- and fourth-edition OS maps, a court house was situated in or
near Boulderstone House, close to the Presbyterian Church on the
south side of the Antrim Road. Templepatrick petty sessions were
abolished in 1971.

TOOME/TOOMEBRIDGE
Main Street
Market House and Court House
1786

The much altered end-of-terrace, two-storey, five-bay former market
house of 1786, located to the east side of Main Street, at the corner of
Roguery Road, served as Toomebridge petty sessions court house. The
market arcade at ground floor is now enclosed by windows and doors.
Five square-headed windows to first floor provided light to an upper
room which housed court sittings. Toomebridge petty sessions were
abolished in 1974.

WHITEHOUSE/WHITEABBEY, BELFAST
Shore Road
Court House

Whitehouse petty sessions court sat in the upper room of Whitehouse
post office, established in 1832, a small detached building on the
corner of Shore Road and Quay Road, at the northern end of
Whitehouse Upper. No longer extant. By the end of the 19th century,
the petty sessions area name had changed to Whiteabbey and the
sessions were being held in a court house on the west side of Shore
Road, just north of the junction with Dillons Avenue. In 1958 the
name of the petty sessions area was changed to Newtownabbey, and
from 1953 to 1977 the former court house served as Whiteabbey Free
Presbyterian Church. Some fabric may remain in the much altered
commercial premises on the site.

ARMAGH
College Hill
County Court House
See Significant Court Houses – A Chronological Selection   **P182**

BALLYBOT (NEWRY)
Kiln Street/Needham (Patrick) Street
Bridewell and Court House
1797

Ballybot bridewell, situated on the north side of Kiln Street, was built in 1797, according to the OS *Memoirs*. A cruciform building with gaoler's accommodation, it had cells for twelve prisoners, though occasionally over thirty were held there, on the ground floor. On the first floor was 'a sessions court 46 feet by 19 with a jury room on each side and a room for the use of the barrister at the end'. A location for petty and quarter sessions until 1900, when Ballybot petty sessions were merged with Newry, the building is no longer extant.

CHARLEMONT
See under Moy, Co. Tyrone

CLONMAKATE
Court House

Clonmakate petty sessions court house was constructed as a court house and constabulary barracks in the mid-19th century on the west side of Clonmakate Road just south of the present Birches Primary School. Clonmakate petty sessions were abolished in 1963 and a modern residence now occupies the court house site.

CRAIGAVON
Central Way
Court House   **#014**
Northern Ireland Works Service
1982-85

The late-20th-century brown-brick, utilitarian court house in Craigavon, now accommodating Magistrates, County and Crown Courts was designed by Northern Ireland Works Service with T.J. McCaw and J.A. Clarke as project architects under Principal Architect W.J. Savage. Construction began in April 1982 and the building was completed in February 1985. Set back from surrounding developments and isolated behind a security wall, this is a multi-bay, two-storey rectangular block with a windowless lift-tower and a full-height glazed element flanking the entrance. The hipped roof is interrupted by two squat pyramidal projections with broad eaves and glazed apexes. 'The unappealing architecture of entrenchment' is the verdict of the *Buildings of Ireland*.

CROSSMAGLEN
Market Square (Cardinal Ó Fiaich Square)
Market House and Court House   **#015**
1865

Replacing an earlier building, Crossmaglen market house was built in 1865 for local landlord Thomas P. Ball. Brett's *Court Houses of Ulster* describes it as 'of five bays; the ground-floor of well-laid black-stone, with granite quoins and three broad central segmental arches; a doorway at either end'. The rendered upper storey had five tall round-headed windows and a central gable with clock which Brett thought 'does not quite amount to a pediment'. It was topped by 'a large bell hanging in a wooden cradle'. The first floor served as the petty sessions court house. Billiard and reading rooms were added by William S. Barber in 1911 and from 1944 the building was being used as a cinema. Crossmaglen petty sessions were abolished in 1965 and the former market and court house was destroyed by fire in July 1974. A new community centre was constructed on the site from 1982 to 1984. Only the ground floor front wall of the old building was retained, screening the centre from the street. The market house bell is on display in the centre's foyer.

FORKHILL
Main Street
Court House

The first building at the south end of the west side of Main Street, Forkhill, is identified on the second-edition OS map (1863-64) as a constabulary barracks and on the third as a court house. Four-bay, two-storey random-coursed stone building with blocked architraves to square-headed windows, an arched surround to the main entrance, and a second, square-headed entrance flanked by double windows. Forkhill petty sessions sittings were transferred to Newtownhamilton in 1971.

KEADY
Market House and Court House
Fitzgibbon Louch
1870

Lewis's *Topographical Dictionary* reports that Keady petty sessions were held 'in the court-house every Friday'. The courts sat in the market house which Lewis considered 'commodiously arranged' but which the OS *Memoirs* reported as 'a very small and insignificant erection, with no point deserving of observation about it'. It was replaced in 1870 by a new market house by architect Fitzgibbon Louch, whose name appeared on the building in mirror writing alongside that of the contractor, John Cullen, in normal script. An exercise in polychromatic Venetian Gothic – stone and red-brick with black and white brick bands – it had a circular clock-tower topped by a conical roof. The building was destroyed by a bomb in 1970 and Keady petty sessions were transferred to Armagh before being abolished in 1971. It was replaced by an unprepossessing brown-brick library.

LOUGHGALL
Main Street
Market House and Court House
1746

'The court house, situated at the north-east end of the town of Loughgall', says the OS *Memoirs*, 'is a plain stone building, roughcast, whitewashed and slated, 52 feet long and 29 feet broad, built in 1746. The upper part of the building is used as a court house and the under as a market house'. No less a figure than Edward Lovett Pearce prepared plans for a replacement, but the four-bay, two-storey 1746 building still stands and, despite losing its whitewash, is still recognisable from the OS *Memoirs* description. Four-arch market arcade to ground floor with four square-headed windows above. Court use continued until 1938 when Loughgall petty sessions were abolished. The building is now a commercial premises.

LURGAN
Church Place
Court House
1802; c. 1830

A nearly square, detached, sessions house is shown on the first-edition OS map of Lurgan, just north of Christ Church. Gothic in style, it had been erected in 1802 with a bridewell below the court room. Renovated c. 1830 at a cost of £1,633, it is described in Lewis's *Topographical Dictionary* as a 'large, handsome, and well-arranged building'. Following the construction of a new court house in 1872, it was demolished.

LURGAN
William Street
Court House   #016
Henry Davison and Thomas Turner
1872

Designed by Henry Davison, Armagh County Surveyor, and Thomas Turner, Lurgan's new petty and quarter sessions court house was constructed in 1872 on a triangular site at the junction of William Street and Charles Street. The contractor was McLaughlin and Harvey of Belfast and the building cost £4,000. Polychromatic, with yellow-brick walls on a black stone plinth, multiple red-brick bands and sandstone dressings. A four-bay, two-storey, pitched-roof block with tall, bridged chimneystacks and a semi-circular apse at its south end below a pedimented gable. This is fronted by a single-storey flat-roofed, elongated porch, rising to a pediment towards its north end and terminating in a carriage arch, with twin round-headed arches on three short stone columns, their capitals richly detailed, leading to recessed opposed entrances. The windows are segmental-headed, except for the two beneath the pediment to the right of the entrance arches, which are round-headed. Four-bay, flat-roofed projection to the rear. Court use ceased following the opening of the court house in Craigavon and in 1996 the building was converted to a licensed premises.

Craigavon (Paul Tierney, 2019) | #014
Crossmaglen (Crown DfC Historic Environment Division, 1973) | #015
Lurgan (Lawrence Collection, NLI, late 19C) | #016

ARMAGH | ULSTER   223

ULSTER

MARKETHILL

Main Street

Court House   #017

Thomas Duff; Consarc Design Group

1842-43; 1999-2000

'Petty sessions are held every Friday' in Markethill, according to Lewis's *Topographical Dictionary*, 'and quarter sessions for the county, alternately with Ballybot, in a neat sessions house'. This court house was one of the few public buildings listed in the village by the OS *Memoirs*. Located at the north end of the west side of Main Street, it was replaced in 1842-43 by a new court house designed by Thomas Duff, who was paid £48 2s 6d for providing the working drawings and specifications. The two-storey, three-bay building in squared and coursed dark stone was originally T-plan, with a wide advanced, pedimented, central bay containing a square-headed Wyatt window in a plain stone surround above a double-door flanked by square-headed windows. Dressed-stone quoins to corners and sill-level platband extending the full width of the building and along the sides. Recessed panels to ground floor of the set-back side bays beside square-headed entrances, with square-headed windows above. Wyatt windows to first floor of side elevations, above small square-headed windows. Rendered block to rear. Octagonal domed lantern to centre of hipped roof. Closed as a court house in 1940 and converted to a clothing factory in 1954. Unoccupied from the mid-1970s, it was added to the Ulster Architectural Heritage Society (UAHS) 'Buildings at Risk' register before being renovated by Consarc Design Group in 1999-2000 at a cost of £894,000 to become a multi-purpose community hall.

MIDDLETOWN

The Diamond

Market House and Court House   #018

1829

'There is a large public building erected in the year 1829', the OS *Memoirs* reports of Middletown, 'the upper part of which is used as a court and session house and the lower part as a market house'. As recorded on a plaque on the building, it was erected by the trustees of a charitable bequest left by John Sterne (1660–1745), Bishop of Clogher. Two-storey, four-bay, hipped-roofed building in ashlar limestone to the front and rubble stone to the sides. Two segmental market arches to centre, now filled in, with entrances in segmental recesses in the slightly advanced end bays. Square-headed windows to first floor. Flanked by two gateways with stone piers providing access to the rear where a large late-20th-century extension has been added. No trace remains of the 'clock and cupola' recorded in 1838. It is now a community hall.

#017 | Markethill (Crown DfC Historic Environment Division, 1973)
#018 | Middletown (Crown DfC Historic Environment Division)
#019 | Portadown (Lawrence Collection, NLI, late 19C)
#020 | Tynan (Crown DfC Historic Environment Division, c. 2010)

NEWTOWNHAMILTON
The Square
Court House

Newtownhamilton, Lewis's *Topographical Dictionary* records, had 'an excellent court-house, in which the quarter sessions for the county were held till 1826, since which time they have been removed'. Described in Brett's *Court Houses of Ulster* as 'a small dull single-storey building on a sloping site, with a basement tucked in at the rear only, a hipped roof, a rendered front, and an arched doorway visible from the street'. It was repeatedly damaged by bombs and subsequently rebuilt as a community centre; only the arched doorway remains. Newtownhamilton petty sessions were abolished in 1979.

PORTADOWN #019

'A large and commodious market-place, with shambles and every requisite, has been recently erected by subscription, and is under the regulation of a committee' (OS *Memoirs*). This is possibly where Portadown petty sessions were held, for the town otherwise lacked a specifically designated court house. No longer extant. The local ratepayers objected to the replacement of Lurgan court house in 1872 on the grounds that they wanted to build a court house in Portadown instead, and plans for Portadown court house were prepared, but nothing came of this. The building identified in a William Lawrence photograph as Portadown court house is in fact the red-brick, twin-gabled town hall, built in 1890 to designs by Thomas and Robert Roe. However, the identification suggests that petty and quarter sessions were in fact held there.

POYNTZPASS
Railway Street
Court House

Petty sessions hearings did not take place in Poyntzpass until 1851, and a three-bay, two-storey, mid-19th-century end-of-terrace house on the north side of Railway Street became the local court house. Pitched roof, quoined on one side, square-headed openings and with a lintelled door surround. Now in use as a restaurant called, appropriately, 'Petty Sessions', though Poyntzpass petty sessions were abolished in 1936.

TANDRAGEE
The Square
Court House

The OS *Memoirs* reports that 'petty sessions are held every alternate Tuesday in Tanderagee, in a house hired for the purpose for 10 pounds paid by the county'. A building at the north end of the west side of the Square is marked as 'Court Ho.' on the third-edition OS map (1905-09). Externally, this presents as a mid-19th-century five-bay, two-storey, end-of-terrace house, with a segmental-arched central entrance, but the entire terrace was in fact replaced behind the façade by local authority housing in the latter part of the 20th century. Tandragee petty sessions were abolished in 1979.

TYNAN
Main Street #020
Court House

The OS *Memoirs* merely records that there was a court house in Tynan, a building in which the petty sessions were held 'every second Wednesday and at Middleton on the alternate Wednesdays' (Lewis's *Topographical Dictionary*). The structure now identified as the former court house is a curiosity, a two-storey, three-bay, three-sided, attached rubble-stone building on the corner where Dartan Ree turns into Main Street. Entrances in the end bays, one in a red-brick surround, and a square-headed window in the centre bay, all set in relieving arches. At first floor, small square-headed windows with red-brick lintels sit on the apexes of the arches. The arches suggest that this may have been built as a market house, with court sittings taking place on the first floor.

BAGENALSTOWN/MUINE BHEAG

Main Street/Bachelors Walk

Court House   #021

Daniel Robertson; []

c. 1825; 1992

Lewis's *Topographical Dictionary* describes Bagenalstown petty and quarter sessions court house as 'a handsome building in the Grecian style, in front of which is a portico with four Doric [sic] pillars'. References in the second (1824) and fifth (1827) Annual Reports of the Inspectors General for Irish Prisons suggest a date of 1825-26 for the building. Erected at the expense of Philip Bagenal, it is attributed to Daniel Robertson who had several members of the extended Bagenal family as clients. A single-celled Roman temple sitting on a slightly raised platform, the court house turns its back on Main Street to face out over its sloping site. Its most distinctive feature is a four-column wide by two deep Ionic portico. The building was restored in 1992 and converted for use as a public library. A single-storey extension was added to the rear while the former courtroom retained some of its fixtures including the judge's bench, which became a checkout desk, and witness box, which served as a reference area.

BAGENALSTOWN/MUINE BHEAG

Fair Green

Court House and Fire Station   #022

1990

A 1990 utilitarian red brick and concrete building occupying a corner of the Fair Green and incorporating the fire service in one wing and a court house in the other. The court house section closed in 2005 when Bagenalstown/Muine Bheag District Court was amalgamated with Carlow.

BORRIS

Main Street

Court House

An irregularly planned petty sessions court house is shown on the 25-inch OS map of Borris, set back from Main Street behind a terraced three-bay, two-storey over raised-basement house of c. 1835 (now part of Step House Hotel) opposite Sir Richard Morrison's monumental turreted gateway to Borris House. No trace of the court house seems to remain. Borris was designated a District Court location in 1924 but not in 1961.

CARLOW

Court Place

County Court House

See Significant Court Houses – A Chronological Selection   P198

#021 | Bagenalstown (c. 1825) (IAA, c. 1985)

#022 | Bagenalstown (1990) (Denis Mortell, 2019)

FENAGH/FENNAGH

Fenagh, or Fennagh, is listed in the 1842 *Petty Sessions Return*, and court order books survive for 1851-74. However, Fenagh had ceased to be a petty sessions location by 1882. A court house remains to be identified.

HACKETSTOWN
Main Street
Court House   #023

Attached, three-bay, single-storey mid-19th-century court house on the north side of Main Street, with a mid-20th-century flat-roofed porch to front. Following the amalgamation of Hacketstown District Court with Baltinglass in 1998, the building became Hacketstown Credit Union.

MYSHALL
Court House

It would appear that Myshall petty sessions were held in the constabulary barracks, which stood just to the west of the grounds of the Adelaide Memorial Church, but is no longer extant.

TULLOW
Barrack Street
Court House   #024
[Thomas Alfred Cobden]
1825-26

The petty and quarter sessions court house in Tullow is a detached, stone-faced building of c. 1825-26, whose façade is enlivened by a modestly pedimented parapet below which are three semi-circular windows at first floor level and two granite-framed entrance doors. The double-height courtroom, with galleries on either side, was lit by a large arched window in the end wall. The *Dictionary of Irish Architects* records that Thomas Cobden carried out work to the Grand Jury room in 1828. He may have designed the whole building. Damaged in 1920 during the War of Independence and subsequently repaired. Tullow District Court was amalgamated with Carlow in 2007 and the building, no longer in use as a court house, has served as both offices and a library.

ARVA/ARVAGH

Main Street/Market Square

Market House and Court House   #025

[John Farrell or William Deane Butler]; []

c. 1833; 2000

Set back from Main Street, the seven-bay (at ground floor) market and court house in Arva has an advanced ashlar middle section consisting of a large arched entrance with three square-headed windows at first floor, surmounted by a pediment with lunette window. Brett's *Court Houses of Ulster* attributes it to William Deane Butler but, based on surviving drawings dated 1833 in the Gosford Estate muniments, the *Buildings of Ireland* prefers John Farrell. The centre block was originally flanked by single-storey wings. These were extended to two storeys c. 1912. Having served a variety of purposes including, partially, a private house, a turf accountant and a travel agency, the building was renovated in 2000 for the Courts Service as a shared facility with Cavan County Council to provide District Court and library facilities. Arvagh District Court was amalgamated with Cavan in 2008.

BAILIEBOROUGH

Main Street

Court House   #026

[]; George Beckett; Patrick Joseph Brady

1817; 1910; 1928

The petty and quarter sessions court house in Bailieborough was built in a classical style for local improving landlord Colonel William Young, c. 1817. Detached, three-bay, two-storey building with a stuccoed façade, hipped roof and broad modillioned eaves. Front porch and bridewell to rear added 1834. Large, double-height courtroom renovated c. 1910 by George Beckett to include a gallery, judge's canopy and jury-box balcony. Further repairs were undertaken by Patrick Joseph Brady in 1928 following a War of Independence fire, and the building was renovated in 2006 for the Courts Service. Bailieborough District Court was amalgamated with Virginia in 2010, and the court house closed. Efforts to convert the building to community use have been ongoing since 2016.

BALLINAGH/BELLANANAGH

Court House

The petty sessions court house in Bellananagh stood on the west side of Main Street at the south end of the village, adjacent to the entrance to Corstruce House. A 20th-century bungalow now occupies the site.

BALLYCONNELL

Church Street

Court House   #027

William Deane Butler; Patrick Joseph Brady

1833; c. 1919

Detached, two-storey petty and quarter sessions court house of 1833 built to replace the existing court house in Ballyconnell which was subsequently converted into a stable by local attorney, Thomas Cochrane. Designed by William Deane Butler, and similar to his court house in Cootehill. Set behind a forecourt, demarcated by a low wall topped by railings. Symmetrical, three-bay, stone façade, the centre bay advanced and pedimented, with string-course dividing ground and first floors. Entrance porch with paired square columns flanked by blind arched recesses. Three square-headed windows to first floor, the centre one larger and tripartite. The return to the rear originally held cells. Interior, including double-height courtroom, refurbished c. 1919 by Patrick Joseph Brady following a fire. Maintenance work was carried out by the Courts Service in 2006. Ballyconnell District Court was amalgamated with Cavan in 2013, since when the court house has been in occasional cultural use.

BALLYJAMESDUFF

Stradone Street

Court House   #028

Joseph Patrick Brady

1927-28

Looking like a congregational hall, Ballyjamesduff court house – originally a school converted to court house use – was rebuilt by Patrick Joseph Brady in 1927-28 following a fire. Set behind railings in its own grounds on Stradone Street, this is a simple, three-bay gable-fronted hall containing the courtroom, with a smaller gable-fronted entrance porch and, to the rear, a second porch and judge's chamber projecting at right angles, both with handsome chimneys. Closed following the amalgamation of Ballyjamesduff District Court with Virginia in 2005.

BAWNBOY

Court House

Bawnboy petty sessions were held in one of a small cluster of what look like vernacular rubble-stone farm outhouses still standing behind the Keepers Arms Hotel.

BELTURBET

The Diamond
Town Hall and Court House   #029
Patrick Joseph Brady
1928

Built in 1928 to designs by Patrick Joseph Brady on the site of, and
to replace, Belturbet's mid-18th-century market house which was
destroyed by fire in 1926, this gable-ended, seven-bay, two-storey
block accommodated a courtroom, county council offices, library and
concert hall. On a plinth overlooking the Diamond, approached by a
flight of six shallow steps which are flanked by stone figures holding
lamps. The central three bays, highlighted by quoins, are recessed
and surmounted by a small pediment containing a clock. Bracketed
string-course and cornice provide a classical emphasis. Round-headed
windows to ground floor, with square-headed entrance and square-
headed windows above. It is no longer in court use, Belturbet District
Court having been amalgamated with Ballyconnell in 2005.

BLACKLION

Main Street
Court House   #030

The end-of-terrace, stone-built market house of c. 1830, restored in
2000 as a tourist centre, accommodated Blacklion petty sessions for
a time. Three-bay, two-storey building with a segmental market arch
(now a window) flanked by square-headed openings to ground floor,
and square-headed windows above. Two further segmental arches in
east side elevation, with a clock in the side gable. By the end of the
19th century, its neighbour but one, the terraced house immediately
adjacent to the site on which the Garda station was later built, had
come to serve as the local court house and dispensary. Blacklion was
designated a District Court location in 1924, but not in 1961.

CAVAN

Farnham Street
County Court House
See Significant Court Houses – A Chronological Selection   P192

COOTEHILL

Market Street

Court House #031

William Deane Butler; []

1831-32; 1978

Cootehill's petty and quarter sessions court house is a detached, two-storey structure described in the OS *Memoirs* as a 'handsome modern building… erected in the years 1831 to 1832'. This makes it slightly earlier than the similar court house in Ballyconnell which is also by William Deane Butler. Set back from the street, the rubble-stone façade, with dressed architraves, quoins and string-course, has an advanced, pedimented central bay with a pedimented doorcase at ground floor and a recently reinstated Wyatt window above. Shallow arched recesses beneath relieving arches flank the entrance door, one containing a recessed square-headed panel and the other a window. Extended and altered internally in 1978. Cootehill District Court was amalgamated with Cavan in 2010. The building remains in local authority use.

DOWRA

Main Street

Court House and Garda Station #032

c. 1930

Dowra became a petty sessions location in 1881 and the court house was set back from the west side of Main Street. A new U-plan building to accommodate both the District Court and the local Garda station was provided c. 1930, built on the site of the previous court house and reflecting the disposition of the buildings it replaced. Detached, six-bay, two-storey structure with significantly advanced end wings, one bay wide by two deep. In the middle is a pair of tall round-headed windows (lighting the centrally placed courtroom) flanked by round-headed doors topped by oculi. Square-headed windows in wings. Rough-cast walls with quoins on corners of wings. Hipped roof with tall brick chimneys, a central ventilator and overhanging bracketed eaves. The courtroom retained its original furniture into the 2000s. Dowra District Court was amalgamated with Ballyconnell in 2006, while the Garda station transferred to a new building across the street before being closed in 2013.

KILLASHANDRA/KILLESHANDRA

Main Street

Market House

Lewis's *Topographical Dictionary* notes that 'a manorial court is held occasionally' in Killashandra 'and petty sessions every alternate Thursday'. Possibly the courts sat in the market house, a 'very neat and well-arranged building' which stood on Main Street where Market Avenue is now.

#029 | Belturbet (NIAH, 2012)

#030 | Blacklion (Paul Tierney, 2019)

#031 | Cootehill (Roger Hill, 1998)

KILNALECK
The Green
Court House

The petty sessions court house in Kilnaleck occupied the mid section of a long, narrow building at a right angle to the Green. This structure would appear to still stand, rubble-walled and with a corrugated iron roof.

KINGSCOURT
Market Square
Market House and Court House
c. 1800

Kingscourt market house is shown on the 25-inch OS map as 'Market House and Court House'. Built c. 1800 and described by the *Buildings of Ireland* as the 'pivotal' building in the town, it stood at the top of Market Square on the west side of Main Street and incorporated an arch which straddled the roadway. Demolished in the mid 20th century, after which the parochial hall was used for court sittings. Kingscourt District Court was abolished in 2005 on amalgamation with Bailieborough.

MOUNTNUGENT/MOUNT NUGENT

Mountnugent or Mount Nugent was a petty sessions location from at least 1842, and court order books survive for 1876-70 and 1895-1914. However, a petty sessions court house has not been identified.

MULLAGH
Court House

Mullagh petty sessions court house is shown on the 25-inch OS map on the north side of the road 200m east of Mullagh crossroads and 2.5km west of Mullagh town, directly opposite the old gates to Mullagh Cottage. A building is shown on the site on the first-edition OS map. The *Irish Builder* of 8 June 1912 reported that a 'special meeting of the Roads Committee of Cavan County Council was held, when Mr. Henry McGeough, builder, Monaghan, was declared the contractor for taking down and rebuilding Mullagh Courthouse at £289 10s. The estimate of the county surveyor, Mr R. N. Somerville, B.E. was £325'. A three-bay, single-storey house with attached shed/garage stands on the site now, presumably the repurposed rebuilt court house.

SHERCOCK
Main Street
Court House and Constabulary Barracks   #033

A long, low market house stood on the south side of the west end of Main Street, the upper floor of which could have been used for petty sessions sittings. Divided into two separate premises, it still retains a tall arched recess in its south gable and, at first floor, seven long tripartite windows set in flat, blocked, surrounds. By the time the 25-inch OS map was published, Shercock court house shared accommodation with the constabulary barracks. This would appear to have been in a detached, three-bay, two-storey building on the south side of the east end of Main Street (opposite the modern Credit Union building). Now a commercial premises. Shercock was a District Court location until 1961 when it became part of the Bailieborough District Court Area.

SWANLINBAR
Court House

The petty sessions court house in Swanlinbar stood on the south side of the Cladagh (or Swanlinbar) River, west of the Methodist church and adjacent to the Fair Green. No longer extant. Listed as a District Court location in 1924, Swanlinbar became part of the Ballyconnell and Bawnboy District Court Area in 1927.

VIRGINIA
Main Street
Market House and Court House   #034
c. 1830; 1930; 2006-08

The early-19th-century market house in Virginia is a tall, three-bay, two-storey block with additions to the rear. Rendered walls with stone dressings. The Main Street façade retains a pair of stone market arches, now filled in and converted to windows. A small fanlit entrance stands between them, with a second entrance (formerly a small window) to one side. Already in use as a court house, the building was purchased by the OPW from the Marquess of Headfort in 1930 and subsequently remodelled as a 'properly equipped' court house. The courtroom retains fittings and furniture from this time. Refurbished in 1973, and again from 2006 to 2008 when the building lost some of its most distinctive features, including the ventilator from its roof, the original mullioned casement windows, and an external cast-iron staircase which provided access to first-floor offices. Still in use.

BALLYVAUGHAN
Court House #035

Although not listed in the 1842 *Petty Sessions Return*, Ballyvaughan had become a petty sessions location by the late 1850s. A photograph by Robert French in the Lawrence Collection in the National Library is titled 'Court House, Ballyvaughan'. It shows a three-bay, single-storey detached, vernacular thatched cottage, with square-headed openings, a door to the right and two asymmetrically sized windows to the left, with a third window in the end gable. This cottage certainly served as a court house on at least one occasion. In her *Three Months' Tour in Ireland, translated and condensed by Mrs Arthur Walter* (London, 1891), Marie-Anne de Bovet recorded that 'there has been a stir in the peaceful village of Ballyvaughan lately, for judgement was given against the murderer of a policeman in a little cottage, which since then has been jokingly named "The Court of Justice of Her Majesty the Queen."' No longer extant.

BROADFORD
Court House

Broadford petty sessions court house was situated at the T-junction in the centre of the village, on the west side of the main village street. Listed in the 1842 *Petty Sessions Return*, but no trace of the court house remains. However, court order books survive for 1898-1911.

CARRIGAHOLT
The Square
Court House

Carrigaholt petty sessions court house shared a premises with the local dispensary at the east end of the terrace on the south side of the Square. The building still stands, a vernacular five-bay, two-storey rubble-stone house.

COROFIN
Bridge Street
Market House and Court House #036
c. 1670

Although bearing an O'Brien coat of arms dated 1876, the market house in Corofin dates from c. 1670. It is a rendered, end-of-terrace, six-bay, two-storey building, standing above the street on a cut-stone raised plinth. Round-headed openings to ground floor and small square-headed windows above. It is shown as 'Court & Market House' on the 25-inch OS map. Three front wall buttresses of c. 1750 were removed in 2005 when the building was renovated for residential use and extended to rear. Corofin District Court was amalgamated with Ennis in 2008.

CRUSHEEN

Lewis's *Topographical Dictionary* states that petty sessions were held in Crusheen 'once a fortnight, and the road sessions for the district, are held here; also a seneschal's court occasionally for the manor of Bunratty, in which small debts are recoverable'. Listed as a petty sessions location from 1842, and court order books survive for 1864-1912. A specific court building has yet to be identified.

DOONASS

According to Lewis's *Topographical Dictionary*, Doonass petty sessions were held weekly on Friday at Clonlara or Cloonlara, where a manorial court was also occasionally held for the recovery of small debts. Listed as 'Doonass' in 1842 and as 'Doonass or Cloonlara' in 1915; no court house has been identified.

ENNIS
Abbey Street
Market House and Court House #037

Courts in Ennis sat in the Franciscan friary from as early as 1571, and then in two succeeding market and court house buildings, one built pre-1642 and damaged in 1690, and its successor built c. 1733-40. This is depicted by William Turner de Lond in his painting of the Market Square, Ennis. James Pain carried out repairs to the building in 1820-21, Michael Fitzgerald carried out alterations in 1825, and John Herbert was appointed contractor in 1830 to keep the court house in repair. After the new court house came into use, the Abbey Street building was demolished in 1852 to make way for the O'Connell Monument, though part of a wall survives in an end-of-terrace four-storey shop and house.

ENNIS
Lifford Road
County Court House
See Significant Court Houses – A Chronological Selection P203

MOUNTSHANNON/MOUNT SHANNON
Court House

Mountshannon was included in Galway until 1900. The court house is indicated on the first-edition OS map as 'Pettit Sessions Ho. & Savings Bank' and on the 25-inch map as 'Petty Sessions House', and located on the south side of the road just east of the point where Mountshannon Court intersects the main village street. The site of the court house is now occupied by an early- to mid-20th-century cottage. Mountshannon became part of Tuamgraney District Court Area in 1924.

NEWMARKET-ON-FERGUS

Lewis's *Topographical Dictionary* records that petty sessions were held in Newmarket-on-Fergus 'on alternate Thursdays, and a court for Lord Egremont's manor of Bunratty is occasionally held by the seneschal, for the recovery of small debts'. Elsewhere Lewis reports that the Newmarket petty sessions were held 'at Rathfoland, on the southern border of the parish [of Kilnasoolagh], immediately adjoining the town'. Slater's 1881 *National Commercial Directory of Ireland* noted the town had a 'court house, in which petty sessions are held every alternate Thursday'. Court order books survive for 1841-1914. Newmarket was listed as a District Court Area in 1924 but not 1961. A specific court house has not been identified.

QUIN
Court House

Quin petty sessions court house is indicated on the 25-inch OS map as being located at the western end of the village on the site where the Village Inn public house now stands.

SCARRIFF

Not a site of a petty sessions court, Scarriff is listed as the place where Tuamgraney District Court would sit in 1950 and again in 1965. Scarriff had its own District Court from 1997 to 2008, with the court sitting in the local GAA club.

SHANNON

Shannon became a District Court Area in 1978. It was amalgamated with Sixmilebridge in 2000 and abolished in 2012. The court sat in Shannon Community Hall.

SIXMILEBRIDGE
Lodge Road
Court House

The court house in Sixmilebridge is a detached, five-bay, single-storey structure with advanced end bays and an off-centre fanlit entrance beside which is a small plaque bearing the title 'Teach na Cúirte'. Original roof replaced with flat roof in 1997. The courtroom retained some original furniture until closure in 2012 when Sixmilebridge District Court was amalgamated with Ennis, after which the building was made available for community use. Behind the court house is a late-18th-century two-storey, six-bay, rubble-stone bridewell with hipped roof, fanlit entrance and round-headed windows in arched recesses. This is now a private residence.

TUAMGRANEY/TOMGRANEY
Court House

According to the 25-inch OS map, the left-hand building of a pair of three-storey houses (once part of a longer terrace) on the east side of the village main street, at the junction with Raheen Road, appears to have served as Tuamgraney petty sessions court house. Two bays wide, with a fanlit entrance, the building has lost its original render, leaving exposed the rubble-stone walls and brick lintels. Tuamgraney (or Tomgraney) was listed as a District Court Area in 1924 but by statutory instrument dated 1950 sittings were moved to Scarriff. Tuamgraney was again listed as a District Court Area in 1961 but in 1965, once more by statutory instrument, sittings were relocated to Scarriff.

TULLA
Main Street
Court House   **#041**
[James Boyd]; []
1837; 2005

Very similar to the court house in Killaloe, and also attributed to County Surveyor James Boyd, Tulla is a variation of the standard late-1830s – early-1840s petty and quarter sessions court house design. It is a detached building with a five-bay, single-storey ashlar main façade, the centre three bays containing tall round-headed windows at first floor level whose sills merge to form a platband. The end bays are slightly advanced, with pedimented entrances surmounted by blank decorative panels. A clock in an ornate pedimented stone frame perches on the parapet above the centre window. Two-storey, three-bay east side elevation, with dressed-stone surrounds to windows. Blank elevation to west side. Single storey return to rear where two large round-headed windows provide light for the courtroom. In court use until 2005, after which it was restored and extended to the rear with grant assistance from the Department of Culture, Heritage, and the Gaeltacht in order to provide a community facility.

WHITEGATE
Court House

A 'Petit Sessions Ho.' is shown on the first-edition OS map of Whitegate, on the west side of the road at the south end of the village. No longer extant. The 1842 *Petty Sessions Return* notes that the petty sessions of Whitegate and Mountshannon (both of which are listed in the Return under Galway) 'are in union, and are held alternately, that is once a month, for the district'. Whitegate is not listed as a petty sessions location after 1842.

Killaloe (Courts Service, c. 2000) | **#039**
Kilrush (Denis Mortell, 2019) | **#040**
Tulla (IAA, c. 1985) | **#041**

CARRIGALINE
Carrigaline Cross Roads
Court House

Carrigaline petty sessions court house occupied a corner building at Carrigaline Cross Roads, opposite the constabulary barracks. The site of this court house is now under the Cork Road Roundabout at the north end of Main Street. Court sittings subsequently transferred to a building 200m south, on the west side of Main Street. Carrigaline District Court was amalgamated into Cork City District Court Area in 2001.

CARRIGBOY/CARRICKBUE/CARRIGBUI (DURRUS)
Main Street
Court House

The first-edition OS map shows a combined 'Police station & Court Ho.' in Carrigboy. By the end of the 19th century this building had disappeared, to be replaced by a separate barracks and a petty sessions court house on the west side of Durrus Main Street. The former court house is still standing, a three-bay, two-storey structure with two ground floor entrances and three round-headed windows to first floor. Now in residential use.

CASTLEMARTYR
Main Street
Market House   #047
1757

Petty sessions and District Court sittings were held in Castlemartyr where the market house is shown as the court house on the 25-inch OS map. This is a three-bay, two-storey structure built in 1757, according to Lewis's *Topographical Dictionary*, for Henry Boyle, Earl of Shannon, whose seat was at Castlemartyr. Rubble limestone walls, aside from the east elevation which is rendered, with dressed limestone quoins. Three-arched market arcade, now filled in, to ground floor, finely dressed with alternating long and short limestone voussoirs. Square-headed windows to first floor former courtroom. Centrally placed square-headed plaque with yellow brick surround at roof level. Castlemartyr District Court was amalgamated with Midleton in 1998. Now in commercial use.

CASTLETOWNBERE/CASTLETOWN BEARHAVEN
Court House

Castletownbere petty sessions court house is shown on the 25-inch OS map on the west side of the town. On the first-edition OS map, it is a police barracks. No trace of this structure remains. District Court sittings continued in the town until 2012, accommodated in local venues including the Beara Bay and Craigies Hotels.

#045 | Bantry (Denis Mortell, 2018)
#046 | Buttevant (Denis Mortell, 2018)
#047 | Castlemartyr (IAA, 1980)
#048 | Charleville (IAA, 1980)

KANTURK

Church Street

Court House   #056

George Richard Pain

1825-27

Kanturk court house is one of a number of petty and quarter sessions court houses built in Cork to George Richard Pain's *Design for a court house and bridewell to be built in the different sessions towns in the County of Cork* dated 6 May 1824. Classical three-bay stone façade, the centre bay advanced and pedimented with a Venetian window between two broad plain pilasters. Pedimented entrances, with blank panels above, in the shallow end bays. Ashlar walls to front and partly to sides before giving way to rubble masonry. Galleried, double-height courtroom with a recessed hooded arch over the judge's bench. Bridewell to rear. Court sittings moved to Mallow in 2010, and the court house became a cultural venue.

KILDORRERY

Main Street

Court House

A two-bay, two-storey terraced house on the north side of Main Street at a gap in the continuous run of buildings is identified on the 25-inch OS map as Kildorrery petty sessions court house. The building is distinguished by quoins, has modestly dressed windows to the first floor and a 19th-century-style shopfront.

KINSALE

Market Square

Market House and Court House   #057

c. 1610

The prominently located and highly distinctive market house in Kinsale was built c. 1610 (NIAH). The building was in use as a court house by c. 1705, from which time the front façade dates. This has a five-bay, red-brick arcade at ground floor, the end arches of which are blind while the centre three are open, though gated, and give access to the covered market. Slate-hung first floor with central Venetian window flanked by square-headed windows. Triple curvilinear 'Dutch' gables, also slate hung, one window in each of the end gables and a pair of windows in the centre, with a clock. Behind the central gable is a bellcote and behind that an octagonal cupola with conical roof topped by a weathervane. Rough whitewashed side and rear façades, with arched carriage entrances and asymmetrically placed square-headed windows. The inquest into the 1915 sinking of HMS Lusitania was held here. The building became the Kinsale Museum in 1958 and court sittings transferred to the Municipal Hall.

Inishannon (Denis Mortell, 2018) | #055
Kanturk (IAA, 1980) | #056
Kinsale, Market House and Court House (IAA, c. 1970) | #057

CORK | MUNSTER   245

MUNSTER

KINSALE

The Mall

Municipal Hall #058

c. 1830

Lewis's *Topographical Dictionary* records that a 'handsome suite of assembly-rooms has recently been built' in Kinsale, 'and on the ground floor of the same building is a reading and newsroom'. Presenting a rather severe face to the Mall, but giving the appearance of a Gothic castle when viewed from the former bowling green over which it looks, Kinsale Municipal Hall was built c. 1830 as assembly rooms. It is shown as a 'Club Ho.' on the first-edition OS map. The street façade has a recessed, arched, central entrance, with two square-headed windows set high in the wall. There are later secondary entrances at each end. Rubble-stone side and east walls, with limestone tooling to pointed windows. The Gothic Revival four-bay, two-storey, east front has tower-like advanced end bays and a crenellated parapet. Burned in 1922 and rebuilt c. 1928, the building has housed local authority offices, the local library and District Court sittings from c. 1958. District Court sittings were moved to Bandon in 2010 because of the increasingly poor condition of the Municipal Hall. The Court returned to Kinsale briefly in 2013, sitting in the 1885 Temperance Hall, Market Quay. At the end of that year, the District Court Area of Kinsale was amalgamated into that of Bandon. The Municipal Hall has become an arts venue.

KNOCKNAGREE

Court House

pre-1842

A petty sessions court house stood set well back from the east side of the road c. 1.5km south of Knocknagree, at a point where the road crosses a small tributary of the Blackwater. The building appears on the first-edition OS map, though not identified as a court house. It is no longer extant.

LISCARROLL

Castle Street

Court House #059

Liscarroll petty sessions court house is shown on the 25-inch OS map as the first and largest of a cluster of buildings strung out along the south side of the road to Charleville to the east of the village centre. The last building in the run was a school and, much expanded, is now the community centre. The court house would appear to still stand. A single-storey, three-bay rendered building with a corrugated iron roof, it most resembles a disused agricultural shed.

#058 | Kinsale, Municipal Hall (IAA, c. 1975)

#059 | Liscarroll (Denis Mortell, 2018)

#060 | Mallow (IAA, 1980)

LISHEENS
Court House

Lisheens rural petty sessions court house is shown on the first-edition OS map, on the south side of what was the main Ballincollig to Ovens road (now the R608), at a point just north-east of what is now Junction 3 on the N22. Although listed as a petty sessions location as late as 1883, court use had ceased by the time the 25-inch OS map was published. The former sessions house is no longer extant.

MACROOM
Barrack Lane
Court House
See Significant Court Houses – A Chronological Selection   **P195**

MALLOW
William O'Brien Street
Court House   **#060**
George Richard Pain; []
c. 1826; 2001

Mallow court house is another of those built to George Richard Pain's *Design for a court house and bridewell to be built in the different sessions towns in the County of Cork* dated 6 May 1824. Classical, three-bay stone façade, the centre bay advanced and pedimented with a large round-headed window (as opposed to Pain's more usual Venetian window) between two broad plain pilasters. Pedimented entrances, with blank panels above, in the shallow end bays. Ashlar walls to front and part sides before giving way to rubble masonry with square-headed windows. Double-height galleried courtroom altered in the late 1970s and again in 1995, yet retains original panelling. Sympathetically refurbished and extended in 2001, with the addition of a two-storey flat-roofed block to the rear to provide consultation and barristers' rooms, staff facilities, and holding cells. A new disabled access entrance on the south side has a cut limestone doorcase salvaged from Manor Vaughan, the residence of Lord Leitrim, near Milford, Co. Donegal. Still in court use.

MIDLETON
Main Street
Court House   **#061**
George Richard Pain; []
c. 1826; 1997

One of a number of petty and quarter sessions court houses built in Cork to George Richard Pain's *Design for a court house and bridewell to be built in the different sessions towns in the County of Cork* dated 6 May 1824. Midleton court house has a classical, three-bay stone façade, the centre bay slightly advanced and pedimented with a central Venetian window between two broad plain pilasters. Pedimented entrances, with blank panels above, in the shallow, full-height end bays. Ashlar walls to front and part sides before giving way to rubble masonry with square-headed windows. Refurbished and remodelled in 1997, with additional repairs in 2003, it is still in court use. Double-height galleried courtroom retains original panelling and built-in furniture.

MILLSTREET
Killarney Road
Carnegie Library   **#062**
Rudolf Maximilian Butler
1912

Built in 1912 to designs by Rudolf Maximilian Butler as Millstreet Carnegie Free Library, with reading rooms and book stores on the ground floor and a large lecture room above. This room was subsequently used as a courtroom. Three large gables with swagged shields to the six-bay, two-storey front façade. Overhanging cornice and eaves and paired casement windows, the original leaded lights of which have long been replaced. The central doorcase was obscured for a time by an entrance porch which has been removed. Renovations in the 1980s included the addition of a second storey to the rear for county council offices and new judge's rooms. Court use ceased in 2009, and the building is now used as local authority offices.

MITCHELSTOWN
New Square
Market House and Court House   **#063**
George Richard Pain
1823

Mitchelstown's 'very neat and well-arranged' market house and petty sessions court house was, according to Lewis's *Topographical Dictionary*, 'erected in 1823, at an expense of £3000, by the Earl of Kingston'. This is confirmed by a plaque on the building. The architect was George Richard Pain. Originally detached, but now terminating a line of buildings on the east side of New Square. Three-bay ashlar façade, the centre bay advanced and pedimented, with a three-arch market arcade at ground floor, now filled in. Three large square-headed windows to first floor, and a platband between the floors. In use as a supermarket.

MITCHELSTOWN
George's Street
Court House   #064
James Rupert Boyd Barrett
1951-53

In 1953 Mitchelstown District Court sittings moved from the market
and court house in New Square to a purpose-built premises on George's
Street, one of the very few mid-20th-century court houses to be built,
and possibly the finest. Asymmetrical, flat-roofed, redbrick and concrete
building designed by James Rupert Boyd Barrett. Set back from the road
behind a garden protected by iron railings with distinctive brick piers.
Five-bay, two-storey office section with adjoining five-bay, single-storey
courtroom wing which has a projecting judge's chamber at the north
end. An additional wing was later added to the rear. Flat-roofed concrete
porch to entrance. Closed 2011 following the amalgamation of the
District Court Area of Mitchelstown into that of Fermoy. Now in local
authority use.

NEWMARKET
Main Street
Market House and Court House   #065
c. 1810

Built c. 1810 (NIAH), Newmarket's former market house was also
used as a petty sessions court house. Ashlar limestone façade with
five-bay arcade at ground floor, the arches now filled in, and three
square-headed windows above. Damaged in 1920 during the War of
Independence, but briefly returned to court use. Newmarket became
part of Kanturk District Court Area in 1927. The former court building
was a school from 1945 to 1954, and subsequently became the Catholic
Young Men's Society (CYMS) hall.

PASSAGE WEST
Main Street/Wesleyan Place
Court House

A petty sessions court house is shown on the 25-inch OS map of
Passage West on what is now Wesleyan Place. The building may have
served originally as a Methodist chapel. No longer extant.

RATHCORMACK
Main Street
Court House

The petty sessions court house in Rathcormack was the middle
building in a terrace of three on the south side of Main Street just east
of Church Street. The fabric of the two-storey, two-bay court house
would appear to be incorporated into the commercial premises which
now occupies the site.

#061 | Midleton (IAA, 1980)
#062 | Millstreet. Perspective view by R.M. Butler, architect, 1912 (R.M. Butler Collection, IAA)
#063 | Mitchelstown, Market House and Court House (IAA, 1980)

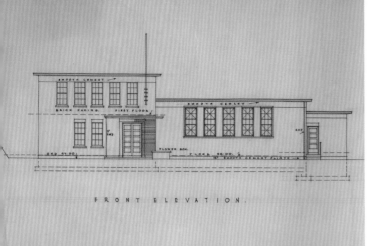

FRONT ELEVATION.

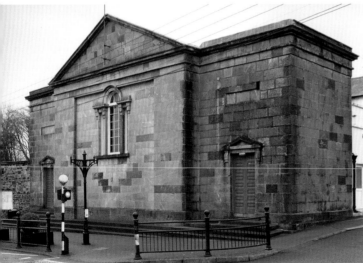

RIVERSTOWN

Old Court

Court House

Riverstown petty sessions court house formed part of a terrace of small buildings shown on the 25-inch OS map opposite the lodged entrance to Riverstown House. Much altered, the terrace is still identifiable though the court house is not. The court house fell out of use in the mid-1960s, though Riverstown remained a District Court Area until amalgamated into Cork City District Court Area in 2001.

ROSSCARBERY

Court House

Lewis's *Topographical Dictionary* describes the court house in Rosscarbery as 'a very neat building' adjoining the constabulary barracks. By the time the 25-inch OS map was published the constabulary barracks had moved to the centre of the town while the court house remained on the west periphery, in New Town, with the former barracks section serving as a dispensary. Rosscarbery was a District Court Area until 1961. The court house still stands, converted – with the adjoining barracks/dispensary – into residential units. The entrance was formerly in the gable end facing the town, protected by the still standing shallow porch whose roof is supported by a pair of Doric columns. The door has been replaced by a single window topped by an oculus above which are two small shields. The porch, and the dressed-stone surrounds to some entrances and windows, are all that remain to hint at the building's former purpose.

SCHULL

Main Street

Court House

Schull petty sessions court house was a detached building on the north side of Main Street; destroyed by fire in May 1920. The Munster and Leinster Bank (now AIB) was constructed on the site in 1933. Schull District Court continued to sit in the local parochial hall until 2011, when it was amalgamated into the Bantry District Court Area.

SHANDANGAN

Court House

Shandangan petty sessions court house stood isolated on the south side of the road just east of Shandangan Crossroads. A pair of modest gate piers, with their rusty gates, is all that remains to indicate the site.

Mitchelstown. Elevation of Court House by James Rupert Boyd Barrett, 1952 | #064
(Boyd Barrett Murphy O'Connor Collection, IAA)
Newmarket (Denis Mortell, 2018) | #065
Skibbereen (Denis Mortell, 2018) | #066

SKIBBEREEN

North Street
Court House   #066
George Richard Pain; []
c. 1826; 1956

One of a number of petty and quarter sessions court houses built in Cork to George Richard Pain's *Design for a court house and bridewell to be built in the different sessions towns in the County of Cork* dated 6 May 1824. Skibbereen court house has a classical, three-bay stone façade, the centre bay slightly advanced and pedimented with a central Venetian window between two broad plain pilasters. Pedimented entrances, with blank panels above, in the shallow, full-height end bays. Ashlar walls to front and part sides before giving way to rubble masonry, now partly rendered, with square-headed windows. Original gallery and dock were removed from the double-height courtroom in 1956 when the building was extended to the rear. Still in use.

TIMOLEAGUE

Mill Street
Market House and Court House   #067

Forming part of the continuous line of buildings on the east side of the north end of Mill Street in Timoleague, this two-storey stone structure had a market house at ground floor and a petty sessions courtroom above. Five-bay market arcade at street level, the end bays narrower than the centre three and having brick arches instead of stone (all of which would have been hidden by a render which is now removed). A keystone-shaped plaque on the centre arch bears the improbably early date of 1700. Three square-headed windows to first floor. Now in commercial use.

TRACTON

Court House

Tracton petty sessions court house stood on the north side of what is now the L3210, opposite the access road to the C of I church. No trace remains, the site being now a pub carpark.

UNION HALL

Court House

Union Hall petty sessions court house was on the north-west side of the village, on a triangular plot bounded by a laneway and the road to Myross School. No longer extant; the site is now occupied by a private residence.

#067 | Timoleague (Denis Mortell, 2018)
#068 | Youghal, Mall House (Denis Mortell, 2018)
#069 | Youghal, Court House (Denis Mortell, 2018)

YOUGHAL

The Mall
Town Hall/Mall House   #068
[]; Wilson Architecture
1779; 2002

Youghal town hall is an imposing, detached, three-bay wide by two-bay deep, former assembly rooms and court house built, according to Lewis's *Topographical Dictionary*, in 1779 on reclaimed slob land. Advanced central bay to entrance front with rendered quoins and a Venetian window arrangement at first floor level above a later barrel-vaulted gated porch. Round-headed windows at ground and first floor of flanking bays. Further stylised Venetian windows to ground and first floors of side elevations. Two-storey glass-box extension to rear added in 2002 to designs by Wilson Architecture. Much altered internally to provide accommodation for a multi-purpose theatre and arts venue as well as court sittings, which returned to the building in 2002 from the Market Square court house and which continue to sit in the building.

YOUGHAL

Market Square
Court House   #069
[Alexander Tate]
1848

The purpose-built petty and quarter sessions court house in Youghal is a detached sandstone block with limestone cornice, string-course, quoins, window and door surrounds. Hipped roof with modillioned eaves. Five-bay entrance front, the end bays slightly advanced and demarcated by quoins, each with a square-headed entrance framed by Tuscan pilasters and surmounted by a round-headed window. Between these, at first floor level, is a distinctive, centrally-placed tripartite round-headed window set in a dressed-stone surround. Similar tripartite windows to first floor of both side elevations where each surmounts a triple square-headed window. The south side has an additional bay with an entrance surmounted by a round-headed window. This is a more decorative version of the court house in Balbriggan, Co. Dublin, by Alexander Tate (1844), which shares the distinctive tripartite round-headed window composition. Both Youghal and Balbriggan also take cues from the standard late-1830s – early-1840s petty and quarter sessions court house design, notably the twin entrances in the end bays, the rectangular plan and the blank ground floor façade beneath the central first floor windows. The courtroom was renovated in the 1960s and 1980s, losing many of its original features, but is no longer in use, court sittings having been moved back to the former town hall on the Mall in 2002.

CLAUDY
Court House
1829

The OS *Memoirs* records that the combined petty sessions house and police barracks in Claudy was 'a plain building of 1-storey… built in 1829 by John Browne Esquire of Cumber House. The road sessions were held here on one occasion but the house proved too small'. Standing on the west side of the former cattle market, now car park, in the centre of the village, the building is now a commercial premises. It has a half-hipped roof and a central shop entrance to the left of which is a blank wall and to the right, two pointed-arch window openings, and a side entrance in porch. Claudy petty sessions were abolished in 1950.

COLERAINE
Castlerock Road
Court House   #070
Stewart Gordon; Charles Littleboy Boddie
1852; 1908

The former market house or town hall in Coleraine's Diamond, erected in 1742 and renovated in 1787, was used for a variety of purposes including the holding of petty and quarter sessions. It was 'a plain rectangular building surmounted by a small cupola in which the town clock is placed… Part of the lower storey was formerly left open (for the use of a market) by means of semicircular arches. It was however, closed up in 1833'. This building was replaced by a new town hall by Thomas Turner in 1859, seven years after a purpose-built court house had been provided west of the Bann on a commanding site at the junction of Castlerock Road and Captain Street, Lower. Designed by County Surveyor Stewart Gordon as a Roman temple in ashlar sandstone, rusticated at ground level, with a tetrastyle Doric portico approached by a flight of steps and sheltering a pedimented entrance flanked by high-level pedimented windows, between which is a shield inscribed with the date 1852. 'Ever since its erection', the *Irish Builder* reported in 1871, 'the glaring structural defects of this building have been commented upon… The Court-house, indeed, seems to have been designed to afford the least amount of accommodation, with the greatest degree of discomfort'. These issues were not addressed until 1908 when the court house was renovated and extended by Charles Littleboy Boddie, who added a rendered single bay, two-storey, entrance wing half-way down the north side of the building and a two-bay by three-bay, two-storey, office wing on the south. Court use ceased in 1985 and since 2001 the building has been a licensed premises.

COLERAINE
Mountsandel Road
Court House   #071
pre-1993

Coleraine's new court house for Magistrates Courts, County Courts and Crown Courts was constructed in a greenfield suburban setting on Mountsandel Road by 1993. Set back from the street behind a fence and security hut, this is a T-plan, two-storey, red-brick building. A central entrance, flanked by towers, fronts a central zinc-roofed office block which separates two pyramid-roofed, glass-topped, courtroom wings.

DERRY/LONDONDERRY
Bishop Street
City and County Court House
See Significant Court Houses – A Chronological Selection   P187

DRAPERSTOWN
High Street
Market House   #072
William Joseph Booth
1827-39

The first floor of the market house in Draperstown was used as a petty sessions court house. It was originally designed in 1827 by William J. Booth, surveyor to the Drapers' Company which owned the town, but not built until a decade later. The market house is the centrepiece of Booth's scheme and is flanked by terraces of two-storey houses originally terminating at one end in an inn and at the other in a dispensary. Three-bay, two-storey, pedimented front with four plain pilasters separating square-headed openings. Broad eaves with distinctive brackets and a square clock tower set back towards the centre of the building. Draperstown public library opened in the building, then referred to as the court house, in 1959. Petty sessions transferred to Magherafelt in 1964. Damaged by fire in 1972 but subsequently repaired, the building remains in library use. Draperstown petty sessions were abolished in 1964.

DUNGIVEN
Market House and Court House
1829

Lewis's *Topographical Dictionary* records that a 'court for the manor of Pellipar is held in the court-house at Dungiven, every third Thursday, for the recovery of debts under 40s… Petty sessions are likewise held monthly in the court-house'. Presumably the courts sat in the market house, which the OS *Memoirs* reported as being 'without architectural pretention'. Built in 1829 for Robert Ogilby at the cost of £1,000, it was a two-storey block in red sandstone with a room for public meetings on the upper storey. No longer extant. Dungiven petty sessions were transferred to Limavady in 1969, and abolished in 1971.

EGLINTON (MUFF)

Main Street
Court House   #073
Michael Angelo Nicholson, James Bridger
1823-24

Michael Angelo Nicholson, the son of Peter Nicholson, author of builders' and carpenters' manuals, was paid by the Grocers' Company for plans for Eglinton court house in 1823. It is likely that these were altered by James Bridger before construction began in 1824; the building was completed at a cost of £1,500. The OS *Memoirs* comments extensively: 'The sessions house stands in the centre of the village, in an open well-chosen situation... It appears to advantage from many points of view. Its proportions, however, those of a square, are not pleasing: the front should have been longer in proportion to the depth... it is a 2-storey building of freestone, comprehending in the upper part a sessions room and agent's office... The front half of the lower storey is occupied by the market. That part of the upper storey mainly over the market house is supported on semicircular arches, which form large entrances to it... In the sessions room is a window of coloured glass tastefully ornamented. On it are the king's and the Grocers' arms'. The stained-glass window does not survive. Eglinton petty sessions were abolished in 1940 and by 1948, with its market arcade filled in, the building was a private residence. Converted to a bank in 1970, it is now home to Faughanvale Credit Union.

GARVAGH

Garvagh is described in Lewis's *Topographical Dictionary* as having a petty sessions court house. While the sessions are noted by the OS *Memoirs*, a court house is not, nor has a court house been identified, although Garvagh remained a petty sessions location until 1979.

INISHRUSH

Court House

The petty sessions court house in Inishrush is noted in passing by the OS *Memoirs* and identified on the third-edition OS map (1904-16) as a small building at the junction of the main village street and Killycon Road, opposite the Orange hall. The overgrown ruin standing on the site may be the remains of the court house.

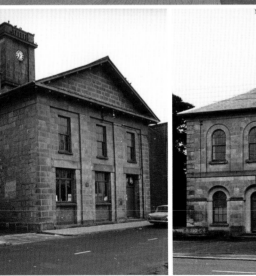

Coleraine (Alistair Rowan/Buildings of Ireland, 1971) | **#070**
Coleraine, Mountsandel Road (Paul Tierney, 2019) | **#071**
Draperstown (Alistair Rowan/Buildings of Ireland, 1971) | **#072**
Eglinton (Alistair Rowan/Buildings of Ireland, 1971) | **#073**

DERRY/LONDONDERRY | ULSTER   253

KILREA

The Diamond
Market House and Court House   #074
William Barnes
c. 1837

According to the OS *Memoirs*, petty sessions in Kilrea were held 'on the first Monday of every month in a private room in Coleraine Street'. However, the *Memoirs* goes on to note that the 'foundations of a good market house have been laid at the northern side of the Diamond and adjacent to Coleraine Street. It will be 50 by 30 feet and is to contain a room for holding petty sessions'. Designed by William Barnes and paid for by the Mercers' Company, it was completed c. 1837. James Turnbull was the clerk of works. Brett's *Court Houses of Ulster* describes it as 'a five-bay two-storey stuccoed building, the hipped roof topped by a simple weathervane. The ground floor had five open archways, four broad and one (for the central doorway) narrow; unusually the arches were carried on cast-iron Doric columns'. Damaged by a bomb in 1972, it was demolished and replaced by a late-20th-century library. Kilrea petty sessions were abolished in 1979.

LIMAVADY

Irish Green Street
Court House   #075
1830

Lewis's *Topographical Dictionary* reports that Limavady has 'a handsome sessions-house, where the general sessions for the county are held in June and December, and petty sessions on alternate Tuesdays; adjoining it is a small bridewell'. Rectangular in plan, with a narrow end facing onto the west side of Irish Green Street, it was built in 1830 at a cost of £950. Later converted to a gospel hall, but no longer extant as Limavady's new gospel hall now occupies the site.

LIMAVADY

Main Street
Court House
Charles Littleboy Boddie
1913-15

A new court house was provided for Limavady in 1915 to designs by County Surveyor Charles Littleboy Boddie. Located on Main Street, it is a seven-bay, single-storey, red-brick building with square-headed windows and an advanced central entrance bay. This extends upward into an Italianate tower, with round-headed windows, topped by a modillioned pyramid roof. 'Not everybody's idea of a court house', comments the *Buildings of Ireland*, 'for this is surely the architecture of Toytown'. The building acquired a not unsympathetic security hut in the late 20th century, and is still in use. Limavady Magistrates' Court sits there weekly, the District Judge sits on a monthly basis to hear small claims and divorce cases, and the court house is also used for additional court sittings from Derry.

#074 | Kilrea (Alistair Rowan/Buildings of Ireland, 1971)
#075 | Limavady (Crown DfC Historic Environment Division, 1973)
#076 | Magherafelt (Ulster Museum, late 19C)
#077 | Moneymore (Alistair Rowan/Buildings of Ireland, 1970)

MAGHERA
Market Houses

Maghera had two market houses: one built in 1824, with a room for petty sessions, and a second, constructed in 1832-33, also with a first floor room for court sittings. No trace of either building remains, nor has another court house been identified, although Maghera petty sessions were not abolished until 1976.

MAGHERAFELT
Union Road
Court House
1804

James Boyle, who compiled the OS *Memoirs* entry on Magherafelt in 1836, provides a detailed description of the court house. Standing at the foot of Broad Street, it was built, he says, in 1804, partly by the landlord and partly by the county. 'It is perfectly plain in its exterior, but solid, substantial and in good order. Its extreme length is 74 feet and width 22 feet. It consists of a spacious hall at one end and 2 jury rooms at the other. The intermediate space is filled up with jury boxes on either side, which open into the jury rooms. Transversely are, at one end, 2 benches for the magistrates, chairman and at the other the dock, with a low partition shutting out the hall. In the centre is the council table, around which are the benches for the attorneys. This is a very comfortable and well planned court house, being commodious, well lit and airy'. This building was converted to the town hall in 1890 by George R. Tipping, as it had been replaced by a new court house.

MAGHERAFELT
Hospital Road
Court House   #076
Thomas Turner and Richard Williamson
1874

Magherafelt's new petty and quarter sessions court house was built in 1874 to designs by architects Thomas Turner and Richard Williamson. Sitting side-on to the street, this is a red brick and black stone exercise in Victoriana. A three-arch loggia (repeated on the street side) stands between two square, squat, pyramid-roofed towers in front of a stepped-gabled hall topped by tall chimneys and containing the double-height courtroom which is lit by porthole clerestory windows. Two taller towers are asymmetrically placed behind the courtroom at either end of a transverse, single-storey, gabled block with paired and single round-headed windows. A three-storey, stepped-gabled office block stands to the side. Sir Charles Brett's poetical analysis was that the building, which is protected now by a high security fence and lodge, had 'strayed from the land of German fairy-tales and German building bricks… a mixture of ogres, dungeons and Kafka (*Court Houses of Ulster*)'. Magistrates Courts and County Courts continue to sit in the building.

MONEYMORE
High Street
Market House and Court House   #077
Jesse Gibson
1817-19

Designed for the Drapers' Company by Jesse Gibson, surveyor for the City of London, Moneymore's first market house was constructed from 1817 to 1819 as the centrepiece of a fourteen-bay range which also included a dispensary and an inn. Referred to by Lewis's *Topographical Dictionary* as 'market and court-house', this is a three-bay, two-storey pedimented building with a round-headed entrance, square-headed windows, small at ground floor and taller above, a first-floor sill-level platband and a tall late-19th-century wooden clock turret which replaced the original cupola. After a new market house was constructed across the street in 1839, court functions stayed in the 1819 building, which became known as the court house. Moneymore petty sessions were abolished in 1979. The former court house is now used as a meeting hall by a variety of organisations including the Women's Institute.

ÁRAINN MHÓR/ARRANMORE

Court House

Árainn Mhór/Arranmore had a petty sessions court and was listed as a District Court location in 1924, but not in 1961. A three-bay, single-storey, vernacular house, still standing on the east side of the road between An Leadhb Gharbh (Leabgarrow) and Fál an Ghabhann (Fallagowan), functioned as both court house and dispensary.

ARDARA

The Diamond

Market House and Court House   #078

c. 1840

Ardara market house is shown on the 25-inch OS map as the court house. It is a two-storey, three-bay building with a granite façade, the middle bay advanced. Central segmental arch, now containing the entrance but formerly leading to an inner courtyard. Dressed-stone doorcases on either side, now converted to windows. Above the string-course a central tripartite window is surmounted by a plain pediment containing a clock. A location for petty sessions and District Court sittings until 1961 (when the District Court was transferred to Glenties), the building subsequently was a library and has been in use as a heritage centre since 1992.

BALLINTRA

Main Street

Court House

Petty sessions were held in Ballintra 'on alternate Mondays', according to Lewis's *Topographical Dictionary*, and the village was listed as a District Court location in 1924. In 1961, Ballintra became part of the Donegal District Court Area. A court house is shown on the 25-inch OS map off Main Street, just south of the RC church. An early-20th-century single-storey hall stands on the site – gable-fronted entrance block, four bays by one, with door set in an arched recess, and a slightly taller three-bay-deep main hall behind.

BALLYSHANNON

Market Street

Market House and Court House

1762

Ballyshannon market house and sessions house stood at the south end of Market Street. Dating from 1762, it was described in the *Buildings of Ireland* as 'a utilitarian rendered lump, unworthy of its position', a verdict with which others apparently agreed, as it is no longer extant.

BALLYSHANNON

The Mall

Court House   #079

Enoch Trevor Owen and Alfred Richard Owen

1880-90s

A new court house for petty and quarter sessions was designed for Ballyshannon in 1880 by OPW architect Enoch Trevor Owen and his son Alfred Richard Owen. A contractor, James Monaghan, was appointed the following year, though the building may not have been completed until the early 1890s. Standing on the north side of the Mall, it has a rendered, two-storey, five-bay symmetrical front consisting of a gabled central block with three tall round-headed windows. Flanking single-bay wings each contain a door with a window above. Now in use as a resource centre.

BALLYSHANNON

Portnason

Court House

HMD Architects

2002-05

In 2005 a new court house for Ballyshannon District Court opened adjacent to a new garda station at Portnason to the west side of the town centre. Designed in a contemporary idiom by HMD Architects, the modest court house sits back from the road behind a large carpark. Chamfered front elevation comprising white rendered walls, oak window, glazed entrance with a zinc canopy and a lean-to office wing. Beside the entrance is an old-Irish judgement text in bronze. The building contains an oak-lined, and oak-furnished, top-lit courtroom, with judge's chambers, facilities for the legal profession, and a secure holding cell for prisoners.

BUNBEG

Court House

A three-bay vernacular cottage, single-storey to front, on a sloping site on the east side of the road north of Bunbeg quay served as the local court house. Heavy continuous buttress to lower part of front façade. In 1997 Bunbeg District Court was abolished and the District Court Area amalgamated with Glenties.

BUNCRANA

Main Street, Lower

Court House   #080

[Jacob Owen]; William James Doherty

1842; 1925

A variant of the standard late-1830s – early-1840s petty and quarter sessions design, Buncrana court house was built in 1842 to replace an 1830 court house provided to the town by Mrs Todd of Buncrana Castle. Tentatively attributed to Jacob Owen by the *Dictionary of Irish Architects*. Set slightly back from the street behind iron railings on a low boundary wall. Five-bay, two-storey main façade; the end entrance bays step forward and are pedimented. Horizontal rustication below sill-level string-course. Square-headed windows with ornate architraves at first floor level. Double-height courtroom with timber dock and benches, reredos to judge's bench, and a public gallery supported on cast-iron columns. The bridewell was located in the basement (later converted to public toilets). Damaged during the War of Independence. Reconstructed in 1925 by William James Doherty, who also rebuilt Carndonagh court house with which Buncrana shares a number of features, including the reredos to the judge's bench, which suggests these are his and not original. Refurbished by the Courts Service in 2000. Still in use.

BURNFOOT

Court House

One part of the substantial two-storey, seven-bay, south-facing semi-detached block at the north end of the village served as Burnfoot petty sessions court house; the other part (now Leo's Café) was a hotel. A District Court location in 1924, in 1926 Burnfoot was amalgamated with Buncrana, and cases could be brought to either court. Burnfoot ceased to be a District Court Area in 1961.

CARNDONAGH

Court House   #081

William Harte; William James Doherty

1873; 1925

Replacing a courtroom located in the long-demolished market house, Carndonagh petty and quarter sessions court house is a late iteration of the standard late-1830s – early-1840s court house model. Designed by the Donegal County Surveyor William Harte and built in 1873 by contractor Robert Colhoun of Derry. Railing and wall erected, 1878. Reconstructed by William James Doherty in 1925, as was Buncrana (hence similarities externally and internally). Detached, two-storey over basement, five-bay building, the end bays with entrances slightly recessed. Rendered façade with horizontal rustication rising to a platband just below the first floor window sills. Square-headed windows with bracketed architraves, the centre three windows, framed by somewhat stylised pilasters, are lower than their neighbours. String-course at the level of the lintels of the end windows. Roughcast render to sides and rear. Double-height courtroom with timber panelling and reredos to judge's bench. Still in use.

CHURCH HILL

Sessions House and School   #082
1842

Combined petty sessions court house and school on the west side of Church Hill village street, almost opposite St Columba's C of I church. Three-bay, two-storey central block flanked by lower two-bay wings. The middle bay is pedimented with the main entrance in a pointed recess topped by a decorative shield bearing the date 1842. Now three separate private houses used for short-term holiday lets.

DONEGAL

Tyrconnell Street
Court House   #083
[]; William James Doherty
1833; 1925

Replacing an earlier court house of 1810 by John McGuiggan, Donegal court house is an irregularly planned detached building constructed in 1833 to designs by an as yet unidentified architect. Built to accommodate petty and quarter sessions, this is an asymmetric four-bay, single-storey block containing a double-height courtroom. There are two-storey over basement offices and former cells to rear, and a split-level two-storey extension. Hipped roof with prominent eaves. Squared-rubble sandstone walls, with dressed-stone corners, window and door surrounds, and decorative panels. Rendered side and rear. On a triangular site adjacent to Donegal Castle and looking towards the Diamond, the front façade's most prominent feature is the porch added in 1891 by Frederick Gahan, obscuring the original large arched window whose cut-stone voussoirs can be seen above the curved pediment of the addition. According to the Bureau of Military History Witness Statement of Liam O'Duffy, Donegal court house was 'completely destroyed' by fire on 7 August 1920 by the Donegal Company of the Irish Volunteers (WS 1,485). Reconstruction was carried out in 1925 by William James Doherty. Maintenance works were carried out in 2006 for the Courts Service. Still a Circuit and District Court venue, the building is now also used by the local Chamber of Commerce.

DRUM (PORTSALON)

Drum (Portsalon) was not a petty sessions location but was listed as a District Court Area in 1924, only to be abolished and amalgamated with Milford District Court Area in 1929.

#082 | Church Hill (Paul Tierney, 2019)
#083 | Donegal (Courts Service, 1995)
#084 | Dunfanaghy (Paul Tierney, 2019)
#085 | Letterkenny, High Road (Courts Service, 2017)

DUNFANAGHY
Market House   **#084**
1845

Lewis's *Topographical Dictionary* notes that petty sessions were held
in Dunfanaghy every Friday. Presumably these would have been held
in the upper room of the market house. This is a detached, two-storey
building facing a neat square and with its back to the sea. A plaque
on the front façade records that the building 'was erected by Alexr
Robt Stewart Esqr of Ards House A.D. 1845'. Originally four bays
wide, with a ground-floor market arcade and square-headed windows
above. An additional bay, slightly set back, was later added to the
east end. Dunfanaghy was a District Court location from 1924; the
Court was transferred to Letterkenny in 1997. The building is now in
commercial use.

DUNGLOE
Main Street
Court House

Petty sessions in Dungloe were held in a semi-detached two-storey
building on the west side of Main Street opposite Sweeney's Hotel.
Some fabric of this building remains. The site is now occupied by a fast
food outlet. Dungloe was a District Court Area from 1924 to 1997,
when it was amalgamated with Glenties.

FALCARRAGH
Court House

Falcarragh petty sessions court house stood isolated on a site north
of the village, adjacent to Falcarragh House. A modern house now
occupies the site. Falcarragh District Court was amalgamated with
Letterkenny in 1997.

GLENTIES
Mill Road
Court House
See Significant Court Houses – A Chronological Selection   **P202**

KILLYBEGS
New Row
Court House

A small petty sessions court house is shown on the 25-inch OS map of
Killybegs in a cluster of similarly-sized structures on the south side of
New Row on the site now occupied by the Anvil Court development.
Killybegs District Court Area was amalgamated with Donegal Town
in 1997.

LETTERKENNY
Justice Walsh Road
Court House
John Hargrave; []
1828-31; 1992

The Donegal Grand Jury Presentments record that in 1831 architect
John Hargrave was paid £60 'for having made plans estimates and
specifications for the Session House and Bridewell at Letterkenny, and
for having superintended the erection of same'. Nine years later, James
McLoughlin received £66 for erecting a gallery in the court house.
Erected for petty and quarter sessions, this is a seven-bay by two-bay,
two-storey (three to rear) detached building. The ground floor is blank,
aside from entrances, as it contained the bridewell. The original main
façade was the three-bay pedimented elevation facing Main Street.
This was flanked by twin single-bay, single-storey entrance porticos.
Following the creation of Justice Walsh Road, a development which
led to the loss of one of the entrance porticos, the long seven-bay
flank of the building was fully exposed, with its projecting central
bay incorporating a tetrastyle portico and recessed entrance. Square-
headed windows to first floor, all with triangular pediments, except
the middle one on the short façade which is segmental. Extended and
renovated in 1992 when the courtroom fittings were replaced. Closed
2018 following the completion of the new Letterkenny Court House.

LETTERKENNY
High Road
Court House   **#085**
OPW   *See also* **P102**
2015-17

A site for a new court house in Letterkenny was acquired in 2008. The
building is one of seven court houses delivered under the 2015 Public
Private Partnership Court House Bundle project, the contract for
which was agreed in 2015 with BAM as the preferred bidder. Detached,
four-storey structure sitting on an elevated site with accessible entrance
forecourt and stepped podium to rear. The austere stone façade is
interrupted by banks of tall recessed glazing. Completed at a cost of
€19.7 million, it contains four courtrooms with associated facilities
including consultation and custodial rooms, areas for victim support
and an office wing linked by a public atrium. Court sittings began in
January 2018 and the court house was officially opened on 12 February
2018 by Mr Justice Frank Clarke, Chief Justice of Ireland, and the
Minister for Justice, Charles Flanagan TD.

LIFFORD

The Diamond

County Court House

See Significant Court Houses – A Chronological Selection   **P171**

MALIN

Court House

The petty sessions court house in Malin occupied a single-storey cottage adjacent to the C of I church on the west side of the triangle at the heart of the village. Two entrances, each with a shallow pedimented porch supported on brackets. Three square-headed windows. Following a War of Independence fire, it was rebuilt in 1927, possibly by William James Doherty, who worked on repairing or rebuilding several other Donegal court houses in this period. Malin ceased to be a District Court location in 1961.

MILFORD

Main Street

Town Hall/Court House/Library   **#086**

c. 1885

Milford had a petty sessions court and was a District Court Area from 1924. The courts sat on the first floor of the town hall, a three-bay, two-storey building constructed on the east side of Main Street c. 1885 for Robert Bermingham Clements, 4th Earl of Leitrim, at a cost of £700 (NIAH). Rubble walls with dressed-stone quoins and voussoirs to central carriage arch and red-brick surrounds to square-headed windows, those to first floor set in gabled dormers. For much of the 20th century the court shared the first floor with the public library, before transferring to the adjacent Milford Hotel. In 1997, a refusal by a judge to hold court sittings in the hotel ballroom because it also contained a bar precipitated the abolition of Milford District Court and the amalgamation of the District Court Area with that of Donegal Town.

MOVILLE

Market Square

Court House

Moville court house was located in Market Square adjacent to the market building. A much altered commercial and residential premises stands on the site, one of whose occupants is the local library. Moville District Court was abolished in 1997 and amalgamated with Carndonagh.

NEWTOWN CUNNINGHAM

Court House

The 25-inch OS maps shows Newtown Cunningham court house located behind what would become the Orange hall. No trace remains. In 1988 Newtown Cunningham District Court Area was abolished. Burt and Castleforward Electoral Divisions were added to Buncrana District Court Area, while Killea and Newtown Cunningham were added to Raphoe.

PETTIGOE

Market House and Court House   **#087**

1836

Adjacent to Pettigoe C of I church, this detached two-storey court house was built as a market house, the OS *Memoirs* noting that it was 'in progress' in February 1836. It also served as a dispensary. The gabled north front, facing the street, has a segmental-arched tripartite window at ground-floor level, originally a market entrance and now flanked by two doors. Two square-headed windows above. The four-bay east elevation, facing towards the church, also has a segmental-arched window at ground floor level, with three square-headed windows above, and is noticeable for the external cut-stone flight of steps leading to a first-floor entrance. Pettigoe District Court was amalgamated with Donegal in 1997. The former court house is now in residential use.

RAPHOE

Market House

The petty sessions in Raphoe were held on alternate Saturdays, in the market house which the OS *Memoirs* describes as 'clever' and Lewis's *Topographical Dictionary* thought a 'neat building and well-arranged'. Brett's *Court Houses of Ulster* provides more details: 'two-storey, three-bay, hipped roof, with single storey ranges at either end enclosing a small market yard, closed by twin square pavilions with slated pyramidal roofs topped by wind-vanes'. No longer extant. Raphoe was designated a District Court location in 1924. Raphoe District Court sittings were moved to Convoy in 1992 and in 1997 Raphoe was amalgamated with Letterkenny District Court.

RATHMELTON

Castle Street

Public Hall/Town Hall   #088

Young & Mackenzie

1878

Rathmelton petty sessions were held on alternate Thursdays, according to Lewis's *Topographical Dictionary*, and the town was designated a District Court location from 1924. The court would appear to have sat in the 'Public Hall' built in 1878 (according to its datestone) to designs by Young and Mackenzie. It is a two-storey gable-fronted block in coursed black rubble with extensive yellow-brick trimmings and twin round-headed entrances below three round-headed lancet windows. In 1961 Rathmelton was included in the District Court area of Milford. The Public Hall was extended in the 2000s, the contemporary wing alluding to the original design.

RATHMULLAN

Main Street   #089

Court House

Rathmullan court house is an attached, single-storey (though with the same roof line as the adjacent two-storey houses), three-bay structure, with two entrances flanking a central large shop window, all of which now have relatively recent 'crazy-paving' surrounds. Paired dentils to eaves hint at a more dignified previous appearance. Now in use as 'The Old Courthouse' antiques and bric-a-brac shop, though the original ceiling of the courtroom remains. Rathmullan ceased to be a District Court Area in 1961.

STRANORLAR

Main Street

Court House   #090

Lewis's *Topographical Dictionary* records the presence of 'a market and court house' in Stranorlar, but no trace of this remains. By the end of the 19th century, Stranorlar court house was located directly opposite Meetinghouse Lane in the middle of a range of buildings on the south side of Main Street. In court use until the 1960s, the building survives, a three-bay, two-storey rendered structure of mid- to late-19th-century domestic appearance; now used as a shop. Square-headed windows to first floor. Rendered string-course and quoins. Shop windows and entrance on west side of ground floor. On the east a round-headed entrance with rendered hoodmould. Stranorlar District Court was abolished on the amalgamation of the Area with Letterkenny in 1997.

TAWNY

Court House

A two-bay single-storey cottage on the west side of the village street served as Tawny (or Tamney) petty sessions court house. Its immediate neighbour to the south (to which it is now joined) was the local dispensary.

ARDGLASS
Kildare Street
Court House

A petty sessions court house is indicated on the third-edition OS map of Ardglass (1899-1904), on the west side of the south end of Kildare Street, opposite Jordan's Castle. This is possibly the three-bay, three-storey, mid-terrace house with two entrances, one round-headed and one square, which stands on the site today. Ardglass petty sessions were abolished in 1936.

BALLYNAHINCH
Market Square
Market House and Court House   #091
1795

Lewis's *Topographical Dictionary* reports that there was a large court house in the square in Ballynahinch, 'built by Lord Moira in 1795, but now in a dilapidated state'. The building was repaired in 1841, gaining a clock and cupola in the process. It is a four-bay, two-storey market and court house standing at right angles to High Street and filling the north side of Market Square. The rubble-stone front wall lost its render during extensive restoration works in 2002. Above a string-course is a deep parapet in coursed squared stone, with end finials and a small central pediment containing the clock. Four-arch market arcade to ground floor, now filled in with glazing, and square-headed windows to first floor courtroom. The building is topped by an eight-pillared open cupola, a 2002 replica of the 1841 original which had been severely truncated in 1957. The building remained in use as both a court and market house until 1935, when the courtroom became home to a working men's club and the ground-floor market was converted to shops. Acquired by Down District Council in 2010, it now accommodates a wide range of community activities.

BANBRIDGE
Victoria Street
Court House   #092
Henry Smyth
1874

Banbridge court house was constructed from 1872 to 1874 at a cost of £2,465 by contractor John Thompson of Belfast to designs by Down County Surveyor Henry Smyth. Prior to its erection, petty and quarter sessions were held in the late-18th-century market house, demolished in 1832 to facilitate the lowering of the central thoroughfare of Newry Street/Bridge Street. The courts then sat in the new market house on the corner of Bridge Street and Scarva Street, 'a large and handsome edifice surmounted by a dome… built by the Marquess of Downshire in 1834, at an expense of £2000' (Lewis's *Topographical Dictionary*). The court house is an Italianate pile consisting of a tall, three-bay, two-storey central courtroom block with lower two-bay flanking wings, 'an opulent and individual extravaganza in stucco', according to Brett's *Court Houses of Ulster,* but now half-hidden behind security walls and fences. Tall chimneys and a parapet with distinctive circular piercings sit on a cornice supported by paired modillions, below which, in the three advanced centre bays, are tall round-headed windows with curved glazing bars and porthole vents. The circular theme continues under the windows, at ground level, where there are three oculi between string-courses, with two more in the inner sides of the wings. Pairs of blind round-headed windows to first floor in side elevations of centre block. Further round-headed windows in the wings which have parapets with the same round piercings as on the central block. Refurbished and extended to the rear in 2004, the double-height courtroom retains a pedimented niche behind the judge's bench. The court house has most recently been used for public hearings of the Northern Ireland Historical Institutional Abuse (HIA) inquiry.

BANGOR
Main Street
Market House and Court House   #093
c. 1830

Bangor petty sessions have moved location on several occasions, starting out in the 18th-century market house and then moving to the first floor of its c. 1830 successor on the corner of Main Street and Hamilton Road. Described by the OS *Memoirs* as 'a small building of recent erection and plain and unfinished appearance', this is a two-storey, five-bay block, the centre three bays advanced and pedimented, with a five-arch market arcade to ground floor, filled in since c. 1860, and square-headed windows in blocked architraves above. The pediment contains a clock but the cupola which once crowned the building was removed c. 1950. Market use had come to an end in the 1860s, when valuation records indicate that it was a school (the Ward School) and a petty sessions court house. Court use ceased in 1887 but the school remained until 1933, when the building became Bangor town hall. In 1952 it was converted to a bank which it remains to the present day.

BANGOR
Hamilton Road
Masonic Hall
John Boyd
1882-83

By 1910, Bangor petty sessions were being held in the Masonic Hall on Hamilton Road, a five-bay, two-storey building erected 1882-83 to designs by John Boyd. This has an elaborately pedimented central entrance and hoodmoulded segmental windows to ground floor. Above the entrance are various Masonic emblems flanked on either side by two round-headed windows. The parapet has a balustrade, finials and a small Dutch-gable pediment.

BANGOR
Quay Street
Bank/Court House
1866

In 1950 the petty sessions were transferred for a period to Newtownards, as it had become 'impossible to fix some convenient place for the holding of Petty Sessions within the Petty Sessions District of Bangor' (NI Petty Sessions Districts and Times Order No. 129, 1950). They returned to Bangor in 1952 to occupy the 1866 Belfast Banking Co. premises on Quay Street, the bank having moved that year to the petty sessions' former home in the market house. Five-bay, two-storey, commercial building, classical, rendered and quoined, with square-headed entrance framed by pairs of Doric pilasters. Round-headed windows in arched recesses to rusticated ground floor, their sills supported by large brackets. Modillion cornice above square-headed windows to first floor, each with a pediment supported by brackets and each fronted by a balustrade. Court use ceased in 2013 and the building was subsequently acquired under the Community Asset Transfer scheme by Open House, an independent music and arts charity which runs an annual summer festival in Bangor.

CASTLEWELLAN
Main Street
Market House and Court House   #094
1764

Lewis's *Topographical Dictionary* reports that petty sessions were held in the market house in Castlewellan, which is described as 'a neat building, with a belfry and clock, surmounted by a spire'. It was originally built c. 1764 for William Annesley as a five-bay, two-storey market house with an arcade of four arches on its north and south sides, and one square-headed entrance on the north side. This led to the stairs which provided access to the first floor room where petty sessions were held. This is lit by square-headed windows in simple dressed-stone surrounds. The *Archaeological Survey of County Down* (HMSO, Belfast, 1966), which records the building as a court house, considers that the church-like square Gothic tower was added to the west end in the early 19th century. Crenellated and pinnacled, with four pointed windows and a clock, the tower lost the spire (noted by Lewis) sometime after 1850. Castlewellan petty sessions transferred to Newcastle in 1977 and were abolished in 1979. The building is now a library.

Ballynahinch (Lawrence Collection, NLI, late 19C) | **#091**
Banbridge (IAA, c. 1970) | **#092**
Bangor, Market House (Lawrence Collection, NLI, late 19C) | **#093**
Castlewellan (Crown DfC Historic Environment Division, 1973) | **#094**
Donaghadee (Crown DfC Historic Environment Division, 1977) | **#095**

COMBER

Comber became a petty sessions location in the 1920s, and had merged with Grey Abbey by the late 1960s. The sessions were relocated to Newtownards in 1969 and abolished in 1971.

DONAGHADEE

New Street
Market House and Court House   #095
Daniel de la Cherois
1819

Daniel de la Cherois, amateur architect and proprietor of most of Donaghadee, designed and paid for the market and court house in the centre of the town. Completed c. 1819, it is similar to, though smaller than, Bangor market and court house. Detached, five-bay, two-storey quoined and rendered building, the centre three bays advanced and pedimented. Market arcade to ground floor with blocked surrounds to arches. Square-headed windows in square-headed recesses to first floor, with sill-level platband. Donaghadee petty sessions were abolished in 1965. The building was renovated c. 1990, when the ground floor was converted to shops and offices and the former courtroom on the first floor became home to Elim Pentecostal Church.

DOWNPATRICK

English Street
County Court House
See Significant Court Houses – A Chronological Selection   P169

DROMARA

Hillsborough Road
Market House and Court House   #096
c. 1835

Built to replace an earlier market house destroyed in a storm in 1829, Dromara market house is set back from the west side of Hillsborough Road, a two-storey, three-bay, hipped-roofed building in squared stone with dressed-stone quoins and simple surrounds to the square-headed openings. Referred to in valuation records of 1865 as a petty sessions house but used as a Masonic hall from at least the 1920s. Dromara petty sessions were abolished in 1965.

#096 | Dromara (Crown DfC Historic Environment Division, 1974)
#097 | Dromore, Market House/Town Hall (Lawrence Collection, NLI, late 19C)
#098 | Florida Manor (Kilmood, Killinchy) (Crown DfC Historic Environment Division, c. 19
#099 | Hillsborough (IAA, early 20C)

DROMORE
Market Square
Market House; Town Hall #097
1732; 1886

The OS *Memoirs* records that the court house in Dromore, 'with a market place underneath, is situated in Market Square. It is a very plain and dirty looking building, 50 feet long and 35 feet broad. Shambles are attached to it'. Erected in 1732, it was used for sittings of a manor court and a court leet as well as petty sessions. This building was replaced on the same site in 1886 by a new town hall in which court sittings took place. It was built by contractor J.H. Burns for £854, but the architect is not recorded. A five-bay by three-bay, two-storey, L-plan exercise in red brick, with segmental market arches to the long east and west sides, those on the east protected by a slate awning on iron supports, and segmental windows to first floor. Round-headed openings, and one oculus, in the gable front which is topped by a square clock tower. Hoodmouldings to most windows and doors. A plaque on the front records that the clock was 'Presented to the Inhabitants by William Cowan Heron JP, Maryville, Holywood, Co. Down'. Dromore petty sessions were transferred to Banbridge in 1976. That same year the cinema, which had occupied part of the town hall on and off since the silent era, closed and the building was converted to library use.

FLORIDA MANOR (KILMOOD, KILLINCHY)
Kilmood Church Road
Court House #098
c. 1822

A rare example of a purpose-built manor court house. Erected c. 1822 for David Gordon of Florida Manor in a vernacular Gothic style, this is a five-bay, single-storey over tall basement (three-storey to the rear) building with hipped roof. The centre bay, approached by a short causeway, is advanced and contains a pointed entrance. It is flanked by pairs of pointed windows and has an eccentric crow-stepped gable-cum-pediment with an inscription in a quatrefoil which reads 'Florida Manor Court House Date of Patent 1638'. The date refers to the original creation of Florida Manor by Charles I. Although built as a manor court house, it accommodated petty sessions sittings until 1922 after which it became a private residence. Extended to the rear c. 1985.

GILFORD
Dunbarton Street
Police Barracks and Court House
c. 1850

Not on the first-edition OS map of Gilford but shown on the second-edition (1862-63) as a constabulary barracks, this building is listed in Griffith's Valuation (c. 1861) as a police barracks and sessions house, and is shown on the third-edition OS map (1809-1904) as a court house, the barracks having relocated to Main Street in 1879. Detached, five-bay, two-storey structure built c. 1850 on the west side of Dunbarton Street, adjacent to the former Gilford Mill millpond. Square-headed windows and doors and rendered walls. Gilford petty sessions were abolished in 1963 and the building, which had been partially occupied by a caretaker since the 1880s, became fully residential. It was damaged by fire in the 2000s and now stands derelict and roofless.

GREY ABBEY
Main Street
Coach House/Court House
1725-35

A five-bay, single-storey, attached structure standing on the west side of the south end of Main Street served as Grey Abbey petty sessions court house. Central round-headed entrance flanked on each side by two round-headed windows. The NI Historic Buildings database records local information suggesting that it was built between 1725 and 1735 as a coaching inn. Having served as a school for a time, it is marked as a court house on the third-edition OS map (1899-1904). Grey Abbey was part of Kircubbin petty sessions area in the 1830s but had acquired its own petty sessions court by 1880. Grey Abbey (or, more correctly, Comber and Grey Abbey) petty sessions were transferred to Newtownards in 1969, and abolished in 1971.

HILLSBOROUGH
The Square
Market House and Court House #099
William Forsyth or James McBlain; David McBlain
c. 1760; c. 1820

The NI Historic Buildings database says Hillsborough court house was built c. 1760, possibly to designs by William Forsyth or James McBlain, and extended c. 1820, to plans possibly by James McBlain Jnr. Sir Charles Brett thought there were two James McBlains, father and son, but research by architectural historian Peter Rankin has established that there was only one James, who had a son, David. The 1760s date derives from notices which appear in the *Belfast Newsletter* from 1763 onwards, but surviving drawings are dated a decade later. There is one drawing for Hillsborough in PRONI by William Forsyth dated in the 1770s (the exact date is obscure), as well as signed but undated drawings by James McBlain for Edenderry market house, Co. Offaly, a building similar to that in Hillsborough. One unsigned and undated drawing for Hillsborough, showing the building as extended, was attributed by Brett to James McBlain, the son, but may now be assigned to David McBlain. Described by the OS *Memoirs* as 'a neat, stone building occupying a space 103 feet long and 64 feet broad. At one end is the sessions court, at the other a market place and between them are the Grand Jury room and caretaker's apartments. It was built by the Marquis of Downshire'. The oldest part of the building is the two-storey section in the centre. Sandstone ground floor with opposed flights of steps to front and rear each leading to a three-arch arcade. Set back above this is a three-bay, square, Palladian upper storey, urn-topped and crowned by a square clock tower and cupola. The single-storey, three-bay by five-bay granite wings are later, that to the north containing the courtroom. These have arcades of arched recesses, the centres containing entrances and the rest windows. These windows are larger on the south side. By the early 1860s the market function had come to an end, and by the mid-20th century the south wing had become the Downshire estate office. In 1959 the building was taken into state care and refurbishment works began. These continued into the 1970s. The estate office became a community hall while the courtroom, with its flagged floor and plain wood furnishings, remained in use until the late 1990s. In 1997 the building was converted to a tourist information and heritage centre, with the courtroom as a central attraction.

HILLTOWN

Main Street
Market House
Thomas Duff
1828

Hilltown market house is listed in the *Archaeological Survey of County Down* (1966) as a court house. Designed by Thomas Duff and built in 1828, this is a fairly typical example of the type, two-storeys and three bays, the centre bay advanced and pedimented, with three segmental market arches to ground floor (long filled in), square-headed windows to first floor, and a louvered cupola. Hilltown is not listed in the usual sources as a location for petty sessions or other courts so it is an open question whether this market house did in fact serve as a court house.

HOLYWOOD

Sullivan Place
Town Hall   #100
William Batt
1873

Lewis's *Topographical Dictionary* records that 'a court leet and baron' is held in Holywood 'every three weeks by the seneschal of the manor, for pleas in civil bill cases to the amount of £10, and pleas of record and attachment of goods and chattels to the amount of £20'. Neither Lewis nor the OS *Memoirs* mention a court house or petty sessions, but the sessions are listed in the 1842 *Petty Sessions Return*. By 1910 at the latest the petty sessions were being held in the town hall, constructed in 1873 to designs by William Batt. The *Irish Builder* described it in 1876 as 'faced with red and white brick, having cement dressings'. A clock tower shown in the accompanying illustration was never built. No longer extant.

KILKEEL

Market House and Court House   #101
c. 1800

A manorial court 'is held in the sessions-house at Kilkeel, once in three weeks, for the manor of Greencastle and Mourne, by a seneschal appointed by the Earl of Kilmorey; its jurisdiction extends over the whole of the barony of Mourne, which is included in this parish, and is the property of his lordship, and pleas to the amount of £10 are determined either by attachment or civil bill' (Lewis's *Topographical Dictionary*). The *Archaeological Survey of County Down* (1966) says this market and court was probably erected c. 1800 and 'was of two storeys, of granite rubble construction… faced with wrought and coursed granite at ground floor, and cement rendered…. The main elevation, of three bays, with central projecting pedimented feature, had a first-floor plat-band and eaves cornice of granite; each bay contained a semi-elliptical arched opening, with key-block, at ground floor, with a rectangular window, formerly sashed, above'. Demolished in 1952.

KILLYLEAGH

According to Brett's *Court Houses of Ulster*, the manor court for Killyleagh was held in a room over a public house. Perhaps Killyleagh petty sessions also sat there. Killyleagh remained a petty sessions location until 1965.

KIRCUBBIN

The OS *Memoirs* state that Kircubbin court house was 'erected in 1835, not yet finished, cost 200 pounds' and that petty sessions and a manor court sat here. While there is a market house on the first-edition OS map, a court house has not been identified and Kircubbin had ceased to be a petty sessions location by 1882.

MOIRA

Main Street
Market House and Court House   #102
c. 1810

J.R. Ward and T.C. McIlroy, in their 'Statistical Report' on Moira for the OS *Memoirs*, considered the market house to be 'a neat, stone building in the centre of the town. It was built and the cost defrayed by Sir R. Bateson'. (Bateson's father had acquired Moira Castle in 1805.) M.M. Kertland in his 'Notes' on Moira, also for the *Memoirs*, was somewhat more dismissive: 'One market house. It is also used as a court house, is very small'. Standing on the corner of Main Street and Meeting Street, this is a three-bay, two-storey structure in coursed basalt rubble with granite dressings. The two similar street fronts each have an arcade of three semi-circular arches to ground floor, square-headed windows to first floor and a slightly advanced central bay, formerly pedimented. The pediments disappeared when the walls were raised during the replacement of the original hipped roof with a pyramidal roof of corrugated asbestos. The family coats of arms which once adorned the tympanums remain. The ground floor became a filling station in 1929 and remained one until 1979. The petty sessions court sat on the first floor until 1960 (when they were transferred to Lurgan, prior to abolition in 1963), after which this was converted to a dancehall. Since 1980, the building has been the Moira Pentecostal Church.

NEWCASTLE

South Promenade

Annesley Hall and Court House

1857; 1893

This single-storey Gothic building acquired its present appearance in 1893, when it was converted to a public hall in memory of Priscilla Cecilia, Countess of Annesley (d. 1891). It is a remodelling of an 1857 school. In court use from 1899 when Newcastle petty sessions were established. Asymmetrical façade with gabled entrance porch flanked by sets of lancet windows, two on the left and three on the right. Gabled end block on right, with projecting bay containing three lancet windows. Rendered, with granite dressings. Pitched roof, tall chimneys, modillioned eaves and decorative barge boards. The building is marked as 'Annesley Hall and Court House' on the third and subsequent editions of the OS map. No longer in court use, Newcastle petty sessions having been abolished in 1979. The building remains a meeting hall and concert venue, while also housing the Annesley Estate office.

NEWRY

Trevor Hill

Court House   #103

Thomas Duff; Henry Smyth; Richard Henry Dorman; NI Department of Finance Architects

1843; 1862-65; 1892; 1993-95

Newry's first court house stood detached in the centre of Margaret Square. Described as old in 1836, it had been built as a market house and converted to court use. Marked as 'Sess. Ho.' on the first-edition OS map, it was demolished, as the OS *Memoirs* records, 'in order to open a free communication with Monaghan Street on the Armagh side of the river, across which a new bridge has lately been erected'. Thomas Duff designed its replacement, a new petty and quarter sessions court house on Trevor Hill, completed in 1843. A two-storey, three-bay by five-bay classical block, rusticated at ground level; the broad centre bay to the front advanced with a hooded entrance and a pediment supported by four Doric pilasters. Square-headed windows to front and side elevations, and a tall lantern, topped by a cupola, provided light to the centrally placed double-height courtroom. The County Surveyor John Fraser, whose own 1837 scheme had been passed over by the Grand Jury, was critical of the finished building, and there were ongoing issues regarding the internal layout in particular. Fraser's successor as County Surveyor, Henry Smyth, carried out extensive alterations in 1862, with further repairs and alterations following in 1865 at a cost reported by the *Dublin Builder* as £1,000. Yet more 'improvements' were carried out by Richard Henry Dorman in 1892. Damaged by a bomb in 1972, and more recently in 2010, it is now hidden behind a high security wall and fence. The court house was largely rebuilt from 1993 to 1995 to meet new court requirements. Only the front façade and side elevations were retained. A large wedge-plan extension with rounded corners was added to the rear, its architectural expression an austere contemporary reflection of the classical language of the original. The building remains in use for Magistrates, County and Crown Courts sittings.

Kilkeel (Lawrence Collection, NLI, late 19C) | **#101**

Moira (IAA, 2000) | **#102**

Newry (Lawrence Collection, NLI, late 19C) | **#103**

NEWTOWNARDS

Conway Square

Town Hall/Market House

Ferdinando Stratford

1771

According to Lewis's *Topographical Dictionary*, a manor court was held in Newtownards 'before a seneschal appointed by the Marquess of Londonderry, every third Saturday, for the recovery of debts not exceeding £10; and a court leet annually, at which various officers are appointed for the manor, and also a constable for the borough, whose sole duty it is to assist in preserving the peace. The general sessions for the county are held here, in June and December, before the assistant barrister for the division of Downpatrick; petty sessions are held on the first and third Saturdays in every month'. It is presumed that these courts sat in the fine assembly rooms available in the still extant town hall, the eleven-bay, two-storey structure built as a market house in 1771 to designs by Ferdinando Stratford for Alexander Stewart of Mount Stewart. Stone-fronted on its south side, rendered on its north, this elegant building has a prominent three-storey central bay, advanced and pedimented on both fronts. A double-height central arch, topped by Palladian windows, is crowned by a tall cupola and flanked by five-bay wings, arcaded at ground floor and with square-headed windows above.

#100 | Holywood, Town Hall (*Irish Builder*, 1 April 1876)

NEWTOWNARDS

Regent Street

Court House   #104

William Francis Caldbeck; Henry Smyth

1849-50; 1863

A purpose-built petty and quarter sessions court house was provided for Newtownards in 1850, designed by William Francis Caldbeck. This is the only court house which can be attributed with certainty to him. In the Royal Hibernian Academy exhibition of 1849 Caldbeck exhibited a 'Design for a Court-house and Bridewell, to be erected at Newtownards, County of Down, for which the Grand Jury awarded the Artist a premium of £25'. *The Builder* magazine reported on 24 August 1850 that there was 'a new court-house erecting at Newtownards, from the designs of Mr Caldbeck, to whom the premium of 25l. was awarded in competition for same. The cost will be about 2,000l'. Caldbeck's own account book for 1844-60, held in the Irish Architectural Archive, records payments relating to Newtownards, beginning with £25 'Cash paid for Premium for N.T. Ards Court House' on 22 May 1849. He was paid £1 on 9 June 1849 for tracings for the court house, £50 'on acct of [work] at N.T. Ards Court House' in November 1849, a further £15 in May 1850 and a final payment of £14 16s 4d, which was 'the Balance of N.T. Ards' on 22 August 1850. The first sessions sat in the court house in June 1850 and, as at Newry, the County Surveyor John Fraser was critical of the new building, in particular its internal arrangements. Architect Henry Smyth enlarged and remodelled the building in 1863. The building was, in Maurice Craig's words, 'a close relative' of the standard late-1830s – early-1840s court house design. It had a five-bay, two-storey centre block, with recessed entrance wings at either end. The three centre bays of the rusticated ground floor were blind, with recessed panels. The end bays had segmental windows to ground floor. The first floor had five square-headed windows in arched recesses, their sills merging to form a platband which traversed the entire façade. So much was fairly typical of a standard court house. However, here the end bays were slightly recessed, whereas the typical standard court house had advanced end bays. There was an eaves pediment above the centre three bays, while the tall attics of the entrance wings had unusual thin paired windows with rounded hoods, all features not found on other standard court houses. Whether these deviations from the standard were due to Caldbeck or Smyth cannot now be ascertained. The court house was demolished in 1968.

NEWTOWNARDS

Regent Street

Court House   #105

NI Department of Finance Architects

1969

The c. 1850 court house in Newtownards was replaced on the same site by the current court house in 1969. It is a twenty-one bay, two-storey, flat-roofed, modernist block with flush glazing, skylights to courtrooms, and a flat concrete porch. A 'justice factory', according to Sir Charles Brett, who took a particular dislike to it, in his *Court Houses of Ulster*. Magistrates and County Courts continue to use the building.

NEWTOWNBREDA
Saintfield Road
Hotel
c. 1830

The OS *Memoirs* recorded in 1832 that Newtownbreda petty sessions were held in the hotel in the village, there being no court house. The hotel itself was said to be 'clean and kept in good order, it being but lately built'. The much altered hotel still stands on the corner of School Road and Saintfield Road, a two-storey, four-bay building with projecting gable-fronted end bays, shop fronts now to ground floor but round-headed windows in arched recesses to first floor of the end bays, and square-headed windows in between. In 1955 the petty sessions transferred to the British Legion Hall, Montgomery Street, Creagh, in 1964 to Creagh Youth Centre, and in 1970 to Malone Rugby Club. They were abolished in 1979.

PORTAFERRY
The Square
Market House and Court House   #106
1752

Built for Andrew Savage as a market house in 1752, a date recorded on a plaque on the building, and listed as a court house in the *Archaeological Survey of County Down* (1966), this detached structure stands in Portaferry's central square. Four-bay, two-storey building, the south or rear façade rendered, with square-headed windows and a central pediment containing a clock. Similar north or front elevation, but with square-headed entrances in the end bays and two arched recesses to the centre, each containing a lunette window. A small bellcote perches on the pediment. Having served as a court house, market house, ballroom and barbershop, the building was in a dilapidated condition when demolition was contemplated in the mid-1960s. It survived to be restored as a community hall in 1971-72. A drawing of 1841 by Frederick Darley for an unexecuted court house may have been intended for Portaferry, based on the fact that the Savage coat of arms appears on the front and side elevations (PRONI D552/B/3/4/44).

RATHFRILAND
Church Square
Market House and Court House   #107
c. 1770

The market house in Rathfriland 'is a handsome building in the centre of the square; the lower part is appropriated to the use of the market, and the upper part contains accommodation for holding courts' (Lewis's *Topographical Dictionary*). Five-bay, two-storey detached building. The end bays, slightly recessed and slightly lower than the centre three, were sympathetically added in 1949-51 at the time court use came to an end. Rendered with stone quoins and voussoirs to ground-floor market arcade. Square-headed windows to first floor. The north end has a single arch surmounted by three windows; there are two arches in the south end below two windows between which is a plaque with the Meade family crest and the date 1951. Latterly a community hall.

SAINTFIELD

Main Street

Market House and Court House   #108

1803

The Orange hall in Saintfield, standing detached on the north side of Main Street adjacent to the C of I parish church, was built in 1803 by Nicholas Price as a market and court house. T-plan, two-storey, three-bay rendered building with a market arcade to ground floor, the arches now filled in, and square-headed windows above. An eaves pediment contains a clock and the hipped roof is topped by a cupola ventilator.

SEAFORDE

Newcastle Road

Alms House/Court House   #109

Peter Frederick Robinson

1828

A picturesque terrace of six alms houses for widows was erected in Seaforde in 1828 to designs by Peter Frederick Robinson at the expense of Mrs Forde of Seaforde House. As indicated on the third-edition OS map (1899-1904), the house at the south end of the terrace was converted to petty sessions court use. Single-storey attached building with broad eaves and a gabled porch. Seaforde petty sessions were abolished in 1936 and the former court house was renovated and returned to domestic use by the National Trust in 1977.

WARINGSTOWN

Where the petty sessions, which Lewis's *Topographical Dictionary* says were held in Waringstown every Monday, sat is not recorded. By 1901, Waringstown petty sessions had transferred to Lurgan.

WARRENPOINT

Church Street

Court House and Town Hall

[]; W.J. Watson

1829; 1887

Warrenpoint court house 'is a small 2-storey house belonging to Roger Hall Esquire. In it is the office of the savings bank. It was fitted up as a court house in 1829' according to the OS *Memoirs*. Now the town hall, this is a two-storey, three-bay house, with rusticated render, the centre bay advanced and containing a square-headed central entrance in a granite architrave. Square-headed windows in simple architraves. Valuation records of the early 1860s show that, as well as being both a savings bank and a court house, the building also accommodated a dispensary. It was acquired by the Warrenpoint Town Commissioners in 1884, at which time the central bay acquired a rectangular panel at eaves level with the inscription 'Town Hall', though court and bank use continued for some time. A public hall was erected to the rear in 1887 to designs by W.J. Watson. Warrenpoint petty sessions were abolished in 1979.

#108 | Saintfield (IAA, 2000)

#109 | Seaforde (IAA, 2000)

BALBRIGGAN
St George's Square
Court House   **#110**
Alexander Tate
1843-45

On a podium which modulates the sloping corner site, Balbriggan court house is a detached, two-storey, five-bay building in coursed blocked stone with dressed-stone cornice, string-course, quoins, window and door surrounds. Hipped roof with broad eaves on paired brackets. Modestly advanced end bays demarcated by quoins, that to the right (west) containing an entrance approached by a short flight of steps, while that to the left (east) has a window. The door and window are framed by Tuscan pilasters which support an entablature and an arched architrave containing a round-headed window. Between these, at first floor level, is a distinctive centrally placed tripartite grouping of round-headed windows in a dressed-stone surround. The façade below this arrangement is blind, aside from an additional Tuscan-pilastered entrance to the left. Square-headed windows in red-brick surrounds in the side elevations, some blind. On the Dublin Street front the central ground floor window is tripartite, and the podium has what appears to be the tops of red-brick window surrounds giving the impression that there is a basement level. Double-height courtroom with fixed wooden furnishings. An idiosyncratic variation of the standard late-1830s – early-1840s petty and quarter sessions court house, and a near replica of the court house in Youghal, Co. Cork, Balbriggan was designed by Alexander Tate who was County Surveyor for the Northern Division of Dublin from 1845 to 1861. However, the Grand Jury refused to grant a presentment for this building, or for Tate's court house in Swords, causing the Lord Lieutenant, as empowered by Section 70 of the Grand Jury Act, 1836, to direct the Board of Works to proceed with the construction, with the Grand Jury forced to meet the cost. The building was completed in 1845 without Tate's direct involvement. Balbriggan District Court was abolished in 1982 and the area absorbed into the Dublin Metropolitan District, but the court house remains in use for District Court hearings.

BLACKROCK (RATHDOWN)
Newtown Avenue
Court House

Pettigrew and Oulton's *Dublin Almanac and General Register of Ireland* for 1837 lists 'Rathdown Petty Session Court' on Newtown Avenue in Blackrock, adjacent to a police station. Neither is listed by 1841.

BLANCHARDSTOWN
River Road
Court House

Blanchardstown was a petty sessions location until Independence. The court house was on the north side of the west end of River Road. Damaged by fire in December 1922 and explosion in January 1923, the building still stands. Now known as Ardee House it is a detached, five-bay, two-storey structure with square-headed openings and a hipped roof with broad eaves. Single bay extension to the east end. Now in office use.

BLANCHARDSTOWN
Grove Road
Court House   **#111**
Scott Tallon Walker (building); Brian O'Connell and Associates (fit-out)
2000-05 (building); 2008 (fit-out)

Blanchardstown was listed as a potential District Court location in 1924 but did not actually become one until the first decade of the 21st century, when a new court house was provided. Adjoining the Blanchardstown Shopping Centre, and adjacent to a leisure centre and the building accommodating the Draíocht Theatre and Blanchardstown Library, Blanchardstown court house is located in a 16,773m² four-storey precast concrete office development clad in terracotta, aluminium and glass. An east-west atrium spine is traversed by four office wings, the one at the east end curved to form a crescent. Designed by Scott Tallon Walker Architects as new offices for Fingal County Council, the building also houses a health centre. The fit-out of the court house section was completed in 2008 by Brian O'Connell and Associates (now O'Connell Mahon Architects) around the existing four-storey glazed atrium, with two copper-clad boxes inserted to create a new entrance lobby and reception. There are two double-height courtrooms, clad in curved cherry veneer and with clerestory windows, for District and Circuit Court use with requisite ancillary facilities including a District Court office, a legal practitioners' room, several consultation rooms, judge's chambers, a jury room, holding cells, public waiting areas and a victim support room.

CABINTEELY
Old Bray Road
Court House   **#112**

The 25-inch OS map shows Cabinteely petty sessions court house and the local dispensary occupying a premises on the south side of the Old Bray Road. Next door was the constabulary barracks which on the map is the building adjacent to the current Garda station. The court house and dispensary were burned by 'Irregular forces' in December 1922 (NAI OPW/6/1/9). A three-bay, two-storey, mid- to late-19th-century house with square-headed entrance and windows still stands on the site, the ground floor partly converted to a retail premises.

CLOVERHILL
Cloverhill Road
Court House
Scott and MacNeill
2001

Completed in 2001 at a cost of €2.9 million, Cloverhill court house is attached to Cloverhill remand prison. The building contains two courtrooms and ancillary offices required for sittings of the High Court and the District Court. Procured with the prison and related facilities through a design and build competition won by Sisk, with Scott and MacNeill as architects. A crank-ended rectangular two-storey block, clad in banded stone. Small square windows in side elevations and glass block projections framing the central entrance.

DRUMCONDRA

Drumcondra Road, Upper

Court House

Having apparently sat in part of the premises that became the Big Tree public house on the corner of North Circular Road and Dorset Street, Lower, by the end of the 19th century, Drumcondra petty sessions had moved to a detached court house building on the east side of Drumcondra Road, Upper, just north of the junction with Richmond Road. It was damaged by fire during the Civil War in February 1923 and is no longer extant. A terrace of early 1930s two-storey red brick commercial and domestic properties now stands on the site. Drumcondra was a District Court Area from 1924 until 1961, but a note in the District Court (New Areas) Order, 1927 (SI No. 103/1927) records that 'pending the provision of suitable Courthouse accommodation at Drumcondra, all cases appropriate to that Court will be heard at Kilmainham'.

DUBLIN

Abbey Street, Lower

Methodist Church

George Francis Beckett

1901-02

Built from 1901 to 1902 to designs by George Francis Beckett, the red-brick, four-storey Methodist City Mission on Lower Abbey Street is described by the *Buildings of Ireland* as 'a busy nondescript mish-mash of nine bays, with four tiers of various window types and advanced curved-topped ends'. The plain, pillared church hall accommodated court sittings for a number of years up to the early 1990s. For a time it housed the court dealing with parking offences in Dublin.

DUBLIN

Bow Street

Commercial Court House

Millar and Symes

1899

The Commercial Court division of the High Court was established in 2004. It was intended that the court would sit in a converted building at 12-13 Bow Street. This is a red-brick late-Victorian office which forms the corner into May Lane. Its most prominent feature is a sandstone entrance porch. Designed by Millar and Symes architects and built in 1899 as the 'Counting Office' of John Jameson and Son by George Moyers, contractor. The Commercial Court has primarily operated from facilities in the Four Courts since its establishment, and the Bow Street building is no longer in court use.

#110 | Balbriggan (Cathy Hayes, 2019)
#111 | Blanchardstown (Courts Service, 2012)
#112 | Cabinteely (IAA, 2019)

DUBLIN

Brunswick Street, North
Richmond Hospital
Carroll & Batchelor
1899-1901

Built by Collen Brothers to designs by Carroll and Batchelor architects, the Richmond Surgical Hospital on North Brunswick Street was opened by the Lord Lieutenant on 20 April 1901. Described by the *Buildings of Ireland* as 'Red brick and terracotta in an English Renaissance idiom, with a lively roofscape, four corner towers, decorative gables and oriel windows'. U-plan, with advanced ward wings terminating in two-storey Italianate loggias framed by copper-roofed towers. To the centre is a gabled entrance block which contained offices and operating theatres. The building closed as a hospital in 1987 and was converted to business incubation units. It was leased for court use in 1996 and five courtrooms were inserted into the ward wings. Court use ceased in 2011 following the completion of the Criminal Courts of Justice in Parkgate Street.

DUBLIN

Castle Street
Dublin Castle   #113
OPW
1922

Dublin Castle was the intermittent seat of the superior courts in Ireland from the 14th century until 1542. Following the destruction of the Four Courts in June 1922, court business relocated briefly to the King's Inns in Henrietta Street and then, on a more permanent basis, to Dublin Castle. The State Apartments were fitted out by the OPW for court use in time for the Easter sittings in April 1923. While minimal changes were made to the physical spaces, suitable furniture was installed and the throne and royal coat of arms, lion and unicorn were removed from the Presence Room. The gilded canopy remained to cover the judges' bench. The superior courts left the Castle in 1931 to return to the rebuilt Four Courts. The Dublin Children's Court continued to sit in Dublin Castle into the latter part of the 20th century.

Castle Street, Dublin Castle. Last sitting of the High Court, July 1931 (Courts Service) | **#113**
Chancery Place (Courts Service, 1995) | **#114**
Chancery Street (IAA, 2019) | **#115**

DUBLIN

Chancery Place

Court House   #114

Jacob Owen; James Higgins Owen

1837-39; 1858-62

Board of Works architect Jacob Owen designed a detached Solicitors and Benchers Hall to the rear of the main Four Courts building, on an axis with the central courtroom block. Linked to this on its east side, Owen placed a Bankruptcy Court building. These were completed in 1839, the costs of the Solicitors Hall being defrayed by the Benchers of the King's Inns. Now linked to the main Four Courts building by a connecting corridor, the Hall was converted to the Law Library following the reconstruction of the Four Courts complex by Thomas Joseph Byrne in the 1920s. From 1858 to 1862, the Bankruptcy Court building was altered and extended to accommodate the Landed Estates Court by Jacob Owen's son James Higgins Owen, also of the Board of Works. At the same time J.H. Owen also added a new wing to the west of the Solicitors Hall to house the Probate Court and additional offices. This west wing was incorporated into the Law Library following the reconstruction but the Bankruptcy Court building continues to be used as a court house for sittings of the High Court. Standing north-east of the Four Courts and facing onto Chancery Place, it is a multi-bay, three-storey block in ashlar granite, rusticated at ground floor, with square-headed windows and a square-headed entrance now approached by an elaborate curved access ramp in polished stone and painted steel.

DUBLIN

Chancery Street

Court House   #115

James Higgins Owen with Enoch Trevor Owen

1865-68

Adjacent to the Central Bridewell and built as the Central Police Court, the Chancery Street court house was designed by Board of Works architect James Higgins Owen with the involvement of Enoch Trevor Owen, and completed by 1868. Eleven-bay by four-bay, single-storey over basement front and sides, the basement area railed, with twin double-height courtrooms rising to a second storey to the rear. The granite walls are smooth at ground floor and rusticated at basement level, where the short windows are round-headed. Square-headed windows flank the advanced and pedimented centre bay where a rusticated arch contains the fanlit entrance. The three-bay by three-bay, hipped-roofed courtroom volumes are each flanked by a circular ventilation tower. Between the courtrooms to the rear is a tall arched recess with rusticated voussoirs containing a double entrance topped by a large fanlight. While the court house was altered internally in the 1980s, the judges' benches retain canopies supported on ornate brackets. Having served as the Dublin District Court, the building was adapted for District Court children's cases in 2015-16 and remains in use.

#116 | Essex Street, East, Dolphin House (IAA, c. 1985)

#117 | Green Street (IAA, c. 1940)

#118 | Henrietta Street, Kings Inns. Perspective drawing by Raymond McGrath, 1941
(Raymond McGrath Collection, IAA)

DUBLIN

Church Street

Bar Council Headquarters

Brian O'Halloran & Associates

1996-97

Filling a site between Church Street and Bow Street, and incorporating the former grain store of the Bow Street Jameson Distillery, this in-fill office development by Brian O'Halloran & Associates was the successful entrant in a concept competition organised by the Bar Council and the RIAI. Offices, consultation rooms, mediation rooms and associated facilities are arranged around a series of internal courtyards. The High Court regularly sat here in the first decade of the 21st century.

DUBLIN

Essex Street, East

Dolphin Hotel; Dolphin House   **#116**

John Joseph O'Callaghan; []

1887-98; 1979-83

The Dolphin Hotel, on the corner of East Essex Street and Crane Lane, was designed by John Joseph O'Callaghan and built from 1887 to 1898. Four-storey, red-brick structure with Gothic detailing in stone and marble, it has been described by Dr Frederick O'Dwyer as 'probably the last important secular Gothic building to be erected in the city' (*The Architecture of Deane and Woodward* (Cork, 1997)). Decorated pediment with gilded dolphin over corner entrance set in a pointed arch and flanked by pointed windows. Another pointed entrance and windows under projecting bay to the centre of the Essex Street front. Foliate string-course between ground and first floor includes the inscriptions 'Dolphin Hotel and Restaurant' and 'Wine Merchants'. Square-headed windows in recessed brick surrounds to first and second storeys, each topped by a relieving arch in brick and stone. Gabled windows to Essex Street attic above cornice punctuated with gargoyles. Rebuilt in 1979 to 1983 as a speculative office building with only the façade retained. Adapted to accommodate sittings of the Dublin District Court from 1984, somewhat ironically, given the reputation of the old hotel bar as a haunt for the legal profession. It remains in use for family law cases.

DUBLIN

Green Street

Court House   **#117**

Whitmore Davis; John Semple; Murray and Denny;

Charles James McCarthy

1792-97; 1842; 1850; 1893

In his *Historical Guide to Dublin* (2nd ed., 1821), G.N. Wright attributes Green Street court house or 'Dublin Sessions House' to Richard Johnston but the Bolger papers in the National Archives of Ireland show that its erection was supervised by Whitmore Davis and it is to him that it is assigned by the *Buildings of Ireland*. Built to replace the inadequate court space available in the Tholsel on Skinner's Row (Christ Church Place), the building opened in January 1797,

its foundation stone having been laid in 1792. Lewis's *Topographical Dictionary* records that it was used for 'the court of quarter sessions, the court of oyer and terminer, the lord mayor's and sheriffs' court, and the recorder's court'. The manor court of Glasnevin, also known as the manor court of Oxmantown, Grangegorman and the Liberties of Christ Church, which had a peripatetic existence, also sat here (as well as in Dun Laoghaire) from at least 1848 until its abolition in 1859. Spanning the space between Green Street and Halston Street, with the Debtors' Prison to the north and the now demolished Newgate Gaol to the south, its position was criticised by J. Warburton, Rev. J. Whitelaw and Rev. Robert Walsh in their *History of the City of Dublin* (London, 1818): 'its confined and unwholesome site adds much, during the sessions in particular, to the insalubrity of that crowded spot'. The court house has two street façades. The nine-bay, two-storey front in ashlar granite on Green Street is the more elaborate. The two end bays on each side are advanced with square-headed windows in full-height arched recesses. Over the three centre bays is a pediment supported by six engaged Portland stone Doric columns, paired at the ends, on either side of which are fanlit entrances. There are three square-headed windows between the columns at ground floor while the five central first-floor windows are round-headed and stand on a sill-level platband which traverses the full façade. The coursed, squared-rubble, seven-bay, two-storey façade on Halston Street also has a pediment, here supported by four engaged Doric columns, with a central fanlit entrance and square-headed windows. Extended by Murray and Denny architects in 1850 and further altered by Charles James McCarthy in 1893. The double-height courtroom was refitted by John Semple in 1842 and some replacement furnishings were inserted in the 1990s. The conical canopy to the judge's bench has been retained. From 1922 to the end of 2009, Green Street housed the Central Criminal Court, with the Special Criminal Court also sitting there from 1972. Since the transfer of these Courts to the Criminal Courts of Justice in Parkgate Street in 2010, Green Street has been used for office accommodation and also houses the Dublin Drug Treatment Court Office.

DUBLIN

Hammond Lane

Court House

The Courts Service has plans to develop a new twenty-two courtroom complex for family law and children's court business on the former Eagle Foundry site bounded by Hammond Lane and Church Street. The complex will also include a new Supreme Court. The project will provide a purpose-built facility where family law cases and cases involving children in Dublin can be held in a dignified, secure and non-threatening environment with all required support services at hand. Currently family law business in central Dublin is spread across four different buildings, where facilities are inadequate: Áras Uí Dhálaigh, Chancery Street, Dolphin House and Phoenix House. The proposed building will increase the capacity of the family and children's courts to deal with this growing area of activity in a modern court building designed with the specific needs of children and family law clients in mind. It will provide the capacity and facilities to support the operation of new legislation and future planned legislation in this area. The proposal is the subject of discussions between the Courts Service and the Department of Justice and Equality.

DUBLIN
Henrietta Street
King's Inns   #118
James Gandon, Henry Aaron Baker, Francis Johnston
1800-17

Composed of separate dining hall and library wings, with caryatid-flanked entrances and a shallow, cupola-topped linking block, the King's Inns building was conceived as the centrepiece of an unrealised development that was to fill the space between the top of Henrietta Street and Constitution Hill with substantial ranges of legal chambers. Construction began in 1800 under the supervision of James Gandon, assisted by Henry Aaron Baker. Gandon resigned from the project in 1808, leaving Baker to complete the dining hall wing. In 1813 the benchers of the Hon. Society of King's Inns agreed that the shell of the unfinished library wing should be altered for use by the prerogative court and as the Registry of Deeds. This work was completed by Francis Johnston in 1817. The prerogative court remained in the building until its abolition in 1857. In 1922 the superior courts briefly transferred to the King's Inns after the destruction of the Four Courts, before relocating to Dublin Castle. The High Court sat in the King's Inns on a semi-regular basis in the latter part of the 20th century.

DUBLIN
Heytesbury Street
Court House

The manor court of the Liberties of St Sepulchre sat in the palace of St Sepulchre on Kevin Street, until its acquisition by government as a barracks in 1803. In their *History of the City of Dublin*, (London, 1818), J. Warburton, Rev. J. Whitelaw and Rev. Robert Walsh record that there 'is now a very handsome court-house erected, with all suitable offices of the register, and a marshalsea contiguous thereto, for the Liberty of Saint Sepulchres… in a new street, which is a continuation of Bride-street'. Shown on the early 25-inch OS map of Dublin (1846-47), the court house was a three-bay structure, the centre bay advanced, set back from the east side of Heytesbury Street (formerly New Bride Street) at the corner with Camden Row (formerly Long Lane). Immediately adjacent, and facing onto the south side of Camden Row, was St Sepulchre's Marshalsea. Neither building is extant.

DUBLIN
Inchicore Road
Kilmainham Court House   #119
William Farrell; OPW   *See also* P144
1820; 2013-16

Kilmainham court house, Lewis's *Topographical Dictionary* records, 'is a spacious and handsome building; and adjoining it is the county gaol, a well-arranged building enclosed by a lofty wall… the whole admirably adapted to classification, and to the employment and improvement of the prisoners'. The Irish Architectural Archive holds drawings for a court house in Kilmainham by Henry, Mullins and McMahon dated 1817, but a plaque in the hall of the building reads

'Architect William Farrell. Opened 3 Oct 1820'. Drawings for the court house by Farrell are held in the Houghton Library, Harvard University. A detached building in ashlar granite on a corner site with two street fronts. The central three bays of the five-bay, two-storey, principal façade on the north are advanced and pedimented. These bays are rusticated at ground floor where there are square-headed entrances, the outer two blind, and have tall round-headed windows to the first floor. The outer bays are broad and have tripartite windows to ground and first floor; those to the ground floor are blind. The two-storey, three-bay east façade has an elaborate entrance in the advanced centre bay, originally intended for use by the Grand Jury and the judges. This is surmounted by a further tripartite window, with square-headed windows in the side bays. The galleried double-height courtroom has a Diocletian window above the arched recess behind the judge's bench and retains its simple wooden furnishings. Closed in 2008 following the transfer of court business to the newly opened Blanchardstown court house. Having stood vacant for a number of years, the court house was handed over by the Courts Service to the OPW in 2013. Following an extensive programme of restoration by the OPW, the court house reopened in 2016 as an integrated element of the highly successful Kilmainham Gaol museum and visitor centre. As well as the preserved courtroom, the building also houses ticket facilities, a bookshop and a café. The restored court house won the Irish Building of the Year award at the Irish Building and Design Awards 2017.

DUBLIN
Inns Quay
Áras Uí Dhálaigh   #120
Henry J. Lyons and Partners
1987

Áras Uí Dhálaigh was commissioned by the OPW to provide accommodation for District and Circuit court sittings, court administration and computer services. Standing on the corner of Inns Quay and Church Street on the site of the Four Courts Hotel, and incorporating as its east flank the retained 1960s extension to the hotel, Áras Uí Dhálaigh was designed by Henry J. Lyons and Partners and completed in 1987. The contractor was John Paul Construction Ltd. A four-storey over basement, concrete frame block, arranged around a central top-lit atrium, is attached to and shares a parapet level with the five-storey 1960s wing. A set-back attic storey clad in copper spans both old and new sections. The full-height expanse of brick of the 1960s façade contrasts with the vertical brick bays and extensive recessed glazing of the new structure. With their brick piers rising through the stone-capped parapet, the bays alternate from narrow to wide on the nine-bay Inns Quay front, a pattern repeated as the building steps back in sections along Church Street. A tunnel connects the building to the Four Courts. District, Circuit and High Court sittings are held here.

DUBLIN
Inns Quay
Four Courts
See P50 *&* Significant Court Houses – A Chronological Selection P174

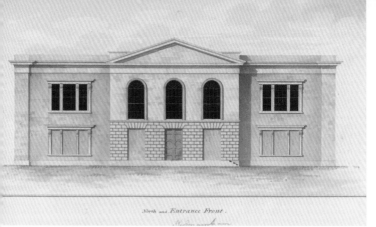

North and Entrance Front.

DUBLIN

Inns Quay (Morgan Place)

Public Records Office/Court of Appeal #121

Enoch Trevor Owen and Robert John Stirling; OPW

1861-66; 2014-15

Initially planned in 1861 as a 'General Law Record Repository' and completed the year before the passing of the legislation which established the Public Records Office of Ireland, the Public Records Office was constructed from 1864 to 1866 to designs by Board of Works architect Enoch Trevor Owen, assisted by Robert John Stirling. The building consisted of two distinct parts, a front office and reading room block with caretaker's apartment, known as the Record House, and a repository or Record Treasury to which the front building was linked by a fireproof interface intended to prevent any accidental fire in the Record House spreading to the Treasury. Externally, the Treasury read as a two-storey over basement block, with segmental-headed windows in a rusticated ground floor and an arcade of ten 30ft high round-headed windows above. Internally, five levels of records galleries in ornamental ironwork were disposed around a central atrium. The Treasury and its contents – the national archives of Ireland – were destroyed in June 1922, but the Record House survived, thanks in no small part to the fireproofing which prevented the conflagration in the repository spreading to the front block. The Record House is a three-storey over basement seven-bay by four-bay building in ashlar granite. The central bay to the front is pedimented and advanced with a single-storey tetrastyle Doric porch. There are recessed square-headed windows in the rusticated ground floor which is separated from the first floor by a cornice. All the first floor windows have pediments while the second floor windows sit on a sill-level platband. Internally, a fine Portland stone staircase provided access to the main internal space which was located on the first floor. This was the Search Room or public reading room, a double height, top-lit volume with an ornate coved ceiling. In court use from 1995, the Search Room was refitted by the OPW in 2014-15 as a courtroom for the Court of Appeal, with judge's chambers, meeting rooms and ancillary facilities provided in the rest of the former Record House. The National Archives of Ireland continues to use the basement and a reduced repository to the rear.

DUBLIN

Mary's Abbey

Court House

The manor court of the Lordship of St Mary's Abbey sat in No. 6 Mary's Abbey into the 1850s, before transferring by 1858 to No. 55 Bolton Street. Neither building is extant. The court was abolished in 1859.

DUBLIN

Merchants Quay

Riverbank Theatre

1962

Built in 1962 as St Anthony's Hall, this three- and two-storey flat-roofed structure in grey brick, concrete and flushed glazing, became the Riverbank Theatre in the early 1990s, and was converted to a court house for family law cases from 1996 to the early 2000s. The building is now the Riverbank Open Access Centre run by the Merchants Quay Ireland charity.

Kilmainham. Elevation of Main Façade, William Farrell, 1820 | #119
(Houghton Library, Harvard)
Inns Quay, Áras Uí Dhálaigh (Denis Mortell, 2019) | #120
Inns Quay (Morgan Place), Public Records Office/ | #121
Court of Appeal (Courts Service, 2015)

DUBLIN
Merchants Quay
Merchants House
1990

A neo-Georgian, post-modern, speculative office building on Merchants Quay, clad in red brick and stone, with a central full-height glazed atrium, houses the office of the Taxing Master of the High Court, and cost adjudication hearings are held in the building. Completed in 1990, this is ostensibly a four-storey, five-bay, building but is larger than it looks as it includes the three-bay block to the west.

DUBLIN
Ormond Quay, Upper
Family Law Facility
1998

A limited architectural competition was held in 1998 for a family law centre on a site on Upper Ormond Quay. The competition was won by Gilroy McMahon architects but the project was not proceeded with.

DUBLIN
Parkgate Street
Criminal Courts of Justice
See **P58** & Significant Court Houses – A Chronological Selection **P210**

DUBLIN
Phoenix Street, North
Phoenix House   #122
Brian O'Halloran and Associates
1999-2001

Brian O'Halloran and Associates secured planning permission in 1999 for this speculative office development taking up most of the block bounded by North Phoenix Street, Stable Lane, Smithfield and Lincoln Lane. Phoenix House, completed in 2001, is a seven-storey building in dark glass and stone cladding, with exposed steel columns on its Phoenix Street front, structured around a full-height central atrium and demarcated by an elliptical tower or prow at its Smithfield end. Phoenix House accommodates the main offices of the Courts Service and contains a number of courtrooms for family law cases.

DUBLIN
St Michael's Hill
Four Courts (old)
See Significant Court Houses – A Chronological Selection   **P167**

DUBLIN
Skinner's Row (now Christ Church Place)
Tholsel   #123
1676-82

In the first volume of their *History of the City of Dublin* (London, 1818) J. Warburton, Rev. J. Whitelaw and Rev. Robert Walsh provide a detailed description of the Tholsel, erected between 1676 and 1682 as the seat of municipal government. Situated on the corner of Skinner's Row (now Christ Church Place) and Nicholas Street, it was 'nearly a square, being 62 feet in front by 68 in depth, two stories high, built of hewn stone, and supported on arches to the north and west, which were not destitute of elegance; in the center of the principal front [on Skinner's Row] two massive columns of the Tuscan order supported a vestibule of a very robust appearance, but in a stile bold and singular; over this vestibule, which was decorated with the city arms, was a window with niches on either side, in which stood the statues of Charles II in whose reign this pile was erected, and of his brother, James duke of York, afterwards the bigoted and unfortunate James II; and over these the royal arms supported by scrolls formed a kind of angular pediment… A spacious open hall, decorated with four massive columns similar to those of the vestibule, and supporting the floor of the upper story, comprehended the entire of the ground-floor, with the exception of the space occupied by the stair-case, and its south-eastern angle, which was appropriated to the Recorder's court; in this court delinquents were tried in the presence of the lord mayor even for capital offences, murder and treason excepted… On the upper floor, and in apartments appropriated to the purpose, the lord mayor, aldermen, commons and sheriffs used to meet to transact city business'. By the time this description was written the building had been semi-demolished because of its 'dangerously ruinous state'. The remainder was gone by 1820, but the statues were moved to the crypt of Christ Church Cathedral, where they still remain.

DUBLIN
Smithfield
Children's Court House
See Significant Court Houses – A Chronological Selection   **P208**

DUBLIN
Store Street
Coroner's Court   #124
Charles James McCarthy; Dublin City Architects Division
1900-02; 2009

Situated on Store Street, on the site of old mill stores for the Custom House, the Coroner's Court was constructed from 1900 to 1902 to designs by Dublin City Architect Charles James McCarthy. The contractor was Thomas Mackey and the cost £4,259. Behind the building was the City Morgue, also by McCarthy (demolished 1999). Red-brick, with sandstone string-courses, mouldings and decoration, the Coroner's Court comprises a single-storey, single-bay, full-height courtroom block, with elaborate stepped gable, and a slightly set-back, two-storey, two-bay office and entrance wing. Three tall round-headed windows provide light to the half-panelled courtroom which has wooden furnishings and exposed timber beams to its partially glazed ceiling. Above the three windows is a large pedimented plaque bearing the inscription

'Coroner's Court'. The arms of the City of Dublin decorate the rounded parapet of the office wing which has a baroque doorcase set in an arched opening. Renovated and extended in yellow brick in 2009 by Dublin City Architects Division, the building remains in coroner use.

DUBLIN

Strand Street, Great

Court House   #125

The Court for the Relief of Insolvent Debtors, established in Ireland in 1821, moved in 1824 from premises on Abbey Street to a court house at 2 Great Strand Street, a three-bay, two-storey red-brick building with a large, central fanlit entrance. The court offices were located in 3 Ormond Quay, which adjoined the court house to the rear. By the mid-1840s, entry to the court house was provided via the Ormond Quay premises. Legislation in 1861 brought changes to insolvency and bankruptcy procedures and by 1868 the buildings were no longer in court use. The former court house was converted to a licensed premises in 2019.

DUBLIN

Thomas Court

Court House

The manor court of Thomas Court and Donore was held, according to Lewis's *Topographical Dictionary*, 'every Wednesday in the courthouse in Thomas-Court, a plain building erected in 1160'. In their *History of the City of Dublin* (London, 1818), J. Warburton, Rev. J. Whitelaw and Rev. Robert Walsh refer to it as 'a very ancient edifice'. No longer extant.

DUBLIN

William Street, South

City Assembly House   #126

[Oliver Grace]

1766-71

The Dublin Court of Conscience was a court for the recovery of small debts whose origins went back to the 12th century. It sat in the Tholsel in Skinner's Row until the early 19th century, before transferring in 1811 to the City Assembly House on South William Street. This is a three-storey over basement, three-bay structure, rusticated stone at ground floor, red brick above, with a fanlit entrance in a columned surround and stone architraves to square-headed windows. It was built between 1766 and 1771, possibly to designs by Oliver Grace, for the Society of Artists in Ireland and incorporated a large, top-lit octagonal public art gallery, possibly the first such space in Europe. Acquired by Dublin Corporation in 1809, the gallery became a council chamber and the room below it was fitted out for the Court of Conscience. In 1852 the Court of Conscience transferred to the gallery/council chamber where it remained until its abolition in 1924. Having served various municipal functions, including as a museum and archives, the City Assembly House was acquired by the Irish Georgian Society in 2012 and restored as its headquarters. The gallery is once again an exhibitions venue.

DUN LAOGHAIRE
Corrig Avenue
Court House

Kingstown (Dun Laoghaire) petty sessions court house and assembly rooms stood on Corrig Avenue from 1846. The court house also shared with Green Street court house sittings of the manor court of Glasnevin (also known as the manor court of Oxmantown, Grangegorman and Liberties of Christ Church) until 1859. By 1866, the building was listed in street directories only as 'assembly rooms'. No longer extant.

DUN LAOGHAIRE
Corrig Avenue
Court House   #127
Roger P. Hofler
1991-92

Court sittings in Dun Laoghaire returned to Corrig Avenue when a new court house designed by Roger Hofler was constructed in 1991-92. This is a post-modern, L-plan court house of seven bays and two storeys. The central entrance bays are advanced and topped with a blue panelled pediment. Built as a single project with the adjacent Garda station, also by Roger Hofler. Rendered walls, rusticated at ground floor, with square-headed windows. Double-height courtroom with clerestory windows and panelled furnishings. Closure of the court house was considered in 2014 but it remains in use for District Court sittings.

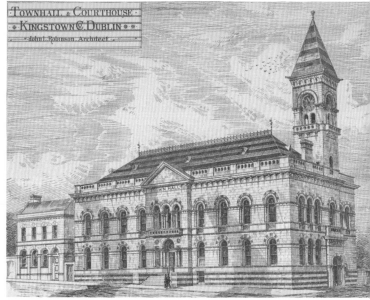

DUN LAOGHAIRE
Crofton Road, Marine Road
Court House and Town Hall   #128
John Loftus Robinson; McCullough Mulvin Architects
1874-80; 1996

In 1866 an architectural competition was held for a new town hall and court house in Kingstown (Dun Laoghaire) but it was not until 1874 that the Town Commissioners approved designs for the building by John Loftus Robinson. The design was modified in 1877 and the corner stone laid on 20 November 1878. Constructed by Michael Meade and Son, the building opened in July 1880 at a final cost of £16,000, almost £4,000 over the tender figure. Standing on a corner site, it is a two-storey, Venetian Gothic block, the town hall facing Marine Road with the court house on Crofton Road looking towards the sea. Built from local granite with Bath stone string-courses, dressings, and frieze set below the broad modillioned eaves. Rusticated plinth and smooth ashlar walls containing recessed round-headed windows with polychromatic arches. The first floor windows have marble columns with foliated capitals while below each window is a foliated shield set in a continuous band between string-courses. The projecting centre bay on the symmetrical Marine Road front is pedimented and 'Town Hall' is inscribed in the frieze beneath the pediment. The Crofton Road court house front is less symmetrical. A shallow porch, topped by a balcony similar to, though smaller than, that of the town hall, has 'Court House' inscribed above the fanlit entrance. Above the porch is a single window. To the left are triple windows at ground- and first-floor

#125 | Strand Street, Great (IAA, 2019)
#126 | William Street, South, City Assembly House.
       View of courtroom, *Evening Telegraph*, 1904 (IAA)
#127 | Dun Laoghaire, Corrig Avenue (Courts Service, 2012)
#128 | Dun Laoghaire, Crofton Road, Court House and Town Hall (*Irish Builder*, 1 Dec 1878)

level, and to the right, in a broad recessed end bay, a double window at first floor and a single window below. Directly above the entrance is a 120ft tall, two-stage clock tower with pyramid roof. The court house front was extended in 1996 by McCullough Mulvin Architects when the entire building became the headquarters for Dun Laoghaire Rathdown County Council.

DUN LAOGHAIRE

George's Street, Upper
Police Court House   #129
John Howard Pentland
1889-90

John Howard Pentland of the Board of Works designed the Kingstown Police Court building, constructed 1889-90 on the north side of Upper George's Street, adjacent to the police station and backing onto the Royal Marine Hotel. Both police station and court house were demolished on a Saturday in October 1992 following the completion of the new court and Garda facilities on Corrig Avenue. A multi-storey residential and commercial building now occupies the site. The court house had a single-storey, five-bay, hipped-roofed front block with square-headed windows and a recessed entrance in a central arch. Behind was a double-height courtroom. The *Irish Times* provides a description of the building on completion: 'We wish it was possible to speak favourably of its external appearance. The interior, however, is admirably arranged. In the centre of the new building is a commodious court, well lighted and admirably ventilated with all the latest improvements, having suitable accommodation for the various classes who from time to time have occasion to visit it… Outside the court are general waiting rooms, as well as a waiting room for ladies unhappy enough to be in trouble because of wandering dogs, or unreasonable domestics' (7 June 1890).

DUNDRUM

Kilmacud Road, Upper
Court House   #130
Deane and Woodward; Mahoney Architecture
1855-57; 2016

The Gothic chapel-like court house in Dundrum, with an attached constabulary barracks, was commissioned from Deane and Woodward architects in 1855 by Sidney Herbert, MP. It was designed by Benjamin Woodward, the contractor was John Askins and the cost was £1,600. The barracks section, which was burned in January 1923 and rebuilt in 1927, was demolished and replaced by a new Garda station in the early 1970s. That replacement was itself replaced in 2016 by Mahoney Architecture, when the original court house wing was integrated into a new expanded Garda station. The gable end of the court house has a pair of double windows set high in the polygonal granite rubble wall, surmounted by red-brick pointed relieving arches containing quatrefoils. The entrance in a pointed surround is in the first bay of the four-bay side elevation and is flanked by buttresses, with double windows set just under the eaves of the steeply pitched roof. Internally, there was a single full-height courtroom with an open-work ceiling. Court use ceased when the District Court Area of Dundrum was abolished in 1982 and transferred to the Dublin Metropolitan District.

Dun Laoghaire, Upper George's Street, Police Court House (RTÉ, 1976) | #129
Dundrum (David Davison, 1970s) | #130
Rathcoole (NIAH, 2002) | #131

HOWTH
Harbour Road
Court House
c. 1840

Built c. 1840 as a place of worship for fishermen, according to a notice in the building recorded by the NIAH, and converted to court use by 1870, Howth court house is a four-bay, single-storey structure on a confined site between Harbour Road and Church Street. There is an entrance porch in the west gable end, beneath an oculus window, and a round-headed entrance in the east end bay of the front façade with three recessed round-headed windows separated by five stylised pilasters whose capitals contain cruciform recesses. Wide surrounds with keystones to openings, stopping just below a string course at impost level. Four oculus windows on the Church Street side of the building where only the top half of the rear wall is visible due to the steep incline. A chimney indicates that the west end bay of the building constitutes a separate chamber from the full-height courtroom, which has a balcony at its east end. Sittings of Howth District Court were transferred to Sutton in 1973. Howth District Court was abolished in 1982 on amalgamation with the Dublin Metropolitan District. The court house became offices and in 2018 was converted to a tourist centre.

LUCAN
Leixlip Road
Court House and Garda Station
c. 1810

Lucan court house was located in the rear or south facing section of the two-storey ashlar building on the Leixlip Road which is now Lucan Garda station. The NIAH suggests it was originally constructed c. 1810. Attributed occasionally to local resident James Gandon, as are several other buildings in the vicinity, it is shown on the first-edition OS map which also shows a 'Police Barracks' across the road and a little further east. By 1864, at the latest, the police had relocated to this building. The north front comprises a pair of three-sided bows projecting beyond a three-bay central section whose fanlit entrance is flanked and topped by square-headed windows. The 25-inch OS map suggests that the south or court house front was similar, with a recessed centre and at least one projecting three-sided bow. Lucan court house closed following the amalgamation of the District Court Area with Dublin Metropolitan District in 1982, and the court house section of the building was subsequently demolished.

MALAHIDE
Church Road
Manor Court Office

In 1475 Edward IV granted the Talbots of Malahide Castle confirmation of the lordship of Malahide with a manor court which could operate as both court leet and baron. Also granted, according to Lewis's *Topographical Dictionary*, was 'full power to hold a court of admiralty and to determine all pleas arising either on the high seas or elsewhere within the limits of the lordship'. The manor court of Malahide continued in existence until 1859, and though no court house is shown on the first-edition OS map, the 'Manorial Court Office' is, standing in a short terrace with the 'Police Station' and the post office on the east side of the north end of Church Road. Although the terrace has been extended, the buildings would appear to be extant and are now in commercial use.

RAHENY (COOLOCK)
Main Street
Court House

Raheny petty sessions area was known as Coolock until 1904. Shown on the first-edition OS map as a schoolhouse, the building which functioned by the end of the 19th century as the area's court house and dispensary stands facing down Main Street, Raheny, on an elevated island site mainly occupied by the ruins of the 1712 C of I Church of St Assam and the associated graveyard. Three-bay, two-storey building with a gabled porch flanked by square-headed windows above which are two dormers. Decorative barge boards and ridge crest. Now a restaurant.

RATHCOOLE (NEWCASTLE)
Main Street
Court House   #131
[William Collen]
1914

The petty sessions court house for the area listed as Newcastle in the 1842 *Petty Sessions Return* and as Rathcoole by 1880 was located, by the end of the 19th century, in Rathcoole on the south side of Main Street. The sessions were held in a still-standing five-bay, two-storey block with square-headed openings, now in commercial use. In 1914 a new gable-fronted court house, helpfully labelled in bold lettering above the entrance 'Court of Petty Sessions Rathcoole' was constructed in an Arts and Crafts style a little further west along Main Street. Based on the similarity of date, inscription and lettering to Rathfarnham court house, the building may be attributed to Dublin County Surveyor William Collen. Rendered, three-bay, two-storey building with quoins to corners, square-headed windows, and a pedimented central entrance. The tympanum is inscribed with the date 1914. Three recessed segmental relieving arches to the sides, those on the east containing an entrance flanked by windows. On the west side is a three-bay, single-storey annex with a gabled canopy over the central door. Although designated a District Court location in 1924, Rathcoole in fact became part of the Kilmainham District Court Area from 1926. The former petty sessions house, one of the last to be purpose built, has most recently been in library use.

RATHFARNHAM

Main Street

Court House   **#132**

William Collen

1912

The court house in Rathfarnham is a detached, single-storey building on the east side of the north end of Main Street. Erected in 1912 to designs by Dublin County Surveyor William Collen, it replaced an earlier petty sessions court house which was located in the terrace of two-storey, two- and three-bay premises a little further north on the west side Main Street. Set-back entrance and office wings to each side. Rendered walls with red brick plinth, chimney stacks, and dressings. Three square-headed windows in centre block, with continuous hoodmoulding, above which is a dentilated string-course and red brick parapet hiding the hipped roof. Between string-course and parapet is a panel with the inscription 'Court of Petty Sessions Erected 1912'. The *Irish Builder* reported that 'the furniture will be movable, so that the building may be used when required for lectures, concerts, and other public purposes' (30 March 1912). Damaged by fire in June 1922, at the start of the Civil War, and subsequently repaired. Still extant but not in use.

RATHFARNHAM

Willbrook Road

School/Court House

c. 1865

In 1977 Rathfarnham District Court sittings transferred from the 1912 court house on Main Street to the former boys' school on the west side of Willbrook Road. This is a rusticated, stone-built, single-storey, three-bay Gothic structure of c. 1865 (NIAH) with three gabled pairs of lancet windows on the street front and an entrance in the south end, protected by a gabled porch. Rathfarnham District Court was abolished in 1982 and the area transferred to the Dublin Metropolitan District. Court sittings transferred to Tallaght in 2000 and the former schoolhouse is now in community use.

SHANKILL
Library Road
Carnegie Library   #133
Rudolf Maximilian Butler
1912

Petty sessions were held in Cabinteely, rather than Shankill, through the 19th and into the 20th century, but in 1924 it was the fast-developing Shankill and not Cabinteely which was designated as a District Court location. It remained one until 1961, and court sittings took place in the still extant Carnegie Library on Library Road, designed by Rudolf Maximilian Butler and constructed in 1912. A distinctive single-storey Arts and Crafts building in rusticated stone and render, with an advanced double-gabled entrance bay containing a hooded doorway, casement windows, and a steeply pitched tiled roof topped by a spire-like ventilator. Butler provided sliding partitions in the main room which, when folded back, created a single large space suitable for social, recreational or, as it happened, court use.

SWORDS
North Street
Court House   #134
Alexander Tate
1843

On the east side of the south end of North Street, Swords court house is a compact five-bay building in coursed rubble limestone. Recessed, single-storey entrance wings flank a full-height centre block, with advanced centre bay containing a tripartite square-headed window set high in the wall. Below the window is a lugged limestone plaque and above it, a terracotta panel. Dressed-limestone quoins, broad window surround, lugged door surrounds, parapet and sill level string-course. Double-height courtroom with wooden furnishings. The court house was designed in 1843 by Alexander Tate, Dublin County Surveyor. As with his court house in Balbriggan, the Grand Jury refused to grant a presentment for the building, causing the Lord Lieutenant to instruct the Office of Public Works to proceed with construction. The contractor was John Russborough and the cost of £420 was levied on the Grand Jury in 1848. Swords District Court was abolished in 1982 and the area transferred to the Dublin Metropolitan District. Damaged by fire in 1998 and subsequently repaired, the court house remains in use for District Court hearings.

TALLAGHT
Old Greenhills Road
Court House
post-1843

The petty sessions court house in Tallaght was located on the east side of the Old Greenhills Road, opposite St Mary's Priory. A post-1843 detached, irregularly cruciform building, it was damaged by fire in February 1923 during the Civil War and is no longer extant.

TALLAGHT
Westpark
Court House   #135
Colette Downey
1996-97

From 1924 Tallaght was part of Kilmainham District Court Area, but as part of the mid-1990s Tallaght development scheme a new court house was provided in what had become since the 1970s a major population centre. Set back from the street behind security railings and hidden by more recent developments, the court house was designed by Colette Downey for South Dublin County Council and completed in 1997. A double-height, gable-fronted courtroom block in red brick, with high-level glazing and an oversailing roof, is flanked by office wings, that on the left containing the main entrance in a white stone-faced cube. The courtroom has an open truss roof and wooden furnishings.

THE WARD
Police Station and Court House

The first-edition OS map shows a 'Police Station & Petty Sessions Ho.' in the V created by the junction of what is now the R130 and R135 at Coolquoy, north of the Ward. By the end of the 19th century this was just a constabulary barracks. A three-bay, two-storey, detached mid-19th-century house stands on the site, most recently used as a commercial premises.

BALLAGH (ARMAGH MANOR)

Ballagh Road

Court House

1853

Armagh Manor is rare example of a purpose-built manor court house. Constructed in 1853 in an isolated rural location for local landlord James Haire of Armagh Manor, this is a T-plan, Gothic Revival structure. Two-storey, gabled east block with ornate bargeboards. Single-storey wing with a slender, three-storey square tower with a tall pyramid roof and an engaged, gabled entrance porch. Having served as a school and a church, it is now boarded up and derelict.

BELLEEK

The OS *Memoirs* notes that the sessions in Belleek were held in a room hired for that purpose. No other court house has been identified. From the mid-1960s the sessions were being held in Wark Hall, a single-storey community hall at the east end of Main Street. Belleek petty sessions were abolished in 1972.

BROOKEBOROUGH

Court House

c. 1849

'An extremely handsome' court house, according to Brett's *Court Houses of Ulster*, Brookeborough court house was built in 1849 for local landlord and MP Sir Arthur Brooke, in a classical style. It was demolished in 1966, Brookeborough petty sessions having been abolished in 1964. The plain pre-1837 market hall, where petty sessions were held before the court house was built, survives as the village's Orange hall.

DERRYGONNELLY

Court House

As recorded on the third- and later edition OS maps, a court house for petty sessions stood at the south end of the village, close to the site currently occupied by the Credit Union. No longer extant. Derrygonnelly remained a petty sessions location until 1979.

DERRYLIN

Main Street

Court House   #136

[]; F.E. Townsend & Son

c. 1850; 1923

Standing on the east side of the road about 200m north-west of Derrylin cross roads, Derrylin court house is a three-bay, two-storey stone-built structure of c. 1850, with an advanced off-centre, gabled entrance bay. Mullioned double windows in dressed-stone surrounds. Those to the ground floor are taller than those at first floor level, and have hoodmouldings, as does the window to the first floor of the gabled block. Stepped hoodmould to entrance. Pitched roof with red-brick chimneys. The building was sold to Callowhill Masonic Lodge No. 453 by the Erne estate for £150 in 1918, and the Lodge held its first meeting there on 24 June that year. It was damaged by fire in June 1920 during the War of Independence and in 1923 tenders were invited for its restoration under the direction of F.E. Townsend and Son, architects. The construction work was carried out by Mr Bloomfield, building contractor, from Brookeborough, and the first meeting in the rebuilt hall took place on 31 March 1924. It remains in Masonic use.

ENNISKILLEN

Bridge Street, East

County Court House

See Significant Court Houses – A Chronological Selection   **P178**

IRVINESTOWN

Church Street

Court House

Listed as Lowtherstown in 1842, Irvinestown remained a petty sessions location until 1979. By the second half of the 20th century at the latest, the court house was located on the north side of Church Street, opposite Derryvullan North C of I church. The three-storey house on the site now may be a reconfiguring of the court house building.

KESH

Main Street

Court House

The petty sessions court house in Kesh was located on Main Street. Still known as the 'Old Court House', it is a single-storey barn with a rendered gable front containing the entrance. Corrugated side walls and roof, with four windows in the side elevations, it is now a mission hall. Kesh petty sessions were abolished in 1979.

LACK

Main Street

Court House

The detached petty sessions court house in Lack stood on the south side of Main Street, immediately to the east of the school. Shown on the second-edition (1860-61) and third-edition (1905-07) OS maps, it is no longer extant. Lack petty sessions were abolished in 1936.

LETTERBREEN

Sligo Road

Court House

Letterbreen petty sessions court house stood beside a constabulary barracks on the north side of the Sligo Road, about 500m west of the village. It was a 'single-storey roughcast barn-like structure', according to Brett's *Court Houses of Ulster*. While the barracks would appear to be still standing, and in domestic use, the court house is not. Letterbreen petty sessions were abolished in 1979.

LISBELLAW

Listed in the 1842 *Petty Sessions Return*, Lisbellaw remained a petty sessions location until 1979. The court house and RIC barracks may have shared a building, though neither one is marked on the various editions of the six-inch OS map.

LISNASKEA

Main Street

Market House and Court House   #137

William Deane Butler

c. 1830

According the OS *Memoirs*, a 'handsome market house built of stone has been erected within 5 years back' in Lisnaskea, 'by and at the sole expense of the Earl of Erne. The ground floor is a spacious opening affording ample accommodation for the oat market… On the first floor are 2 rooms, one small one and the other of considerable size, suitable for an assembly room and capable of holding 150 persons'. Brett's *Court Houses of Ulster* attributes it to William Deane Butler and says that the first floor rooms were converted to court use in 1837. It is shown as 'Town Hall & Court Ho.' on the third-edition OS map (1905-07). A two-storey, T-plan block with market arcade at ground floor, a second arcade of relieving arches at first floor, a central pediment with a clock, and a cupola, it was bombed in 1971 and subsequently dismantled. A modern bank building stands on the site, its pediment and clock the only allusions to its predecessor. Lisnaskea petty sessions were abolished in 1979.

#136 | Derrylin (Paul Tierney, 2019)

#137 | Lisnaskea (Alistair Rowan/Buildings of Ireland, 1970)

#138 | Newtownbutler (Oak Healthy Living Centre, 2015)

NEWTOWNBUTLER
Bridge Street
Court House   #138
William Deane Butler
1828-30

In January 1828, John Creighton of Crom Castle, Co. Fermanagh,
wrote to the Chief Secretary complaining that the court house in
Newtownbutler was in such a poor condition that the magistrates
were unwilling to hold petty sessions there (NAI CSORP/1828/106).
Construction of a replacement petty and quarter sessions court house
and bridewell began in 1828 and the building was completed in
mid-1830 at a cost of £1,077 18s. The builder was Jonathan Tilson of
Belturbet, and the architect William Deane Butler (who also designed
the town's market house, a very similar building to his now-demolished
market house and court house in Lisnaskea). Rendered with stone
quoins, this is a T-plan building whose double-height courtroom
block has a simple, unadorned pediment to the gable front addressing
the street. Two-storey office and accommodation wings. Damaged
by a bomb in 1971, it was adapted for use as a church hall and is now
Cherish Community Centre. Newtownbutler petty sessions were
abolished in 1979.

ROSSLEA
Main Street
Court House

Rosslea petty sessions court house was situated in the terrace of
modest two-storey houses and commercial premises on the west side
of Main Street, almost opposite the junction with Church Street. The
building appears to be still standing, though Rosslea petty sessions
were abolished in 1964.

SHANMULLAGH
Gardrum Road
Court House

Shanmullagh is listed as a petty sessions location in the 1842
Petty Sessions Return. The isolated rural sessions house, which
is mentioned in passing in the OS *Memoirs*, is shown on the
first-edition OS map, a T-plan building at a crossroads on the
Gardrum Road about 1km west of Letterbreen. Court use had
ceased by the 1880s. A modern farm house now occupies the site.

AHASCRAGH
Main Street
Court House

Ahascragh petty sessions court house was located in the middle of a terrace of buildings on the west side of Main Street, just north of the graveyard. The 19th-century terrace survives and the former home to the courts is now a three-bay, two-storey house.

ARDRAHAN
Market Square
Court House

The finest building in Ardrahan is the constabulary barracks of c. 1860, a three-bay, two-storey stone block on the west side of Market Square. It is now the Garda station. A semi-detached, three-bay, two-storey house on the south-east side of the Square served as Ardrahan petty sessions court house.

ATHENRY

Lewis's *Topographical Dictionary* reports that a portreeve's court was held in Athenry, 'not in any fixed court-house or place, but in different parts of the town'. Athenry was a location for petty sessions from at least 1842, and District Court sittings from 1924. In 1936 tenders were invited for the erection of new court houses designed by Limerick architect Patrick J. Sheahan at Athenry, Ballygar, Gurteen and Mountbellew. These were not proceeded with. Athenry District Court sat in the Canon Canton Memorial Hall on Church Street, constructed from 1931 to 1933 by the town's Total Abstinence Association to the designs of a local engineer named Powell. This is a rendered, three-bay, two-storey structure with single-storey entrance annex and round-headed windows, the centre one at first floor level blind and containing a name plaque. Court sittings subsequently moved to Athenry Community Hall, Clarke Street, a rendered, four-bay, two-storey shed with stepped gable. Athenry District Court was abolished in 2011 and the District Court Area merged into that of Loughrea.

BALLINAMORE
Court House

Ballinamore petty sessions court house was located in the western end of a sequence of buildings opposite Ballinamore Park which included the post office and the constabulary barracks. While Ballinamore Park is no longer extant, the other buildings still stand and are mainly in use as a licensed premises. The former court house was part of what is now a single-storey, three-bay cottage.

BALLINASLOE
Society Street
Court House   #139
Henry Clements/William Deane Butler
c. 1840

Henry Clements, County Surveyor for Galway from 1834 to 1838, submitted plans for a court house in Ballinasloe in 1838. The extant building is a solid example of the standard late-1830s – early-1840s petty and quarter sessions court house design. As such it is almost identical to the court houses in Clifden and Oughterard and can therefore be attributed to Clements, or to William Deane Butler, on the basis of his having been paid for the plans and supervision of the construction of Clifden court house. Symmetrical, modestly articulated, ashlar limestone, five-bay, two-storey building terminated on either side by set-back single-storey entrances with pedimented doorcases. Slightly advanced end bays and slightly recessed windows, square-headed at first floor level with sills merging to form a platband. Two round-headed windows at either end of the ground floor flank three framed panels. Internally, the original double-height courtroom was subdivided in 1996 for District Court use, and further maintenance work was carried out in 2006. To the rear is the former bridewell. An early-20th-century post box bearing the royal insignia of Edward VII stands in front of the building.

BALLYGAR
Main Street
Court House   #140
1838

Small scale, single-storey stone building, with pedimented porch, situated at right angles to Ballygar Main Street, adjacent to the RC church. A second, flat-roofed porch has been added to the right. Used for petty sessions and District Court sittings from the 1850s to the 1940s. The District Court Area ceased to exist in 1961. Refurbished as a community centre in 2016. In 1936, tenders were invited for the erection of new court houses designed by Limerick architect Patrick J. Sheahan at Athenry, Ballygar, Gurteen and Mountbellew. These were not proceeded with.

BALLYMOE
Court House

The petty sessions court house was located on the west side of the southern end of Ballymoe. The site is now occupied by a public house and the post office.

CARNA

District Court sittings, and before them petty sessions, took place in Carna until 2008 when the District Court Area was abolished, and the Electoral Divisions amalgamated with Derrynea. While a petty sessions court house has not been identified, the District Court has used a variety of venues including the Parish Hall, the Carna Bay Hotel and the Údarás na Gaeltachta office building.

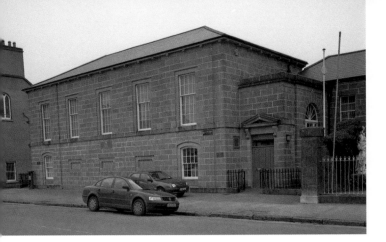

CASTLETOWN

While Castletown is not listed in the 1842 *Petty Sessions Return*, its petty sessions court order books survive for 1860-63 and 1866-1913. A court house has yet to be identified.

CLEGGAN

Cleggan became a petty sessions location in 1901 and court order books survive for 1902-14. Where the court sat has not yet been established.

CLIFDEN
Galway Road
Court House   **#141**
William Deane Butler
1840

Clifden petty and quarter sessions court house was under construction in 1840 when the Board of Works provided a £1,000 loan. A presentment for £95 was made to William Deane Butler at the Galway Summer Assizes of 1845 for providing working plans for and superintendence of the building of the court house, including nine visits from Dublin to inspect the works. A typical example of the standard court house of the late-1830s – early-1840s. Symmetrical, modestly articulated, five-bay, two-storey building, terminated on either side by set-back single-storey entrances with pedimented doorcases and lunette windows in end walls. Rendered façade with slightly advanced end bays and limestone dressings to windows, square-headed at first floor level with sills merging to form a platband. Two segmental-headed windows at either end of the ground floor flank three small recessed panels, the central one of which contains a window. The internal arrangements can be read in the façade; a well lit double-height courtroom at first floor level above holding cells on the ground floor. The courtroom is intact, with semi-circular canopy over judge's bench, witness box and stepped public gallery. Renovated 2018, and still in use for District and Circuit Court sittings.

CLONBUR
Court House

Clonbur became a petty sessions location at some point between 1880 and 1883. The court house is shown on the 25-inch OS map as part of a terrace opposite the diminutive four-arched, pyramidal-roofed market house. It would appear to survive as a three-bay, two-storey private house.

DERREEN

Court House

Derreen petty sessions court house was a small detached building behind a short terrace of three two-storey roadside cottages which still stands. It is possible that any remaining fabric may now have been incorporated into the easternmost surviving cottage. Derreen District Court was abolished in 2004, and the District Court Area amalgamated with that of Tuam.

DERRYNEA/DOIRE AN FHÉICH

Court House   #142

Derrynea petty sessions area was created in 1902. Located close to the village of Costelloe, the court house is a modest three-bay, two-storey structure still with a stone plaque above its entrance identifying it as 'Teach na Cuirte'. Advanced central entrance bay with set back wings all under a broad pitched roof. No longer in use as a court house, though Derrynea District Court continues to sit in rented premises nearby.

DUNMORE

High Street
Court House

A detached court house is shown on the 25-inch OS map of Dunmore, on an island site in the centre of High Street. No trace of this building remains. Dunmore District Court sat in the local community centre until it was merged with Tuam in 2008.

EYRECOURT

Market Street
Market House and Court House   #143
pre-1749

John Wesley is recorded as having preached in the market house in Eyrecourt in May 1749, and in 1760 he preached in the court house, almost certainly the same building. Marked as 'Court Ho. & Sch.' on the first-edition OS map, and a location for petty and quarter sessions, according to Lewis's *Topographical Dictionary*, it subsequently became the town hall. Five-bay, two-storey, detached building, the central three bays of the main, west, front are advanced and topped with a truncated pediment. A central fanlit entrance is flanked by blind arched recesses. Tall segmental recesses in the end bays formerly contained a square-headed window (left) and an entrance (right). Five square-headed windows to the first floor. Above the centre window is a rectangular panel. Full-height return to rear. The shell remains impressive despite the current absence of roof, windows, floors or internal walls.

#143 | Eyrecourt, Market House and Court House (Billy English Collection, IAA, c. 1970)
#144 | Eyrecourt, Court House (IAA, c. 1975)
#145 | Galway, Town Court House (IAA, 2002)
#146 | Gort (IAA, c. 1970)

EYRECOURT
Church Lane
Court House   #144
c. 1825

By the latter part of the 19th century Eyrecourt petty sessions had relocated from Market Street to a building on Church Lane shown on the first-edition OS map as a bridewell. Originally constructed c. 1825 (NIAH), this is a cruciform structure of two storeys, rendered, with two entrances, a lean-to extension to the front, and walled enclosure to the rear. Only the security bars on the first floor windows hint at its former functions. It is no longer in use, Eyrecourt District Court having been amalgamated with Ballinasloe in 2008.

GALWAY
Courthouse Square
County Court House
See Significant Court Houses – A Chronological Selection   P186

GALWAY
Courthouse Square
Town Court House   #145
Alexander Hay; O'Riain and Associates Architects
1825; 1995

Attributed to local architect Alexander Hay, Galway Town court house echoes, without mimicry, its slightly earlier antecedent, the County Court House, which it directly faces. Its monumental façade, with its fine, almost fully recessed, tetrastyle Doric portico, derives from, but is smaller in scale than, its more imposing neighbour. Its side elevations, with their tall arched recesses, also take cues from the earlier building. A second Doric portico enlivens the otherwise relatively plain five-bay, three-storey rear façade. The building served as court house and town hall until 1885, after which court sessions ceased and the building was renamed the Town Hall. In the 1950s it became a cinema and in the mid-1990s, having become dilapidated, it underwent an extensive refurbishment programme by O'Riain and Associates Architects, to be repurposed as a municipal theatre. The theatre was officially opened on 1 February 1996 by the then Minister for Arts, Culture and the Gaeltacht, Michael D. Higgins.

GARRAFIN

Garrafin became a petty sessions location in 1901 and court order books survive for 1902-14. Where the court sat has not yet been established.

GLENAMADDY
Greggs Road
St Bridget's Hall
1909

St Bridget's Hall in Glenamaddy is a six-bay, single-storey building bearing a datestone for 1909 (and a plaque commemorating its restoration 1992-94). Rough stone architraves to windows and prominent central entrance porch. The building has served a variety of uses, including town hall, school and court house. Although not a petty sessions location, Glenamaddy became a District Court Area in 1926 and remained one until 2008. The building is now a theatre venue.

GORT
The Square
Court House   #146
c. 1815

According to Lewis's *Topographical Dictionary*, petty sessions were held in Gort 'every Saturday, and the October quarter sessions for the county are held in the court house, which was erected in the square in 1813, and comprises a court hall, grand and petty jury, rooms and keepers' rooms'. Standing on the north-east side of Market Square, the attached two-storey over part-basement, limestone-faced court house closes the vista from Church Street. A ground-floor arcade consists of a central deeply recessed entrance, with iron gates, flanked by square-headed windows in shallow arched recesses. Above the platband the central bay breaks forward slightly and is surmounted by an entablature. The three first-floor windows are round-headed. The double-height courtroom, used for District Court sittings, was altered c. 1970 and again in the early 1990s. It remains in use.

GURTEEN/GORTEEN

Gurteen was listed as a location for petty sessions from 1842, and as a District Court location in 1924 but not 1961. Where the court sat has not yet been established. In 1936, tenders were invited for the erection of new court houses designed by Limerick architect Patrick J. Sheahan at Athenry, Ballygar, Gurteen and Mountbellew. These were not proceeded with.

HEADFORD
Bridge Street
Court House   #147
c. 1880

The court house in Headford is a small, detached, three-bay vernacular building of c. 1880, adjacent to the Garda station. The central entrance door lead directly to the courtroom which was lit by small windows set high in the wall. In use until Headford District Court was abolished in 2008 and the District Court Area amalgamated with Tuam.

KILLIMORE/KILLIMOR
Court House

Listed as Whitegate in the 1842 *Petty Sessions Return*, a detached 'Petty Sessions Court Ho.' is shown in the first-edition OS map beside a school on the north side of the street at the east end of Killimore village. A later two-storey house and commercial premises now occupies the site. Killimore was a District Court location from 1924 until 1961.

KILRONAN
Court House

Kilronan was a location for Aran petty sessions and was a District Court location from 1924. Halla Rónáin, the local community hall, had been used for District Court sittings but these now take place in a local hotel.

KINVARA
Courthouse Road
Court House   #148
c. 1840

The court house in Kinvara is a rendered, five-bay, single-storey building with entrances in the end bays, each with plain stone surrounds. These flank three tall round-headed windows. Gutted in 1920 during the War of Independence, it was subsequently rebuilt. No longer in use as a court house following the closure of the District Court in 2008. It has been home to Kinvara Area Visual Arts since 2015.

LAWRENCETOWN
Court House

A court house for petty sessions is indicated on the 25-inch OS map of Lawrencetown as a small detached circular building on an island site in the east 'square' of the dumbbell shaped village. It was shown as a market house on the first-edition OS map. No trace remains.

LETTERFRACK
Court House

Letterfrack was not listed as a petty sessions location in the 1842 *Petty Sessions Return*, though nearby Renvyle was. Letterfrack had become the designated petty sessions location by 1880 and the 25-inch OS map shows a court house located adjacent to the Temperance Hotel, built by the Quaker Ellis family c. 1850. The hotel was later known as Casson's Hotel. The court house was an L-plan, two-storey structure with a pedimented window at first floor level of its road façade, but little or no trace of this building remains.

#147 | Headford (Courts Service, 1996)
#148 | Kinvara (Courts Service, 1996)
#149 | Loughrea (IAA, 2002)

LETTERFRACK
Quaker Meeting House/Court House

Latterly, the Letterfrack District Court sat in the former Quaker Meeting House, built by the Ellis family in the 1850s, a simple three-bay hall with rubble limestone walls, square-headed windows, and small extensions at either end. No longer in use as a court house as Letterfrack District Court was amalgamated with Clifden in 2006.

LOUGHREA
Fair Green
Court House   #149
[1821]

Somewhat set apart from the town centre, but originally sited to be adjacent to the now vanished gaol, Loughrea court house is a detached, two-storey, T-plan ashlar limestone building. According to Slater's *National Commercial Directory of Ireland* (1846), it was built in 1821. However, it is not shown on the first-edition OS map, published in 1838-39. Turning its back to the town, the three-bay front elevation looks out over Lough Rea. With banded rustication to ground floor, it has a recessed central bay which contains a stylised entrance portico formed by pairs of squared Doric pilasters. Square-headed windows at ground and first floor, and at first floor in the three-bay back range. Hipped roof, with broad modillioned eaves. Some original features survive in the double-height galleried courtroom, including panelling and door surrounds. Maintenance work was carried out in 2006 to ensure the building remained fit for Circuit and District Court sittings. Still in use.

MAAM
Court House   #150
c. 1870; 1925

Built c. 1870 (NIAH), Maam court house is an isolated modest Roman temple standing on a limestone plinth and approached by a flight of five steps. Portico *in antis* with squared stone columns. Rendered walls and pediment. Square-headed windows to side elevations. Burned in 1923 and reconstructed in 1925. Closed in November 2004 on the amalgamation of Maam District Court Area into that of Oughterard. Currently unoccupied.

MILLTOWN
Court House

The petty sessions court house in Milltown was part of a small cluster of structures on the east side of the road to Tuam, south of Milltown Bridge and opposite the RC church. A public house on the site may include fabric from the court house.

Maam (NIAH, 2008) | **#150**
Mountbellew (IAA, 2019) | **#151**
Oughterard (IAA, 2019) | **#152**

MOUNTBELLEW

Ballygar Road
Court House   #151

Mountbellew petty sessions court house is shown on the 25-inch
OS map attached to the parochial house. The former court house
is still standing, a two-storey, four-bay mid-19th-century house
with square-headed windows to first floor, quoins to corners, and
shopfronts to ground floor. In 1936, tenders were invited for the
erection of new court houses designed by Limerick architect
Patrick J. Sheahan at Athenry, Ballygar, Gurteen and Mountbellew.
These were not proceeded with and Mountbellew District Court sat
in the local community centre, also on Ballygar Road, until it was
merged with Ballinasloe in 2007.

MOYCULLEN

Court House

Moycullen became a petty sessions location in 1875 and a court house
is shown on the 25-inch OS map on the north side of Moycullen
crossroads, near the constabulary barracks. No trace remains.

ORANMORE

Dublin Road
Court House

Oranmore petty sessions court house was part of a terrace of buildings
which included the adjacent constabulary barracks. Three of the
terraced buildings remain on the Dublin Road, the middle one of
which, a three-bay two-storey house, was the former court house.

OUGHTERARD

Main Street
Court House   #152
Henry Clements/William Deane Butler; []
1845; 2012-14

Oughterard is an example of the late-1830s – early-1840s standard
petty and quarter sessions court house design. Very similar to
Ballinasloe and Clifden and therefore attributable to William Deane
Butler or possibly the County Surveyor Henry Clements. Set back
behind railings, this is a symmetrical, modestly articulated, five-bay,
two-storey building terminated on either side by set-back single-storey
entrances with pedimented doorcases. Slightly advanced end bays
with recessed segmental-headed windows to rusticated ground floor.
These flank three panels, the centre one of which contains a window.
Five square-headed windows to first floor, set in architraves and with
their sills merging to form a platband. Closed as a court house in 2008,
when the District Court Area was amalgamated with Spiddal, the court
house was restored 2012-14 for community and library use. Internally,
the original double-height courtroom retains only the canopy to the
judge's bench to indicate its former use.

#153 | Portumna (NIAH, 2009)
#154 | Spiddal (Courts Service, 1996)
#155 | Tuam (Courts Service, 1995)
#156 | Woodford. Engraved view of Constabulary Barracks and Court House,
        Illustrated London News, 5 November 1887 (NLI)

PORTUMNA

Clonfert Avenue

Court House #153

Henry Clements/William Deane Butler

1845

Detached, four-bay, two-storey, ashlar-limestone classical court house which, with the bridewell to the rear, the *13th Annual Report of Commissioners of Public Works (Ireland)* described as being 'nearly complete' in 1845. Portumna is a truncated version of the late-1830s – early-1840s standard petty and quarter sessions court house design as found elsewhere in Galway at Ballinasloe, Clifden and Oughterard. As such, it is attributable to the County Surveyor Henry Clements or, possibly, William Deane Butler, who was responsible for Clifden. It has four, as opposed to five, bays, and lacks the entrance wings. Instead, the slightly advanced end bays each have framed square-headed entrances. Between them at ground floor are two blank panels. Square-headed windows at first floor, below cornice and parapet. Similar windows in three-bay east side, but blind windows in two-bay west side. The double-height courtroom retains some of its original features, including the canopy over the judge's bench and the public gallery accessed via a stone staircase. The roof of the court house failed in 1894 due to heavy rains, filling the interior with 7ft of rubble. The building was subsequently repaired. No longer in use as District Court sittings were transferred to Loughrea in 2008.

RECESS

Not a petty sessions location before 1907. A court order book survives for Recess for the period 1913-14. Where the court sat has not yet been established.

ROUNDSTONE

Court House

According to William Makepeace Thackeray in his 1843 *Irish Sketch Book*, the 'sessions-room' in Roundstone was 'an apartment of some twelve feet square, with a deal table and a couple of chairs for the accommodation of the magistrates, and a Testament with a paper cross pasted on it to be kissed by the witnesses and complainants who frequent the court. The law-papers, warrants, &c., are kept on the sessions-clerk's bed in an adjoining apartment, which commands a fine view of the court-yard – where there is a stack of turf, a pig, and a shed beneath which the magistrates' horses were sheltered during the sitting'. The petty sessions court house is shown at the north end of the village on the 25-inch OS map, close to, if not actually, the two-bay, two-storey cottage used as the local public library.

SPIDDAL

School/Court House #154

1887

The petty sessions court house in Spiddal is shown on the 25-inch OS map on the site now occupied by W.A. Scott's Church of St Enda, built 1903-07. The boys' school of 1887, similar in footprint to the demolished court house, was subsequently converted for District Court and library use. Single-storey, five-bay building with central, gabled entrance porch. Court sessions ceased in July 2013 following amalgamation with the District Court Area of Derrynea. The building continues in library use.

TUAM

Dublin Road

Court House #155

c. 1835

Detached, three-bay court house, set back from the Dublin Road on the outskirts of Tuam, shown with a bridewell to the rear on the first-edition OS map. The bridewell was later replaced by a sports centre. The court house is rendered, with a taller advanced central bay, an eaves parapet and square-headed openings. It closed in 2005, when District Court sittings moved first to the former Old Grove/Bon Secours hospital and then, in early 2018, to premises on the Weir Road, Tuam. The renovation of the former court house is under active consideration.

WILLIAMSTOWN

Court House

The petty sessions court house in Williamstown formed a terrace with the dispensary and post office. A portion of this terrace survives now as two attached houses. Williamstown District Court sat in GAA facilities and, from 1998, in Williamstown parochial hall. It was merged with Dunmore in 2004.

WOODFORD

Court House #156

The petty sessions court house in Woodford stood attached to the constabulary barracks on the north side of a narrow road off the west side of the main village street. An 1887 *Illustrated London News* engraving shows the three-bay, two-storey constabulary barracks with an entrance porch bearing a VR (Victoria Regina) plaque above the door and armoured shutters to the first floor windows. The entrance porch became a two-storey turreted affair in the early 20th century but the entire barracks was demolished c. 2000 to be replaced by a detached house. To the right in the engraving is the more modest court house, a two-bay, single-storey building with a lined rendered façade. Despite not having any electricity, the court house was in use until 1999 and remains extant. Woodford District Court was amalgamated with Portumna in 2000.

ABBEYDORNEY
Bridge Road
Court House   #157

Petty sessions hearings were held in Abbeydorney court house until c. 1919. It is a three-bay, single-storey cottage once isolated at the west end of the village but now integrated into the continuous development on the north side of Bridge Road. Pitched roof with brick chimneys and rubble stone walls with brick surrounds to square-headed openings.

ANNASCAUL
Court House

Annascaul court house was located at the west end of the village in a cluster of small houses. No trace remains. The site is now a park containing a statue of Polar explorer Tom Crean. Annascaul District Court sat in the local community hall until it was amalgamated with Dingle in 2005.

BALLYBUNION

Only a location for petty sessions from 1894, Ballybunion was designated a District Court location in 1924. Prior to 1975, the District Court sat in a number of venues including a former cinema but when this was deemed unsuitable it transferred to Listowel where it remained until the abolition of Ballybunion District Court in 1984, and the amalgamation of the Area with Listowel.

BALLYLONGFORD
Main Street
Court House

A location for petty sessions, Ballylongford court house stood on the east side of the south end of Main Street, practically the last building in the village on the 25-inch OS map. It does not appear to have survived.

BLACKWATER/CLOVERFIELD/TEMPLENOE
Court House

Lewis's *Topographical Dictionary* records that 'petty sessions for the Blackwater district are held monthly, at Clover Field, in the adjoining parish of Templenoe'. A 'School and Petty Sessions Court Ho.' is shown on the first-edition OS map, standing on the north side of the road, c. 300m east of Templenoe C of I church, at a site later occupied by Templenoe House. Cloverfield was listed in the 1842 *Petty Sessions Return*, but had ceased to be a petty sessions location by 1880.

BROSNA
The Square
Court House

Brosna became a petty sessions location in 1875. The petty sessions court house occupied the south end building in the terrace on the west side of the Square, a two-storey, three-bay structure with pitched roof and square-headed openings. Now in use as a licensed premises.

CAHERDANIEL
Court House   #158

Caherdaniel court house stands at the west end of the terrace of buildings on the south side of the village. A venue for petty sessions and District Court sittings until 1961, when Caherdaniel became part of Waterville District Court Area, the four-bay, two-storey, stone-built structure was latterly a take-away restaurant but this is now closed.

CAHIRCIVEEN
New Market Street
Court House   #159
Henry Stokes
post-1846

Designed by County Surveyor Henry Stokes, but not shown on the first-edition OS map of the town (1846), this detached, T-plan, petty and quarter sessions court house, set behind a low wall, has a compact classical façade composed of four Doric pilasters surmounted by a plain entablature and a pediment with a blind oculus. Central doorcase with pediment supported on brackets. The walls are banded below a string-course in line with the base of the door pediment. Two-storey side elevations with 1970s fenestration. Interior refitted in 1974. The building is partly occupied by county council offices while remaining in court use.

CASTLEGREGORY
Tailor's Row
Court House

Castlegregory court house was a T-plan, detached building set in its own grounds at the junction of Main Street and Tailor's Row. Also known as Merville, it is now a private residence, though the boundary wall remains as it was during its court house days. Castlegregory was a venue for petty sessions and District Court sittings until 2005, when the District Court was amalgamated with Tralee. In its latter years, the District Court sat in the local community hall.

CASTLEISLAND
Court House and Library
[Valentine Denis Doyle]
1929

#160

This L-plan building on a corner site opened in 1929, with one wing for Castleisland library and one for court use. It replaced, or is possibly in part a rebuilding of, the Carnegie Free Library by Rudolf Maximilian Butler, which itself was burned in 1920 by the Black and Tans. Possibly by Valentine Denis Doyle, Kerry County Surveyor 1920-43, who is known to have made plans for a new library in Castleisland in 1927. With a pedimented doorcase on the angle of the corner, the seven-bay court house wing has blind windows to ground floor, with distinctive keystones to the architraves, matched by smaller keystones on the first floor windows. A recessed bay at the end contains a second entrance. From 1937 to 1962 the building housed a boys' secondary school. The courtroom space was also used as a cinema and, latterly, a badminton hall. Court acoustics were reported to be difficult. Court sittings in Castleisland came to an end in 2011 on amalgamation of the District Court Area with Tralee.

CAUSEWAY
Court House

Causeway petty sessions court house stood on the south-west corner of the crossroads in the middle of the village. An L-plan structure consisting of a two-storey, three-bay front block with blank gable end on the corner, and a two-storey, two-bay wing to the rear with second entrance. Now in use as a commercial premises. Causeway district court was amalgamated with Tralee in 1994.

COOLMAGORT

Coolmagort is listed in the 1842 *Petty Sessions Return* and court order books for Coolmagort petty sessions survive for 1851-66 and 1872-1909. Where the petty sessions sat has yet to be identified.

Abbeydorney (Denis Mortell, 2018) | **#157**
Caherdaniel (Denis Mortell, 2018) | **#158**
Cahirciveen (Denis Mortell, 2018) | **#159**
Castleisland (Denis Mortell, 2018) | **#160**

DINGLE

The Mall

Court House   #161

Henry Stokes

1836–45

Dingle petty and quarter sessions court house is a three-bay, I-plan structure in coursed sandstone. The recessed centre bay on the Mall façade, which was originally the back of the building, accommodates a mid- to late-20th-century right-angled flight of steps leading to an entrance in the side of the right-hand bay. Three tall round-headed windows are set high in the walls, with Diocletian windows in side elevations. The former entrance loggia remains in situ at what is now the rear of the building. Double-height galleried courtroom with built-in furniture. A drawing for Dingle court house is in the National Archives, OPW drawings collection, signed by Henry Stokes on paper watermarked 1836. The contractor was Thade Donoghue and the building was completed in 1845. It remains in use as a court house, though local authority offices in the building were given over to arts use in 2003.

GUNSBOROUGH

Court House   #162

Anecdotal evidence indicates that an early-19th-century small, Gothicised cottage-schoolhouse later functioned as Gunsborough petty sessions court house. The building is no longer extant. Gunsborough petty sessions area became Ballybunion petty sessions area in 1894.

KENMARE

The Square

Court House   #163

c. 1735

The court house in Kenmare is a six-bay, two-storey, detached double-pile structure built c. 1735. Originally a barracks, the building is denoted as a court house on the first-edition OS map, and accommodated petty and quarter sessions. It was also in part a revenue office, and served as an auxiliary workhouse during the Famine. Burned in 1920, it was rebuilt and reopened in 1927. The second bays from each end push forward and are gabled with decorative barge boards. Between them is a porch providing shelter to the off-centre entrance. Hoodmouldings to ground-floor windows. Four-bay side elevation with shopfront entrance. The render has been stripped from much of the façade, exposing the rubble walls. The building was refurbished in 1994 and is shared between the Courts Service and Kenmare Heritage Centre.

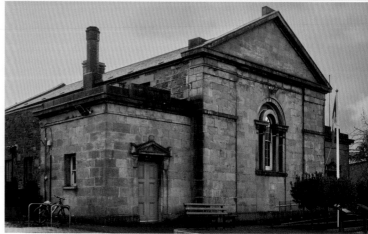

#161 | Dingle (Denis Mortell, 2018)
#162 | Gunsborough (IAA, late 19C)
#163 | Kenmare (Denis Mortell, 2018)
#164 | Killarney (Denis Mortell, 2018)

KILLARNEY

Fair Hill

Court House   #164

George Richard Pain

1826-27

Built 1826-27 for petty and quarter sessions, Killarney court house is a variant of the Pain's *Design for a court house and bridewell to be built in the different sessions towns in the County of Cork* of 6 May 1824 and the only version of this scheme to be built outside Cork. Detached, with a fine classical stone façade of three bays. Tall pedimented courtroom section with a Venetian window framed by broad pilasters. Lower wings on each side contain the entrances with pedimented door surrounds and rectangular pediments to parapets. The cut stone continues around the sides before giving way to rubble walls. Red-brick surrounds to ground-floor windows in the wings and stone to windows of the centre block, which is two-storey at the rear. The single courtroom, which was remodelled c. 1976, was described in 2007 as being in 'dire' condition. Refurbishment works were completed in 2008 and the building remains in court use.

KILLORGLIN

Market Road

Court House   #165

c. 1869

Gothic Revival church apparently built as a private chapel for Lord Ventry in or about 1869 and converted to court use to accommodate Killorglin petty sessions in the mid-1890s. Formerly standing isolated in the centre of a large plot stretching the full width between Market Road and New Line Road, but now encroached upon on all sides by later buildings. Set back from Market Road behind a small courtyard delineated by railings and a gate with stone piers. Pointed-arch doorway in gabled entrance front, surmounted by three lancet windows. Further lancet windows to body of former nave. Hammer-beam roof to what became the courtroom, which was fitted out with plain furnishings including a panelled judge's bench on a raised platform. Court use continued until 2017 when the building was 'temporarily' closed on health and safety grounds, and District Court sittings transferred to Cahirciveen.

KILPADDER

Kilpadder petty sessions were listed in the 1842 *Petty Sessions Return* and were abolished in 1893. Lewis's *Topographical Dictionary* records that petty sessions were held every third Monday in nearby Kilgarvan, but a court house remains to be identified.

Listowel (Lawrence Collection, NLI, late 19C) | **#166**
Killorglin (Denis Mortell, 2018) | **#165**
Milltown, rear (Denis Mortell, 2018) | **#167**
Sneem (Lawrence Collection, NLI, late 19C) | **#168**
Tarbert (Brian Carey, 2019) | **#169**

LISTOWEL
Courthouse Road
Court House   #166
Henry Stokes
c. 1842

Listowel is a variant of the standard late-1830s – early-1840s petty and quarter sessions court house design, as interpreted on this occasion by the Kerry County Surveyor, Henry Stokes. Set at the back of what is now a large square terminating Courthouse Road. Five-bay, two-storey main block with lower set-back entrance wings to the sides. The end bays have large square-headed windows framed by broad plain stone pilasters which terminate in a platband at first floor sill level. Above this are Wyatt windows whose ornate architraves have pediments crowned by anthemia. Simpler architraves to middle three first-floor windows. The single-storey projecting block to centre of the ground floor is a 19th-century addition. Double-height courtroom with arched recess for judge's bench and original furnishings. The building remains in court use.

MILLTOWN
Church Street   #167
Court House and Bridewell
c. 1830

Milltown former petty sessions court house and bridewell of c. 1830 is very similar to Tarbert, Co. Kerry, and Glin, Co. Limerick. Three-bay, two-storey central block, bowed to the rear, with two-bay single-storey flanking wings. Square-headed windows to main block and lunettes to wings. Set behind a high stone wall with dressed-stone gateway topped by a heavy entablature with the inscription 'Bridewell'. Converted to residential use in the late 20th century.

PORTMAGEE
Court House

Portmagee was a location for petty sessions, and the existing building at the start of the terrace facing the sea to the east of the Quay is marked on the 25-inch OS map as the court house. Three-bay, two-storey house with semi-hipped roof, wide entrance in the end gable, and a single-storey return.

RATHMORE
Court House

With the larger constabulary barracks and the smaller post office, the court house in Rathmore is one of very few buildings in the village on the 25-inch OS map. From the map it would appear the court house had two projecting bays, but no trace of this structure remains. Rathmore District Court was abolished in 1984 and the area amalgamated with Killarney and Millstreet.

SNEEM
South Square
Court House   #168

Sneem petty sessions court house stood at the end of Chapel Lane (now Church Street) on the west corner of South Square (Fair Green) in a cluster of buildings which included a school and the constabulary barracks. A William Lawrence photograph shows the court house to have been a two-storey, three-bay building with a central entrance and square-headed windows. In his Bureau of Military History Witness Statement (WS 958), Denis J. O'Sullivan described how the court house was burned by Irish Volunteers in June 1920 because it was adjacent to the actual target, the RIC barracks. Mid-20th-century houses now occupy the site. Sneem District Court subsequently sat in the community centre in North Square until it was amalgamated with Kenmare in 2005.

TARBERT
Court House and Bridewell   #169
1831

The detached, seven-bay, single- and two-storey sandstone court house and bridewell in Tarbert was built in 1831. Very similar to Milltown, Co. Kerry, and Glin, Co. Limerick. Three-bay, two-storey central block, bowed to the rear, with two-bay, single-storey flanking wings. Two-bay, single-storey flat-roofed blocks were later added at right angles to the wings. Limestone quoins and surrounds to windows of central block. Lunettes to wings with dressed-stone surrounds. Grilles to lunettes and first floor windows. Square-headed doorway with limestone surround. Rubble boundary wall, with railings to front and a robust entrance to forecourt with heavy entablature, including a panel bearing the word 'Bridewell'. Court house use ceased in the mid-20th century. Derelict by the 1980s. In 1987 the Bridewell Project Group was formed to restore the building and in 1993 it opened as a visitor centre. Tarbert District Court Area was amalgamated with the District Court Area of Listowel in 2001.

TRALEE
Ashe Street
County Court House
See Significant Court Houses – A Chronological Selection   P197

VALENTIA

Valentia petty sessions were listed in the 1842 *Petty Sessions Return* and court order books survive for 1906-11. A petty sessions court house has yet to be identified. Valentia became part of Cahirciveen District Court Area in 1924.

WATERVILLE

Waterville was not listed as a location for petty sessions, but became a District Court Area in 1961. The District Court sat in the local community centre until amalgamated with Cahirciveen in 2005.

ATHY

Emily Square

Market House and Court House #170

[]; [Sir Richard Morrison]; []

c. 1740; 1804-09; 1913

Athy market and court house is a substantial early-Georgian building of c. 1740. It was originally two-storey and T-plan, with an open ground floor arcade. Rubble-stone with dressed-stone string-courses and surrounds to windows and doors. Extended to front and rear c. 1804-09 by Sir Richard Morrison, according to Richard Butler, given the Morrison-esque sculptured panels added to the main façade. Identified as 'Town Hall' on the 25-inch OS map. Attic storey added, 1913. Accommodated, *inter alia*, Macra na Feirme, the Masonic Order, Athy UDC and Revlon ladies' foundation garments manufacturers. Acquired from the Duke of Leinster in 1975 by Kildare County Council for £9,000. Restored 1983-90. Now in civic, museum, fire brigade and library use.

ATHY

Barrow Quay

Corn Exchange/Court House #171

Frederick Darley; Foley and O'Sullivan; Deaton Lysaght Architects

1857; 1926-28; 2000-01

'As pretty a building as any in Ireland', according to a contemporary newspaper report, Athy Corn Exchange was commissioned by the Duke of Leinster from Frederick Darley and opened for business on 6 October 1857. Complaints soon followed regarding ventilation and lighting, and by 1863 the Corn Exchange had closed. The building was subsequently acquired as a court house for petty and quarter sessions. Detached, two-storey, Tudor Revival structure with distinctively shaped gables, pinnacled dormers, and four-arch external loggias on either side of the courtroom. Square-headed window openings, with granite lintels, and arched doorways with granite surrounds. Single-storey entrance porch at north end (later converted to public toilet). Burned during the War of Independence and reconstructed by Foley and O'Sullivan, architects and engineers, 1926-28. Refurbished for the Courts Service by Deaton Lysaght Architects 2000-01, at a cost of IR£1 million, to accommodate District and Circuit Courts.

BALLYMORE EUSTACE

Barrack Street

Court House

A mid- to late-19th-century detached, two-storey, three-bay house still standing at the west end of the north side of Barrack Street was formerly Ballymore Eustace petty sessions court house.

CARBURY

Court House

[]; Joseph John Bruntz

[]; 1923-24

Carbury petty sessions court house, as indicated on the 25-inch OS map, is still standing. It is a two-storey, three-bay, pitched-roofed building with a window in the first floor of the gable end, set back from the east side of the road just north of Carbury C of I parish church. The *Irish Builder* reported that Joseph John Bruntz, architect, rebuilt Carbury 'Police Barracks and Courthouse' after a fire, 1923-24, suggesting that court sittings had relocated to the constabulary barracks, a two-storey, three-bay house with gabled porch, on the north-east corner of the village centre. Carbury ceased to be a court location in 1924.

CASTLEDERMOT

Carlowgate/Barrack Road

Court House #172

c. 1880; c. 1920

The 25-inch OS map of Castledermot shows a court house located on the west side of Carlowgate at the Market Square end of the street, adjacent to the constabulary barracks on Barrack Road. The *Carlow Nationalist* newspaper reported in June 1920 that 'the courthouse and police barracks' at Castledermot had been destroyed by fire and went on to note that 'the Courthouse was a very substantial granite building, and was the property of the Duke of Leinster, and the barracks, which formed an annexe of the courthouse, had only been vacated by the police the previous day'. The barracks was repaired to incorporate the court house. It still stands, a three-bay, two-storey structure with hipped roof, ruled and lined rendered walls, square-headed windows and a dressed-stone door surround with simple pediment, below which is a plaque bearing the building name 'Castledermot Courthouse'. Used as a library until 1979, it subsequently became a community centre.

CELBRIDGE

Main Street

Court House #173

c. 1775

Stone-built, gable-fronted, two-storey, three-bay court house adjacent to Kildrought House. The late-18th-century main block has red-brick surrounds to windows, which are square-headed, except for that above the entrance, which is round-headed. Dressed-stone doorcase, with lintel supported on brackets, and oculus in gable. To left and right are later, gable-fronted, single-storey asymmetric wings, each now incorporating a segmental-arched shop window. Celbridge had a petty sessions court and was listed as a District Court location in 1924, but was part of Lucan District Court Area by 1927. The court house became the town hall and, following renovation and alterations in 1985, is now in commercial use. In 2013 a statue by local sculptor Jarlath Daly of Arthur Guinness, who was born in Celbridge in 1725, was erected in front of the building.

CLANE
Main Street
Court House

Clane petty sessions court house stood on the east side of Main Street, adjacent to the constabulary barracks (which was itself adjacent to the presbytery). The barracks still stands, converted to commercial use, but the court house building has been replaced. Clane District Court was abolished in 1967 and the area amalgamated with Naas.

CLONDUFF

Clonduff was listed in the 1842 *Petty Sessions Return*, but had ceased to be a petty sessions location by 1882. No court house has been identified.

CURRAGH
Court House

Curragh petty sessions court house, constabulary barracks and resident magistrate's house stood in a cluster on the east side of what is now the R413, just to the south of Lumville House. The court house and magistrate's quarters were destroyed in November 1922. No trace remains of any of these buildings.

DONADEA
Court House

The first-edition OS map shows Donadea 'School & Court Ho.' located north west of Donadea Castle, on the west side of the road bounding the Donadea estate. By the time the 25-inch map was produced this building had become a rectory and Donadea petty sessions court house stood across the road from the castellated Kilcock Lodge entrance to Donadea estate, adjacent to a dispensary and close to Donadea school. The small schoolhouse is extant. Some fabric of the court house may survive in the single-storey block, with chamfered corners and round-headed windows in its gable ends, which forms part of the sprawling residential and commercial (former post office and public house) property on the site.

KILCOCK
Courtown Road
Court House   #174
c. 1965

Kilcock court house is a detached grey-brick, single-storey, T-plan block with glazed central entrance in an otherwise blank main façade. Above the entrance, the set-back, timber-fronted roof of the double-height courtroom rises in a distinctive sweep. A relatively rare example of a mid-20th-century purpose-built court house, Kilcock was branded 'probably the worst in Europe' by a District Court judge in 2016. It was closed for renovations that year and sittings of Kilcock District Court were relocated to Naas.

#170 | Athy, Market House and Court House (IAA, c. 1975)
#171 | Athy, Court House (Corn Exchange) (Denis Mortell, 2018)
#172 | Castledermot (Denis Mortell, 2018)
#173 | Celbridge (Denis Mortell, 2018)

KILCULLEN
Court House

A pre-1830s terraced house on the west side of the main street of Kilcullen, west of the River Liffey, bears the nameplate 'The Old Courthouse'. This petty sessions court house is a two-storey, three-bay building with square-headed windows, double-width on the ground floor, and round-headed central doorcase. A very similar building immediately adjacent was the constabulary barracks.

KILDARE
Dublin Street
Court House   #175
John Hargrave
1829

The detached, three-bay, two-storey petty and quarter sessions court house in Kildare was built to designs by John Hargrave. Plans of the building dated 1829 were lost in the Public Records Office fire of 1922. The contractor was Denis Hays. Double-height courtroom to the front of the building, retaining original panelled fittings, and two-storey offices to the rear. Rendered, with square-headed windows, those to the front topped by recessed panels, a platband at sill level and broad modillioned eaves. The main façade is flanked by two entrance gates providing access to the rear and fronted by four substantial octagonal limestone piers which have lost their chains or railings. The projecting entrance porch was added c. 1840. Closed in 2010, when Kildare District Court Area was amalgamated with Naas.

MONASTEREVIN
Market Square
Market House and Court House   #176

The building that is now the Bank of Ireland on the corner of Dublin Street and Main Street (Market Square) formerly housed Monasterevin petty sessions court house. Extensively altered in the late 19th century from when the first floor square-headed windows with brick surrounds date, and remodelled in the 20th century, the building originated as Monasterevin's mid-18th-century market house. Market use is still hinted at by the three arched entrances (two of which are now closed) with pilasters and prominent keystones on the south or Market Square façade. The ground-floor windows on the east or Dublin Street façade have similar stone frames.

NAAS
South Main Street
County Court House
See Significant Court Houses – A Chronological Selection   P183

NEWBRIDGE

Eyre Street

Court House   #177

1858

Newbridge court house was a detached, gable-fronted, three-bay, two-storey structure erected, according to a datestone in the gable, for local landlord Eyre Powell in 1858. Set back from the street behind a small square, with arched entrance flanked by two round-headed windows and three square-headed windows above. The *Kildare Observer* opined in 1903 (23 March) that the court house was an 'ugly building' with 'still uglier surroundings'. Leaking and draughty, its 'condition is a reproach to the town of Newbridge'. The building survived, despite such low consideration, for almost a century. The ground floor became a health centre in 1980 and the building was refurbished c. 1990. Destroyed by arson in April 2002. The gutted remains were eventually demolished in May 2004. Newbridge District Court Area was amalgamated with Naas in May 2002.

RATHANGAN

Main Street

Court House

c. 1820

A three-bay, two-storey terraced house of c. 1820 on the south side of Main Street is shown as Rathangan court house on the 25-inch OS map. Rendered façade with rendered quoins. Square-headed windows and door which has a minimalist surround with prominent keystone and blocking. Rathangan had a petty sessions court and was a District Court Area from 1924 to 1961, when it became part of Kildare District Court. The building is still extant and is in residential use.

ROBERTSTOWN (KILMEAGUE)

Grove Lane

Court House

Robertstown (or Kilmeague, as the petty sessions area was sometimes called) petty sessions court house stood on the west side of Grove Lane on a corner site now occupied by private residences. It is possible some fabric remains, in particular in the double flight of steps to one of the front doors.

BALLYRAGGET

Castle Street
Court House

Ballyragget had a petty sessions court which met in a detached court house located on the east side of the south end of Castle Street. The five-bay, single-storey dwelling which stands on the site may include some fabric from the original court house building. The District Court Area of Ballyragget was abolished in 1998 on amalgamation with Castlecomer.

CALLAN

Green Street
Court House   #178
William Deane Butler
1838-40

Identical petty and quarter sessions court houses were built at Callan and Urlingford, designed by William Deane Butler for the Kilkenny Grand Jury at the instigation of the County Surveyor, Samson Carter, whose own 1836 scheme for Callan had been rejected. The Board of Works annual report for 1840 noted that the building was 'considerably advanced'. An example of the standard late-1830s – early-1840s petty and quarter sessions court house design, it is a detached, two-storey, five-bay centre block with single-storey recessed entrances at either end, each with a pedimented doorcase. That on the north side is incorporated into a triumphal arch with an identical entrance to the adjacent Bank of Ireland (on stylistic grounds attributable also to William Deane Butler). The arch itself provides access to the constabulary barracks (Garda station) behind the bank. An unsympathetic additional storey has been added to the south entrance. The end bays of the centre block advance slightly, with segmental windows in channelled ashlar at ground floor level. Between these were three blind recessed panels, the outer two of which were converted to windows when the building was repurposed as offices in 2005. String-course at first floor sill level. Five large square-headed windows to first floor courtroom with cut-limestone surrounds incorporating distinctive cornices. Callan District Court was amalgamated with Kilkenny in 2003 and the building was sold for commercial redevelopment that year. In front of the court house stands a monument by Peter Grant (1935-95) commemorating Edmund Ignatius Rice (1762-1844), founder of the Irish Christian Brothers, who was born nearby.

CASTLECOMER

Kilkenny Street/Market Square
Market House and Court House   #179
Henry Aaron Baker
1809

Commissioned by the Dowager Countess of Ormonde, the architect Henry Aaron Baker exhibited his design for the market house in Castlecomer in the Society of Artists of Ireland exhibition of 1809, when the building was described as 'now erecting'. Single-bay, double-height central block, crowned by a tall timber lantern, with pedimented single-storey projecting pavilions on either side. Round-headed central entrance, with prominent keystone, above which is a platband and a tripartite segmental window and clock. Pedimented entrances in each pavilion wing, surmounted by blank panels. These three entrances have been closed since c. 1880, when the building was converted to petty and quarter sessions court use, with new rear-facing entrances provided in porches behind the pavilions. Further tripartite segmental windows in stone surrounds to sides of pavilions, and also the sides and rear of main block. Single-storey addition to rear. Refurbished in 1997. Closed in 2012 when the District Court was amalgamated with Kilkenny.

FRESHFORD

Bridge Street
Court House

The petty sessions court house in Freshford was part of the terrace on the west side of Bridge Street, and some fabric may remain in the two-storey commercial and domestic buildings which occupy the site.

GORESBRIDGE

Bridge Street
Court House

Goresbridge petty sessions court house stood on the south side of Bridge Street on a site now occupied by a filling station. Listed as a District Court location in 1924, Goresbridge District Court was transferred to Gowran in 1934.

GOWRAN

Main Street

Court House   #180

Patrick O'Toole and Joseph Wright

1855-56

The court house in Gowran is an austere limestone-faced, three-bay, two-storey building on a slightly sloping site on the south side of the east end of Main Street. Hipped roof with projecting eaves. Stone frieze, quoins and plinth. Square-headed windows with restrained surrounds to ground floor, and central entrance approached by a double flight of steps. Three blind-arched recesses to first floor have been replaced by three square-headed windows. Two-bay rendered side elevations. Built in the mid-1850s to designs by Patrick O'Toole and Joseph Wright, possibly on the site of a 1730s almshouse, and certainly on the site of the pre-1840 'Sessn Ho.' shown on the first-edition OS map, the exterior of which, as depicted in a drawing by R. Gibbs of c. 1810, would appear to have been retained. By the end of the 19th century, it accommodated both the petty sessions court house and a constabulary barracks. The building remained in court house use into the second half of the 20th century but had become derelict by 1973, after which it was converted to a private residence. Gowran District Court was abolished in 1983 and the Area amalgamated with Thomastown.

GRAIGUENAMANAGH

Main Street

Market House and Court House   #181

c. 1800

Identified as the court house on the 25-inch OS map, Graiguenamanagh market house, built for Henry Welbore Agar-Ellis, 2nd Viscount Clifden, is set at the back of a small square at the south end of Main Street. Two-storey, five-bay main façade. The building's most distinguishing feature is the arcade formed by four stone pilasters. These rise full height to support arches with rubble spandrels topped by an understated pediment containing a small oculus. This is a return to the original configuration as, by the mid-1970s, the building had lost its pitched roof and pediment, and acquired a partial third storey. The end bays are blank, aside from rectangular panels at first floor level, while the centre bays now have segmental entrances with segmental windows above. The south façade has a tall window set in an arched stone surround. Petty sessions and District Courts sat in rooms on the first floor. Much altered, it is now in use as a commercial premises. Graiguenamanagh District Court was amalgamated with Thomastown in 1986.

#178 | Callan (Courts Service, 1995)

#179 | Castlecomer (IAA, c. 1975)

#180 | Gowran. Perspective view by R. Gibbs, c. 1810 (IAA)

#181 | Graiguenamanagh (Lawrence Collection, NLI, late 19th century)

INISTIOGE
Hundred Court
c. 1600

Small, three-storey roofless tower on the east side of Inistioge, adjacent to the former boys' school, built c. 1600 and known locally as 'the Hundred Court'. It has been suggested that it served as a manorial court house and later as a petty sessions court house. While there is no indication that petty sessions were held in the village, Inistioge corporation was headed by an official with the title of 'portreeve' who, according to Lewis's *Topographical Dictionary*, 'with two or more of the burgesses, holds a court of record, with jurisdiction extending to £20 late currency, every month'. This may be the last court to have used the building, if in fact it was ever used for court purposes at all.

JOHNSTOWN
The Square
Court House

Johnstown petty sessions court sat in the building on the south side of the corner where Church Street intersects with the neat village square. Now a shop.

KILKENNY
High Street
Tholsel   **#182**
1761; c. 1986

An imposing presence on High Street, Kilkenny Tholsel was built in 1761, possibly to designs by William Colles, who executed the stonework. The ground floor is open, with a double arcade of five arches supported on Roman Doric columns. Three square-headed windows in blocked architraves to first floor. Hipped roof, topped by a three-stage octagonal cupola with clock and weathervane. This is the third in a succession of tholsels on the site and, as with its two predecessors, it served as a court house (as did the church of the Holy Trinity Priory, or Black Abbey, in North Abbey Street on an intermittent basis in the 17th century). Court sittings took place in the Tholsel's large first-floor room or 'Great Council Chamber', at least until the court house in Parliament Street became operational c. 1790, after which the Tholsel served primarily as municipal offices. Gutted by fire in 1985, it was subsequently repaired.

KILKENNY
Parliament Street
County Court House
See **P68** & Significant Court Houses – A Chronological Selection **P176**

KILMACOW
Court House

Kilmacow petty sessions court house was located in front of the graveyard in the centre of Kilmacow Lower. No longer extant.

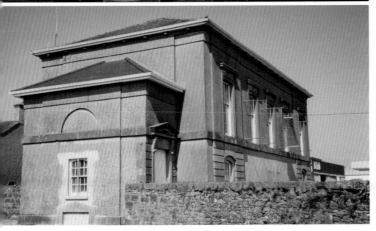

Tholsel, Kilkenny (IAA, late 19C) | **#182**
Piltown (Denis Mortell, 2019) | **#183**
Thomastown (NIAH, 2002) | **#184**
Urlingford (Courts Service, 1995) | **#185**

KILMAGANNY
Mill Street
Court House

The petty sessions court house in Kilmaganny stood on the west side of the road leading north from the village, opposite the constabulary barracks. Towards the end of 1920, the local battalion of Irish Volunteers received orders to destroy Kilmaganny court house. However, the building was reprieved at the last minute when it was learned that it was private property, 'owned by a Miss Moore who was a great supporter of the Movement in Dublin'. (Bureau of Military History Witness Statement, Nicholas Carroll, WS 1705). An extensively altered and modernised dwelling known as the Old Courthouse stands on the site now, two-storey, three-bay with recessed single-storey, single-bay wings and blind dormers. Kilmaganny was a District Court Area from 1924 to 1961 when it became part of Callan District Court Area.

KILMANAGH
Court House

A small, single-storey, three-bay cottage at the west end of Kilmanagh, on the south of what is now the L1009, functioned as the local petty sessions court house. Though altered and extended, and now in residential use, it is still known as 'The Court House'.

LIMETREE

At a Grand Jury meeting on 29 December 1831, the petty sessions district of Limetree was defined as being 'in and through the Parishes of Tullamaine, Lislone and Dirreen, Burnchurch, Grange and Grove, and Castleinch and Brownstown'. Located half way between Kilkenny and Callan, Limetree was listed in the 1842 *Petty Sessions Return*, but had ceased to be a petty sessions location by 1882. Court order books survive for 1851-55.

PILTOWN
Main Street
Market House   #183
c. 1830

Piltown Garda station was formerly Piltown petty sessions court house and before that it was Piltown market house. Lewis's *Topographical Dictionary* reported that a patent for a market in Piltown had been obtained but was not yet established, although a 'handsome building' had been erected at the expense of the 3rd Earl of Bessborough for use as the market house. Instead, the building was 'appropriated to the use of the R.C. day-school, the Protestant Sunday-school, and all public meetings'. Of two storeys and three bays, the ground floor arcade, with prominent keystones and string-course at impost level, was originally open but now contains round-headed windows on either side of a recessed entrance. Three paired square-headed windows to first floor. Semi-circular stairwell to rear. Court use had ceased by 1926, when the building was derelict. It was subsequently repaired and altered for Garda use.

ROSBERCON

Rosbercon was listed in the 1842 *Petty Sessions Return* and court order books survive for the period 1870-99. A petty sessions court house has yet to be identified. Rosbercon petty sessions merged with New Ross in 1900.

STONEYFORD
Court House

Forming part of a still-standing short terrace of three mid- to late-19th-century two-storey houses on the north side of Main Street, little of the original fabric of Stoneyford petty sessions court house appears to remain.

THOMASTOWN
Logan's Street
Court House   #184
c. 1824

Thomastown court house is a classical, gable-fronted, three-bay, single-storey building, probably originally detached. 'Sessions House' is inscribed on a plaque just below the gable, which is surrounded by a course of dressed stone to form a pediment. Double-height centre block with central square-headed window in a shallow segmental-arched recess. Lower, recessed entrance wings on either side with dressed-stone door surrounds. Completed by 1824 and used for petty and quarter sessions, and District Court sittings from 1924. Court use ceased in 2007 when Thomastown District Court was amalgamated with Kilkenny. Now an arts centre.

URLINGFORD
Main Street
Court House   #185
William Deane Butler
1838-40

Identical petty and quarter sessions court houses were built at Callan and Urlingford, designed by William Deane Butler for the Kilkenny Grand Jury at the instigation of the County Surveyor, Samson Carter. As at Callan, Carter's own 1836 scheme for Urlingford had been rejected. Urlingford is also a version of the standard late-1830s – early-1840s court house design. The Board of Works annual report for 1840 notes that the building was in progress. Set back from the road and directly facing the slightly earlier St Mary's RC church, this is a detached court house with a five-bay, two-storey centre block and single-bay recessed entrance wings at either end. Pedimented doorcases to entrances. The end bays of the centre block advance slightly, with segmental windows in channelled ashlar at ground floor level. Between these are three recessed blind panels. String-course at first floor sill level. Five large square-headed windows to first floor courtroom with cut-limestone surrounds. Renovated in 1996 to accommodate use as library. Urlingford District Court was amalgamated with Thurles in 2005.

ABBEYLEIX
Stucker Hill/Upper Main Street
Court House   #186
c. 1820

Raised above the street – the entrance is approached by a flight of ten steps – Abbeyleix petty and quarter sessions court house was constructed c. 1820, and leased to the Grand Jury by the de Vesci family of Abbey Leix. It is set back behind a wall topped with cast-iron railings and with cast-iron double gates. Two-storey, five-bay symmetrical block with hipped roof, corner quoins, square-headed windows in lugged architraves and a central pedimented doorcase. Court use ceased c. 1910, when court business was transferred to an adapted former schoolhouse on the Ballacolla Road. The old court house was subsequently reduced in size by the removal of the rear section and is now in office use.

ABBEYLEIX
Ballacolla Road
Court House   #187
1910

For most of the 20th century, the court house in Abbeyleix was located on the south side of the Ballacolla Road. It is a gable-fronted, two-bay, two-storey block with recessed single-storey wings on either side, that on the east extending into a two-bay, two-storey caretaker's cottage. Rendered walls with red-brick quoins and surrounds to doors and windows. Segmental-arched central entrance at ground floor above which are two square-headed windows surmounted by a date plaque for 1910. This date may refer to the alteration of an existing building to court house use, as a schoolhouse with a similar footprint is shown on the site on the first-edition OS map. This building also appears on the 25-inch map, though without designation. No longer in court use, Abbeyleix District Court having been amalgamated with Portlaoise in 2001.

BALLACOLLA
Court House

The petty sessions court house in Ballacolla stood adjacent to the constabulary barracks on the north-west corner of the village crossroads. A two-storey, five-bay private residence now occupies the site of, and may incorporate, the barracks but the court house is no longer extant.

BALLICKMOYLER
Court House   #188

A two-storey, four-bay, mid-19th-century terraced house, on an elevated terrace on the north side of the main village square, was formerly Ballickmoyler petty sessions court house.

BALLYBRITTAS
Court House

A modern bungalow now occupies the site on the south side of the main street at the west end of Ballybrittas where the small semi-detached cottage designated as the petty sessions court house once stood.

BALLYLINAN
Court House   #189
c. 1830

Set in the V formed by the approach roads at the south end of Ballylinan is a two-storey, L-plan block of c. 1830. Shown on the first-edition OS map, it is composed of the interlocking former petty sessions court house (facing west) and constabulary barracks (facing north). Stone walls with brick surrounds and stone hoodmouldings over the square-headed windows. Pavilion-style flanking porches. Now in residential use.

BORRIS-IN-OSSORY
Main Street
Court House   #190
1826-30

Plans and estimates for the petty and quarter sessions court houses in Borris-in-Ossory and Stradbally were submitted to the Board of Works in 1826 as part of a loan application for £2,700. The loan was drawn down in 1828. Almost identical to Stradbally, Borris-in-Ossory court house is a two-storey, detached building standing side-on to the street and facing a small forecourt. The main front is sufficiently suggestive of the standard late-1830s – early-1840s court house design to speculate that Borris-in-Ossory and Stradbally were early prototypes. It has three recessed panels at ground-floor level flanked by pedimented entrances in the end bays. Above are five tall, round-headed windows, separated by stylised stone pilasters and with half-architraves which merge into a string-course. The end windows are blind, aside from their semi-circular glazed tops. Five-bay side or street elevation. The end bays are rusticated at ground floor with oculus windows. Above, two pilasters frame square-headed windows, that on the left being blind. The centre bays are rendered with three square-headed windows on each floor, the lower ones set in lugged architraves and those above topped by stone mouldings supported on brackets. The middle windows on each floor are blind while the ground floor window on the right has been converted to a door. Borris-in-Ossory was a District Court Area until 1961 when it became part of the Rathdowney Area. The court house was subsequently used as county council offices but has been derelict for most of the 21st century, despite repeated calls for its renovation.

CASTLETOWN

Castletown was listed in the 1842 *Petty Sessions Return*, and listed as Castletown and Coolrain in 1882. Court order books survive for 1851-86 and 1897-98, but Castletown had ceased to be a petty sessions location by 1905 and a petty sessions court house has not yet been identified.

CLONASLEE
Main Street
Court House   #191
pre-1840

The building that functioned as Clonaslee petty sessions court house stands on the south side of the triangular green at the west end of the village. It is an L-plan, three-bay, two-storey pre-1840 house with part-pitched and part-hipped roof and a modern porch. The west side elevation has an entrance flanked by two windows, with two further windows at first floor, all set in segmental recesses. It is shown on the first-edition OS map as a schoolhouse. Clonaslee was a District Court location until 1961, when it became part of the Mountmellick Area. Now a private residence.

DURROW
Oldchapel Street
Court House   #192
1830s

Built in the 1830s, though not shown on the first-edition OS map, Durrow court house is a detached, three-bay, double-height structure with recessed single-bay, single-storey porches on either side containing pedimented doorcases. Three tall, square-headed windows to main block. Random rubble-stone walls with dressed-stone quoins, cornice, window surrounds, platband at sill level, and corbels to broad eaves. Set back from the street behind cast-iron railings. Ventilator at apex of hipped roof. A District Court location until 1961, when Durrow became part of the Abbeyleix Area, the court house subsequently functioned as a Fórsa Cosanta Áitiúil (FCÁ) hall. Renovated in 2008 to accommodate Durrow library, a community museum and meeting space.

KILLEANYTOHER/KILLEANY TOGHER

Killeanytoher is listed in the 1842 *Petty Sessions Return*, but had ceased to be a petty sessions location by 1882. No court house is shown on the first-edition OS map.

#186 | Abbeyleix, Court House (19C) (Denis Mortell, 2018)
#187 | Abbeyleix, Court House (20C) (Denis Mortell, 2018)
#188 | Ballickmoyler (IAA, 2019)
#189 | Ballylinan (Denis Mortell, 2018)

MOUNTMELLICK

O'Moore Street

Court House   #193

Alexander Harrison

1839-40

Set back from the street behind iron railings, Mountmellick court house was completed in 1840 by builder William Dunne to designs by the County Surveyor Alexander Harrison. Originally I-plan, with a narrow double-height courtroom, lit by three round-headed windows in the side walls, topped and tailed by wider two-storey, three-bay, office and entrance blocks. The street façade is a simple classical composition, four Doric pilasters supporting a plain entablature and pediment and framing three square-headed windows on both ground and first floor. Quoined corners and channelled rustication to ground floor. The entrance was located to the right hand side of the front block. In 1998 the District Court Area of Mountmellick was abolished and amalgamated with the District Court Area of Portlaoise. Between 2003 and 2011 the court house underwent two phases of restoration and extension to accommodate Mountmellick civic offices and library.

MOUNTRATH

Market Square

Market House and Court House   #194

[Richard Castle or Francis Bindon]; []; [] Campbell

c. 1750; 1838; 1853

Variously attributed to both Richard Castle and Francis Bindon, Mountrath market house was erected c. 1750 and stood in the centre of the Market Square. Lewis's *Topographical Dictionary* considered it 'a respectable building' and noted that petty sessions were held here each Thursday. Lewis also reported that a 'new court-house and bridewell are about to be erected' in Mountrath but in 1838 the Grand Jury authorised expenditure on the upper rooms of the market house to make them more suitable for quarter sessions. On 5 February 1853 the London *Builder* magazine reported: 'We are informed that the new court-house at Mountrath, in the Queen's county, is finished. The accommodation contained therein is more extensive than those (generally speaking) through the country. It is stated that the inhabitants of the locality find that the arrangements, which have been designed under difficulties arising from limited space, answer the required purposes satisfactorily. Mr Campbell superintended the execution of the works'. As it would seem that no new separate court house was built in Mountrath in the 1850s, this report presumably relates to further alterations carried out to the market house. Court use continued into the 20th century. Five bays wide by one deep, with an open market arcade at ground floor and large square-headed windows above. The end bays of the main façade projected slightly and the hipped roof was topped by a cupola. Palladian window in south end. Recorded in *Broadsheet*, an RTÉ television magazine programme, in early 1962, when it was already in poor condition and a straw poll of local citizens condemned it as both an eyesore and a traffic hazard, it was subsequently demolished.

MOUNTRATH

Shannon Street

Court House and Library

c. 1960

Following the demolition of Mountrath market house, a new court house and library building was provided c. 1960 on Shannon Street. This was a utilitarian, flat-roofed rectangular single-storey structure, the front elevation divided between the court (on the left) with a recessed entrance framed by two large windows, and the library, with a smaller entrance flanked by narrow slit windows. Mountrath District Court was amalgamated with Portlaoise in 2001, and the court house and library have since been replaced by a new library and civic offices building.

NEWCHURCH

The otherwise unidentified Newchurch is listed in the 1842 *Petty Sessions Return*, but had ceased to be a petty sessions location by 1882.

PORTARLINGTON

Market Square

Market House and Court House   **#195**

1730s

The Market House in Portarlington is designated 'Court House' on the 25-inch OS map. It was probably built in the 1730s and was certainly standing when John Wesley preached here in 1749. Petty sessions use began in the 1820s and a prison cell was installed in 1824. Detached, three-bay, two-storey, almost square building standing in the middle of Market Square. Tall, hipped, M-profile roof. The centre bay of the main façade steps forward. Three open arches at ground floor and three tall, square-headed windows light the room used for court sittings. In use as a garage for over forty years.

PORTARLINGTON

Main Street

Court House and Library   **#196**

1995

In 1995 a new court house and public library building opened at the south end of Main Street, Portarlington. It is a single-storey, nine-bay structure, the centre three bays recessed, with a double-hipped, pyramidal roof structure. Separate entrances to court and library. Court use ceased in 2012 when Portarlington District Court was amalgamated with Portlaoise and the building was subsequently altered for library use only.

#194 | Mountrath (IAA, c. 1960)
#195 | Portarlington, Market House (Maurice Craig Collection, IAA, 1948)
#196 | Portarlington, Court House and Library (Denis Mortell, 2018)
#197 | Rathdowney (Denis Mortell, 2018)
#198 | Stradbally (IAA, 2019)

PORTLAOISE
Main Street
County Court House
See Significant Court Houses – A Chronological Selection P181

RATHDOWNEY
Church Street
Court House

The petty sessions court house in Rathdowney was located in a mid-19th-century terrace on the south side of Church Street at a right angle to the street and facing what was a Methodist chapel but is now a site occupied by a school. Still standing, it is a single-storey, three-bay stone building with pitched roof. Two entrances, one each side of a large square-headed window.

RATHDOWNEY
Mill Street
Court House and Library #197
c. 1970

Rathdowney acquired a somewhat perfunctory library and court house c. 1970, when this red-brick and rough-cast five-bay, single-storey building was erected on Mill Street. Gated recessed entrances in end bays, with brick piers and entablatures containing signage. The entrance on the right was for the court house. Three windows, the centre one larger than its neighbours. In use as a court house until Rathdowney District Court was amalgamated with Portlaoise in 2004, the building is now used exclusively by the library.

STRADBALLY
Court Square
Court House #198
[]; Milligan Reside Larkin Architects
1830; 2009-10

Plans and estimates for the petty and quarter sessions house in Stradbally were submitted with those for Borris-in-Ossory to the Board of Works in 1826 as part of a loan application for £2,700. The loan was drawn down in 1828 and Stradbally has a datestone for 1830. Very similar to Borris-in-Ossory; both court houses are obviously by the same hand. Described in Lewis's *Topographical Dictionary* as 'a neat building and attached to it is a small bridewell containing three cells, two day-rooms and an airing yard'. Commanding the large square to the back of which it stands, the two-storey, five-bay front presents as a variation of the late-1830s – early-1840s standard court house, possibly making this and Borris-in-Ossory prototypes for that design. It has three recessed panels at ground floor level flanked by entrances in the end bays, the pedimented tops of which sit proud of a platband at first floor sill level. The half-architraves of the five first floor round-headed windows merge into a string-course. The windows are separated by stylised stone pilasters. Five-bay side elevation. The end bays are rusticated at ground floor with oculus windows. Above, two pilasters frame square-headed blind windows. The centre bays are rendered with three square-headed windows on each floor, the lower ones set in lugged architraves and those above topped by stone mouldings supported on brackets. A District Court location until 1961, when it merged with Portlaoise, the court house was subsequently converted to library use. Renovated and extended to the rear in 2009-10 by Milligan Reside Larkin Architects for Laois County Council at a cost of €1.2 million to provide a revamped library and an arts centre with exhibition space, a recording studio, and accommodation for artists-in-residence.

TIMAHOE

'In Timahoe', Daniel O'Byrne records in his *History of the Queen's County* (Dublin, 1856), 'are a dispensary, a post-office, a loan-fund, and a petty-court-house, these important and public services may be principally attributed to Joseph Edge Esq, who is a gentleman of very excellent character'. The petty sessions had been established in 1844 and were abolished in 1886. Court order books survive for 1851-86, but which building served as the court house remains to be identified.

BALLINAMORE

Main Street
Court House   #199
Thomas Dugall Hall; []
1838; c. 1930

Thomas Dugall Hall, County Surveyor for Leitrim, 1836-57, was responsible for the design and construction of Ballinamore petty and quarter sessions court house, which Lewis's *Topographical Dictionary* notes 'has been recently erected, to which is attached a bridewell containing four cells, with apartments for the keeper; the cost of the building was £2200, of which £1200 was lent by Government, to be repaid by instalments'. Set back from Main Street behind a forecourt, Ballinamore is a three-bay, two-storey building with an ashlar main façade. The end bays step forward. Three segmental-arched recesses at ground floor level, the outer two now containing entrances and the central one a blind window. Above, three tall square-headed windows, prominent cornice with parapet, and small stylised pediment. Badly damaged by fire in October 1920, when it was targeted by the local Irish Volunteers. Re-covered with a flat concrete roof c. 1930, when the double-height courtroom was also refitted. The furnishings survive, including gallery, jury box and judge's bench, though the court house is in an increasingly dilapidated condition after court use ceased in 2010, following the amalgamation of Ballinamore District Court with Carrick-on-Shannon. A gable-fronted building to the rear of the court house – the bridewell or accommodation block – was converted into a genealogical research centre in 1994.

CARRICK-ON-SHANNON

St George's Terrace
County Court House
See Significant Court Houses – A Chronological Selection   P191

CARRICK-ON-SHANNON

Shannon Court
Court House   #200
Burke Kennedy Doyle (BKD)
1997

Set back from a peripheral road, and facing a housing estate rather than addressing the street, the new court house in Carrick-on-Shannon was commissioned after the old court house became unusable. It opened in April 1997. The architects, Burke Kennedy Doyle, noted that the project brief called for the provision of 'a modern Courthouse which is at the same time both dignified and unintimidating'. The reconstituted stone façade curves to shelter the entrance and is punctured by a cedar-clad projection at first floor level. Flat roof which over-sails the walls on slender steel supports. Rendered side and rear elevations. An internal curved colonnaded space separates entrances, offices and courtrooms. Three main courtrooms are provided – Circuit Court, District Court and Family Law Court. The court house won the 1998 RIAI Western Regional Award for buildings over £200,000.

CARRIGALLEN

Mohill Road
Court House

A petty sessions court house stood behind the market house in Carrigallen in a short terrace of two buildings on the Mohill Road. Neither court nor market house survive.

CLOONE

Court House

Cloone petty sessions court house stood in a terrace on the west side of the village street on the site where St Mary's RC church was constructed in 1970.

DROMAHAIR

Market Street
Court House

On the 25-inch OS map, a court house is shown in the middle of the 'Market Place' on the south side of what is now Market Street, Dromahair. No trace remains. In 1965 Dromahair District Court sittings were relocated to Drumkeeran.

DROMOD

Main Street
Court House and Constabulary Barracks   #201
c. 1840

Dromod's architecturally complementary petty sessions court house and constabulary barracks were built c. 1840 (NIAH) and form a T-plan assemblage, with the court house at the top of the T. Gable-fronted, two-storey, rubble-stone building now with a tripartite window at ground floor level and a double window above. A cut-stone relieving arch above the ground floor window is now intersected by the first floor window and is suggestive of an earlier configuration. Plain, two-bay north side with two small windows in brick surrounds. Entrance in south side. Altered and fully integrated with the former barracks during the 20th century to serve as the residential wing of Dromod Garda station, which itself closed in 2013.

DRUMKEERAN

Court House   #202

McDonell and Dixon Architects

1936

The court house in Drumkeeran is an unusual and distinctive T-plan, gable-fronted Arts and Crafts building, incorporating an early petty sessions house (the top of the T). Maurice Craig in the Foras Forbartha *Buildings of Architectural Interest in County Leitrim: Preliminary Survey* (1976) considered it 'faintly art-nouveau' and suggested the architect might be E.H. Carson, but it is too late to be by him. It is, in fact, by McDonnell and Dixon Architects and was built c. 1936. Set back from the street on a raised platform. Tall pitched roof with splayed corner buttresses to the entrance front. Central entrance flanked by paired windows with a tripartite window above, all with dressed-stone surrounds. Additional stone detailing to tops of buttresses and gable. The courtroom was intact until 2006, when court use ceased on the amalgamation of Drumkeeran District Court with Manorhamilton. More recently used as a youth club and café.

DRUMSHANBO

Barracks Square

Court House

The petty sessions court house in Drumshanbo shared a premises with the dispensary and stood adjacent to the constabulary barracks (later Garda station) on the corner of Barracks Square and Carrick Road. Two-storey, three-bay, mid-19th-century house now in commercial use. Drumshanbo was a District Court location until 1961 when it became part of the Carrick-on-Shannon District Court Area.

DRUMSNA

Court House

Set back from the road immediately to the west of the gate to Mountcampbell House, no more than the lower portions of the exterior walls of the small rectangular petty sessions court house in Drumsna remain.

KESHCARRIGAN

Court House

Keshcarrigan petty sessions court house stood attached to the east end of the fine, five-bay, two-storey stone constabulary barracks, later Garda Station. No longer extant.

KILTYCLOGHER

Main Street

Market House and Court House   #203

post-1831

Lewis's *Topographical Dictionary* records that Kiltyclogher, 'which consists of about 25 houses, has been recently built by C. H. Tottenham, Esq., under the north-eastern range of the Glenfarne mountains. A market is held every Friday in a good market-house and is well attended'. Bearing a plaque with the Tottenham family coat of arms, the name Sarahville which the Tottenhams gave the town on its establishment, the initials C.H.T. (Charles Henry Tottenham) and the date, 1831, the market and court house stands on the south-west corner of the crossroads at the centre of the village. The date may refer generally to the establishment of the town, rather than specifically to the market and court house itself, as the building is not shown on the first-edition OS map of 1835-6. Three-bay, two-storey structure in rubble stone with hipped roof and broad eaves. At ground floor level, two wide segmental market arches with blocked voussoirs. Narrower round-headed entrance to left. Square-headed windows with dressed-stone architraves, sills and hoodmouldings to first floor. Kiltyclogher was a District Court location until 1961 when it became part of the Manorhamilton Area. The building is now in use as a heritage centre.

KINLOUGH

Court House   #204

Kinlough petty sessions court house is shown on the 25-inch OS map as the second building in the terrace on the east side of the village main street, north of the Rossinver C of I church. On the map, the first building in the terrace is identified as a school. It is still standing, though the original court house and its immediate neighbours to the north have been demolished and replaced. The most northerly building in this terrace is now a restaurant and guest house called 'The Court House', a name which reflects the fact that court sittings relocated here in 1918 when the building was extended. This is a one- and two-storey structure, four bays on the west front (facing the main street) and five on the north, including paired entrances and a carriage arch. Yellow-brick eaves course and chimneys, rendered quoins and dressed surrounds to doors and windows. Kinlough ceased to be a District Court location in 1961, becoming instead part of Ballyshannon District Court Area.

#203 | Kiltyclogher (IAA, 2002)
#204 | Kinlough (Paul Tierney, 2019)
#205 | Manorhamilton (IAA, c. 1975)
#206 | Mohill (Leland Duncan Collection/Davison and Associates, 1892)

MANORHAMILTON

Main Street
Court House #205
1819; c. 1920

Set well back from the street behind a courtyard fronted by low curved
walls with tall gate piers and iron gates, Manorhamilton court house
is a three-bay, single-storey structure with hipped roof, yellow-brick
cornice, and three large round-headed windows set in stone arches.
The entrance is in a wing set back on the left. The OS *Memoirs* notes
that 'the court house was built about 1819 and cost 2,400 pounds.
There are 3 prisoners' rooms, 1 for the court, 2 for the petty jury and
1 for the grand jury'. Referred to as 'Courthouse and Bridewell' on the
first-edition OS map, and used for petty and quarter sessions. Two-
storey mid-19th-century extension to rear. Altered c. 1920. Courtroom
has an open-truss roof, plaster canopy to judge's bench, and furniture
by W. Haslett and Son. Major refurbishment was proposed 2005-08
but was not proceeded with. Manorhamilton remains a District Court
location, with the court sitting now in the Glens Centre on New Line, a
converted Methodist chapel of c. 1820 (NIAH).

MOHILL

Station Road
Court House #206

Mohill had a single-storey classical court house (bearing similarities
to that at Maam, Co. Galway) which stood on the east side of Station
Road at the intersection with Hill Street. As shown in an 1892
photograph, it was pedimented and had a tetrastyle portico with
squared columns. Long gone; a three-storey, gable-fronted commercial
premises now occupies the site. From 1936 to 1938, McDonnell and
Dixon Architects, Dublin, put forward a number of alternative designs
for a new court house on a site on Causey Street, south of the old
court house on the east side of Station Road. These designs ranged
from large court houses occupying the entire site, to a small building
sharing the site with a separate health clinic. Regardless of size, all
had a common plan – an entrance lobby at the east end, a central
double-height courtroom, and an office wing at the west end. While a
clinic was constructed, a court house was not. The site is now occupied
by Mohill fire station. The District Court sat in the Canon Donohoe
Memorial Hall constructed in 1911 at the west end of Main Street. The
District Court Area of Mohill was amalgamated into the District Court
Area of Ballinamore in 2005.

Mohill, Proposed Court House. Elevation by McDonnell and Dixon Architects, 1938
(McDonnell and Dixon Collection, IAA)

FOYNES
Court House

Foynes petty sessions court house stood on the south side of the main street immediately east of St Senan's RC church. The site is now occupied by a late-20th-century flat-roofed bank building. Foynes was a District Court location until 1938, when the court was transferred to Shanagolden.

GALBALLY
The Square
Court House

The petty sessions court house in Galbally was located in the centre of a still-standing mid-19th-century terrace of two-storey, two- and three-bay houses and commercial premises on the east side of the Square.

GLIN
Main Street
Court House and Bridewell   #213
c. 1830

Very similar to Milltown and Tarbert, Co. Kerry, the detached former bridewell and petty sessions court house of c. 1830 in Glin is set back from the street on a sloping site behind a wall with railings and a monumental stone gateway. Lewis's *Topographical Dictionary* records it as 'a substantial bridewell, containing six cells, two day-rooms, and two spacious airing yards'. Walls of rough stone, laid in brick-like courses, with dressed-stone surrounds to openings. Three-bay, two-storey centre block with hipped roof and square-headed entrance and windows. Recessed, two-bay, single-storey wings with round headed windows. In use as a library since the late 1970s.

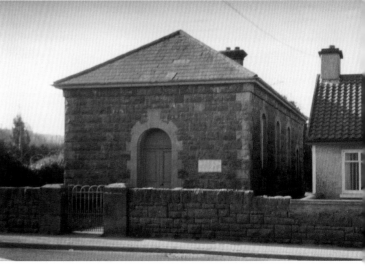

HOSPITAL
Lower Main Street
Court House

The petty sessions court house in Hospital stood adjacent to the earlier constabulary barracks (later Garda station) on the west side of Lower Main Street. Mid-19th-century, five-bay, two-storey terraced building, much altered and now in use as a shop. Hospital was made a District Court location in 1927, but the Statutory Instrument (SI No. 103/1927 - District Court (New Areas) Order, 1927) stated that 'pending the provision of suitable Courthouse accommodation at Hospital, all civil cases appropriate to that Court will be heard at Bruff'.

#210 | Bruff (Roger Hill, 1998)
#211 | Castleconnell (NIAH, 2006)
#212 | Dromcolliher (Roger Hill, 1998)

KILFINNANE
Market Square
Court House   #214

The market house in Kilfinnane was used for court sittings. It was a two-storey, three-bay building erected c. 1760 but only the ruins of the ground-floor market arcade still stand. Lewis's *Topographical Dictionary*, which records that the market house was repaired in 1836, notes 'a small bridewell has recently been built and the sessions house, which is large and convenient, is about to be repaired'. The 25-inch OS map shows the petty sessions court house occupying part of the substantial two-storey, six-bay building on the south-east side of Market Square immediately adjacent to the market house. Pitched roof and rendered façade with square-headed windows to first floor. Ground floor openings have been much altered. Kilfinnane District Court was abolished in 1998 and amalgamated with Kilmallock.

KILMALLOCK
Market Square
Workhouse/Court House   #215
George Wilkinson; Ahrends Burton Koralek (ABK) Architects
1841; 2008-10

The petty sessions court house in Kilmallock was originally located on the north side of Lord Edward Street. A filling station now occupies the site. In 1925, the seven-bay, two-storey entrance building of Kilmallock Union Workhouse was converted to court use. The 1838 Act for the More Effectual Relief of the Destitute Poor in Ireland (1 & 2 Vict., Cap. 56) provided for the division of Ireland into over 130 Poor Law Unions, each managed by a Board of Guardians, and the construction of a workhouse in each Union. The task of building all the new workhouses was given to one architect, George Wilkinson. To solve the problem of having to construct so many buildings in such a short space of time, Wilkinson in effect designed one workhouse which could be replicated in a variety of sizes across the country. He chose a Tudor domestic idiom, with picturesque gabled and dormered entrance buildings to provide reception or 'probationary' facilities at ground floor and a meeting room for the Board of Guardians above. Kilmallock, which received its first admissions in March 1841 and was intended to accommodate 800 people, is a typical example. From 2008 to 2010 the workhouse entrance building, the only surviving part of the original workhouse complex, was gutted and extended as part of a €2.5 million civic precinct by Ahrends Burton Koralek (ABK) Architects which also includes a new library and civic offices. A double-height entrance hall was created within the retained external walls, and a walnut-panelled courtroom. New facilities include private meeting rooms and accommodation for legal practitioners and their clients. The complex won Best Public Building in the 2010 RIAI Architecture awards.

LIMERICK

Merchants Quay

County Court House

See Significant Court Houses – A Chronological Selection   **P184**

LIMERICK

Bridge Street

City Court House /Gerald Griffin Memorial Schools   **#216**

[]; []; Joseph P. O'Malley

1763-65; 1846; 1906-07

Limerick City Court House was built at the corner of Quay Lane (now Bridge Street) in 1640, court sittings having taken place in the 15th-century tholsel up to that point. The court house was altered and extended in 1685, and then replaced by a new City Court House on the same site in 1763-65. Having served as a court house for 80 years, and following the construction of a replacement City Court House, this building was acquired by the Christian Brothers in 1845 and altered in 1846 for use as a school. It was altered again in 1906-07 by Joseph P. O'Malley, who raised the roof to accommodate four additional classrooms. Despite these substantial changes, which included the addition of a stone Celtic cross to the apex of the pediment, the building retains a civic presence, thanks in large measure to the austere classicism of its limestone façade. It is a four-bay, two-storey structure, the centre two bays advanced, quoined and pedimented. Large round-headed windows to ground floor front and side elevations, set in Gibbsian architraves with platband at impost level. Smaller round-headed windows above (square-headed on the side). Between the middle windows at first floor level is a niche containing a bust of Fr Gerald Griffin, the 19th-century Limerick-born novelist, poet and playwright after whom the school came to be named. To the right is a pedimented entrance gate on which is inscribed 'Christian Brothers Schools'.

LIMERICK

Merchants Quay (St Augustine Place)

City Court House   **#217**

James Pain

1843-45

In 1834 Henry Hill prepared plans for a new Limerick City Court House on St Augustine Place to replace the earlier City Court House on Bridge Street. This scheme was not proceeded with and instead the new City Court House was completed to designs by James Pain in 1845. Standing partially on the site of the city gaol and at a right angle to the County Court House, this was a five-bay, two-storey classically proportioned building. The centre three bays were advanced and quoined with a central pedimented entrance at ground floor, flanked by square-headed windows, and three square-headed windows above, the central one topped by a cornice supported on brackets. Tripartite windows in end bays, those at first floor elaborately pedimented. Repaired in 1911 by Joseph J. Peacocke. Demolished in 1988 to be replaced by a new civic offices complex including a new court house.

#216 | Limerick, Bridge Street, City Court House/Gerald Griffin Memorial Schools (IAA, 198?)
#217 | Limerick, Merchants Quay (St Augustine Place), City Court House (IAA, c. 1975)
#218 | Limerick, Merchants Quay, Civic Centre Court House (Judith Hill, 2019)
#219 | Limerick, Mulgrave Street, Limerick Court House (Neil Warner, Courts Service, 2018)

LIMERICK

Merchants Quay

Civic Offices and Court House #218

Burke Kennedy Doyle and Partners (BKD)

1988-90

Competition-winning, post-modern 'Civic Centre' by Burke Kennedy Doyle and Partners consisting of a large office block for Limerick Corporation, new council chambers and a new court house. On the site of the former City Court House, at a right angle to the County Court House. The competition brief had called for a civic centre which was 'an inviting place to go, with any sense of monumentality restricted to limited elements of the complex such as Council Chambers and Law Courts'. A three-bay tubular steel portico fronts an internal glazed 'street' which separates the four-storey office building on the east from the separate council chamber and court house on the west. Clad in Ballinasloe limestone, the court house presents as a robust, enclosed block. The ancillary facilities, including offices and judges' chambers, are in a two-storey section on the west side with windows looking out over the river, while the sloping courtroom roof gives the building a distinctive profile. Internally, the double-height, top-lit courtroom features exposed steel beams and timber panelling.

LIMERICK

Mulgrave Street

Limerick Court House #219

OPW *See also* P94

2016-18

Located on the site of the former artillery barracks on Mulgrave Street, and adjacent to Limerick Prison, the new Limerick Court House opened in February 2018. Designed by the OPW, with Wilson Architecture acting for the contractor BAM, it is one of the seven court house developments included in the 2015 Public Private Partnership Courts Bundle project. The protected 1807 gable-fronted gate lodges of the barracks have been retained and integrated into the Mulgrave Street façade of the new building. They are now flanked by a pair of Portland stone-clad boxes on the corners of the building, which float on darker limestone walls and are punctured by recessed glazing. These projections, separated by areas of glazing, repeat on the other façades and are the external expression of the internal disposition of six courtrooms on the first floor of the building. The main entrance, set between the original gate lodges, leads to a glazed stair hall with access to consultation rooms, the jury assembly area, legal practitioners' rooms, court offices and victim support services. Flights of steps at each end provide access to the nearly symmetrically arranged courtrooms. These are high-ceilinged, naturally lit, wood-lined spaces and include, at 200 m², the largest courtroom in Ireland. A former gunpowder magazine of c. 1810 has also been retained and integrated into the new building. The Supreme Court sat here in March 2018, only the second time in its history it has sat outside Dublin.

MURROE/MOROE
Court House

Standing on the west side of the village street, immediately adjacent to a filling station, Murroe petty sessions court house is a single-storey, three-bay building with a pitched roof and square-headed windows. A District Court location until 1961, the building was converted to a dispensary in 1963 by Patrick J. Sheahan, who added a flat-roofed entrance block to the street front. It remains in use as Murroe Health Centre.

NEWCASTLE WEST
Bishop Street
Court House   #220
1841; c. 1925

A more sophisticated than usual variant of the standard petty and quarter sessions court house of the late-1830s – early-1840s, Newcastle West was completed in 1841. Set back from the street behind a wall and forecourt, this is a five-bay, two-storey rectangular block with hipped roof and overhanging bracketed eaves. Round-headed windows to first floor set in arched recesses. Advanced end bays of channelled ashlar with vermiculated quoins and surrounds to windows and entrances. These entrances are surmounted by ornate stone balconies on stone brackets. Channelled ashlar to otherwise blank centre three bays of the ground floor. Extension to rear. Destroyed by local Irish Volunteers, 1921 (Bureau of Military History WS 1,021) and subsequently reconstructed c. 1925. Double-height courtroom with gallery supported on square timber piers. Still in use as a court house.

PALLASGREEN NEW/PALLAS GREAN NEW/CAPPAMORE
Tipperary Road
Court House

Pallasgreen petty sessions court house was located on the north side of the Tipperary Road at the east end of Pallasgreen New. No longer extant. Pallasgreen became a District Court Area in 1961. In 1978 the venue for sittings of the District Court was moved from Pallasgreen to Cappamore. The name of the District Court Area was changed to Cappamore in 1980, and in 1998 Cappamore District Court Area was abolished and merged with Newport.

PALLASKENRY
Main Street
Court House

The petty sessions court house in Pallaskenry was located on the west side of Main Street at the south end of the village. No longer extant.

PATRICKSWELL
Court House

Patrickswell had a small petty sessions court house located on the south side of the main village street, directly opposite St Patrick's Well. No longer extant.

RATHKEALE
Main Street
Court House and Bridewell   #221
James Pain/Michael Fitzgerald; []
1843; 1977-83

Lewis's *Topographical Dictionary* reports that the court house in Rathkeale 'is a large and convenient old building, but much out of repair'. In 1843 a Mr Fitzgerald won the contract to construct a new bridewell and court house for petty and quarter sessions to designs by James Pain. This was probably the same Michael FitzGerald who had designed the bridewells at Ennistymon and Tulla, Co. Clare, was responsible for alterations to Ennis court house, 1825, and who worked on several C of I churches in Limerick, Tipperary and Offaly. Originally a T-plan, two-storey, five-bay, classically proportioned building. The centre three bays are advanced and have a pediment containing a clock and topped by a bellcote. An additional bay was added to the east side and a two-storey, two-bay extension on the west. The bridewell was at ground floor level, hence the lack of windows here. The principal entrance to the court house was at first floor level, approached by a double flight of stone steps and flanked by large square-headed windows with rendered architraves. Above the entrance is a recent commemorative plaque. Court use ceased in the early 1970s when the court moved to Rathkeale Carnegie Library building. Internally much altered, especially following restoration works which began in 1977, as the building had fallen into disrepair and its demolition was mooted. Reopened in 1983 by President Patrick Hillery as a community centre.

RATHKEALE

New Line

Library and Court House #222

Francis C. Hartigan; EML Architects

1907; 2008

Rathkeale Carnegie Library is an eight-bay, two-storey rectangular block. Two bays on each end are advanced and gable-fronted. Square-headed windows and doors to ground floor. Dormer windows to centre bays. Described by Brendan Grimes (*Irish Carnegie Libraries* (Dublin, 1998)) as 'a plain and uninteresting piece of work', it was designed by architect and engineer Francis C. Hartigan and opened in 1907. The first floor was converted to District Court use in the early 1970s. Following an architectural competition, the building was refurbished in 2008 by EML Architects as part of a €2.5million project which included the construction of a new extension to accommodate Limerick County Council local area offices and meeting rooms. The ground floor windows of the centre bays were replaced by a floor-to-ceiling glazed porch. Court use ceased following the amalgamation of the District Court Area of Rathkeale into the District Court Area of Newcastle West in 2010.

SHANAGOLDEN

School/Court House #223

Main Street

c. 1910

Shanagolden became a District Court location in 1938 on the transfer of the court from Foynes. In 1985 part of the former national school on the east side of Main Street – a single-storey, six-bay block with advanced, gabled entrance porches on each end – was converted to a court house. Shanagolden District Court was amalgamated with Rathkeale in 2003.

ARDEE
Castle Street
St Leger's Castle/Court House   #228
15th cent.; 1805-10; 1860s

Four storeys tall with projecting towers on the Castle Street front, St Leger's Castle in Ardee was reputedly first built in the 13th century. While the existing fabric is in fact 15th-century and later, it remains the largest fortified medieval townhouse to survive in Ireland. Though much altered, the castle retains some early elements, including a barrel-vault at ground floor, a murder hole, a spiral staircase in the south tower, some corbelled rooms, as well as one ogee and several loop windows. By the mid-18th century the building was in use as a gaol. It was reportedly in ruins in 1804, when it was acquired by the Louth Grand Jury. Renovations were carried out between 1805 and 1810, during which the building lost its original roof but gained a crenellated parapet. A double-height balconied courtroom was provided at first-floor level. In 1825 a bridewell was created in the building and, sometime after that, a new three-bay entrance block was inserted between the projecting towers, crenellated, with a pointed-arch entrance and square-headed windows in brick surrounds. In 1863 John Neville, County Surveyor, built a new two-storey, five-bay bridewell to the rear. Court use continued into the 1990s.

ARDEE
Fair Green
Mid-Louth Civic Services Centre   #229
van Dijk Architects
2006

Located at Fair Green, Ardee, the Mid-Louth Civic Services Centre provides offices and workshop facilities for Louth County Council and the Office of Public Works, and a new District Court House for the Courts Service. Designed by van Dijk Architects and opened in June 2006, the exterior of the L-plan complex is composed primarily of continuous wooden fenestration, with zinc gables and a red brick spine. There are two single-storey parallel asymmetrical office and service wings, one of which has a sloping 'green' roof which overhangs to form a sheltered walkway. The universally accessible court house element, which cost €2.3 million, is the tallest part of the complex and includes a non-jury courtroom, a legal practitioners' room, consultation rooms, prisoner holding facilities, judge's chambers, and segregated circulation routes for prisoners, judiciary and members of the public. Its slopping roof incorporates continuous windows behind louvres which admit natural light to the high-ceilinged, wood-panelled courtroom.

CARLINGFORD
Newry Street
Court House   #230
c. 1935

Carlingford court house was built c. 1935 in a contemporary stripped classical idiom to replace a petty sessions court house which had stood on the same site. (The former coastguard station of 1848 by Jacob Owen, further south on Newry Street, was also apparently used as a court house before becoming a constabulary barracks and, later, Garda station.) Single-storey block set behind curving walls topped with railings and flanked by pedestrian gates. Three-bay front with plain pilasters on the corners. A flight of five steps leads to the central entrance set in a shallow flat-roofed porch, on either side of which are narrow windows, and above which is a plaque bearing the inscription in an Irish font 'Teach Cúirte'. Above this again is a string-course and squared pediment. Round-headed windows to sides. Carlingford District Court was abolished in 2007 and amalgamated with Dundalk. Now in use as a library.

CASTLEBELLINGHAM
Main Street
Court House

Castlebellingham's small petty sessions court house was part of the row of buildings on the west side of the south end of Main Street, on the site now occupied by the late 20th-century 'Coach House' commercial and residential development. Castlebellingham became a District Court location in 1924 and remained one until 1961, when it was transferred to the District Court Area of Dunleer.

COLLON
Main Street
Market House and Court House   #231
pre-1822; 1990s

On the east side of Market Square, Collon market house also served as the petty sessions court house. Gable-fronted, three-bay, two-storey centre block, originally flanked on both sides by a single-storey, five-pillared, open market portico terminating in a single-bay, two-storey pavilion. The range to the north was demolished by the mid-20th century, with only the back wall remaining, while on the south the portico was enclosed. The centre block was originally rendered. It has square-headed windows and doors, a stone string-course at first floor sill level, and a tall belfry with copper dome and weather vane. The building gained a single-storey, two-bay wing to the north on conversion to residential use in the 1990s. At the same time it lost its render, leaving exposed the rubble masonry with red-brick corners and surrounds to the openings. The centre gable still contains a clock which a plaque on the building records as having been donated by a Rev. Bradshaw in 1822.

DROGHEDA

West Street

Tholsel #232

George Darley; William Henry Byrne

1770; 1890

Drogheda's first tholsel was built in the mid-15th century and located in the Bull Ring. Court sessions were held there and in other locations in the town including, as recorded in the statute rolls of the parliament of Ireland for the reign of Edward IV, in a 'wretched hut' near Sunday's Gate and a thatched house near Mount St Oliver. The Bull Ring tholsel was replaced in the mid-17th century by a new wooden building on the corner of West Street and Shop Street. This in turn was demolished in 1765 to be replaced on the same site in 1770 by the current tall, narrow, classical building. The architect was George Darley whose design had been approved by Christopher Myers over a rival scheme by Hamilton Bury. Bury was compensated with the position of overseer on the construction. The tholsel accommodated Drogheda Corporation and served as a court house for assizes and county courts as well as petty sessions. It is a two-storey structure with a three-bay entrance front on West Street and a four-bay side elevation on Shop Street. The centre bay of the West Street façade is advanced and has an eaves pediment. There are round-headed windows and entrance to ground floor, the voussoirs of the relieving arches in which they are set continuing into horizontal channelling of the surrounding rustication. At first floor level are square-headed windows in ashlar walls with those on the West Street pedimented. The building is surmounted by a three-stage clock-tower crowned by a lead dome. The first two stages are square, the second one containing four clock faces, while the top is octagonal with engaged Ionic columns and oculus windows. In 1861 John Neville prepared plans for improving the tholsel, which was referred to as 'the Courthouse', but these were not proceeded with and by 1884 the building was recognised as increasingly unsuitable for court use. Following the construction of the new court house and municipal building at the Cornmarket, the tholsel was leased to the Hibernian Bank and conversion work to facilitate the new occupier was carried out in 1890 by William Henry Byrne. It remains in bank use.

DROGHEDA

Fair Street

Cornmarket and Court House #233

Francis Johnston (Cornmarket); Patrick John Lynam (Court House)

1796 (Cornmarket); 1887-90 (Court House)

Francis Johnston submitted plans for the Cornmarket in Drogheda in 1787 but nine years would pass before the building was completed. An enclosed square, with two wings of sheds on the east and west sides, a wall on the north side, and the main range on the south side facing onto Fair Street. Here, a central three-bay, two-storey block, with arcade to ground floor and square-headed windows above, is topped by a tall wooden lantern and weathervane and flanked by single-storey wings terminating in the pavilion-like gabled ends of the side ranges. In 1885, following ongoing issues at the tholsel in West Street, where conditions had become so poor as to lead to worries that the assizes might be removed from Drogheda altogether, the Grand Jury requested that the Corporation make a site available at the Cornmarket for a new court house. The building was also to be 'reserved to the Corporation of Drogheda for Municipal purposes' so long as this did not 'at anytime interfere with the assizes, County Courts or Petty Sessions'. Plans submitted in 1887 by the County Surveyor Patrick John Lynam were accepted. Attached to the north side of Johnston's Fair Street centre block, this plain single-storey building with square-headed windows and pedimented entrance took up almost half the market square, much to the annoyance of market-goers, who complained of being 'huddled together in the corners'. It cost £3,000 and opened in 1890. Altered and extended in the early 20th century; court use continued into the 1980s. The building remains in use as Louth County Council offices.

DROGHEDA

St Patrickswell Lane

Court House #234

OPW See also **P88**

2015-17

Having left the increasingly cramped facilities in the Cornmarket, court sittings in Drogheda moved to St Mary's Hall on Old Hill in the 1980s and thence to temporary facilities in Dyer Street. A site adjacent to Drogheda Garda station and overlooking the Boyne was acquired in 2000 for a new court house for Drogheda. However, the construction of the new facility was delayed until the initiation of the 2015 Public Private Partnership (PPP) Court House Bundle project, with construction firm BAM as the preferred bidder. The court house was designed by the OPW. Construction began in 2015 and the building was officially opened in July 2017, making Drogheda the first court house to be delivered under the PPP. Standing on a stepped plinth, the external expression of the new court house is dominated by henge-like, full-height stone-clad uprights interspersed with deeply recessed shafts of glazing. Light wells carry natural light deep into the building. Two centrally placed, wood-lined double-height courtrooms have been provided, designed for jury and non-jury courts, with requisite ancillary accommodation for judges, staff, practitioners, jurors, witnesses and persons in custody.

#232 | Drogheda, Tholsel (IAA, 1977)

#233 | Drogheda, Cornmarket and Court House (IAA, 1978)

#234 | Drogheda, St Patrickswell Lane, Court House (Barrow Coakley Photography, 2017)

#235 | Ravensdale (IAA, 1974)

DUNDALK

Market Square

County Court House

See Significant Court Houses – A Chronological Selection   **P188**

DUNLEER

St Brigid's Hall, Upper Main Street, a finely detailed gable-fronted, red-brick building with terracotta elements including name and date, was constructed in 1902 on the site of, and may include fabric from, Dunleer petty sessions court house. Alfred Augustine Murphy carried out repairs and alterations to 'the Courthouse in Dunleer' in 1939, but it is not clear what building is being referred to. Dunleer remained a District Court location until 2007 when it was abolished and merged with Drogheda.

LOUTH

Court House

Louth petty sessions court house stood on the south side of the Dundalk Road at the east end of the village. A private residence now occupies the site.

MELL

Waterunder Road

Court House

pre-1835

Mell petty sessions court house stood at the junction of Waterunder Road and Barrack Lane, 1km north-west of the centre of Drogheda. It is shown as a police station on the first-edition OS map, and as 'Mell Court House' on the 25-inch map. No longer extant.

RAVENSDALE

Court House   #235

The small, mid-19th-century petty sessions court house at Ravensdale stands on the east side of the road, just south of Ravensdale Bridge. Classical in appearance with a pedimented entrance front, the tympanum having a royal coat of arms, and quoins to corners. A blind recessed panel is set above the central entrance which is framed by a lugged architrave. Square-headed windows in red-brick surrounds to side elevations. Damaged by fire in 1921 during the War of Independence and subsequently repaired. A sign above the entrance bears the inscription 'Antiques', indicating a commercial use, but the building is currently unoccupied.

RIVERSTOWN

A Riverstown is listed in the 1842 *Petty Sessions Return* but it is not clear which of the three locations associated with this name in Louth is being referred to. Riverstown was no longer listed as a court location by 1882.

TERMONFECKIN

Court House

The petty sessions court house and dispensary in Termonfeckin stood on the north-east corner of the crossroads at the north end of the village. In 1890 it was described in the *Drogheda Conservative* as 'a standing disgrace to the Grand Jury of the County Louth'. The complainant continued: 'At present it is in the most filthy and dilapidated state. There is hardly a whole pane in any of the windows, and the magistrates, solicitors, and others, whose business compels them to be there, suffer the greatest amount of discomfort. On entering the building the smell of damp is such that one would encounter on descending into a vault, and the various law books which lie upon a shelf on the side of the bench, are covered with blue mould; and if requisitioned for the enlightenment of the magistrates they would have to be fingered very gingerly or they would drop asunder'. The building was burned in July 1920 during the War of Independence and subsequently rebuilt as a private residence.

ACHILL/ACAILL

Court House   #236

[Thomas Patrick Flanagan]

1938

A petty sessions court house was provided in 1839 at Dorrary Point on the north side of the road at the west end of Achill Bridge. In 1938 a new, single-storey, L-plan court house was constructed at the east or mainland end of the bridge, beside the Garda station. Somewhat ecclesiastical looking, thanks to the three-arched open portico to the front. This is surmounted by a pediment with a large roundel containing the date of construction. An upgrading of the court house was undertaken in 2006. Despite fears that Achill District Court might be abolished, the court house remains in use. The court houses in Ballycroy and Kilkelly, Co. Mayo, built in 1939, are sufficiently similar to be derivatives of Achill. All three are presumably by the same hand, possibly that of County Surveyor Thomas P. Flanagan.

BALLA

Main Street/Market Square

Court House   #237

[Henry Brett]

1843; 2000

The formerly detached court house in Balla, bearing a datestone of 1843, stood adjacent to the 1806 RC church (converted to a dance hall in 1920) on the north side of Market Square. A building is clearly shown on the site on the first-edition OS map which for Mayo was published 1837-39, so the date 1843 may refer to the conversion of an already existing structure to court use rather than a new building. The work – converting or building anew – may have been carried out by the Mayo County Surveyor Henry Brett. Three-bay, two-storey block with a central entrance at ground floor, above which are three small square-headed windows set just below the eaves. The building is now integrated into, and dwarfed by, Balla Community Resource Centre which stands on the site of the church, and opened in 2000, the same year that Balla District Court was amalgamated with Castlebar.

BALLINA

Kevin Barry Street

Court House   #238

1840s; 1930s

A court house is shown in Ballina on the first-edition OS map, a T-plan building on the same site on Kevin Barry Street (formerly Francis Street) as the current court house. Described in 1828 as being 'defective in size, in arrangement, and in most other requisites', it was upgraded or replaced in the 1840s, possibly by Mayo County Surveyor Henry Brett. Set behind iron railings and gates with large tapered pedimented stone piers, this is a classical petty and quarter sessions court house of two-storeys and five-bays, the centre three bays advanced and gabled. Simplified, round-headed Gibbsian stone doorcase centrally placed in the main façade, with the door now replaced by a lunette window. This is flanked by round-headed niches linked by a stone string-course at impost level. In the end bays are round-headed recesses which

#236 | Achill (Paul Tierney, 2019)
#237 | Balla (Special Collections, Mayo Library, Castlebar, c. 1900)
#238 | Ballina (Courts Service, c. 1995)
#239 | Ballinrobe (IAA, 2004)

formerly contained square-headed windows. That on the right remains but that on the left is now obscured by a later gabled entrance porch. Square-headed windows to first floor. Altered and extended in the 1930s, and extensively refurbished in 1995, when the double-height courtroom was refitted. Still in court use.

BALLINDINE
Station Road
Court House

The petty sessions court house in Ballindine was located on the north side of Station Road. No trace remains, an industrial shed now occupying the site.

BALLINROBE
Main Street
Market House and Court House   #239
pre-1767

Described in Lewis's *Topographical Dictionary* as 'a neat building well adapted to [court] purpose, and affording also accommodation for the market', Ballinrobe's mid-18th-century market house and court house was extant by 1767 at the latest. John Wesley preached here in 1775. Five-bay, two-storey building, with a weathervane-topped ventilator over centre bay, set behind a small eaves pediment containing a split lunette window and a clock. The ground floor was formerly an open market arcade, with stone surrounds to arches and string-course at impost level. The arches were infilled with doors and windows towards the end of the 19th century. Tall windows to first floor, where the assembly rooms were used for petty and quarter sessions. With Castlebar, it was also one of two venues for the Mayo county assizes until c. 1840, when Castlebar became the sole venue. While the former market had a number of uses from grain store to public house, the courtroom, with its broken pediment over the judge's bench and iron railing separating the public area from the court, remained in use and intact into the 21st century. In 2010 the Electoral Divisions of the District Court Area of Ballinrobe were amalgamated into the District Court Area of Castlebar. The court house was re-roofed in 2017 and various heritage uses for the building continue to be proposed. A post-box of 1897-1901 is located between the second and third arches from the right.

BALLYCASTLE
Main Street
Court House   #240
pre-1838

A pre-1838 vernacular, three-bay, single-storey cottage, one of a terrace of such houses on the north side of Main Street, formerly functioned as Ballycastle court house. Now with a two-bay 19th-century-style shopfront entrance, the building is owned by the Ballinglen Arts Foundation and has served with the adjoining two-storey house as the Ballinglen Arts Centre and Gallery since 1997. Ballycastle District Court continued to sit in the Arts Centre until abolished in 2008 and amalgamated with Ballina.

BALLYCROY

Court House   #241

[Thomas Patrick Flanagan]

1939

Adjacent to the cemetery on the north side of Ballycroy village, this simple five-bay court house was built in 1939, according to a datestone on the gable end. The render on this end is decorated with square-headed panels flanking a round-headed central recess to give the impression that this was the entrance front. (A window has recently been inserted into the centre panel.) This treatment of the gable is similar to, though less elaborate than, the decoration to be found on the nearly identical court house in Kilkelly, also dated 1939. Both Ballycroy and Kilkelly show similarities to Achill, which has an actual gable porch and entrance and was built the year previously. All three may be by the Mayo County Surveyor Thomas P. Flanagan. Having been a court location since before 1882, Ballycroy District Court was abolished in 2011, and the District Court Area amalgamated with that of Achill (Acaill). The court house was subsequently used by Ballycroy Development Co.

BALLYGLASS

Court House

The petty sessions court house in Ballyglass was a nearly square two-storey structure attached to the south side of the constabulary barracks (later Garda station). Still standing but ivy-clad and derelict.

BALLYHAUNIS

Main Street

Court House   #242

c. 1875

On the corner of Main Street and Barrack Street, and set back from the street behind a low wall and wrought-iron railings, the detached, four-bay, hipped-roofed limestone court house in Ballyhaunis was built c. 1875. The centre bays are single-storey with large square-headed windows lighting the central double-height courtroom with its timber panelled judge's bench. The end bays project very slightly and are two-storey, with recessed square-headed doors at ground floor and short square-headed windows above. Single-bay side elevation. Refurbished 1995-97. The court house closed at the end of 2013 following the amalgamation of the District Court Area into that of Castlebar.

BELLAVARY

Court House/Police Barracks

A combined police barracks and petty sessions court house is shown on the first-edition OS map of Bellavary, at the east end of the village. The building was still standing when the 25-inch map was produced, but was not in use by either police or court. No longer extant.

#244 | Belmullet, Civic Centre (Paul Tierney, 2019)
#245 | Cong (NIAH, 2010)
#246 | Kilkelly (Paul Tierney, 2019)

BELMULLET
William Street
Court House   #243

The two-storey, four-bay building, incorporating a carriage way, standing in the middle of the terrace on the south side of William Street directly opposite the end of Chapel Street functioned as Belmullet court house. Closed in 2000, with sittings moving to Ballycroy, on foot of complaints from judges and other court users over the poor facilities available. As there were no judge's chambers, judges were required to arrive in court attire and enter the building through the front door alongside members of the public, defendants and other court attendees. Now occupied by Údarás na Gaeltachta and the local library.

BELMULLET
Church Street
Civic Centre (including Court House)   #244
Mayo County Council
2005-07

A new Civic Centre was built in Belmullet from 2005 to 2007 as a joint project between the Courts Service, Mayo County Council, who provided design input, Údarás na Gaeltachta and the Belmullet Arts Group. Composed of a sequence of white-walled volumes linked by single-storey stone-clad elements, the building includes an auditorium/cinema, recording studio and exhibition rooms (collectively Áras Inis Gluaire or Erris Arts Centre), the local library, a café, offices for the four agencies and a simple modern courtroom with wooden furnishings.

BINGHAMSTOWN (SALEEN)/AN GEATA MÓR
Court House

Binghamstown is listed as a petty sessions location in the 1842 *Petty Sessions Return*, and Lewis's *Topographical Dictionary* records that the petty sessions were 'held in a court-house every Thursday'. However, the court house is not marked on the first-edition OS map, and Binghamstown had ceased to be a petty sessions location by 1880.

CASTLEBAR
The Mall
County Court House
See Significant Court Houses – A Chronological Selection   P190

CHARLESTOWN (LOW PARK)
Market Square
Court House

Charlestown petty sessions were listed throughout the 19th century as Low Park. By 1907 the petty sessions were being listed as 'Low Park (in Charlestown Courthouse)', with the court house in question being the four-bay, two-storey mid-19th-century structure at the east end of the terrace on the south side of Market Square. This building is now a pharmacy. Charlestown became a District Court location in 1924 and remained one until 2008, with court sittings taking place in the local community hall.

CLAREMORRIS
Ballyhaunis Road
Court House

Claremorris court house, which Lewis's *Topographical Dictionary* describes as 'a large building, about a quarter of a mile from the town', stood on the north side of the Ballyhaunis Road. The interior was depicted in an engraving by Aloysius O'Kelly published in the *Illustrated London News*, 26 November 1881, which reported on the opening of new land courts in Ireland under the Land Law (Ireland) Act 1881 (see pp. 16-17). This shows a crowded double-height courtroom viewed from the back, looking towards a pedimented judges' bench where three judges are presiding. Against the right hand wall is a gallery supported on square wooden posts and on the left is the jury box, behind which is a large window. Built for petty and quarter sessions, the court house continued in use until the latter part of the 20th century, before being demolished and replaced by a two-storey, eight-bay commercial office development. In 1969 a part of Claremorris Town Hall was made available for District Court sittings. In 2008, the suggestion circulated locally that a new court house would be built in Claremorris but in 2011 the District Court Area was amalgamated with Castlebar.

CONG
Abbey Street
Court House   #245
1853

The small Gothic petty sessions court house in Cong is situated on the north side of Abbey Street and faces directly down the road to Ashford Castle. Single-storey, three-bay structure with rubble-stone walls and dressed-stone surrounds to openings. Projecting central entrance porch, with door set in pointed arch, flanked by paired lancet windows. Above the entrance is a datestone reading 'Courthouse 1853'. Now a tourist office.

CROSSMOLINA
Chapel Street
Court House

A three-bay, two-storey, mid-19th-century house in the terrace on the west side of Chapel Street is shown on the 25-inch OS map as Crossmolina court house. Flanked on one side by a set of steps leading to the rear. Latterly a public house. Crossmolina District Court was amalgamated with Ballina in 2000.

FOXFORD
Market Square/Pound Street
Court House

Shown on the first-edition OS map, a market and court house was located in the Market Square (Davitt Street) in Foxford, immediately adjacent to the C of I church. This was demolished in the mid-19th century, at which point the court house transferred the short distance to the end-of-terrace, two-storey premises on the west side of Pound Street, almost opposite the church, where it remained until Foxford District Court was abolished in 2008 and the Area amalgamated with that of Ballina.

HOLLYMOUNT
Court House

The petty sessions court house in Hollymount was located in the left end house of the four-house terrace still standing at the south end of the west side of the broad main street. Hollymount was a District Court location until 1961, when it became part of the Ballinrobe Area.

KILKELLY
Swinford Road
Court House   #246
[Thomas Patrick Flanagan]
1939

Kilkelly petty sessions were established in 1896, but the simple, rectangular five-bay court house was not built until 1939, according to a datestone on the gable end. The render here is decorated with four plain pilasters separating square-headed panels which flank a round-headed central recess. The tympanum of the pediment-like gable contains a large roundel with the date AD 1939. All of this decoration serves to give the impression that this was the entrance front, whereas the entrances are actually located in the five-bay east side. This treatment of the gable is similar to, though more elaborate than, that of Ballycroy, also dated 1939. Both these court houses show sufficient similarities to Achill to suggest that they are by the same hand, possibly that of Thomas P. Flanagan, County Surveyor. Kilkelly District Court was amalgamated with Ballyhaunis in 2000 and the former court house became a library.

KILLALA
Courthouse Street
Court House

Meetinghouse Street in Killala was so called because there was a Methodist meeting house located on the south side of the street, just north of the sharp elbow-turn it takes halfway along its length. A much altered, gable-fronted, two-storey building stands on the site. Just at the elbow, on the north side of the street, was Killala court house. Both meeting house and court house are shown on the first-edition OS map, along with a market house, south of the court house. The Methodists have left, the market house is gone, and the road is now Courthouse Street. Lewis's *Topographical Dictionary* records that petty sessions 'are held in a private house every Friday' and a pair of two-storey, early- to mid-19th-century houses, one two-bay, one three, still stand on the court house site. One of these functioned as the court house. Killala District Court was amalgamated with Ballina and Ballycastle in 2000, by which time the court had been sitting in the local community hall.

KILMAINE

Petty sessions were held in Kilmaine on Wednesdays, according to Lewis's *Topographical Dictionary*, and the village was a District Court location from 1927 to 1939 for summary jurisdiction only. No designated court house has been identified.

KILTIMAGH
James Street
Court House
c. 1860-70

A detached, two-storey, three-bay building of c. 1860-70 on the east side of James Street (formerly George Street) was Kiltimagh court house. Set back from the street behind a low wall, the court house had stone surrounds to square-headed openings, quoins to corners, and an eaves pediment below which the two first floor windows were grouped. In 2011 the District Court Area of Kiltimagh was amalgamated with Castlebar. The court house was demolished c. 2015 and replaced by a private residence.

LOUISBURGH
The Square
Market House and Court House   #247

Petty sessions were held in Louisburgh in the market house on the Square. The Square itself was laid out in 1795, but the market house as it now stands on the north apex post-dates the first-edition OS map (1837-39). The angled side walls match those of the former constabulary barracks on the west corner. Three-bay market arcade facing the Square with two further arches in the angled gables, all now filled with windows and doors. Square-headed windows to the first-floor rooms which housed the petty sessions. The building is now a pharmacy. Louisburgh had a summary jurisdiction District Court from 1927 to 1961, when it became part of the Westport District Court Area.

NEWPORT
Castlebar Street
Court House   #248

Lewis's *Topographical Dictionary* comments that Newport court house 'in which the sessions are held, is a small neat building'. By the end of the 19th century, Newport court house was located towards the east end of the terrace on the north side of Castlebar Street, east of the former railway bridge. A six-bay, two-storey, mid- to late-19th-century structure, possibly originally comprising two houses, with a carriage arch and two entrances at ground floor, one with a later window to the side, and six square-headed windows above. The east end was hollowed out internally to create a double-height courtroom accessed directly from the street and lit by the first-floor windows. The west end remained two-storey, with the court office on the first floor. The courtroom was refurbished in 1989 and the court house remained in use until 2000, when the District Court Area was amalgamated with Westport.

SWINFORD

Davitt Place

Court House   **#249**

Henry Brett

1838-40

Built from 1838 and opened in 1840, Swinford court house is a variation of the standard petty and quarter sessions court house of the late-1830s – early-1840s, as interpreted in this instance by Mayo County Surveyor Henry Brett. Very similar to the court house in Westport. Standing prominently on a corner site, this is a detached two-storey building with a five-bay front on Davitt Place and three-bay sides, with a single-storey, single-bay block to the rear. Hipped roof, and dressed-stone quoins, eaves cornice and window surrounds. The external render is a later addition. Two square-headed entrances set in channelled stone in the modestly advanced end bays of the Davitt Place façade. Between them is a blank wall with a long recessed panel. A platband delineates ground floor from first, where five square-headed windows are provided. The side façades have three small square windows at ground floor and three large square-headed windows above. A number of the windows in the side elevations are blind. Internally, the courtroom retained its original furniture, including judge's bench with pedimented canopy, into the 21st century. Plans for a major refurbishment were developed by the Courts Service from 2005 to 2008 but not proceeded with and the court house was closed in 2013. In 2016 funding was provided to convert the former court house into a Creative Hub for Swinford under the Rural Economic Development Zones scheme.

WESTPORT

Castlebar Street

Court House   **#250**

Henry Brett

1838-40

Westport court house is a variation of the standard petty and quarter sessions court house of the late-1830s – early-1840s and practically identical to the court house in Swinford. It is therefore attributable to the same County Surveyor, Henry Brett, and to the same construction period of 1838-40. Certainly extant by 1846 when it is referred to in *Slater's Directory* as 'a neat substantial stone building'. Situated on the corner of Castlebar Street and Distillery Road, this is a detached, two-storey stone building with a five-bay front and three-bay sides and a single-storey, single-bay block to the rear. Hipped roof with tall stone chimneys on side walls. Rough stone with dressed-stone quoins, platband, eaves cornice and window surrounds. Two square-headed entrances set in channelled stone in the modestly advanced end bays of the Castlebar Street façade. Between them is a blank wall with a long recessed panel. Five square-headed windows to first floor. The side elevations have three small square windows at ground floor and three large square-headed windows above, some of which are blind. Internally, the courtroom ceiling was lowered in the early 1990s to provide office accommodation above, though the judge's bench retained its large flat canopy. Further refurbishment works were carried out 2000-02. The court house closed in 2013 due to what were referred to as serious health and safety risks posing an immediate danger to judges, staff, the public and others using the building, since when court hearings for the Westport District have been heard in Castlebar.

NAVAN
Ludlow Street
Court House   #256
1801

Gable-fronted, two-storey over raised basement rubble-stone petty and quarter sessions court house. Dressed-stone quoins and three large round-headed windows at first floor level beneath a pediment with blind oculus. Erected in 1801 on the site of Navan's 17th-century tholsel, and on display in the building now is a stone uncovered in 1977 with the inscription 'Edmund Manninge was overseer of this work in the year of Our Lord 1632. On whose soul the Lord have mercy'. The court house continued in use into the second half of the 20th century before becoming, in succession, a supermarket, a bank, and a solicitor's office. It is now a dental clinic. Little trace of the original interior remains, and nothing of the original entrance arrangements. Iron railings at street level now screen a modern glazed shopfront by Clancy Architects, 2016.

NAVAN
Canon Row
Court House   #257
Freyer and Taylor
2003

In November 1897, the *Irish Times* reported that James Franklin Fuller was preparing plans for a new court house in Navan for Meath Grand Jury. This was not proceeded with, nor was the 1947-48 proposal by the Dublin-based architectural practice, William H. Byrne and Son, for a new court house to be built on a site between the railway station and the County Council offices (which they also proposed to expand) on Railway Street. Navan District Court did not acquire a building of its own again until 2003, when a two-storey late-20th-century mixed-use commercial building on Canon Row was adapted by Freyer and Taylor architects, at a cost of €600,000, to provide facilities, including courtroom with judge's chambers, an office for the District Court clerk, consultation rooms, legal practitioners' room and a holding room for prisoners. In use from October 2003, it was officially opened in April 2004. In 2012 criminal court sittings were relocated to Trim due to the inadequacy of holding cells in Navan, among other issues. Family law and civil sittings are still held in the Canon Row court house. A new court house for Navan was among the proposals detailed in Project Ireland 2040.

OLDCASTLE
The Square
Market House and Court House   #258
c. 1750

The market house in the Square of Oldcastle is recorded on the 25-inch OS map as being both a market house and court house. Three-bay, two-storey structure built c. 1750 for the Napier family of Loughcrew House. Triple market arcade in the central bay. Modern alterations include a flat roof, unsympathetic windows and shallow battlements to parapet. In use as retail premises. Oldcastle District Court was amalgamated with Kells in 2006.

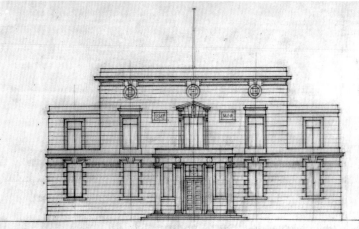

#255 | Julianstown (Paul Tierney, 2018)
#256 | Navan, Ludlow Street, Court House (Paul Tierney, 2018)
#257 | Navan, Proposed Court House. Elevation by W.H. Byrne & Son Architects, 1947 (W.H. Byrne & Son Collection, IAA)

SLANE
Chapel Street
Court House #259
c. 1800

The 25-inch OS map shows Slane court house occupying one of a pair of opposing c. 1800 houses standing perpendicular to Chapel Street, facing each other across a small forecourt. That on the south side was the court house. It has a three-bay, two-storey entrance front with pedimented porch. Unlike its near twin, the building which accommodated the court house has a second entrance (for the court) in its gable end or street front, approached by a short flight of steps at a right angle to the building. Slane District Court was amalgamated with Navan in 1973. Having served for a time as a credit union, it is now in private use.

SUMMERHILL
The Green
Court House

Summerhill petty sessions court house was a small semi-detached building on the west side of the Green. No longer extant.

TRIM
Castle Street
County Court House
See Significant Court Houses – A Chronological Selection **P185**

Oldcastle (Paul Tierney, 2018) | **#258**
Slane (Paul Tierney, 2018) | **#259**

BALLYBAY

Main Street

Market House   #260

William Walker

1848

The fine market house in Ballybay also functioned as a court house. Replacing an earlier version shown on the first-edition OS map as a detached building standing in the middle of Main Street, the market house was built in 1848 to designs by William Walker. A 'perfectly balanced classical essay', according to the *Buildings of Ireland*, this is a four-bay, two-storey, limestone block with a four-arch open ground-floor market arcade. Ashlar piers support the dressed-stone arches which have prominent keystones and iron gates. Dressed-stone platbands, one just above the keystones, and a second at first floor sill level. Square-headed first floor windows set in dressed-stone architraves. The centre two bays are advanced and pedimented, the pediment containing a red-brick roundel. Between the centre first floor windows is a plaque with the date 1848 in Roman numerals. Hipped roof with broad eaves supported by brackets. The south façade is blank while the north side, on Church Street, has two blind windows to the first floor and a later red-brick offshoot at ground floor level. External steps to the rear provide access to the first floor which accommodated court functions. Ballybay District Court was amalgamated with Monaghan in 2007.

CARRICKMACROSS

Market Square

Court House   #261

Edward V. Forrest; Hamilton Young Lawlor Ellison Architects

1837-44; 2000-02

Set behind railings on a raised plinth at the back of a small square facing directly down Main Street, the court house in Carrickmacross is a solid example of the standard late-1830s – early-1840s petty and quarter sessions design. As is often the case, the building can be attributed to the local County Surveyor, in this case Edward V. Forrest, who was asked to provide drawings in 1837. He made some modest changes to the basic template, in particular the decorative elements such as architraves and door surrounds. A five-bay, two-storey stone-built centre block with recessed single-bay, single-storey entrance wings at each end. The end bays of the main block are slightly advanced and have segmental-headed windows at ground floor. Between these are three recessed panels, the centre one glazed. Tall, square-headed first floor windows set in dressed-stone surrounds, their sills merging into a platband. Completely refurbished by Hamilton Young Lawlor Ellison Architects for the Courts Service in 2000-02. Due to the presence of dry rot, the building had to be stripped back to the external walls and rebuilt to meet the requirements of a contemporary court house, including a universally accessible courtroom with advanced audio facilities, judge's chambers, practitioners' and meeting rooms.

#260 | Ballybay (IAA, c. 1975)

#261 | Carrickmacross (Roger Hill, 1998)

#262 | Castleblayney (Lawrence Collection, NLI, late 19C)

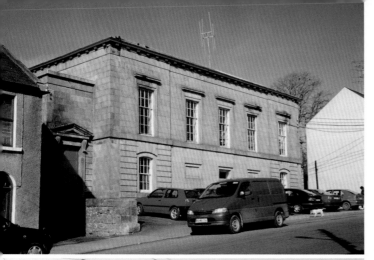

CASTLEBLAYNEY

Market Square

Court House and Market House   #262

1859

Castleblayney had a late-18th-century market house in Market Square, described in 1801 as neat, with spacious rooms and a belfry. Near this, by the 1830s at the latest, was a separate sessions house. In 1856, the Grand Jury decided to replace both with a new combined market and court house for petty and quarter sessions. Erected on the old market house site, this is a large, classical building with a three-bay, two-storey entrance front at the west end, in front of which is a railed, semi-circular platform. Round-headed openings at ground floor set in relieving arches, square-headed windows above, a decorated platband in between. The centre bay is slightly advanced with a small round eaves pediment containing a clock, behind which was a tall cupola with copper dome. The east end is a reflection of the west, though without the advanced centre bay, entrance, clock or cupola. The long side elevations maintain the pattern of relieving arches containing round-headed windows at ground floor and square-headed above. The eight-bay south side is two-storey with four deeply recessed centre bays, in front of which is a single-storey arched loggia. The three centre bays of the seven-bay north side project significantly with round-headed windows to ground and first floor. On this side the site drops sharply to accommodate a seven-bay, basement level, rusticated market arcade with niches in the chamfered corners of the advanced centre block. Internally, a double-height courtroom had a gallery on cast-iron supports and a canopied judge's bench. The building remained in use as a court house and library until the 1990s. Empty since 2003, it is now a roofless shell. Court sittings moved first to the town hall and then to nearby Hope Castle. In 2010, Castleblayney District Court was amalgamated with Carrickmacross.

CLONES

McCurtain Street

Court House   #263

Edward V. Forrest

1837-42

Clones court house is a standard late-1830s – early-1840s petty and quarter sessions building, and a near twin of Carrickmacross. It is also by County Surveyor, Edward V. Forrest, who was asked to produce designs in 1837. Set back from and slightly raised above the street. Five-bay, two-storey, stone-built centre block with recessed single-bay, single-storey entrance wings at each end. The end bays of the main block are slightly advanced and have segmental-headed windows at ground floor. Here the voussoirs of the segmental arches continue into the channelled ashlar of the end bay ground-floor walls. The centre bays have three recessed panels at ground floor, the centre one glazed. Large square-headed first-floor windows set in dressed-stone surrounds, their sills merging into a platband. Hipped roof with bracketed eaves. Pedimented entrance door in each side wing. Double-height, galleried courtroom with canopied judge's bench. Refurbished for the Courts Service 2007. Closed 2014 following the amalgamation of Clones District Court with Monaghan, since when the building has been used for community, municipal and cultural purposes.

EMYVALE
Main Street
Court House

A five-bay, single-storey, end-of-terrace structure on the east side of Main Street at the corner with Glaslough Road served as Emyvale petty sessions court house from 1847 to 1920, according to a plaque on the building. Subsequently a parochial hall and now in use as an oratory.

MONAGHAN
Church Square
County Court House
See **P76** *&* Significant Court Houses – A Chronological Selection **P196**

NEWBLISS
Main Street
Court Houses   **#264**
c. 1820

Lewis's *Topographical Dictionary* gives a litany of significant buildings in Newbliss including a 'neat' market house, 'a good inn', a Presbyterian meeting house of 1816, a school and a dispensary. He conspicuously fails to mention either a court house or petty sessions and yet Newbliss had two buildings which served as the local court house. The former Mail Coach Inn on the east side of Main Street at the north end of the village is identified on the 25-inch OS map as a court house. This is a three-storey, three-bay, L-plan building of c. 1820 with a fanlit central door flanked by square-headed windows set in arched recesses, and Wyatt windows to the first floor of the end bays. At the other end of the village, on the west side of Main Street, is a building which has more recently served as Newbliss court house. Also built c. 1820, this was formerly a three-bay, two-storey, L-plan detached block, extended by one bay on the left to incorporate a now filled-in carriage arch. The central entrance bay is recessed, and there are tripartite windows in segmental-arched recesses at ground floor with square-headed windows above. This building has also accommodated local authority offices. Current proposals are for it to be adapted for use by the Tyrone Guthrie Centre. Newbliss ceased to be a court location in 1924, becoming part of Clones District Court Area.

ROCKCORRY
Newbliss Road
Market House and Court House   **#265**
[Benjamin Hallam]
1805

Prominently located in the centre of Rockcorry, the market house, which also accommodated petty sessions, was built in 1805, possibly to designs by Benjamin Hallam, who laid out the village for Thomas Charles Steuart Corry in the first decade of the 19th century. Three-bay, two-storey, almost square block with a set-back extension to the right side. Hipped roof and rendered walls with plaster quoins to corners. Advanced pedimented centre bay on main front, a plaque in the tympanum bearing the inscription 'TCSC AD MDCCCV'. Tall recessed arches on three façades, tied together by a platband at impost level. Flanking the arches are decorative panels with chamfered corners, while the arches themselves are filled in with shopfronts and entrances at ground floor, and single square-headed windows above. Square-headed windows to first floor of main front, set higher than the windows in the arches. External stairs to extension. Not currently in use.

BANAGHER

Cuba Avenue
Court House

Banagher petty sessions court house stood on the north side of Cuba Avenue, a short distance from the corner with Main Street. Burned in the War of Independence; no trace remains. In 2008 Banagher District Court, which had sat above a former dance hall in the town and later in a school building on Cuba Avenue, was abolished and the Electoral Divisions of the District Court Area of Banagher were amalgamated into Birr and Ballinasloe.

BIRR

Townsend Street
Court House   #266
pre-1810

Built before 1810 to replace an earlier sessions house, Birr court house, which is similar to, or derived from, that in Daingean, was described by Thomas Lalor Cooke in his 1826 *Picture of Parsonstown* as a 'handsome, convenient building sufficiently extensive for the business of the county. The Bench, Jury-boxes, &c. are prettily contrived, and unlike to session houses in general, there is a good outside hall to the one now being described. The Grand Jury Room is spacious in proportion to the criminal business to be transacted in it'. Set back slightly from the street behind railings, this is a rendered, five-bay, two-storey building, the façade extended by carriage and access gates to each end, and the parapet dramatically castellated. The centre three bays are recessed with a round-headed central entrance door (for a time obscured by an entrance porch) flanked by round-headed windows, and three square-headed windows to first floor. The gabled end bays have arched recesses with a string-course at impost level. Each arch contains a square-headed window at ground floor, that on the right being blind, and a tall round-headed window above. Four-bay sides with tall round-headed windows to first floor. The courtroom has a wooden gallery supported on square wooden piers, and a plaster canopy over the judge's bench. The ceiling was replaced with acoustic panels in 1990, though the original rose was retained. A renovation programme was being planned in 2008 but was postponed, and the court house closed in 2013, with court sittings transferred to Tullamore.

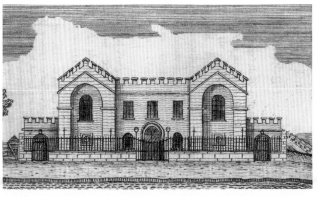

Birr (*The early history of the town of Birr or Parsonstown*, T.L. Cooke (Dublin, 1826), Offaly History)

CLARA

Church Street
Court House   #267

A two-storey, three-bay, detached mid- to late-19th-century house on the north side of Church Street, immediately west of St Brigid's RC church, functioned as Clara petty sessions court house. Burned in 1920 and subsequently repaired. Clara was a District Court location for summary jurisdiction only from 1924 to 1961, when it became part of the Kilbeggan District Court Area. The former court house served as a technical school and branch library before becoming the parish centre.

CLONBULLOGUE

Court House   #268

Clonbullogue became a court location in 1880. Valuation records indicate that from 1884 the petty sessions court house occupied the three-bay, two-storey house with prominent entrance porch on the east side of the triangular village green, just to the south of the constabulary barracks (later Garda station). The court house had itself previously been a police barracks, and became a private residence in 1923. It stands now with its render removed, exposing rubble-stone walls and brick window surrounds.

CLONYGOWAN

Court House

Clonygowan constabulary barracks and court house are shown on the 25-inch OS map as two attached buildings on the west side of Fair Green, close to the site now occupied by Clonygowan Health Centre. No trace of either building remains.

KILCORMAC (FRANKFORD)
Main Street
Court House

The first-edition OS map of Kilcormac or Frankford shows a 'Petit Sessions Ho.' on Main Street. The map is ambiguous but the building in question may be on the north side of the west end, close to the junction with the road to Ferbane. On the 25-inch map no court house is identified in the town, with the possible site of the petty sessions house occupied by a post office. This building is still standing, a two-bay mid-terrace house with double shopfront to ground floor. The NIAH says that the three-bay, two-storey house with recessed fanlit entrance and advanced outhouse wings which now functions as Kilcormac Garda station was built c. 1800 as a petty sessions court house, but it is clearly marked on the 25-inch OS map as Ballyboy Rectory. For the latter part of the 20th century, Kilcormac District Court sat in the stepped-gabled Fiesta Ballroom at the east end of the town. The District Court was abolished in 2007 and amalgamated with Birr.

KINNITTY
Schoolhouse and Court House   #271
[Arthur Cluskey]
c. 1820

Kinnitty Community Centre now occupies the former schoolhouse built c. 1820 which came to accommodate petty sessions court sittings. It is possible that the 1810 elevations and plan by Arthur Cluskey for a 'Proposed Free School at Kenetty' held in the Erasmus Smith Schools Archive show the original appearance of the school. The plan would seem to correspond with that on the 25-inch OS map. However, the elevation as its stands is Gothic, not classical. It is a three-bay structure of rubble stone, each bay gable-fronted, the centre one rising to a second storey. Segmental arch to centre contains a recessed entrance, with single pointed-arched windows on each side and above. Much altered and extended to the rear.

MONEYGALL
Court House

Moneygall's petty sessions court house was set back from the road on the north side of the village street just west of the village centre and adjacent to the dispensary. The dispensary has gone, aside from its roadside wall and gate, but some trace of the court house may remain in the lower wall of the industrial shed which stands on the site.

MOYSTOWN
Court House

Moystown petty sessions court house was located on the south side of the road (now the R357), c. 2.7km north-west of Moystown Cross. An isolated, rural court house; some fabric may remain in the six-bay, two-storey residence to be found on the site.

SHINRONE
Main Street
Court House   #272

The first-edition OS map shows a 'Petit Sessions Court Ho.', on the south side of Shinrone Main Street, adjacent to a 'Female School'. No longer extant; a public house now stands in the vicinity. By the late 19th century, the building on the south corner of Main Street and the Roscrea road was Shinrone constabulary barracks. The building immediately beside this had become the petty sessions court house, a single-storey, three-bay cottage with round-headed entrance and two round-headed windows. Now in residential use.

THOMASTOWN (RATH)
Court House
pre-1838

A small, rural, petty sessions court house stood on the south side of the road 200m east of Rath/Tinnacross crossroads, itself just east of Thomastown Demesne. Shown on the first-edition and 25-inch OS maps, and located directly opposite what is now the entrance to Grennans agricultural supplies premises, it is no longer extant.

TULLAMORE
Cormac Street
County Court House
See Significant Court Houses – A Chronological Selection   **P199**

BANAGHER

Cuba Avenue

Court House

Banagher petty sessions court house stood on the north side of Cuba Avenue, a short distance from the corner with Main Street. Burned in the War of Independence; no trace remains. In 2008 Banagher District Court, which had sat above a former dance hall in the town and later in a school building on Cuba Avenue, was abolished and the Electoral Divisions of the District Court Area of Banagher were amalgamated into Birr and Ballinasloe.

BIRR

Townsend Street

Court House   #266

pre-1810

Built before 1810 to replace an earlier sessions house, Birr court house, which is similar to, or derived from, that in Daingean, was described by Thomas Lalor Cooke in his 1826 *Picture of Parsonstown* as a 'handsome, convenient building sufficiently extensive for the business of the county. The Bench, Jury-boxes, &c. are prettily contrived, and unlike to session houses in general, there is a good outside hall to the one now being described. The Grand Jury Room is spacious in proportion to the criminal business to be transacted in it'. Set back slightly from the street behind railings, this is a rendered, five-bay, two-storey building, the façade extended by carriage and access gates to each end, and the parapet dramatically castellated. The centre three bays are recessed with a round-headed central entrance door (for a time obscured by an entrance porch) flanked by round-headed windows, and three square-headed windows to first floor. The gabled end bays have arched recesses with a string-course at impost level. Each arch contains a square-headed window at ground floor, that on the right being blind, and a tall round-headed window above. Four-bay sides with tall round-headed windows to first floor. The courtroom has a wooden gallery supported on square wooden piers, and a plaster canopy over the judge's bench. The ceiling was replaced with acoustic panels in 1990, though the original rose was retained. A renovation programme was being planned in 2008 but was postponed, and the court house closed in 2013, with court sittings transferred to Tullamore.

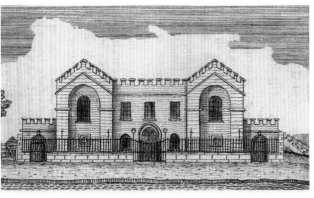

Birr (*The early history of the town of Birr or Parsonstown*, T.L. Cooke (Dublin, 1826), Offaly History)

CLARA

Church Street

Court House   #267

A two-storey, three-bay, detached mid- to late-19th-century house on the north side of Church Street, immediately west of St Brigid's RC church, functioned as Clara petty sessions court house. Burned in 1920 and subsequently repaired. Clara was a District Court location for summary jurisdiction only from 1924 to 1961, when it became part of the Kilbeggan District Court Area. The former court house served as a technical school and branch library before becoming the parish centre.

CLONBULLOGUE

Court House   #268

Clonbullogue became a court location in 1880. Valuation records indicate that from 1884 the petty sessions court house occupied the three-bay, two-storey house with prominent entrance porch on the east side of the triangular village green, just to the south of the constabulary barracks (later Garda station). The court house had itself previously been a police barracks, and became a private residence in 1923. It stands now with its render removed, exposing rubble-stone walls and brick window surrounds.

CLONYGOWAN

Court House

Clonygowan constabulary barracks and court house are shown on the 25-inch OS map as two attached buildings on the west side of Fair Green, close to the site now occupied by Clonygowan Health Centre. No trace of either building remains.

DAINGEAN

Main Street

Court House   #269

c. 1810; 1930s; 1980s; 2012

Prominently located on the east side of the south end of Main Street, and set back behind a substantial forecourt, the large court house in Daingean was built c. 1810 to replace an earlier court house of 1760 on the same site. The scale of the building is explained by the fact that Daingean, or Philipstown, as it used to be known, was the seat of the county assizes until Tullamore court house was built in the 1830s. Similar in elevation to the court house in Birr and of the same vintage. The building has been attributed to James Gandon, but Edward McParland dismisses this suggestion in his *James Gandon: Vitruvius Hibernicus* (London, 1985), commenting that Daingean should be excluded from any list of Gandon's work 'on grounds of quality'. Rendered, five-bay, two-storey building, the centre three bays recessed with an arcade of three arches to ground floor, the voussoirs merging into the channelled rusticated stonework. The outer arches contain tall round-headed windows while the centre has a squat square-headed entrance with a modern concrete canopy. A platband separates ground and first floor and standing on this are four square Doric pilasters supporting a parapet with lugged panels topped by a pair of ball finials. The pedimented end bays have full-height arched recesses, with string-course at impost level. These bays are quoined at ground floor and contain a round-headed window, and later square-headed door, above which is a round-headed niche. There are three urn finials to each pediment. Three-bay side elevations, with tall round-headed windows to first floor. The double-height courtroom had a wooden gallery (similar to that in Birr) and imposing panelled judge's bench. The building was substantially altered in the 1930s, and the subject of an AnCO restoration programme in the 1980s. It has served *inter alia* as a local authority office, dancehall, bingo hall, fire station and youth centre. Further restoration works were carried out in 2012 which included the reopening of some blocked-up windows. Daingean District Court Area was abolished in 1997, recreated in 1998, and finally amalgamated with Tullamore in 2001.

#266 | Birr (IAA, c. 1975)
#267 | Clara (Michael Goodbody, 1920)
#268 | Clonbullogue (Amanda Pedlow, 2019)

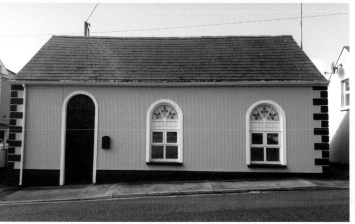

EDENDERRY

O'Connell Square

Market House and Court House #270

Thomas Duff; []

1826; 1950

Detached, T-plan, two-storey, five-bay by three-bay market and court house built in 1826, as recorded by a dated keystone, to designs by Thomas Duff and paid for by Lord Downshire. This was at least the fifth scheme to be proposed for a market house in Edenderry since 1791. Channelled rustication to market-arcaded ground floor, smooth ashlar above with large square-headed windows which light the first-floor courtroom. A sill-level platband circumscribes the building. The market arches were closed in 1950 during alterations following a 1940s fire and the ground floor has served as a ballroom, museum, and county council offices. The three centre bays on the main front are slightly advanced and pedimented. The pediment once held the Downshire coat of arms and later a small clock, the circular recess for which is still visible. Topping the building is a tall, square, louvred ventilator with dome and weather vane, into which a four-faced clock has been inserted. The centre three bays of the rear (north) advance considerably and are pedimented. Here the walls are of rubble stone, with dressed-stone window surrounds, pediment, coping and roundel. Court functions ceased in 2014 following the amalgamation of Edenderry District Court with Tullamore. The building now serves as local authority offices.

FAHY

Court House

Fahy's isolated rural petty sessions court house stood on the north side of the Edenderry road, east of Rhode and just west of the right-angle turn the road takes to circumvent Ballyburly rectory. Shown as a schoolhouse on the first-edition OS map. The curtilage is still discernible and the two-storey extended vernacular house on the site may retain some court house fabric.

FERBANE

Court House

Not recorded as having had petty sessions, Ferbane became a District Court location in 1924 with the court sitting in rooms rented for the purpose. The District Court was transferred from Ferbane to Cloghan in 1979. Cloghan District Court was in turn abolished in 1984 and the Area merged with Kilcormac.

KILCORMAC (FRANKFORD)
Main Street
Court House

The first-edition OS map of Kilcormac or Frankford shows a 'Petit Sessions Ho.' on Main Street. The map is ambiguous but the building in question may be on the north side of the west end, close to the junction with the road to Ferbane. On the 25-inch map no court house is identified in the town, with the possible site of the petty sessions house occupied by a post office. This building is still standing, a two-bay mid-terrace house with double shopfront to ground floor. The NIAH says that the three-bay, two-storey house with recessed fanlit entrance and advanced outhouse wings which now functions as Kilcormac Garda station was built c. 1800 as a petty sessions court house, but it is clearly marked on the 25-inch OS map as Ballyboy Rectory. For the latter part of the 20th century, Kilcormac District Court sat in the stepped-gabled Fiesta Ballroom at the east end of the town. The District Court was abolished in 2007 and amalgamated with Birr.

KINNITTY
Schoolhouse and Court House   #271
[Arthur Cluskey]
c. 1820

Kinnitty Community Centre now occupies the former schoolhouse built c. 1820 which came to accommodate petty sessions court sittings. It is possible that the 1810 elevations and plan by Arthur Cluskey for a 'Proposed Free School at Kenetty' held in the Erasmus Smith Schools Archive show the original appearance of the school. The plan would seem to correspond with that on the 25-inch OS map. However, the elevation as its stands is Gothic, not classical. It is a three-bay structure of rubble stone, each bay gable-fronted, the centre one rising to a second storey. Segmental arch to centre contains a recessed entrance, with single pointed-arched windows on each side and above. Much altered and extended to the rear.

MONEYGALL
Court House

Moneygall's petty sessions court house was set back from the road on the north side of the village street just west of the village centre and adjacent to the dispensary. The dispensary has gone, aside from its roadside wall and gate, but some trace of the court house may remain in the lower wall of the industrial shed which stands on the site.

MOYSTOWN
Court House

Moystown petty sessions court house was located on the south side of the road (now the R357), c. 2.7km north-west of Moystown Cross. An isolated, rural court house; some fabric may remain in the six-bay, two-storey residence to be found on the site.

SHINRONE
Main Street
Court House   #272

The first-edition OS map shows a 'Petit Sessions Court Ho.', on the south side of Shinrone Main Street, adjacent to a 'Female School'. No longer extant; a public house now stands in the vicinity. By the late 19th century, the building on the south corner of Main Street and the Roscrea road was Shinrone constabulary barracks. The building immediately beside this had become the petty sessions court house, a single-storey, three-bay cottage with round-headed entrance and two round-headed windows. Now in residential use.

THOMASTOWN (RATH)
Court House
pre-1838

A small, rural, petty sessions court house stood on the south side of the road 200m east of Rath/Tinnacross crossroads, itself just east of Thomastown Demesne. Shown on the first-edition and 25-inch OS maps, and located directly opposite what is now the entrance to Grennans agricultural supplies premises, it is no longer extant.

TULLAMORE
Cormac Street
County Court House
See Significant Court Houses – A Chronological Selection   **P199**

AUGHRIM
Court House

The rural petty sessions court house at Aughrim is shown on the first-edition OS map as a small building on the north side of the road between Elphin and Hillstreet, about 150m east of Aughrim C of I church. Neither church nor sessions house are still extant.

BALLAGHADERREEN
Court House #273
c. 1880

The detached, five-bay, two-storey court house in Ballaghaderreen was built c. 1880 to terminate the vista down the recently extended Main Street. Random block-stone building, with dressed-stone pilaster-like quoins framing the end bays. Dressed stone also to the square-headed window and door surrounds, bracketed cornices to entrances and platband to centre three bays separating ground and first floor. Hipped roof. The building now has three entrances to the front, one central and one in each of the end bays. The right side of the building was converted to a Garda station c. 1930 while the left side accommodates local authority offices. The much altered first-floor courtroom continues in use.

BALLINLOUGH
Court House

A freestanding, two-storey building set at a right angle to the east side of the village street, opposite Kiltullagh C of I parish church, served as Ballinlough petty sessions court house. Three-bay front with square-headed windows above a modern shopfront. Ballinlough was a District Court location from 1924 until 1961, when it became part of the Castlerea District Court Area.

BALLINTOBER
Court House

The petty sessions court house is shown on the 25-inch map of Ballintober on the west side of the road at the north end of the village. A three-bay, two-storey residence now occupies the site. Further south, on the same side of the street, adjacent to Daly's shop, is an attached two-bay, single-storey front wall, all that remains of an otherwise vanished building, bearing a sign which reads 'Ballintubber Courthouse'. A door and window remain. Ballintober was a District Court location from 1924 until 1961, when it became part of the Castlerea District Court Area.

BALLYDANGAN

Ballydangan was listed in the 1842 *Petty Sessions Return*, but had ceased to be a petty sessions location by 1882. It has not been possible to establish where the court sat.

BALLYFARNON
Court House #274
1863

Terminating the south end of the village 'square', in front of the former Fair Green, Ballyfarnon court house is a five-bay, two-storey, roughly-rendered, pitched-roofed building with segmental lights above entrances in the end bays and square-headed windows to ground and first floor. A plaque in the centre of the façade records that it was 'Erected by T.C. McDermottroe, 1863'. The court entrance was on the left, and the unassuming courtroom had 20th-century furnishings. Closed in 2006 following the amalgamation of Ballyfarnon District Court with Boyle, it is now brightly painted, thanks to the efforts of the local Tidy Towns committee.

BALLYFORAN
Court House #275

Ballyforan's former petty sessions court house is a small, two-storey, two-bay, pitched-roof, vernacular building whose gable end stands on the south side of the village street opposite the former parochial house. Just to the east of this a new court house was provided in the 1950s. Vaguely modernist courtroom block, fronted by a lower entrance porch and flanked on the right by an office wing and on the left by a link to the adjacent health centre, all flat-roofed with square-headed openings. The courtroom doubled as a library. Closed in 2006 following the amalgamation of the District Court Area of Ballyforan into the District Court Area of Ballinasloe.

BELLANAGARE/BALLINGARE
Court House

The petty sessions court house in Bellanagare occupied an end-of-terrace house on the south side of the village main street. A much altered two-storey, five-bay building stands on the site. The channelled plaster to ground floor and fragments of hoodmouldings hint at its former use, as do the two entrances which formerly flanked three full-height round-headed windows. A further full-height round-headed window is in the gable end. One of the entrances has acquired a later porch, while two of the windows have been truncated and replaced at ground level by a single rectangular window.

BOYLE

The Crescent
Court House   #276
Samuel Jackman
1826-29

Shown on the first-edition OS map as 'Court Ho. & Bridewell', and on the 25-inch OS map simply as 'Court House', Boyle court house was built for petty and quarter sessions in 1826-29 to designs by local builder and architect Samuel Jackman. Three-bay, two-storey, classical ashlar stone façade on the Crescent, flanked by single-storey gate wings providing access to the rear. Four full-height pilasters support a cornice and chamfered rectangular pediment. The pilasters separate an arcade to the ground floor in which the three arches are blind, except for glazed lunettes to the outer two. String-course between ground and first floor. Square-headed windows to first floor and six-bay, rendered, side elevations. Stone panels with swagged chains above the side gates. Other plaques on the façade commemorate Patrick Pearse, and Count Plunkett, whose election as Sinn Féin MP for North Roscommon took place in the court house in February 1917. Galleried, double-height courtroom, with elaborately canopied judge's bench. Altered c. 1960 and again in 1984, when the bridewell section was converted to local authority offices. Closed since the amalgamation of Boyle District Court with Carrick-on-Shannon in 2011. The following year Boyle Courthouse Development Company was formed and in 2017 restoration work began.

BRIDESWELL

Court House

There was a small petty sessions court house on the south-east corner of Brideswell's broad T-junction. No trace remains.

CASTLEREA

Barrack Street
Court House   #277
Godfrey Wills
1843-45

In the National Archive's OPW collection is a set of eight drawings on paper watermarked 1843, signed by Godfrey Wills, for the court house at Castlerea, Co. Roscommon. The Board of Works provided a loan for the construction of the court house in 1845. As built, Castlerea court house is a solid example of the standard late-1830s – early-1840s petty and quarter sessions court house. Rendered, five-bay, two-storey over basement block with dressed-stone detailing. The quoined end bays are advanced to front and back, with square-headed entrances to front in partly lugged surrounds. Between the entrances at ground floor are three recessed panels. Five round-headed windows with stone architraves to first floor, the sills merging to form a platband. Hipped roof with modestly overhanging eaves and a pair of tall stone chimneys. Three-bay side elevations with square-headed windows. Five-bay rear elevation, with advanced end bays and three round-headed windows to the middle bays of the first floor. Double-height centrally placed courtroom, with original furnishings, including wooden gallery on square timber piers, and panel-backed judge's bench. The court house is now in use as local authority offices.

#273 | Ballaghaderreen (NIAH, 2000)
#274 | Ballyfarnon (Paul Tierney, 2019)
#275 | Ballyforan (Paul Tierney, 2019)
#276 | Boyle (Maurice Craig Collection, IAA, 1978)

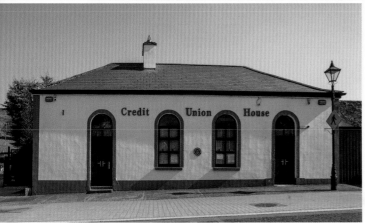

COOTEHALL
Court House

Isolated rural petty sessions house on the east side of the road just over 1km north of Cootehall Bridge, opposite the modern housing development at Quay West. The single-storey, five-bay residence with gabled porch standing on the site may incorporate some of the old court house fabric.

CROGHAN
Court House

The petty sessions court house in Croghan occupied a single-storey, five-bay house on the west side of the village street, just south of the two-storey, three-bay former constabulary barracks. Still standing and in use as a private residence.

ELPHIN
Main Street
Court House   #278
c. 1940

Elphin petty sessions court house was located in the end building of a terrace of small houses on the west side of Newline Road (formerly New Street). The terrace is no longer extant. A new court house was provided on the north side of Main Street, almost opposite the Bank of Ireland. Built c. 1940, according to the NIAH, and replacing a previous house on the site, this is a two-storey, five-bay building with arched surrounds to the two entrances in the end bays. Between these are three tall square-headed windows, lighting the ground-floor courtroom, with five square-headed windows to the offices on the first floor. The court house had become home to Elphin Credit Union by the mid-1990s. Elphin District Court was abolished in 2003 and the Area merged with Strokestown.

FOUR ROADS (FOUR ROADS MOUNT TALBOT/COOLDERRY)
Court House

Listed as 'Four Roads Mount Talbot' in the 1842 *Petty Sessions Return*, and as Coolderry in 1882, Four Roads petty sessions court house is shown on the 25-inch OS map standing on the west side of the road at a minor junction half a kilometre north of Four Roads itself. No trace remains.

FRENCHPARK
Market Place
Court House   #279

The L-plan, single-storey, stone building on the south-east corner of Market Place in the centre of Frenchpark, across the road from the now derelict market house, was Frenchpark court house. While a building with the same footprint is clearly visible on the first-edition OS map, the publication of which predates the market house, it was not identified as a sessions or court house. The first floor of the market house may have accommodated petty sessions sittings after it was built c. 1840, but these had moved to the corner building by the time the 25-inch map appeared. This is a rubble-stone building with a three-bay front facing the market house consisting of an entrance and two square-headed windows in dressed-stone surrounds. Two windows in gabled end which extends into a set-back, two-bay wing with an entrance and window. Frenchpark ceased to be a District Court location in 1961 when it became part of the Ballaghaderreen District Court Area. In 1993, the former court house was converted to gallery use and it has also served as a theatre.

HARRISTOWN (CASTLEREA PRISON)
Court House
2000-02

Harristown court house at Castlerea Prison was built 2000-02 and is a nearly square single-storey block with blank rendered walls. Clerestory windows and a hipped roof to courtroom section, adjoining which is a lower entrance and office wing with inward sloping roof.

HILLSTREET
Court House

The building in which Hillstreet petty sessions were held stands on the north side of the village street just west of the village centre. It had previously served as a schoolhouse (as indicated on the first-edition OS map). A three-bay, two-storey vernacular structure, it is now derelict.

KEADEW
Court House   #280
c. 1840

The petty sessions court house in Keadew stands on the middle of the north side of the village main street. A detached, single-storey, four-bay, hipped-roof building of c. 1840, with round-headed entrances at each end and two round-headed windows in between. Now in use as the local credit union.

#281 | Roosky (Courts Service, 1995)
#282 | Roscommon, Market House and Court House (IAA, c. 1950)
#283 | Strokestown (Courts Service, 1995)

LECARROW

Court House

early-19th century

Lecarrow petty sessions court house is an early-19th-century single-storey vernacular building on the east side of the road, just to the south of Lecarrow bridge. Still standing, though now partially roofless, and partially converted to a shed with corrugated iron roof.

LOUGHGLYNN

Court House

Loughglynn petty sessions area was created in 1895. The court house occupied one of a row of single-storey cottages on the north side of the main village street, at the location where the Garda station now stands.

ROOSKY/ROOSKEY

Main Street

Court House   #281

An end-of-terrace two-storey, three-bay, mid-19th-century house standing on the north side of Main Street, about halfway between the river and railway bridges, served as Roosky petty sessions court house. In the early- to mid-20th century the court transferred to a detached two-storey house on the opposite side of the street. Small square-headed first-floor windows are suggestive of this also being a mid-19th-century structure. Much altered in the mid-20th century. Changes included the widening of ground-floor windows, the addition of a single-storey projecting porch to right, and the provision of a flat concrete projecting lintel to the entrance. Plain ground-floor courtroom with simple judge's bench. Roosky remained a District Court location until 2003, when it became part of the Strokestown District Court Area.

ROSCOMMON

Market Square

Market House and Court House   #282

George and John Ensor; Goldie and Child

1762; 1833-69

As recorded in an anonymous pamphlet entitled *Account of how the court house in Roscommon fell down* (Dublin, 1719), the market house and court house in Roscommon collapsed in March 1719. Over 200 people were killed or injured. A replacement market and court house was not constructed until 1762. Designed by architect George Ensor (though his half-brother, John Ensor, also signed the contract), this was a two-storey, hipped-roofed, stone building dominating the centre of Market Square. The three-bay main entrance front faced the old gaol to the north and had full-height arched recesses in the end bays, each with a fanlit entrance. To the rear, or south, there was a market arcade at ground floor, above which were tall, round-headed windows in Gibbsian surrounds. Section XCVII of the 1796 *Act for the Amendment of Public Roads, for directing the power of Grand Juries respecting presentments etc* (36 Geo. III c. 55) noted that the 'court-house at Roscommon requires further room for the convenience of business' and authorised the Roscommon Grand Jury to provide a new market house

and convert the market section of the existing building to court use. It would appear that a separate market house was not built and, following the completion of the new county gaol in 1818, agitation increased to replace the court house on an alternative site. This was accomplished by 1827, and the former court house was sold to the parish priest, Fr John Madden, in 1829 and converted to a Catholic church. The necessary alterations were carried out from 1836 (according to Maurice Craig) or 1844 (according to the NIAH) or, possibly as late as 1869 (when the *Irish Builder* reported that Goldie and Child were carrying out major extensions). The building acquired a cruciform plan with the addition of a new south-facing entrance front, topped by a tall cupola spire, and an extension on the north to the former front, now rear. Church use ceased in 1903 following the completion of Walter Glynn Doolin's Church of the Sacred Heart, and the former court house became the Harrison Memorial Hall. Named in honour of local doctor John Harrison, it was used for a variety of leisure purposes including as a concert and dance hall, the local YMCA headquarters and a badminton venue. Dilapidated by the early 1970s, it was purchased in 1976 by the Bank of Ireland, which combined two existing local branches in the building. The bank opened for business in March 1980.

ROSCOMMON

Abbey Street

County Court House

See Significant Court Houses – A Chronological Selection   **P193**

STROKESTOWN

Church Street

Court House   #283

1826-c. 1832

In his capacity as inspector of civil buildings for the Board of Works, Francis Johnston approved plans for a new court house and a separate bridewell in Strokestown in 1826. Lewis's *Topographical Dictionary* notes that the court house and bridewell 'have been recently erected'. Strokestown court house stands on the north side of the west end of Church Street. Behind it was the former bridewell. The bridewell was constructed in 1832 with a grant from the Board of Works. It was burned by local Irish Volunteers in July 1920. The slightly later court house is a hipped-roofed, T-plan building with a two-storey, two-bay, quoined, street front flanked by single-storey wings. The wing to the right contains the entrance and that to the left – extended to two storeys in the 1930s – has a window at ground floor. Blind square-headed windows to ground floor of centre block. Double-height, galleried courtroom with round-headed niche behind the judge's bench. Strokestown remains a District Court Area but the court house is no longer in use.

TULSK

Court House

Although not marked on the 25-inch OS map, a rare omission, Tulsk petty sessions court house was described in a 2014 local history blog as the 'long low building next to the current petrol station'. Still standing but roofless.

BALLINAFAD
Court House

Ballinafad petty sessions court house stood isolated on the west side of the road, just over 1km north of the village. A modern bungalow now occupies the site.

BALLINTOGHER (SOOEY)
Court House
c. 1810

Listed as Sooey from 1842 to at least 1887, by 1900 the name of this petty sessions area had changed to Ballintogher, and the court house was located in the east end of Kingsfort House in the centre of Ballintogher village. Built as a single dwelling c. 1810 (NIAH), this seven-bay, two-storey building was subdivided into a four (west) and a three (east) bay section, each with a gabled porch. The east end has returned to domestic use.

BALLYDOOGAN

Included in the 1842 *Petty Sessions Return*, court order books survive for Ballydoogan petty sessions for 1857-61 and 1869. Ballydoogan had ceased to be a petty sessions location by 1882. A court house remains to be identified.

BALLYMOTE
Court House   #284
1813/14

The OS *Memoirs* records that Ballymote court house was built in 1813 or 1814 at a cost of £600. It is shown on the first-edition OS map as a detached building terminating the east end of Teeling Street. Just to the north on the map is a smaller block. This is the three-bay wide, by one-bay deep, two-storey, stone-built house to which the court house is now attached, the attachment having occurred by the time the 25-inch OS map was produced. The court house was altered c. 1930 to provide local authority offices. From 1984 it also accommodated the local library. As it stands this is a rendered, four-bay, single-storey, hipped-roofed building with tall, round-headed windows set in recesses. The main entrance is directly beneath the second window from the right. The double-height courtroom had a recessed niche behind the judge's bench. The court house closed in 2011 on the abolition of Ballymote District Court and its amalgamation with Sligo.

COLLOONEY
The Square
Court House

The two-storey market house, with portico by Collooney-born architect and engineer Sir John Benson, which used to stand on the west side of the Square in Collooney may have accommodated court sittings in its first floor rooms. An end-of-terrace, three-bay, two-storey mid-19th-century house on the south side of the Square functioned as Collooney court house from at least the late 19th century. Rendered, with plaster quoins. Two entrances to ground floor flanking a central square-headed window. Three windows to first floor, their tops set just below the eaves of the pitched roof. Collooney District Court was abolished in 2003 and the Area amalgamated with Sligo.

COOLANEY
Court House   #285

Lewis's *Topographical Dictionary* reports of Coolaney that in the 'centre of the village is the court-house, where petty sessions are held on alternate Wednesdays'. Standing on the west side of the street, towards the north end of the village, Coolaney petty sessions court house, as identified on Sligo County Council's *Record of Protected Structures*, is a mid- to late-19th-century, two-storey, end-of-terrace building with a carriage entrance on the left and a gabled porch with two side windows on the right. Between these is a square-headed window with three windows to first floor. The adjoined building on the right serves as Coolaney community centre, while the former court house is now in residential use.

DROMORE WEST (COMCALL)
Court House

A two-bay, two-storey house attached to a long, single-storey barn on the Easky road served as the petty sessions court house in Dromore West (or Comcall, as it was recorded in the 1842 *Petty Sessions Return*). Now windowless, with a corrugated iron roof. Dromore West was a District Court location for summary jurisdiction only until 1961, when it became part of Easky District Court Area.

EASKY
Court House   #286
c. 1870; 1990s

Set back from the road behind a stone wall and cast-iron gates, Easky court house is a single-storey, stone-built, Y-plan building. It has a central gable-fronted, pitched-roofed courtroom block with simplified Venetian window to front, and entrances on each side. This is flanked by one-bay wide, hipped-roofed wings. Round-headed windows to front of wings, with square-headed windows and door to sides. Extended to the rear in the 1990s. Exposed rafters and modern roof-light in courtroom. A court house is shown on the site on the first-edition OS map, though the NIAH suggests that the present structure dates to c. 1870. Easky District Court was amalgamated with Sligo in 2011, since when the court house has been used as a community centre and latterly a residence.

ENNISCRONE/INNISCRONE (DOONEEN)
Court House

Listed as Dooneen in the 1842 *Petty Sessions Return*. The 25-inch OS map shows a small petty sessions court house on the north side of the road, about 1km east of Enniscrone, opposite the road to Corballa. No trace remains. In the mid-1960s a single-storey, flat-roofed, T-plan local authority office was constructed on Pier Road, incorporating a courtroom. Court use continued until 2008, when the Electoral Divisions of the District Court Area of Enniscrone were amalgamated into Easky District Court Area. The building now houses the local library.

GRANGE (ARDNAGLASS)
Court House   #287
1891

Listed as Ardnaglass in the 1842 *Petty Sessions Return*, and as Grange in 1882, Grange petty sessions court house was built in 1891, according to a plaque above the main entrance, for William Cowper Temple of Classiebawn Castle. Slightly elevated above the east side of the main road to the south of the village, it has rough, squared stone walls with dressed-stone window and door surrounds, sharply pitched roof and brick chimney. A three-bay front overlooks the main road, with a gabled entrance porch on the left, a large window and a second entrance on the right. The porch has a pronounced batter, and both doors are set in pointed segmental-arched, dressed-stone surrounds. Large pointed-arch window in the north end and two square-headed windows in the south. Single window in rear façade. In use until Grange District Court was abolished in 2008 and amalgamated with Sligo. The court house is now occupied by the Grange and Armada Development Association and a Spanish Armada Visitor Centre.

MULLAGHROE/GURTEEN (GORTEEN)
Court House

On the 25-inch OS map Mullaghroe consists of a short cluster of adjoined buildings on the west side of the road, c. 3km east of Gurteen, with a constabulary barracks at one end and a petty sessions court house at the other. Bypassed by the R294, the range of two-storey, mid-19th-century buildings is still standing, though now in a semi-ruinous condition. Listed as 'Gurteen or Mullaghroe' in the 1842 *Petty Sessions Return* but just Mullaghroe in 1882. Sittings of Mullaghroe District Court, which had summary jurisdiction only, were transferred to Gurteen in 1955, though where the court sat has not been established. Gurteen ceased to be a court location in 1961.

RIVERSTOWN
Court House

The petty sessions court house in Riverstown was a small structure on a corner site just north of the constabulary barracks (later Garda station). The building, which also functioned as a dispensary, is no longer extant. Riverstown District Court sat in the parochial hall. It was abolished in 2008 and the District Court Area amalgamated with that of Ballymote.

SKREEN
Court House

Lewis's *Topographical Dictionary* notes that petty sessions in the parish of Skreen were 'held at Ardnaglass once a fortnight', but no petty sessions court house is shown on either the first-edition or the 25-inch OS map. Skreen was designated a District Court location from 1924 until 2006, when the District Court Area was abolished and amalgamated with Easky. The court sat in the local community hall.

SLIGO
Teeling Street
Court House
1785; 1810; 1816

A sessions house stood in Castle Street, Sligo, at the time of the 1641 Rebellion. By the mid-18th century the sessions house had moved to a site on the south side of Church Lane (now occupied by a public house) and in 1785 a new court house was built in Old Market Street. This was extended in 1810 and again in 1816 and stood immediately adjacent to the old gaol, leading to the street being variously referred to as Gaol Street or Correction Street for the first half of the 19th century. In 1865 it became Albert Street and in 1898 Sligo Corporation renamed it Teeling Street. The court house was a five-bay, two-storey structure, the centre bay advanced, with a large entrance hall, two courtrooms, a Grand Jury room and various offices. Described by Lewis's *Topographical Dictionary* as 'a well arranged building, but too limited for public business' and by the *Sligo Chronicle* in 1856 as 'antiquated, and out-of-date, and moreover, contemptuously shoved into a corner by the neighbouring buildings', in 1874 the Grand Jury decided to replace the court house and gaol with a new court house on the same site, and the old court house was demolished.

SLIGO
Teeling Street
County Court House
See Significant Court Houses – A Chronological Selection   P206

TEESAN/TEESON

Listed as Teeson in the 1842 *Petty Sessions Return*, Teesan had ceased to be a petty sessions location by 1882. No court house is shown on the first-edition OS map.

TOBERCURRY/TUBBERCURRY
Teeling Street
Court House

The petty sessions court house in Tobercurry was located in a long narrow building on the south side of the west end of Teeling Street, adjacent to the constabulary barracks. In his Bureau of Military History

Witness Statement (WS 1,278), John C. Brennan of the Third Battalion, Sligo Brigade, Irish Volunteers, provided a detailed account of the burning of the court house in early 1920. 'The burning', he noted, 'created a favourable impression on the civilian population as the job was carried out in an efficient manner and all records of the Court such as decrees and fines imposed and papers dealing with dog licences etc. were destroyed. This operation had a fine moral effect on the Volunteers who carried out the job'. The building was subsequently repaired and is still standing. A long, two-storey structure with gabled end to the street, it now functions as Gallagher House Resource Centre.

TOBERCURRY/TUBBERCURRY
Humbert Street
Teach Laighne
McCullough Mulvin Architects
2003

Tobercurry was designated a District Court location from 1924 though efforts to provide a suitable venue continued for the rest of the 20th century. A parliamentary question in 1969 elicited a reply from the then Minister for Justice, Michael Moran TD, that he was not aware of any plan by Sligo County Council to construct a court house in Tobercurry. In 1973 a prefabricated structure was provided, with wooden walls and clerestory windows. Finally, in 2003, Teach Laighne, a new civic centre, opened on Humbert Street, incorporating a library, county council and HSE offices, and District Court facilities. Designed by McCullough Mulvin Architects and incorporating a pair of existing mid- to late-19th-century houses on the site, this is a two-storey structure with random rough stone walls to front and side, flush glazing, a zinc roof and a recessed entrance set in a full-height concrete porch. According to the architects, the project was 'an opportunity to explore modern concepts of urbanity in a small Irish town: the front façade is directly on the street and the plan opens back into a series of narrow fingers echoing the original house plots, inviting access deep into the scheme'. The courtroom and library share the same space, with the shelves on wheels to allow for easy reconfiguration. The project won an RIAI Award in 2004.

Tobercurry (Christian Richters, 2003)

ARDFINNAN
off Main Street
Court House
#288

Ardfinnan petty sessions court house stood in a laneway known as the Boreen, just off the south side of Main Street. A two-storey structure with gabled dormers, it is still extant and known as the 'Old Courthouse'.

BALLYNONTY/BALLYNUNTY
Court House

The building at the north end of the terrace on the east side of the road at Ballynonty is shown on the first-edition OS map as a petty sessions court house. A mid- to late-19th-century three-bay, two-storey attached house stands on the site. In the first years of the 20th century Ballynonty petty sessions were transferred to the court house in Killinaule.

BALLYPOREEN

Ballyporeen was listed in the 1842 *Petty Sessions Return*, and remained a petty sessions location into the 20th century. However, a court house has not been identified. Ballyporeen became part of the Clonmel District Court Area in 1924.

BANSHA
Barrack Street
Court House

The petty sessions court house in Bansha stood on the east side of Barrack Street, just to the south of the constabulary barracks (later Garda station). Still standing, this is a two-storey, three-bay, end-of-terrace building with pitched roof and square-headed openings.

BORRISOKANE
Fair Green
Court House
1840s

The petty sessions court house in Borrisokane was built in the mid-1840s and stood detached on the west side of the Fair Green on the site delineated on the first-edition OS map as 'Intended for Court House and Gaol'. The court house was burned in June 1921 during the War of Independence. A pair of semi-detached three-bay, single-storey houses now occupies the site.

BORRISOKANE
Ballyhaden Road
Workhouse/Court House
George Wilkinson; []
1851-52; c. 1925
#289

Following the destruction of the Fair Green court house in 1921, a section of Borrisokane Union Workhouse was converted for court use. This is a late example of one of George Wilkinson's workhouses. On foot of the 1838 *Act for the More Effectual Relief of the Destitute Poor in Ireland* (1 & 2 Vict., Cap. 56), Wilkinson had been assigned the task of providing a workhouse in each of over 130 Poor Law Unions. By the time Borrisokane Workhouse was being built from 1851-52, Wilkinson had moved away from the Tudor domestic idiom of the first wave of workhouses, with their picturesque gables, dormer windows and barge-boards. The plan had also evolved. At Borrisokane (as at others of the same type such as Portumna or Tobercurry) a pair of long, unadorned, hipped-roofed, two-storey blocks stood at the front of the complex. These accommodated offices of the Board of Guardians and the Workhouse Master as well as school and work rooms on the ground floor with dormitories above. At a right angle to these, and dividing the space behind into separate yards, was the centrally placed dining hall/chapel block, to the rear of which were two further accommodation wings, parallel to those at the front. To the back of the site was the infirmary. A six-bay, ground-floor section at the right-hand end of the right-hand front block was converted to court use with minimal intervention or embellishment. From 1942 Borrisokane Community College occupied much of the rest of the workhouse and remains on the site. Refurbished in 2001; in 2011 Borrisokane District Court was abolished and amalgamated with Nenagh.

BORRISOLEIGH
Lower Main Street
Court House
#290

A semi-detached, single-storey, six-bay building on the south side of Lower Main Street served as Borrisoleigh court house. Pitched roof and square-headed openings, with two entrances, each flanked by a pair of windows. Borrisoleigh was a location of a District Court exercising summary jurisdiction only from 1924 until 1961 when it became part of Templemore District Court Area. Now in residential use.

TIPPERARY

CAHIR/CAHER

The Square
Market House and Court House   #291
c. 1770

Described by Lewis's *Topographical Dictionary* as 'a neat and
commodious building', the market house in Cahir was built c. 1770. It
is shown on the first-edition OS map as 'Court Ho.' but on the 25-inch
map as 'Townhall'. For much of the 20th century the building was
used as a commercial premises but in 1984 it was converted back to
court use, with a library on the ground floor. It is a five-bay, two-storey
building dominating the north end of the Square. Single-bay, lower and
narrower annex to rear. The ground floor, where library use continues,
has been altered considerably and the front façade now comprises
large rectangular floor-to-ceiling shop windows into one of which
is set the entrance. At first floor are three round-headed windows,
flanked by niches in the end bays, all with prominent keystones to their
architraves. The hipped roof has broad eaves and is crowned by a clock
tower topped by a weathervane. The first-floor former courtroom was
plain and unadorned. Cahir District Court was abolished in 2008 and
the Area transferred to Cashel.

CAPPAWHITE/CAPPAGH WHITE

Main Street
Court House   #292
1931

The three-bay, two-storey attached house, with pitched roof and
square-headed openings, on the north side of Main Street to the west
of the junction with Church Street, was Cappawhite petty sessions
court house. The attached house to its west was the constabulary
barracks. In 1930, John O'Dwyer, engineer, prepared plans for a
new parochial hall for parish priest Fr Edward Ryan. The hall was
completed in 1931, as commemorated by a plaque on the front
wall, and subsequently became Cappawhite court house. Standing
on the south side of Main Street, this is a severe, cement-rendered,
five-bay, two-storey block, with three entrances to ground floor
– square-headed at each end, wider segmental-headed and fanlit
to centre – separated by pairs of segmental-headed windows. Five
segmental-headed windows to first floor with string-course at sill
level. Pitched roof topped by ventilator. In 1998 the District Court
Area of Cappawhite was abolished and the Electoral Divisions which
comprised that Area were amalgamated with Thurles.

MUNSTER

#288 | Ardfinnan (Denis Mortell, 2019)
#289 | Borrisokane (NIAH, 2004)
#290 | Borrisoleigh (Denis Mortell, 2019)
#291 | Cahir (IAA, 1976)

CARRICK-ON-SUIR

Greenside South

Court House   #293

Samuel Jones

1837

Built beside the bridewell (later constabulary barracks and subsequently Garda station) on the south side of the Fair Green to the north of the town centre, Carrick-on-Suir court house is an unadorned example of the standard late-1830s – early-1840s petty and quarter sessions court house design, one of three nearly identical such court houses in Tipperary. The others are in Clogheen and Tipperary Town. In this case the architect was Samuel Jones, County Surveyor for Tipperary, 1834-52, who submitted the plans in 1837. His variation on the standard is a five-bay, two-storey hipped-roofed building. Atypically, the end bays containing the regular simply-pedimented entrances are slightly recessed. Above the entrances are single square-headed windows. At ground floor the centre three bays are blank while at first floor there are three tall, round-headed windows lighting the courtroom, their sills merging into a platband which extends the width of the building and around the sides. Similar round-headed windows to rear elevation. Three-bay side elevations with square-headed windows to ground and first floors. The double-height courtroom, which retains some of its original simple furniture, is still in use.

CASHEL

The Green

Court House

1818

The 'Bridewell & Sessions Ho.' in Cashel is delineated on both the first-edition and the 25-inch OS maps, a T-plan building facing onto the Green on the south edge of the town. Constructed in 1818, when Cashel was the location for county quarter sessions as well as weekly petty sessions. Lewis's *Topographical Dictionary* tells us that the 'county court-house and prison… form a neat and substantial pile of building of stone: the former is sufficiently adapted to the transaction of business; and the latter, to which the city magistrates also commit prisoners, contains eight cells, three day-rooms, and two airing-yards'. The Cashel Urban District Council housing scheme Treacy Villas has occupied the site since the early 1930s.

CASHEL

Commandant P.J. Hogan Square

Court House   #294

c. 1910

A new court house was provided in Cashel c. 1910 in what is now
Commandant P.J. Hogan Square but was formerly Cashel barracks, 'a
handsome range of building, occupying three sides of a quadrangle'
(Lewis's *Topographical Dictionary*). The court house terminates the
square, replacing the smallest of the original barracks blocks. The
others have since given way to a Garda station, school and post office.
The court house itself has a two-storey central block, with single-storey
recessed wings. To the centre is a square-headed entrance topped by
bracketed lintel and flanked by square-headed windows framed by
blocked plaster pilasters and quoins. Large round-headed window to
first floor, on both sides of which are moulded decorative panels and
pilasters supporting the cornice. The central pediment has a plaque
bearing the inscription 'Cashel Courthouse' in block capitals. There are
lunette windows in the first-floor sides of the central block. The wings
have square-headed entrances to the front, again framed by moulded
pilasters, and square-headed openings to the sides. Two tall round-
headed windows to rear which, with the lunettes, light the single
courtroom. This has a horseshoe gallery and panelled judge's bench
with a simple canopy. The court house remains in use.

CLOGHEEN

Barrack Hill

Court House   #295

Samuel Jones

1841

Detached court house set back from the street behind a low wall
topped by railings with tall, stone gate piers and iron gates. Shown
as 'Court Ho.' on the first-edition OS map, a two-storey, three-bay
elevation presents itself to the street, with three square-headed
windows to each floor, divided by a platband. This is the side elevation
of what is another example of the standard petty and quarter sessions
court house of the late-1830s – early-1840s. Identical in most respects
to Carrick-on-Suir and Tipperary, it is also by Samuel Jones, Tipperary
County Surveyor, who submitted his plans in 1837. A plaque to the
front elevation gives the building date as 1841. As at Carrick, the end
bays of the entrance front are slightly recessed and contain the simply-
pedimented entrances. Above the entrances are single square-headed
windows. At ground floor the centre three bays are blank while at first
floor there are three tall round-headed windows, their sills merging
into the platband which extends the width of the building and around
the sides. Similar round-headed windows to rear light the plain
double-height courtroom. Court use ceased when Clogheen District
Court was abolished in 1998 and the District Court Area amalgamated
with Cashel.

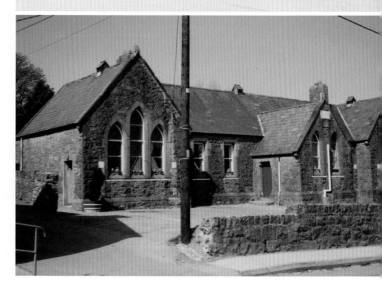

#296 | Dundrum (NIAH, 2005)
#297 | Fethard (IAA, c. 1980)
#298 | Killenaule, St Mary's Hall (Courts Service, 1995)

CLONMEL
Sarsfield Street
Main Guard
See Significant Court Houses – A Chronological Selection **P168**

CLONMEL
Nelson Street
County Court House
See Significant Court Houses – A Chronological Selection **P179**

CLOUGHJORDAN
Main Street
Court House

A three-bay, two-storey, mid- to late-19th-century attached house on the north side of Main Street functioned as Cloughjordan petty sessions court house. Cloughjordan was designated a District Court location in 1924 but District Court (Areas) Order 1926 (SI No. 52/1926) included the provision that 'Suitable accommodation for the District Court not having yet been provided at Cloughjordan by the Local Authorities, as required by law, all cases arising in the Court Area will, until further notice, be heard at the Court at Roscrea'. The former court house has most recently been a restaurant.

DUNDRUM (CLONOULTY)
School/Court House   **#296**
1824

Dundrum petty sessions were listed as Clonoulty in the 1842 *Petty Sessions Return*, with a note that they had 'altered to Dundrum'. Dundrum petty sessions court house was located to the west of the village, south of the confluence of roads formerly known as Pounds Cross Roads, at the junction of the current R661 and L5217. Built in 1824, according to a dated plaque on the building, it is designated as Dundrum School on the first-edition OS map. Still extant, this is an elegant single-storey, T-plan building, with hipped roof, rendered walls, large square-headed windows in dressed-stone surrounds, stone quoins, porches with limestone pediments, and a rendered bellcote. Dundrum was a District Court location from 1924 until 1961, when the District Court Area was divided between Cappawhite and Cashel.

Lorrha (Denis Mortell, 2019) | **#299**
Mullinahone (NIAH, 2006) | **#300**
Newport (Michael O'Boyle, 2018) | **#301**

FETHARD

Main Street

Alms House/Market House and Court House #297

c. 1610

One of the earliest extant buildings to have been used as a court house, this multi-bay, two-storey structure was built c. 1610 as an alms house by Sir John Everard, whose family owned Fethard from the 15th century until the 1750s. Rendered walls with off-centre gable, surmounted by one of a number of tall octagonal stone chimneys. Central archway, now partially glazed, to ground floor, and other irregularly dispersed openings of various ages including: 17th-century windows to façade, gables and rear elevation; 17th-century Tudor-arch doorways to first floor at rear; 1820s square-headed windows to front; and a 1990s door. Three 17th-century carved limestone plaques to front façade, comprising two armorial plaques of the Everards and Dunboyne Butlers and one crucifixion plaque. Also one 20th-century plaque commemorating Patrick Pearse. Internally some 17th-century features remain, including corbels that supported the original first floor, and three large fireplaces at first-floor level. Charitable use had ceased by 1758 and the building was designated as Fethard Market House on the first-edition OS map. Petty sessions sittings were held in the building through the 19th century, while over the course of the 20th century, aside from court use, the building has also accommodated a fire station, a scout unit, and a dance hall. Since 2017, following a €1.6 million refurbishment, it has housed a horse museum. Fethard was designated as a District Court location in 1924. In 1961 it became part of the Clonmel District Court Area.

GOLDEN

Main Street

Court House

Golden petty sessions were held in a still-extant five-bay, two-storey, mid- to late-19th-century terraced house on the south side of the village main street.

KILLENAULE

River Street

Court House #298

The building that served as Killenaule petty sessions court house is set back from the north side of River Street. Much altered, it currently presents as a two-storey, three-bay block with one square-headed entrance and two infilled arched openings to ground floor, and three square-headed windows above. It accommodates a fast-food restaurant, with residential use to first floor. Killenaule was a District Court location until 2008 when it became part of Cashel District Court Area. Latterly the court sat in St Mary's Hall, the single-storey Gothic former schoolhouse adjacent to St Mary's RC church.

#302 | Roscrea (Roger Hill, 1998)
#303 | Templemore (Roger Hill, 1998)
#304 | Thurles (Courts Service, 2009)
#305 | Tipperary (IAA, late 19C)

LORRHA
Court House   #299

Lorrha petty sessions court house occupied the west end building of
a short single-storey terrace on the south side of the road facing St
Rodhan's Abbey. The building to the east end of the terrace was the
post office. Still standing, though now in private use, this is a fine
example of the vernacular 19th-century petty sessions court house.
Its original function can still be read in its four-bay façade, with two
entrances flanking two small central windows.

MULLINAHONE
Killaghy Street
Court House   #300

A tall, pitched-roofed, three-storey, five-bay building facing south
down Killaghy Street functioned as Mullinahone petty sessions court
house. The building seems to have started life as a watermill and was
later a barracks, but was designated 'Court Ho.' by the time of the
first-edition OS map. While the former court house retains its roof, all
openings are now blocked up.

NENAGH
Banba Sqaure
County Court House
See Significant Court Houses – A Chronological Selection   P201

NEW INN

New Inn petty sessions were listed in the 1842 *Petty Sessions Return*,
but abolished in 1873. No court house is recorded.

NEWPORT
Custom Gap Road
Court House   #301
1862

Consisting of a double-height courtroom block with a single-storey
entrance wing to the right hand side, Newport court house was built
in 1862 in front of its companion bridewell. This pair of buildings
replaced a 'Court Ho. and Gaol' located to their north on the west
side of the Square, at the top of what was once called Jail Street (now
Custom Gap Road). Hipped roof and rough stone walls, with dressed-
stone quoins and surrounds to entrances and windows. Extended in
1875, as commemorated on an inscribed plaque on the rear wall which
reads, 'E. Parker/Newport/July 16 1875'. Three large, square-headed
windows are set high in the courtroom block. These provide light to
what was a plain, partially panelled courtroom with furnishings dating
from c. 1925, when the building was refurbished following a War of
Independence fire. Newport ceased to be a District Court location in
2008 on being included in the Nenagh District Court Area.

ROSCREA
Gaol Road
Court House   #302
Jacob Owen
1840

Although County Surveyor Samuel Jones included Roscrea on the list
of court houses for which he had prepared plans in 1837, the actual
building is unlike the others on his list – Carrick-on-Suir, Clogheen,
and Tipperary – all of which are standard late-1830s – early-1840s
court houses. In fact it was Jacob Owen of the Board of Works who
was paid for his work on Roscrea court house in 1840, and the
building was sufficiently extant to be included on the first-edition
OS map of the town produced in 1839-41. Standing on the south
side of the west end of Gaol Road, the detached building comprises
a three-bay, double-height courtroom block with modestly advanced
single-storey entrance wings on each side. Pitched roof and random
masonry walls to courtroom block, with three tall round-headed
windows in plain dressed-stone surrounds set in brick arches and a
dressed-stone platband below sill level. Brick surrounds to entrances,
and to square-headed windows in sides of hipped-roofed wings. The
courtroom was renovated in 1989 and again in 1998. Roscrea District
Court was abolished in 2011 and the Electoral Divisions of the Area
were amalgamated into the Area of Nenagh, since when the court
house has been used for heritage purposes.

TEMPLEMORE
Bank Street
Court House   #303
1937

Lewis's *Topographical Dictionary* notes that in Templemore 'petty
sessions are held every Wednesday in the court or market-house, a
handsome decorated building in the centre of the town'. Built in 1816,
the market house was burned by British forces in 1920, and acquired
its present appearance with loggias on each side when reconstructed
by T.F. McNamara from 1925 to 1927 for Templemore Urban District
Council to serve as the town hall. Before the end of the 19th century
the petty sessions had left the market house and transferred to the old
gaol on Gaol Street (now Bank Street). In 1937 the present court house
was built on the same site. An unprepossessing, gable-pedimented
T-plan building with a square-headed entrance, flanked by two
small windows, sheltering under a flat concrete canopy. An inscribed
arch in the render is used as a guide for painting the building name,
formerly in Irish, 'Teach na Cúirte', latterly in English, 'Templemore
Courthouse'. Templemore District Court was abolished in 2011, and
the District Court Area amalgamated into that of Thurles.

THURLES

O'Donovan Rossa Street

Court House   #304

[]; [William Vitruvius Morrison]; []; Deaton Lysaght Architects

1828; 1830s; 1960s; 2007-09

An ecclesiastical-looking building – a tall nave with side aisles – Thurles petty and quarter sessions court house has a double-height, open-pedimented, limestone-fronted, courtroom block, with single storey wings on each side. Built in 1828 adjacent to the already-existing gaol (now Premier Hall) on what was then Pudding Lane (later Brittas Street, now O'Donovan Rossa Street), on a site given by the 2nd Earl of Landaff in 1819. Altered in the 1830s, possibly to designs by William Vitruvius Morrison, with William Tinsley as contractor, the building may then have acquired its wings and the bow-end to the courtroom. Further substantial alterations took place in the 1960s, when the wings were advanced to be flush with the centre block and were fronted with windows. The triple arcade entrance was also blocked up at this time. Deaton Lysaght Architects carried out an extensive rehabilitation of the building for the Courts Service from 2007 to 2009. The ground-floor entrance arcade was reopened and fitted with deeply recessed frameless glass. The external stone work was repaired as was the set of three round-headed windows above the arcade whose sills form a platband which extends the width of the building and down the sides, marking the point where the lean-to roofs of the wings meet the walls of the courtroom. The wings themselves were cut back and made blind to the front, giving the courtroom block prominence, and a new office extension was added to the rear. This is a two-storey over basement block, linked to the old building by a double-height atrium, and is clad in pre-patinated copper and white stucco. A new entrance was provided to the side, marked by a green copper surround. Internally, a new entrance hall was created at the back of the long courtroom from which it is separated by a partition. This is decorated on the courtroom side with hardwood acoustic panels which match the bespoke furniture. A particularly innovative feature of the courtroom is a universally accessible 'rising witness box'. The project was shortlisted for the 2009 RIAI Awards for best accessible building.

TIPPERARY

St Michael's Street

Court House   #305

Samuel Jones

1837-39

The third (alphabetically) of the standard late-1830s – early-1840s petty and quarter sessions court houses for which Tipperary County Surveyor Samuel Jones submitted plans in 1837, Tipperary court house is a near copy of those in Carrick-on-Suir and Clogheen. Built c. 1839, with James Keyes Fahie as contractor, it was sited in front of the gaol. As at Clogheen, its side elevation faces the street. Again, this is a five-bay two-storey hipped-roofed building, the end entrance bays being slightly recessed. Above the entrances are single, square-headed windows. At ground floor, the centre three bays are blank while at first floor there are three tall, round-headed windows lighting the courtroom, their sills merging into a platband which extends the width of the building and around the sides. As in several other standard court houses, including those by Jones, the platband passes behind the simple pediments of the entrances. Three-bay side elevations with square-headed windows to ground and first floors. The building had been extended to the rear by the time the 25-inch OS map was published (1901-05), converting the rectangular plan shown on the first-edition OS map to a T-shape and altering the configuration and orientation of the double-height courtroom, which also acquired two galleries on square wooden piers. The building closed in 2010 when part of the ceiling collapsed, and District Court sittings transferred to the nearby Excel Heritage Centre.

AUGHER
Market House and Court House
1830

The OS *Memoirs* notes that a market house was built in Augher in 1830 with a room for petty sessions on the first floor. Lewis's *Topographical Dictionary* described it as 'the only public building in the town'. No longer extant.

AUGHNACLOY
Moore Street
Market House
c. 1810

Aughnacloy was a petty sessions location and the sessions presumably took place in the market house as no court house is listed. Brett's *Court Houses of Ulster* and the *Buildings of Ireland* both consider it to be c. 1810. The market house has a two-storey, three-bay, stone-built centre block with square-headed openings and a platband at first floor sill level. This is flanked by lower wings on each side containing full-height arched gateways. The whole composition is thrown somewhat off-balance by an odd gabled tower with pointed window at the south end. Aughnacloy petty sessions were abolished in 1979.

BALLYGAWLEY
Meeting House Street
Court House

Ballygawley court house is a mid-19th-century four-bay, two-storey attached building, standing on the corner of Meeting House Street and Main Street. Round-headed openings to ground floor (aside from a recent additional entrance) with square-headed windows above in simply pedimented architraves. Pointed window to first floor of side wall. Semi-hipped roof. Now in office use, the petty sessions having been abolished in 1972.

CALEDON
Main Street
Court House   #306
William Murray; Manor Architects
c. 1822; 2005

Caledon court house is a 'neat and substantial building', according to the OS *Memoirs*, 'erected for the purpose for which it is used, together with the dispensary and inn which may be said to constitute 1 building, by the Earl of Caledon at a cost of 3,000 pounds, about the year 1822'. The *Buildings of Ireland* attributes it to William Murray. Constituting the south end of the three-building asymmetrical row, the court house is a three-bay, two-storey structure. The dressed-stone centre bay is advanced, with a pediment supported on stylised pilasters and a broad segmental-arched entrance. Above the arch is a triple window, and above the pediment a tall chamfered turret, louvred and with four clock faces, topped by a cupola and weathervane. Rubble-stone walls to end bays, framed in dressed stone, with single square-headed windows in dressed-stone surrounds to each floor. Caledon petty sessions were abolished in 1971 and the court house was renovated by Manor Architects in 2005. It is now occupied by the Caledon Regeneration Partnership.

CARRICKMORE
Court House

The petty sessions court house in Carrickmore is shown on the third-edition OS map (1900-07), forming part of the terrace on the north side of the village main street. A four-bay, two-storey private residence now occupies the site.

CASTLEDERG
The Diamond
Market House and Court House   #307
George Hagherty
1828

'The market place' in Castlederg 'with a court house and police barrack attached to it was built in 1828', the OS *Memoirs* reports, 'and cost 300 pounds, which was defrayed by [local landlord] Sir Robert Ferguson. The architect was Mr George Hagherty of Londonderry'. As shown on the first-edition OS map, this was composed of four ranges around a central courtyard, and stood in the centre of the Diamond. Much changed over the years, it is no longer extant. In 1863 John McCurdy prepared plans for a new court house in Castlederg to be erected as part of improvements to the town by J.G. Smyly, QC. The court house was to be a gable-fronted centrepiece to a row of shops, with residential accommodation above, but the scheme was never executed. Castlederg petty sessions were abolished in 1979.

CLOGHER
Main Street
Court House
[]; John Hargrave
c. 1805; 1832

Set back from the west side of Main Street, Clogher court house is a single-storey, five-bay, stone-built structure which Brett's *Court Houses of Ulster* suggests was erected in 1805. Enlarged in 1825; the OS *Memoirs* stated in 1835 that it had been 'recently very much improved'. This must refer to works carried out in 1832 by John Hargrave at a cost of £300. Used for quarter as well as petty sessions. Ashlar walls with central round-headed entrance set in a Gibbsian surround and square-headed windows in blocked architraves. In the 1990s, a squat pyramid-roofed security lodge and new railings were placed in front of the building. Following the transfer of court sittings to Dungannon in the mid-2000s, the court house was sold to a Christian outreach charity. The security hut has been demolished and the building now hosts a café.

COAGH
Urbal Road
Court House

Coagh petty sessions court house is shown on the third-edition OS map (1900-07) on the east side of Urbal Road, adjacent to the Presbyterian church. No longer extant. Coagh petty sessions were abolished in 1964.

COOKSTOWN
Chapel Street
Court House   #308
John Welsh Leebody and Vincent Craig
1898-1900

Built to replace an early-19th-century market house and court house, Cookstown petty and quarter sessions court house was constructed in 1898-1900 by contractors Messrs Stewart of Belfast at a cost of £3,550. It was designed in a hybrid Scots Baronial style by John Welsh Leebody, County Surveyor for the Southern Division of Tyrone, 1895-1933, and Vincent Craig. 'Decidedly odd and decidedly ugly' is the verdict of the *Buildings of Ireland*. A three-stage, broad-eaved, pyramid-roofed corner tower, with a fanlit entrance to ground floor, adjoins a three-bay block with paired square-headed windows to ground floor, segmental-headed windows above, and a central eaves pediment with blind oculus. Rough-stone walls with cut-stone dressings. One- and two-storey side elevation with tall windows to the plain double-height galleried courtroom with an open-truss wooden ceiling. Bombed in 1972, the building then acquired sheet-metal fencing and a security pillbox which have since been removed. Closed in the mid-2000s, it was for sale in 2018, with planning permission granted for change of use to restaurant/mixed use development or for conversion into four apartments with additional development to the rear.

#306 | Caledon (Alistair Rowan/*Buildings of Ireland*, 1970)
#307 | Castlederg, Proposed Court House Range.
        Elevation by John McCurdy, 1863 (McCurdy & Mitchell Collection, IAA)
#308 | Cookstown (Crown DfC Historic Environment Division, 1973)

DONEMANAGH/DUNNAMANAGH

Donemanagh was listed in the 1842 *Petty Sessions Return*, and ceased to be a court location before 1959. Where the court sat remains to be clarified.

DROMORE
Main Street
Court House
1879

On 22 June 1880, as recorded in Hansard, Thomas Sexton, MP for Sligo, asked Hugh Law, MP for Londonderry and Attorney-General for Ireland, if he was aware that 'about a year ago, the Magistrates of Tyrone, assembled at the Omagh Quarter Sessions, resolved to form a new petty sessions district, comprising a number of townlands in the county of Tyrone, and a few in the county of Fermanagh… that a court-house was accordingly erected at Dromore, and several petty sessions held there, but that the Court of Queen's Bench being appealed to on the subject, delivered a judgment quashing the whole proceedings'. Law corrected Sexton; the Queen's Bench had merely removed the townlands in Fermanagh from Dromore petty sessions district and while the court was currently suspended it was hoped that it would resume shortly. Having started life as a school, a simple five-bay, single-storey building on the west side of the north end of Main Street would appear to be the court house in question, and continued to function as Dromore court house into the second half of the 20th century. Dromore petty sessions were abolished in 1979 and the former court house is now Dromore Bethel Hall.

DUNGANNON
Savings Bank Street
Court House
Richard Taylor
1792

In 1792 County Surveyor Richard Taylor was commissioned by Tyrone Grand Jury to design a new court house in Dungannon. A single-storey, three-bay block with elaborate architraves to windows and a tall pedimented centre bay fronted by a tetrastyle Ionic portico, the court house was in disrepair by the early 1820s and had to be replaced. It was converted to a bank and was later home to the *Tyrone Courier*. The building lost its portico to a bomb in 1972 and, though semi-derelict, still stands at the end of Savings Bank Street, terminating the vista up George's Street.

Dungannon, George's Street (Crown DfC Historic Environment Division, 1973) | **#309**
Dungannon, Killyman Road, Court House (Paul Tierney, 2019) | **#310**
Fivemiletown (Crown DfC Historic Environment Division, 1973) | **#311**

DUNGANNON
George's Street
Court House   **#309**
John Hargrave
1830

Lewis's *Topographical Dictionary* notes that Dungannon's new court house 'is a spacious and handsome building, erected in 1830; under it is the bridewell, containing a day-room and four large cells for male prisoners, with a yard, day-room, and cells for female prisoners; the same accommodation for debtors, and apartments for the keeper'. Designed by John Hargrave to replace the 1792 court house on what is now Savings Bank Street, and paid for in part by a £764 7s 5d loan from the Board of Works, this was a three-bay, two-storey ashlar-fronted building with an eight-bay side elevation extending to three storeys as it descended the William Street hill. Four full-height pilasters to front supported a prominent cornice, above which was a heavy parapet with a central royal coat of arms. Square-headed windows in arched recesses flanked a later projecting entrance porch. The tall square-headed windows to first floor sat on a sill-level platband. Demolished in the 1990s, and therefore outlived by the building it superseded; a leisure centre now stands on the site.

DUNGANNON
Killyman Road
Court House   **#310**
CPD Architecture
2002

Designed by CPD for the Northern Ireland Courts Service and constructed by McLaughlin and Harvey contractors at a cost of £9.4 million, Dungannon's newest court house opened in December 2002. Protected by fencing and a round security lodge, it is a pale-brick building with a tall main block featuring a fully glazed gable wall under an oversailing parabolic roof supported on exposed steel trusses. This is flanked by lower, set-back, two-storey wings. The building houses two main courtrooms, a juvenile court and an informal courtroom, and is used for Magistrates Courts, County Courts and Crown Courts sittings.

FINTONA

Fintona was listed in the 1842 *Petty Sessions Return*. The petty sessions were not abolished until 1979 but a specific court house has not been located.

FIVEMILETOWN
Main Street
Court House   **#311**
1831

The petty sessions court house in Fivemiletown was erected in 1831, according to a date plaque on the front facade, by Colonel Montgomery, the proprietor of the town, who also provided shambles, a constabulary barracks and boys' and girls' schools. Integrated into the terrace on the north side of Main Street, this is a two- and three-storey building, irregularly windowed, with a carriage arch and three entrances, two of which are set in surrounds with stylised pediments. The OS *Memoirs* considered it 'a common kind of building'. Fivemiletown petty sessions were abolished in 1979 and the former court house is now in commercial use. The ornate clock which adorns its façade was damaged by a car bomb in 1972 and stopped working. It was repaired and reinstated in 2014.

GORTIN
Main Street
Court House

Petty sessions were held in Gortin every second Friday, according to Lewis's *Topographical Dictionary*. The third-edition OS map (1900-07) shows a court house located on Main Street in the centre of the village, indicating that one of the pitched-roofed, two-storey terraced houses was appropriated for a time for court purposes. In 1960 Gortin petty sessions were transferred to Plumbridge.

MOY
The Diamond
Market House and Court House
1828

The petty sessions area of Moy was listed as Charlemont, Co. Armagh, in the 1842 *Petty Sessions Return*, and as Moy, Co. Tyrone, in 1882. By 1907 there were two separate petty sessions areas, Moy, and Charlemont and Blackwatertown, though the latter had ceased to exist by 1915 and there seems to have been only one designated court house at any given time. Lewis's *Topographical Dictionary* records that a 'very commodious market-house and a spacious market-place have been constructed [in Moy] by the Earl of Charlemont, who is the proprietor of the town'. The first floor was used for petty sessions and the building is indicated as 'Ct. Ho.' on the third-edition OS map (1900). A stone-built, two-storey structure erected in 1828, according to the OS *Memoirs*, it was a focal point in the middle of the south side of the Diamond. Five-arch market arcade at ground level with a three-bay first floor surmounted by a central pediment containing a finely carved Charlemont coat of arms. Having served as a garage for several years, the building was damaged by a bomb in 1972 and subsequently demolished. When they vacated the market house in the mid-1950s, court sittings moved to the former Hibernian Hall on the east side of Claremont Street, now also no longer extant. Moy petty sessions were abolished in 1964.

NEWTOWNSTEWART

Townhall Street

Town Hall

1880

According to the OS *Memoirs*, petty sessions were held in Newtownstewart 'one Thursday in every month, in the petty sessions room hired for the purpose near the post office… The number of outrages committed is small, and they are generally the result of drunken riots'. Following the construction of the attached three-bay, two-storey, gable-fronted town hall on the east side of Townhall Street in 1880, the monthly petty sessions moved to the first-floor hall of that building. Newtownstewart petty sessions were abolished in 1964.

OMAGH

High Street

County Court House

See Significant Court Houses – A Chronological Selection   **P189**

PLUMBRIDGE

In 1960 Gortin petty sessions area was renamed Plumbridge on the transfer there of court sittings. Plumbridge petty sessions area was abolished in 1976. Where the sessions sat in Plumbridge has not been established.

POMEROY

The Diamond

Market House and Court House

1881-82

Brett's *Court Houses of Ulster* says that the market house in Pomeroy was built c. 1850, though the NI Historic Buildings database says it was built in 1881-82, on the site of what appears to have been a pre-1834 dwelling house. An 1882 valuation record indicates that the ground floor was used as a corn, egg and butter market, with the petty sessions court on the first floor. Located on the south side of the Diamond, this is a four-bay, two-storey building, rendered with red-brick blocked surrounds to openings. These surrounds have been painted for many years. A broad segmental carriage-arch is flanked by two narrower segmental arches with a round-headed entrance in the end bay to the right. Square-headed windows to first floor, that over the carriage-arch wider than the others. Court use continued until 1972, when the petty sessions were transferred to Cookstown (and abolished in 1977), with commercial use at ground floor. Now empty and dilapidated.

SIXMILECROSS

Market House

c. 1840

Petty sessions in Sixmilecross were presumably held in the market house, which Brett's *Court Houses of Ulster* dates to c. 1840 and records as a 'very derelict' two-storey, five-bay hipped-roofed building of random stone with granite dressings. The building is no longer extant and the petty sessions were abolished in 1964.

STEWARTSTOWN

Hillhead

Court House

Stewartstown petty sessions court house is located on the third-edition OS map (1900-07) on the west side of Hillhead. It stood just north of the national school and the McNeece Memorial Hall, and south of the constabulary barracks. The school and hall are still there but the court house and barracks are gone. Stewartstown petty sessions were abolished in 1964.

STRABANE

Derry Road

Court House

[]; John Hargrave (repairs)

1807; 1825-26

Erected in 1807 at a cost of £1,200 and repaired in 1825-26 by John Hargrave, Strabane court house is a tall, two-storey over high basement, three-bay structure, the centre bay advanced, quoined and pedimented. The main entrance is accessed by a steep flight of narrow steps. Above the entrance is a tall segmental-headed window while the tympanum of the pediment contains a painted royal coat of arms. Surrounded by a high concrete security wall with steel mesh cages, the court house continues to be used by Magistrates Courts and County Courts.

TRILLICK

Market House

'Here', Lewis's *Topographical Dictionary* reports of Trillick, 'is a good market-house, recently repaired by Gen. Mervyn Archdall, of Trillick Lodge, the proprietor of the town and adjacent lands, in which a market is held every Tuesday, chiefly for butter and provisions'. The market house is shown on the third-edition OS map (1900-07) as a court house. Set back from the south side of Main Street, this is a plain building with a four-arch arcade to ground floor, now filled in, with entrances in the end bays and windows in the middle two. There are square-headed windows to first floor. A platband separates the floors. Trillick petty sessions were abolished in 1961, since when the building has had a variety of uses including dancehall and community hall.

ARDMORE

Duffcarrick Road
Court House
pre-1840

A two-storey, five-bay, pitched-roof building on the west side of Duffcarrick Road served as Ardmore petty sessions court house. Two entrances, side by side in the centre, with square-headed windows on each side and at first floor level. Though not marked as a court house, a building is shown on the site on the first-edition OS map (1839-41). Latterly in residential use. Ardmore was a location for a District Court, exercising summary jurisdiction only, from 1924 until 1961, when it became part of Youghal District Court Area.

BALLYMACARBRY

Court House   #312

Ballymacarbry petty sessions court house was located at a T-junction on a bend in the road (R671) east of the village centre, the first building in the second terrace (as one approaches from the village). A two-storey, pitched-roofed structure, taller than its neighbours, it is now part of a licensed premises. Ballymacarbry was made a District Court location in 1924, but a 1946 District Court Order (SI 384/1946) noted that, pending the provision of a suitable court house at Ballymacarbry, all cases appropriate to that court would be heard at Clonmel.

CALLAGHANE

Court House and Constabulary Barracks

A 'Police Station' is shown on the first-edition OS map, on the west side of the road c. 270m north of Callaghane Bridge. By the time the 25-inch OS map was published, it had become a combined petty sessions court house and constabulary barracks. No longer extant.

CAPPOQUIN

The Square
Market House and Court House   #313
c. 1775; c. 2000

Cappoquin market house was built c. 1775 (NIAH) and functioned as Cappoquin court house for much of the 19th and 20th centuries. It is an end-of-terrace, two-storey, three-bay, hipped-roofed building facing onto a small square at the confluence of Main Street, Barrack Street and Cook Street. Two market arches with chunky stone voussoirs and keystones face the square. A third is in the side elevation on Barrack Street. Formerly open, all are now filled with modern shopfronts following an extensive renovation of the building c. 2000. Square-headed windows to first floor where the courtroom was located. Access to this floor, which is now in residential use, was provided via an external staircase at the south end of the building. On the abolition of the District Court in 2008, Cappoquin became part of the Lismore District Court Area.

CARRICKBEG

Rack Hill
Court House

The petty sessions court house in Carrickbeg, on the Waterford side of the Suir opposite Carrick-on-Suir, was adjacent to the constabulary barracks on Rack Hill. Now in residential use, it still stands as a four-bay, single-storey building with entrances in the end bays framing two square-headed windows. Later dormer windows to attic.

CLASHMORE

Court House   #314

At the north end of the continuous terrace on the west side of the village main street, almost opposite the C of I church, a four-bay, two-storey building with a semi-hipped roof was Clashmore petty sessions court house. A carriage arch on the left provides access to the rear. Four square-headed windows to first floor of main façade with a tripartite segmental window in end wall. Now in commercial use.

DUNGARVAN

T. F. Meagher Street
Court House   #315
1825-32; 1995

In 1825 plans for a new court house and bridewell for Dungarvan were approved by Francis Johnston in his capacity as inspector of civil buildings. Johnston noted, however, that the windows in the male corridor overlooking the female prison yard should be 'kept up as high as the ceiling will admit, and also to be so sloped upwards that no communication can be had through them' (NAI CSORP/1826/825). The *First Annual Report of the Commissioners of Public Works* recorded in 1832 a grant of £880 2s 10d for the erection of Dungarvan court house. Lewis's *Topographical Dictionary* reports that the 'quarter sessions of the peace for the western division of the county are held here in January, April, and October; and petty sessions are held every Thursday… The county sessions-house is a neat and well arranged building, at the entrance into the town from the bridge; and attached to it is a bridewell, containing ten cells, two day-rooms, and two airing-yards'. So neat and well arranged was the building that efforts were made from 1835 to 1837 to have the county assizes transferred permanently to Dungarvan from Waterford. Set back from the street behind railings, the court house is a classical building comprising a central two-storey, three-bay block with flanking single-bay, single-storey wings. The ground floor of the central block is rusticated, with an arcade of blind segmental recesses. Above are three tall, round-headed windows set in an ashlar wall and standing on a sill-level platband. These are separated by four plain pilasters supporting a plain entablature and pediment. The wings are slightly recessed and have pedimented square-headed openings, that to the right an entrance and that to the left a window, each surmounted by a decorative panel. Rendered four-bay side elevations. Part rendered and part rubble-masonry wall to rear, where the wings are two-storey. Renovated in 1995, when the courtroom acquired its current somewhat austere fitout. Still in use for District and Circuit Court sittings.

KILBARRY MEADOW

Kilbarry Meadow was listed the 1842 *Petty Sessions Return*, though no return was received, and no court house is recorded.

KILMACTHOMAS
Main Street
Court House   #316
c. 1880

End of terrace, single-storey, three-bay court house located mid-way along the south side of Kilmacthomas Main Street. Built c. 1880 and renovated c. 1980. Pitched roof with decorative ridge tiles. Rendered walls, quoined to front where there are two tall round-headed windows and a round-headed entrance. Square-headed windows to side. Kilmacthomas was a District Court location until 2007 when it became part of Dungarvan District Court Area. The court house was subsequently converted to library use.

LISMORE
West Street
Court House   #317
[John Carr]; []; Shaffrey Associates
[1799]; c. 1890; 2004-06

In a letter dated 23 August 1799, the architect John Carr of York discussed his plans for a new court house in Lismore commissioned by the local landlord, the Duke of Devonshire. The building was to include a market hall on the ground floor, cells for male and female prisoners, and 'proper accommodation' for the clerk of the peace and the jury. It was to be of stone and to cost about £1,000. Whether Carr's plans for the court house were those executed is not known, but the main façade of the present building certainly could be his. Protected by a curve of iron railings, this is a three-bay, two-storey classical composition in ashlar granite, with a central pedimented pavilion flanked by lower, slightly set back wings. Below the pediment is a large round-headed window in an arched recess with string-course at impost level corresponding with the eaves of the wings. A second string-course at sill level extends the width of the building, taking in the sills of the square-headed windows in the wings before continuing down the sides. Below the lower string-course is a platband which also continues around the sides, while the central entrance has a cut-stone Doric surround with entablature. Random-stone six-bay, two-storey side elevation on Chapel Street, with a pair of Diocletian windows to the first floor of the taller central bays. The building was considerably altered c. 1890, when it acquired its somewhat incongruous square Italianate clocktower. Burned by local Irish Volunteers in early 1920 during the War of Independence, it was subsequently repaired and remained in use as a court house until 1985, when the facilities were deemed no longer suitable. In 1991 a heritage centre, tourist information centre and craft shop were established on the ground floor while the first floor was used by the local drama society. From 2004 to 2006, Shaffrey Associates architects carried out an extensive and sympathetic programme of works to allow the return to the building of the District Court. The main internal space, the former courtroom,

was reconfigured to serve both as a court and a theatre. Dismountable courtroom furniture has been provided which can be removed and stored when the courts are not sitting. Necessary ancillary facilities were provided, including a lift, family law court and a canteen. The layout of the heritage centre was rationalised and an extension was added to the side, a timber-framed glazed structure with load-bearing masonry walls clad in timber, copper and lime render. The building remains in court and cultural use.

PORTLAW

Market Square

Court House   #318

1854

John Skipton Mulvany

Portlaw petty sessions court house is the central two-storey element in an otherwise single-storey nine-bay court house and school complex standing at right angles to, and set back from, the south side of Factory Road (now Market Square) at the edge of the former Portlaw cotton mill grounds. Built in 1854, almost certainly to designs by John Skipton Mulvany, who carried out a considerable amount of work at Portlaw for the Malcomson family, proprietors of the cotton mill. This included the Malcomson residence, Mayfield, workers' housing, and the reconfiguring of the village in the 1850s on a polyvium plan. Originally built as a multi-purpose hall, the court house is a three-bay block with an arcade of segmental-arched openings to ground floor, pedimented round-headed windows at first floor level, and Mulvany's distinctive heavy modillions to the cornice. Flanked by two- and one-bay classroom blocks which step back progressively, all five elements of the complex originally had Belfast-truss curved roofs covered with tarred canvas produced in the Malcomson mill. Obscured now by the industrial buildings of Clodagh Business Park and a recent housing development on the south side of Market Square, the complex is still standing, though derelict and roofless.

STRADBALLY

High Street

Court House

Lewis's *Topographical Dictionary* records that petty sessions were held in Stradbally once a fortnight. By the end of the 19th century, they were held in the last (east) house in the eastern-most terrace on the south side of High Street. The local dispensary was also located in the terrace. An attached, two-storey, three-bay building, the former court house is still standing and in domestic use.

TALLOW

Convent Street

Court House

The Lismore Castle archives contain a number of proposals for an elaborate market house in Tallow, each with an arcade at ground floor, a first-floor room for court sittings and a clocktower. None of these was executed. A four-bay, two-storey terraced building incorporating a carriage arch on the east side of Convent Street, close to the junction with Chapel Street, functioned as Tallow petty sessions court house, according to the 25-inch OS map. Now in commercial use. Tallow District Court sittings subsequently moved slightly north on Convent Street to St Patrick's Parish Hall, a five-bay, two-storey terraced building erected in the late 19th century as a temperance hall. In 2000 a story in a Sunday newspaper of a judge taking a mobile phone call during a sitting of the District Court in Tallow, where the accommodation was described as 'frugal', resulted in a successful action of libel being taken against the newspaper by the judge. Tallow became part of the Lismore District Court Area in 2008 on the abolition of Tallow District Court.

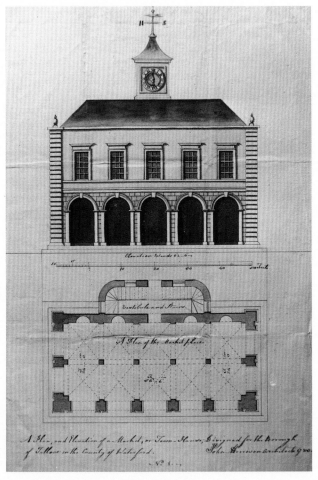

Tallow, Proposed Market House. Plan and Elevation by John Harrison, Architect, 1783 (IAA)

TRAMORE

Patrick Street

Court House

Tramore petty sessions court house was located at the junction of Patrick Street and Pond Road. Much altered, it is still extant. Tramore District Court, which sat in Tramore House on Pond Road, and in Tramore GAA hall, was abolished in 1983, and the District Court Area merged with Waterford.

VILLIERSTOWN

Quay Road

Court House

Villierstown petty sessions court house was constructed in the mid to late 19th century to the south-west of the village centre, adjacent to the already existing police station of c. 1820. Still standing but much altered to convert it to residential use, the building bears a name plaque reading 'The Old Court House'.

WATERFORD

County Court House and City Court House

William Richards' and Bernard Scalé's 1764 *Map of the City and Suburbs of Waterford* shows two separate court houses, both located in the parish of St Patrick. The county court house was on High Street while the city court house was located on Broad Street. The city court house was described as 'an handsome structure, the outside whereof is supported by a range of columns of the tuscan order; the front of the building serves for a corn market-house; and the inner part for a court-house where the assizes for the city, the quarter-sessions, and other assemblies relating to city affairs are held. Above stairs, are apartments for the grand and petty juries' (Charles Smith, *The ancient and present state of the county and city of Waterford* (1746)). The city court house had vanished by 1830. The county court house on High Street was identified on an 1830 map as the 'Old Courthouse', but it too is no longer extant.

WATERFORD

Ballybricken Green

Court House and Gaol

See Significant Court Houses – A Chronological Selection   P173

WATERFORD

Catherine Street

County Court House

See P120 *&* Significant Court Houses – A Chronological Selection P204

ATHLONE

Pearse Street (formerly King Street)

Court House

pre-1834

Athlone tholsel was constructed in 1587 on the east side of the River Shannon. Initially a wooden structure, it was rebuilt in stone in 1703. A centre for local government, the tholsel would have accommodated court sittings of various kinds. In 1834 it was demolished because of its dilapidated condition, by which time a dedicated court house had been constructed on the west side of the Shannon. This court house is shown on the first-edition and 25-inch OS maps of Athlone, standing on the same site as the current court house. As Lewis's *Topographical Dictionary* reports 'Quarter sessions for the Athlone division of the county of Roscommon are held here in March and October, and at Roscommon in June and December'. Athlone petty sessions were also held in the court house and, separately, Brawney petty sessions for the borough area east of the Shannon. Brawney petty sessions merged with Athlone in 1899. The court house was demolished in 1914.

ATHLONE

Pearse Street (formerly King Street)

Court House   #319

Arthur Edward Joyce

1914-16

By 1911 Athlone court house was considered both 'very antiquated' and a danger to public health. 'The sewerage system is defective beyond repair, and the offensive matter lodges in the pipes. As a result the atmosphere is impregnated with an obnoxious and very dangerous odour' (*Irish Builder*, 8 July 1911). The County Surveyor, Arthur E. Joyce, had recommended the demolition of the building and its replacement, but as the court house served both counties Roscommon and Westmeath, and as Roscommon County Council had refused to fund a replacement, nothing had happened. By 1914 the logjam was overcome and a new court house, designed by Joyce, was commissioned. Built on the site of the 1830s building, this is a three-bay, two-storey rendered structure, rusticated at ground floor with a large segmental entrance flanked by square-headed windows. Squared Doric pilasters on either side of the entrance rise the full height of the building to support a pediment. Square-headed windows to first floor, the centre one adorned with an iron balcony. Broad modillioned eaves. At its opening in June 1916, Judge Drummond described it as 'probably the best Sessions Courthouse in Ireland' (*Irish Builder*, 10 June 1916). Extended to the rear in a number of phases. Internally, the austere, double-height courtroom was renovated in 1995, and remains in use.

BALLYMORE

Low Street

Court House

A detached, three-bay, two-storey, mid-19th-century quoined house set back from the south side of the main road, at the junction with the L1240, at the east end of the village, served as Ballymore petty sessions court house. Now in residential use.

BALLYNACARRIGY/BALLYNACARGY

Schoolhouse and Court House

The first-edition OS map shows 'Ballynacarrigy Free School and Petit Session House' standing just north of the village centre, on the east side of the road. The site is now occupied by St Brigid's National School, a single-storey, six-bay building with recessed central double entrance and two gabled classrooms.

BALLYNACARRIGY/BALLYNACARGY

Main Street

Court House   #320

c. 1955

By the end of the 19th century petty sessions had moved from the Free School north of Ballynacarrigy to a premises on the west side of the south end of Main Street. No longer extant, having been demolished c. 1955 to make way for a new purpose-built court house. This is a single-storey, single-bay building, gable-fronted and pebble-dashed, with semi-circular steps leading to an entrance in a red-brick porch with a flat concrete roof. An official harp emblem surmounts the door. Square-headed windows to side elevations. Curved quadrant flanking walls provide an element of civic presence. Ballynacarrigy or Ballynacargy District Court Area was amalgamated with the District Court Area of Mullingar in 2001.

CASTLEPOLLARD

The Square

Market House and Court House/Town Hall   #321

[]; Patrick John O'Loughlin

c. 1810-20; 1926

Lewis's *Topographical Dictionary* notes of Castlepollard that 'in the centre is a square, in which stands the market house'. Probably built in the second decade of the 19th century, the market house is shown on the first-edition OS map. By the time the 25-inch map appears, the building is delineated as 'Market & Court Ho'. As recorded in a Bureau of Military History witness statement (James Maguire, WS 1,439), the building was burned in 1921 by Irish Volunteers. It was rebuilt as Castlepollard town hall in 1926 to designs by Patrick John O'Loughlin, Borough Surveyor of Athlone, Co. Westmeath, 1915-31. In its post-1926 guise, this is a hipped-roofed, two-storey, three-bay by six-bay building standing detached in the Square. The quoined front (north) façade has a single-storey enclosed entrance porch with corner pilasters and a fanlit entrance. Square-headed windows to ground and first floor, separated by a string-course. Between the first floor windows is a plaque with the inscription 'Town Hall A.D. 1926'. A vehicular access on the east side, protected by a concrete porch, is a reminder that the building for a time also served as Castlepollard fire station. A plaque on the west side commemorates local TD Michael Joseph Kennedy. An external staircase to the rear (south) provides access to the timber-panelled first-floor room reserved for District Court sittings. These sittings transferred to Mullingar in 2008. In 2018 the local authority was proposing to refurbish the building.

CLONMELLON

Main Street

Court House   #322

A two-storey, three-bay, end-of-terrace house on the south side of the village main street, immediately adjacent to the gates of St John's C of I church, served as Clonmellon petty sessions court house. Early 19th-century, with three small square-headed windows to first floor. Double window to ground floor, and entrance with top and side lights. An external flight of stairs on the east end provided access to the first-floor courtroom.

COLLINSTOWN

Market House and Court House

A small, square-plan, early-19th-century market and court house stood detached in the centre of Collinstown village square. Demolished c. 1950.

DELVIN (CASTLETOWN-DELVIN)

Main Street

Court House   #323

Florence Mahony; []

1849-52; 1920s

The 1849 Westmeath Grand Jury presentments record the erection of a sessions house at Castletown-Delvin. Designed by Florence Mahony, County Surveyor for Westmeath, 1834-61, the building was completed in early 1852, though some payment was withheld from the contractor, John Meagher, as parts of the building were not satisfactorily finished. A detached, single-storey, three-bay gabled building of partially rendered rubble stone with dressed-stone surrounds to the square-headed openings and a blind oculus in the gable pediment. Extended in the 1920s. Delvin District Court was amalgamated with Castlepollard in 2001, and the former court house was used as Delvin Youthreach centre, an alternative education provider. The court house was demolished in 2005 and the site redeveloped to include a new Youthreach building and residential units.

GLASSAN/GLASSON

Court House, Dispensary and Post Office   #324

A single-storey, three-bay, early-19th-century, L-plan house on the west side of the village street served as Glassan petty sessions court house. Hipped-roofed with wide eaves and decorative ridge tiles. Hoodmouldings to square-headed windows. Although it was shown solely as the dispensary on the first-edition OS map, in an unusual combination the building came to be the village post office and dispensary, as well as court house.

KILBEGGAN

The Square

Market House and Court House   #325

1828

Attached five-bay, two-storey market house. 'Built AD 1828 by Patrick Phylan', as stated on a plaque on the building, with costs mainly met by local landlord Gustavus Lambert. Described by Lewis's *Topographical Dictionary* as 'a neat plain building of limestone'. By the time the 25-inch map was produced, the building was identified solely as a court house. Modestly advanced and pedimented end bays. Later internal divisions left the north end bay, with its own three-bay front on Upper Main Street, as a separate premises. Square-headed windows to first floor in lugged architraves with a market arcade to ground floor where the walls are ashlar. The end arches contain entrances with bracketed surrounds and side lights. These acquired large fanlights in 2005 when the building was renovated and converted to county council offices and a branch library, Kilbeggan District Court having been amalgamated with Tullamore in 2001. The three centre arches, one of which had remained open and had retained its iron gates, received fanlight windows as part of these works and the squared limestone rubble of the first floor was rendered.

#323 | Delvin (NIAH, 2004)

#324 | Glassan (Paul Tierney, 2019)

#325 | Kilbeggan (IAA, 1976)

#326 | Killucan (IAA, 1976)

KILLUCAN

The Square

Market House and Court House   #326

1838

Tall and shallow, coursed-rubble, three-storey, five-bay market house built by local stonemasons William and Thomas Keegan and completed in 1838. Also used as a court house. Set back from the street behind a square enclosed by recent railings with stone piers. Dressed-stone segmental-arched market arcade to ground floor, the south arch now infilled in brick. Advanced and pedimented centre bay, with two-storey arched recess above ground floor and painted clock face in tympanum. Square-headed windows in dressed-stone surrounds to first and second storeys. Covered external stairs on north end where the building was formerly attached to a now-demolished range which closed off the north side of the square. Single-storey open sheds to south side. Currently in a semi-derelict condition. Killucan District Court, which sat in Killucan Working Men's Club and Community Centre, was amalgamated with Mullingar in 2008.

KNOCKDRIN

Knockdrin was listed the 1842 *Petty Sessions Return* and was still a petty sessions location in 1905, but had ceased to be one by 1907. A court house remains to be identified.

MOATE

Main Street

Court House   #327

John Hargrave

1826-28

'Attractive and unusual', according to the *Buildings of Ireland*, Moate court house is a two-storey, three-bay, bow-fronted classical building built by contractor Daniel Gaven in 1828 for petty and quarter sessions. The architect was John Hargrave. Francis Johnston had approved the plans in 1826 in his capacity as inspector of civil buildings. This court house replaced a previous court house built 1798-1800, which the Grand Jury considered too small and too remote. Rectangular plan, with the narrow end set back from the street and a bridewell to the rear. Four evenly spaced, full-height Tuscan pilasters divide the gently curved ashlar limestone façade and support a plain frieze, cornice and parapet. Three plain square-headed entrances, the central one formerly blind. Three square-headed windows to first floor, their sills merging to form a platband which extends to meet the entablature of flanking carriage arches. Square-headed windows set high in the rendered side elevations light the double-height courtroom. Having also served for a time as Moate fire station, the court house accommodated Moate District Court, Moate Boxing Club and Moate Museum until 2002, when the District Court Area was amalgamated with that of Athlone. The building was altered to accommodate Moate branch library in 2013.

Moate (IAA, 1985) | **#327**
Multyfarnham (Paul Tierney, 2019) | **#328**
Rathowen (Paul Tierney, 2019) | **#329**
Tyrrellspass (IAA, c. 1960) | **#330**

MULLINGAR
Mount Street
County Court House
See **P114** *&* Significant Court Houses – A Chronological Selection **P194**

MULTYFARNHAM
Court House   #328

As identified on the first-edition OS map, Multyfarnham 'Petty Sessions Ho.' is on the east side of the street at the north end of the village, across the road from the former constabulary barracks. Formerly detached, it is now the last building in the terrace. A single-storey, six-bay building, with a semi-hipped roof, square-headed openings and rough stone walls, the former court house has two entrances, one in an advanced porch. Multyfarnham had a District Court with summary jurisdiction only from 1924 until 1961 when it became part of Mullingar District Court Area. The building is now a guest house and restaurant.

RATHOWEN
Court House   #329

The petty sessions court house in Rathowen is the first building on the east side of the road as one approaches the village from the south. Almost opposite the former constabulary barracks (later Garda station), the building is shown as a school on the first-edition OS map and as a court house on the 25-inch map. Set back from the road behind a stone wall, this is a five-bay, single-storey structure, with pitched roof, rendered walls, an off-centre entrance and four small square windows set high in the façade.

ROCHFORT
Court House
pre-1837

The building which served as Rochfort rural petty sessions court house and school is shown on the 25-inch OS map on the west side of what is now the N52, just south of Tally Ho or Tallyho Stud. A gate lodge for Tudenham Park stood adjacent. The court house and school would appear to be included on the first-edition OS map but without designation. No trace remains. Rochfort petty sessions had merged with Tyrrellspass by 1905.

TYRRELLSPASS
The Crescent
Police Barracks and Court House   #330
1820s

Prominently located on the Crescent, across the road from St Sinian's C of I church, Tyrrellspass petty sessions court house was originally built as a police barracks. Developed under the patronage of the Countess of Belvedere, most of the Crescent was complete by 1818, with the exception of the school, which was completed in 1823, and this building, which is of a similar date. In the latter part of the 19th century it changed from police to court use. Five-bay, two-storey, Georgian block with ashlar limestone façade. Central round-headed fanlit entrance with square-headed windows to ground and first floor. Eaves pediment over centre three bays, with clock in tympanum, and topped by a domed bellcote. Tyrrellspass was a District Court location from 1924 until 1961 after which the court house fell into dereliction. In 1988 it was converted to residential use.

ARTHURSTOWN
Strand Road
Court House

A mid-19th-century two-storey, two-bay, rendered and quoined end-of-terrace house facing the sea on Strand Road served as Arthurstown petty sessions court house, having previously, it would seem, served as the local dispensary. Now in residential use.

BALLYCULLANE (BAILISTOWN/BAYLESTOWN)
Court House

The isolated rural petty sessions court house at Ballycullane or Bailistown (Baylestown) is shown on the first-edition OS map on the east side of what is now the R734, about 1.5km south-west of Ballycullane village. It had ceased to be a court house by the time the 25-inch map was produced. Some fabric may remain in the small cottage and corrugated agricultural building on the site. Ballycullane became a District Court location in 1924 and remained one until 1986. In a written answer to a parliamentary question the then Minister for Justice, Alan Dukes, TD, noted that he was 'aware that the premises in which Ballycullane District Court has been held are in a very dilapidated condition. The premises are so unsuitable that, in the view of the District Justice who sits there, it is not fitting to the dignity of the court that sittings should continue there and he has, therefore, ceased to hear cases at Ballycullane'. The District Court Area was consequently abolished and the District Electoral Divisions which comprised it were amalgamated in part with the District Court Area of New Ross and in part with that of Wexford.

BUNCLODY
Church Street
Court House   #331

Located on the east side of Church Street, directly opposite the C of I school building, a much altered three-bay, two-storey attached house functioned as Bunclody court house. The present appearance of the building, belies the fact that the court house was located on the site from at least the late 1830s until the mid-20th century. Subsequently venues, including the Meadowlands Ballroom, were rented in the town on a *pro tem* basis for court use. Bunclody District Court Area was abolished in 2000 and the constituent Electoral Divisions amalgamated with Enniscorthy.

CLONROCHE
Court House
pre-1840

The pre-1840 petty sessions court house in Clonroche was the middle of a group of buildings on the north side of the village street which, by the end of the 19th century, also included the post office on the west and the dispensary on the east. The post office building – the largest of the three – is now a two-storey, three-bay private residence to which the single-storey former court house and dispensary are annexed as a wing.

DUNCORMICK
Court House

The petty sessions court house in Duncormick was located in the three-bay, single-storey building at the west end of the stepped terrace of buildings on the south side of the village street. Square-headed entrance in end bay, with two square-headed windows. The houses to the west were formerly the constabulary barracks.

ENNISCORTHY
Court Street
Court House   #332
1820

On a corner site, set back from Court Street behind railings, Enniscorthy court house is, according to Lewis's *Topographical Dictionary*, 'a neat building, erected at the expense of the county' and which contained one of the two 'newsrooms' in the town. A T-plan structure with hipped roof and rendered, ruled-and-lined walls, it was built for petty and quarter sessions by the Grand Jury in 1820, the year after the similar court house in Gorey was completed. New Ross court house is a later variant of the same design. Single-bay, single-storey courtroom wing at the foot of the T, with simple pilasters to the corners, opposing entrances in a flat-roofed shallow porch with blind wall, and a cornice and blocking-course which, awkwardly, does not meet the cornice of the transverse rear wing. The double-height courtroom is lit from the sides by three square-headed windows in plain architraves, and retained timber fittings and furnishings into the 2000s. The rear wing has entrances on both sides, with a single square-headed window to first floor and single windows in the end walls. In his Bureau of Military History witness statement (WS 1,294), Sean Whelan of the North Wexford Brigade, IRA, describes being held prisoner in Enniscorthy court house when it was occupied by British army troops under the command of a Captain Yeo: 'I was in this veritable hell of mental and physical torture for about three weeks before being transferred to the military detention barracks, Cork. It was one of the high spots in my life to stand and watch the courthouse go up in flames before we (the Republicans) evacuated the town in the Civil War of 1922'. The court house was subsequently repaired and remained in use until 2004, when Enniscorthy District Court sittings transferred to a location in Ardcavan Business Park just outside Wexford town. Enniscorthy District Court Area was abolished in 2011 and Electoral Divisions divided between Gorey and Carlow. Aughey O'Flaherty Architects have been appointed to refurbish the original court house for Wexford County Council.

FERNS
Main Street
Court House

At the end of the 19th century, the petty sessions court house in Ferns was a small end-of-terrace building, immediately adjacent to the dispensary and across the road from the constabulary barracks, which was itself just east of the school. The school building, now much extended, is extant. The site of the barracks is now the carpark for the RC Church of St Aidan completed in 1975 and, while part of the terrace of single-storey, two-bay houses in which they stood survives, the court house and dispensary do not.

GOREY
Main Street
Market House and Court House   #333

Lewis's *Topographical Dictionary* records that the market house in Gorey 'is a plain but commodious building, situated in the centre of the town; the upper part, formerly used as a court-house, is now appropriated to the use of the parochial school'. A five-bay, two-storey building, the centre three bays slightly advanced, with a rusticated stone arcade at ground floor, a red-brick first floor and eaves pediment, square-headed windows, a stone platband, cornice and surround to pediment, a clock in the tympanum, and a cupola ventilator. A mid-18th-century building, the market house acquired its present appearance sometime after court sittings had moved to the purpose-built court house further west along Main Street. Having been a private residence for the first half of the 20th century, the market house became headquarters to Gorey Town Commissioners in 1950 and remained in local authority use until 2011. It has also served as a library and, latterly, a tourist office. Plans were drawn up in 2018 by Reddy Architecture and Urbanism for Wexford County Council to restore the building and add a new retail, performance and exhibition space to the rear.

GOREY
Main Street
Court House   #334
1819

Almost identical to the court house in Enniscorthy, Gorey petty and quarter sessions court house is presumably by the same hand. Lewis's *Topographical Dictionary* says that it 'is a neat and appropriate building… erected in 1819, at the expense of the county' making Gorey a year younger than its near twin. The later court house in New Ross is also based on this design. On a site donated by local landlord Stephen Ram and set back from Main Street behind railings, this is a T-plan building with hipped roof and rendered walls. The courtroom wing – the foot of the T – is a single-storey block with a cornice and blocking-course. There are opposing entrances and a window with architrave in a projecting corniced porch. This is flanked by niches topped by distinctive keystones matching the one above the porch window. The double-height courtroom was lit from the sides by three square-headed windows in architraves decorated with the same distinctive keystone, which is also to be found above the doors and windows of the transverse block to the rear. This has entrances on both sides, with a single square-headed window to first floor and single windows in the end walls. The court house was extended to the east in the 19th century and to the west in the mid-20th century. Burned in 1922 and subsequently repaired. Having also accommodated Wexford County Council's Gorey offices, and the town library, the court house closed in 2010, when court sittings were relocated to new facilities in Gorey Civic Square.

GOREY
Gorey Civic Square
Court House   #335
Hall Black Douglas Architects
2010

Gorey's new court house is part of the Gorey Civic Square development by Hall Black Douglas Architects. The other components are civic offices for Wexford County Council and a new library. There are also some residential units. A long, sleek one- and two-storey block, the court house forms the south side of the Square. A full-height projecting canopy at the west end fronts a glazed entrance foyer with a slatted wooden *brise-soleil*, a design feature shared with all three public buildings in the complex. Glazing gives way to grey stone cladding and minimal fenestration where the main courtroom is situated in the centre of the building. This is a double-height volume, panelled and furnished in wood, and lit by clerestory glazing. The €4 million facility also includes judge's chambers, consultation rooms for solicitors and clients, a secure interview room, space for Gardaí and legal practitioners, and two prisoner cells in the lower ground floor level. The court house was a joint project by the Courts Service, Wexford County Council and the HSE, which shares the building with Gorey District Court.

KILLINICK
Court House

Killinick petty sessions court house was located in the terrace on the south side of the village street. Demolitions and insertions have occurred over the course of the 20th century but some fabric from the court house may remain in the much altered buildings on the site.

NEW ROSS
Quay Street
Tholsel   **#336**
1749; 1806

Prior to the construction of a purpose-built court house in 1832, court sittings in New Ross, including quarter and petty sessions, had been held in the tholsel, a five-bay by three-bay, two-storey, classical, stone building on the corner of Quay Street and South Street. According to an inscription on a plaque on the main façade, the tholsel was erected in 1749 and rebuilt in 1806. It has on occasion been erroneously attributed to William Kent, including by no less a source than the *Irish Builder*. Ground floor arcade, the Gibbsian arches filled in probably since 1806 with a square-headed entrance and square-headed windows in lugged mouldings. Square-headed windows, in lugged and keystoned architraves, to first floor, their sills merging to form a continuous platband. Cornice with parapet on which sit four (out of an original five) urns. Hipped roof and two-storey clock tower, square at the base, chamfered above, with pedimented lunette windows under a square dome. The building remains in local authority use.

NEW ROSS
Priory Street
Court House   **#337**
1832

The third and last Wexford petty and quarter sessions court house, after Enniscorthy and Gorey, to be built to a similar design. Lewis's *Topographical Dictionary* reports that it was completed in 1832 at an expense of £1,334, the cost defrayed by the county. On a raised site set back from Priory Street at the corner with Cross Street, this is a rendered T-plan building. As at Enniscorthy and Gorey, the courtroom is contained in a single-bay, single-storey front wing, here with simple corner pilasters and frieze and a single entrance protected by an open, hipped-roofed, quoined porch with solid end wall. The double-height, galleried courtroom is lit from each side by three round-headed windows in plain surrounds. The rear block has entrances on each west-facing side surmounted by rectangular panels, and a five-bay, two-storey east façade. Refurbished in 2006, the court house closed following the 2011 amalgamation of the Electoral Divisions of the District Court Area of New Ross into those of Wexford and Kilkenny. The building is currently unoccupied.

OULART
Court House

An attached building nearly opposite the constabulary barracks (later Garda station) at the south end of the village served as Oulart petty sessions court house. Originally a tall, three-bay, single-storey, rendered and quoined house with a pitched roof, it was altered to a single-bay building with a central shopfront. Now integrated into the licensed premises on the site.

TAGHMON
Ross Road
Court House

The petty sessions court house in Taghmon occupied the two-storey, three-bay by one-bay building on the corner of Main Street and Ross Road, diagonally opposite the constabulary barracks. It has a filled-in archway on the right and a fanlit doorcase with columns. Square-headed first floor windows in simple architraves. Now a licensed premises.

WEXFORD
Commercial Quay
County Court House   #338
Sir Richard Morrison; James Barry Farrell
1803-07; 1862-63

A 1764 description of Wexford noted that in the 'midst or heart of the Main Street is the Bullring, where the courthouse, with an excellent clock etc, stands'. This court house was destroyed during the 1798 rebellion and, as recorded in George Griffith's *Chronicles of Wexford* (1877), at the summer assizes of 1803 Sir Richard Morrison was paid £34 2s 6d for a plan and estimate for a replacement. The site chosen was a prominent one on Commercial Quay, which Morrison was also involved in developing, opposite Wexford Bridge. Changes to the plan occurred as construction progressed but the court house was sufficiently complete for the summer assizes of 1807 to be held there. The building was never considered fully satisfactory and was subject to a continuing programme of works culminating in an extensive enlargement and alteration by County Surveyor J.B. Farrell in 1862-63. An 1820 view of Wexford includes the front façade of the court house and shows a two-storey, three-bay, hipped-roofed centre block, with a columned and pedimented entrance, flanked by pedimented courtroom wings. The accuracy of the view is confirmed by Lewis's *Topographical Dictionary*, which reports that the court house 'situated on the quay, opposite to the end of the bridge, is a neat structure, erected at the expense of the county, and consists of a centre and two wings, with its entrance under a pediment supported by two columns'. This makes Wexford court house strikingly similar to Morrison's court house in Portlaoise. Presumably the plan was also similar, with a large

#334 | Gorey, Court House (NIAH, 2005)
#335 | Gorey, Civic Centre (Denis Mortell, 2019)
#337 | New Ross, Court House (NIAH, 2009)

entrance hall providing access on each side to the two courtrooms and in the middle to the central stair hall. The building, post its 1862-63 alterations, is shown in a late-19th-century photograph. The centre block is now set back, or rather the wings have been extended by two bays, and is fronted by a single-storey tetrastyle Doric portico topped by a balustraded wall decorated with roundels and a rectangular panel. The fronts of Morrison's courtroom wings would appear to have been reinstated. These, as at Portlaoise, each have a central arched recess containing a blind square-headed window in a dressed-stone architrave and flanked by round-headed niches above which are carved decorative panels. The court house became the headquarters of Wexford County Council from 1898 but in June 1921 it was set ablaze by the local Irish Volunteers and almost completely gutted. Until 1962 a surviving portion was used as a scout hall. The building was subsequently demolished and replaced by a petrol station which has since closed. The site is currently a carpark, though redevelopment is under consideration.

WEXFORD

Westgate

County Gaol/County Court House

Sir Richard Morrison; William Fitzgerald Barry

1811-12; 1929-31

Following the destruction of the Commercial Quay court house in 1921, court sittings moved to the former county gaol at Westgate. Attributed to Sir Richard Morrison, the gaol complex, including its massive castellated Gothic gatehouse, was built 1811-12. Acquired by Wexford County Council in 1905, it subsequently served in part as St Brigid's Female Certified Inebriates' Reformatory and in part as a barracks. Burned in June 1921, the former gaol buildings were repaired and repurposed by County Surveyor William Fitzgerald Barry from 1929 to 1931 to accommodate county council offices and court use. The five-bay, three-storey sandstone building immediately behind the gatehouse became the court house. Externally the building's appearance hardly altered; the square-headed windows were retained as was the fanlit entrance with its plain stone doorcase. Internally, a double-height courtroom was created with a public gallery fronted by decorative wrought-iron railings. Below the gallery was an internal porch while the judge's bench was backed by a panel with a scrolled pediment. In local authority use since the transfer of court business to the new court house on Belvedere Road in 2018.

WEXFORD

Belvedere Road

Tate School/County Court House

See **P128** & Significant Court Houses – A Chronological Selection **P211**

ARKLOW
Parade Ground
Court House   **#339**
John Robert Hampton; []
1843; early 20th century

Lewis's *Topographical Dictionary* records that the 'petty sessions for
the barony of Arklow are held every Thursday, in a neat court-house
rented by the magistrates for that purpose, and of which the lower
part is appropriated to the use of the savings' bank'. In 1842 the Grand
Jury acquired a site for a new court house. Set back from the north
side of Main Street on the Parade Ground, this was bounded on the
east by the post office (still extant) and on the west by a large U-plan
police station (now demolished). The County Surveyor, John Robert
Hampton, was responsible for the new court house, possibly with
external assistance. The involvement of William Deane Butler or
William Caldbeck is suggested by Brendan O'Donoghue (*The Irish
County Surveyors 1834-1944* (Dublin, 2007)). Of these, Butler is by
far the more likely. Joseph McDaniel was the builder and the court
house was completed in 1843. Intended to accommodate petty and
quarter sessions, it is a five-bay, two-storey block, the centre three bays
advanced and rusticated at ground level. All five bays have segmental
windows, set in corresponding recesses, to ground floor with square-
headed windows to first floor. The entrances are located in the sides of
the advanced central section and are topped by blind square-headed
windows. Rendered with stone quoins, sill-level platband, cornice and
blocking course. The court house was extended by two bays on the
west end in the early 20th century. The single-storey courtroom was
refurbished and refurnished c. 1980, and remains in use.

AVOCA/OVOCA
Main Street
Court House

Detached, mid-19th-century vernacular petty sessions court house
on the west side of Avoca's Main Street, north of the bridge. Four-bay,
split-level block with pitched roof, recessed entrances in the end bays,
their steps now removed, and two tall square-headed windows. The
rear façade has two lunette windows set high in the wall and a single
lower ground-floor entrance. External steps to an entrance in the north
gable end, and another entrance in the south. A plaque on the front
wall records the fact that the building was formerly a court house.
Now a heritage centre.

BALTINGLASS
Market Square
Court House   **#340**
[]; Foley and O'Sullivan; Newenham Mulligan and Associates
pre-1795; 1926; 1999

A two-storey over raised basement, five-bay building on an island
site in Market Square, facing down Main Street, Baltinglass court
house was originally erected in the mid- to late-18th century. Richard
Johnston, architect, signed an estimate of £558 10s for repairs to the
building in 1795. Further repairs and improvements were carried out
by Wicklow Grand Jury in 1828 and again in 1830. The first-edition OS
map shows a barracks behind the court house. The basement came to
serve as a bridewell, but this was after 1837, when Lewis's *Topographical
Dictionary* reports that a separate bridewell was 'inconveniently
situated' in the town. A house was erected to the north c. 1850 and
expanded to provide municipal offices towards the end of the 19th
century. Foley and O'Sullivan, architects and engineers, reconstructed
the building after it was damaged by fire in April 1920. The works
were completed in 1926. Rendered, with cement blocked architraves
to the square-headed windows, its most obvious external feature is
the pair of opposed granite stairs leading to the entrance porch with
its hoodmoulded openings and granite pediments. Internally, the
double-height courtroom contained a free-standing dock, high-level
jury box and niche behind the judge's bench. Repaired and extended by
Newenham Mulligan and Associates, 1999, the complex accommodated
court use and the local library. The court element closed in 2013
following the amalgamation of Baltinglass District Court with Carlow.

BLESSINGTON
Main Street
Market House and Court House   **#341**
1838-45

Lewis's *Topographical Dictionary* notes in 1837 that a 'neat building, the
upper part of which is used as a girls' school, and the lower as a court
for holding the petty sessions… has been erected at an expense of £800
by the Marquess of Downshire'. While a small attached market house
is shown on the first-edition OS map of Blessington (1838), a court
house is not. In 1838 work began on a new market and court house.
The estimated cost was almost £800 and construction was supervised
by local tradesman Patrick Kearney, who had to guarantee that he was
not associated with ribbonmen or other illegal organisations to secure
the contract. Building works were protracted but the market house was
certainly complete by 1845. It is a detached, ashlar granite two-storey,
three-bay block, the centre bay slightly advanced and pedimented
with the Downshire arms in the tympanum. The front and sides of
the ground floor have an arcade of arched recesses. Those in the end
bays to the front were formerly open and gated but now contain fanlit
entrances. The rest are blind, aside from the end bay of the south-west
side which contains a square-headed door. One string-course at impost
level, and a second separating ground and first floor, where there are
plain square-headed windows. Rendered rear elevation with irregular
fenestration. The building remained in court use until 1971, when a
change in ownership and an increase in rent prompted Blessington
District Court sittings to be transferred to St Joseph's Hall. Blessington
District Court was amalgamated with Naas in 2000. The market and
court house is now occupied by Blessington Credit Union.

BRAY

Main Street

Court House   #342

William Deane Butler; Foley and O'Sullivan

1841; 1926

A pre-1760 court house stood at the south end of Main Street where Bray town hall was subsequently erected. A new court house was built in 1841, on the site of a 1790s market house at the opposite end of Main Street, by contractor Edmund William O'Kelly. It is a detached, three-bay, two-storey classical building, designed by William Deane Butler for petty and quarter sessions. The entrance front faces south and has an advanced and pedimented centre bay, the date inscribed in the tympanum. Over the pediment was an acroterion which doubled as a chimney stack. Single-storey entrance porch, above which is a niche in a stone surround. Rendered walls with stone quoins, platband, pilasters to porch and architraves to square-headed windows, those to the front are blind. Recessed panels between ground and first floor windows on the three-bay west elevation, but not on what was originally a two-bay east elevation. The north front, overlooking Bray Bridge, has two entrances at ground floor and a single window to first floor. Burned in April 1921 during the War of Independence, it was reconstructed by Foley and O'Sullivan, architects and engineers, in 1926. It was presumably at this point that the building changed from an L to a rectangular plan with the addition of a flat-roofed extension on the north-east corner. Damaged by fire again in 1981, the court house was closed. It has subsequently served as a heritage centre (closed 2007) and commercial premises.

BRAY

Boghall Road

Court House   #343

Cooney Jennings Ltd

1984

Brown-brick, utilitarian building designed by Cooney Jennings Ltd and constructed in a zone of industrial buildings off the south side of Boghall Road to replace Bray's fire-damaged 1841 court house. Single-storey courtroom block linked by a lower, single-storey, flat-roofed, entrance to a two-storey office wing, both main blocks having hipped roofs with oversailing eaves. The plain double-height courtroom has clerestory glazing, wood panelling behind the judge's bench and wooden furnishings. Closed when the new court facilities in the Civic Centre on Main Street opened in 2007, though its reopening has been contemplated due to capacity issues in the new Civic Centre court house.

BRAY

Main Street
Civic Centre   #344
Colum Ó Broin and Partners
2002-06

Completed in 2006, Bray's most recent court house was designed by Colum Ó Broin and Partners and forms part of the Cualann Centre, Bray's civic centre, which also contains offices for Bray Town Council, a headquarters for the Health Service Executive, and the Mermaid Arts Centre. Adopting the same contemporary architectural language as the other buildings in the complex by the same firm, the court house is a four-storey, multi-bay structure distinguished by its black granite entrance front topped by a tall lantern-like glazed shaft. Glass-walled, double-height circulation spaces provide access to the three naturally lit courtrooms, which are panelled in light wood with dark wood furnishings. Other facilities include judge's chambers, a jury room, legal practitioners' room, consultation rooms, offices for the staff of the District Court with a public counter and separate interview room, victim support room, media room and holding cells for prisoners. The court house is used for District and Circuit Court sittings.

CARNEW

Court House and Police Barracks

Lewis's *Topographical Dictionary* records that Carnew petty sessions 'are held on alternate Saturdays, in a neat building erected by Earl Fitzwilliam, over which is the constabulary police barrack, this town being the residence of the chief constable of the Tinahely district'. The first-edition OS map shows a 'Police Station' (but no sessions house) opposite All Saints C of I church, inside the wall of Carnew Castle just west of the castle gate. Some traces of blocked-up openings in the wall may relate to this structure. By the time the 25-inch OS map was produced in 1907-09, the constabulary barracks was occupying the five-bay, two-storey, end-of-terrace building on the south side of the street, immediately adjacent to Carnew Castle wall. However, Carnew had ceased to be a petty sessions location by 1900.

DUNLAVIN

Market Square
Market House and Court House
See Significant Court Houses – A Chronological Selection   **P170**

#342 | Bray, Main Street, Court House (IAA, 2000)
#343 | Bray, Boghall Road, Court House (IAA, 2019)
#344 | Bray, Civic Centre Court House (Courts Service, 2006)

ENNISKERRY

Church Hill

Court House   #345

c. 1820

Enniskerry petty sessions court house stands on the west side of Church Hill, a three-bay, single-storey building, which the NIAH suggests is c. 1820. Round-headed central entrance flanked by tall, narrow round-headed windows. Simple mouldings to openings and gable pediment. Now in use as a restaurant.

NEWTOWNMOUNTKENNEDY

Market House and Court House

Newtownmountkennedy, Lewis's *Topographical Dictionary* reports, 'chiefly consists of one wide street, with a small markethouse in the centre, which being disused as such for a long time, is now called the court-house'. It is so marked on the 25-inch OS map, where it is shown as a rectangular detached structure in the middle of the village street at the junction with the side road leading past St Joseph's RC church. At a meeting held on 8 October 1956, Wicklow County Council considered a memorial from Newtownmountkennedy ratepayers requesting the removal of the court house on the grounds that it was 'an eyesore in the middle of the village' and a danger to traffic, while 'alternative housing of the District Court could be provided locally at a cheap rental'. The council agreed and rented Kilmacullagh Auditorium for District Court sittings. The court house was demolished. Newtownmountkennedy ceased to be a District Court location in 1961.

RATHDANGAN

Rathdangan was listed in the 1842 *Petty Sessions Return*, but had ceased to be a petty sessions location by 1882. No court house is shown on the first-edition OS map.

RATHDRUM
Brewery Lane
Flannel Hall/Court House   #346
[John Lascelles]; []
1793; 1891-92

Erected by Earl Fitzwilliam at the cost of £3,500, Rathdrum Flannel Hall on Brewery Lane was a large square building composed of four wings around a central yard. No less than five schemes for the hall are recorded from 1789 to 1793; the last is by John Lascelles or Lassels and is dated 1793, the year the building was constructed, so on this basis it may be attributed to him. By the 1830s the flannel trade in Rathdrum was extinct and Lewis's *Topographical Dictionary* could report that parts of the building 'which forms a spacious square, and above the principal entrance of which is an escutcheon of Earl Fitzwilliam's arms, are now used for a court-house, a R. C. chapel, and schools'. Damaged by fire in 1891, the surviving east wing of the Flannel Hall was repaired in the following year as a court house, magistrates' room and a caretaker's house. The west side also survives, but the north and south ranges are gone. A single-storey, nine-bay, hipped-roofed block, now with a 20th-century flat-roofed extension across the central seven bays to the front. There are hints of its early origins in the round-headed entrances, mouldings and platband to the end bays. Plain interior. The court house closed when Rathdrum became part of Wicklow District Court Area in 2007. Now occupied by Rathdrum Development Association.

RATHNEW

Rathnew was listed in the 1842 *Petty Sessions Return*, but had ceased to be a petty sessions location by 1882. No court house is shown on the first-edition OS map.

REDCROSS

Redcross was listed in the 1842 *Petty Sessions Return*, but had ceased to be a petty sessions location by 1882. Court order books survive for 1866-69, but no court house has been identified.

#347 | Shillelagh (Edward Cassidy, 1998)
#348 | Tinahely, Market House (IAA, 2019)
#349 | Tinahely, Court House (IAA, 2019)

SHILLELAGH (COOLKENNA/COOLKENNO)

Main Street

Court House   **#347**

Fieldsend

1893

Shillelagh petty sessions were listed as Coolkenna or Coolkenno until 1892. The otherwise unknown Mr Fieldsend is credited by the *Wicklow Newsletter* (6 February 1892) with being the architect of the court house in Shillelagh, which was built in 1893. The costs were defrayed by the 6th Earl Fitzwilliam. Single-storey, five-bay building with a lower, single-bay extension on the east end, which is shown on the 25-inch OS map as a bank. Rendered, with stone quoins to corners and to advanced centre bay which is gabled and contains a round-headed entrance beneath a blind oculus. Pitched roof with wide bracketed eaves and decorative barge-boards. Square-headed windows and a square pedimented clocktower topped by a cupola and weathervane. Open-trussed roof to timber-panelled courtroom. Closed in 2000 following the amalgamation of Shillelagh District Court with Gorey, the building is now a community centre.

TINAHELY

Market Square

Market House and Court House   **#348**

1804

Until the construction of the purpose-built court house in 1843, Tinahely petty sessions were held in the upper floor of the market house, erected in 1804 by William Bourke, mason, for Earl Fitzwilliam as part of the rebuilding which followed the destruction of the town during the 1798 rebellion. It is a detached, two-storey, square building whose hipped roof is topped by a short clock tower. Triple-arched stone market arcade to front, with single arches in each side, all now filled in. Stone quoins and square-headed windows to the first floor with sill-level stone platband. The west side has a double flight of opposed steps, similar to those at Baltinglass, leading to a first-floor round-headed entrance flanked by square-headed windows.

TINAHELY

Market Square

Court House   **#349**

William Hampton

1843

The Wicklow Grand Jury presentments for 1843 record the payment of £246 to a Thomas Symes to build Tinahely court house. Construction was supervised by the County Surveyor, William Hampton, who presumably adapted plans received from elsewhere, as this is a version of the standard late-1830s – early-1840s petty and quarter sessions court house. Four-bay centre block (as opposed to the more normal five) with lower, recessed entrance wings on each end and a hipped roof hidden behind a continuous parapet. The end bays of the centre block are modestly advanced and rusticated at ground level, where there are single segmental-headed windows in segmental recesses. As is usual in the standard design, the centre bays are blind at ground floor, the bare look here dissipated by two raised decorative panels. Square-headed windows to first floor, their sills merging to form a broad platband which extends the full width of the building and returns around the sides to be interrupted by the single round-headed windows in the end walls. The platband passes behind the pediments of the entrances in the recessed wings. Above the pediments are niches. Tinahely was a District Court location until 1961, when it became part of the Shillelagh District Court Area. By the 1980s the building, which had served as a dance hall and cinema, was in a state of disrepair. Restored through local fundraising efforts and a youth employment scheme, the court house opened as a cultural centre in January 1996. The former double-height courtroom is now a galleried arts space.

WICKLOW

Market Street and Kilmantin Hill

See Significant Court Houses – A Chronological Selection   **P172**

INDEX TO ARCHITECTS AND BUILDERS

ACKNOWLEDGMENTS AND BIOGRAPHIES

The editors would like to thank the following who have provided assistance in the preparation of this publication:

Mr Justice Frank Clarke, the Chief Justice.

Brendan Ryan and Eva Font of the Courts Service.

Aisling Dunne, Anne Henderson, Simon Lincoln,
Eve McAulay and Ann Martha Rowan in the Irish Architectural Archive.

Gerard Bourke, Eoin Bradley, John Cahill, Richard Calder, Edel Collins,
Pat Cooney, David Cloney, Liam Egan, Derek Fortune, John Furlong,
Patrick Gannon, Gerry Gleeson, Michael Grace, Elaine Hanna, Ger Harvey,
Michael Haugh, Declan Holmes, Audrey Jennings, Carolyn Kenny, Stefan Mathews,
Keith Milsom, Kevin McLoone, Charlie Moore, Sean Moylan, Saskia O'Connor,
Michael O'Doherty, Jim O'Sullivan and Cliodhna Rice in the Office of Public Works.

Richard Butler, Michael Byrne, Brian Carey, Christine Casey, Elisabeth Churchard,
Maureen Costello, Michael Cowman, Nigel Curtin, David Davison, Kyrle Delaney,
Mairead Delaney, Conor Downey, Honora Faul, Úna Forde, Cathy Hayes,
Judith Hill, Roger Hill, Susan Hood, Niamh Howlin, Frank Keohane,
Anthony Kirby, John Kirwan, Paul Larmour, Niall McCullough, Elizabeth Mayes,
Edward McParland, Hazel Menton, Daniel Morehead, Denis Mortell, Tom Mulligan,
Valerie Mulvin, Kate Murphy, Conor Murray, Michael O'Boyle, Frederick O'Dwyer,
T.J. O'Meara, Amanda Pedlow, Alan Phelan, Margaret Quinlan, Zoe Reid, Stephen
Scarth, Philip Smith, Terence Reeves-Smyth, Joanne Rothwell, Alistair Rowan,
Orlaith Styles, Andrew Tierney, Paul Tierney, John Tuomey and Jane Wales.

Paul Burns is Head of the Infrastructure Services Directorate of the Courts Service.

Judith Hill is a professional architectural historian with a PhD in architectural history from TCD and a Diploma in Architecture from the RIBA.

Niamh Howlin is an Associate Professor at the UCD Sutherland School of Law, researching legal history and criminal justice.

Eve McAulay holds a PhD in architectural history from TCD and is an archivist with the Irish Architectural Archive.

Ciaran O'Connor is State Architect and Principal Architect, Director of Architectural Service and Head of Major Projects at the Office of Public Works.

Colum O'Riordan is CEO of the Irish Architectural Archive.